Get the eBook FREE!
(PDF, ePub, Kindle, and liveBook all included)

We believe that once you buy a book from us, you should be able to read it in any format we have available. To get electronic versions of this book at no additional cost to you, purchase and then register this book at the Manning website.

Go to https://www.manning.com/freebook and follow the instructions to complete your pBook registration.

That's it!
Thanks from Manning!

Praise for the First Edition

. . . masterfully blends the basics of programming with the effective use of AI tools to produce code.

—Mehran Sahami, Stanford University

This is such a well-thought-out book from the point of view of someone just starting to code post generative AI tools.

—Ana Bell, MIT

You are about to learn programming with one of the most exciting human task supporters of this century . . .

—From the foreword by Beth Simon, UC San Diego

This book accelerates your Copilot programming learning journey beyond what I ever thought possible.

—Austin Z. Henley, Carnegie Mellon University

This book is an excellent first, forward-thinking step toward working with, not futilely fighting against, the AI-assisted programming boom.

—Max Fowler, University of Illinois at Urbana-Champaign

You cannot compete with AI, instead you should learn how to complement your work with AI. This book is a great resource to get you started on that journey.

—Srihari Sridharan, Thoughtworks

An amazing textbook about how to learn Python programming with AI, written by expert teachers. AI is revolutionizing the way we learn to program. Get on board with Leo Porter and Daniel Zingaro.

—Mikael Dautrey, ISITIX

Embracing the future of programming education, this book is a beacon for educators navigating the brave new world of LLMs. Essential reading for the modern classroom.

—Ildar Akhmetov, Khoury College of Computer Sciences

Learn AI-Assisted Python Programming,
Second Edition

LEO PORTER
DANIEL ZINGARO
FOREWORD BY BETH SIMON

MANNING
SHELTER ISLAND

For online information and ordering of this and other Manning books, please visit
www.manning.com. The publisher offers discounts on this book when ordered in quantity.
For more information, please contact

Special Sales Department
Manning Publications Co.
20 Baldwin Road
PO Box 761
Shelter Island, NY 11964
Email: orders@manning.com

Manning Publications Co.
20 Baldwin Road
PO Box 761
Shelter Island, NY 11964

Development editor:	Rebecca Johnson
Technical editor:	Peter Morgan
Review editor:	Dunja Nikitović
Production editor:	Kathy Rossland
Copy editor:	Julie McNamee
Proofreader:	Mike Beady
Typesetter:	Dennis Dalinnik
Cover designer:	Marija Tudor

ISBN: 9781633435995
Printed in the United States of America

Dan thanks his wife, Doyali, for trading some of their time, again, to help this book exist.

Leo thanks his wife, Lori, and his children, Sam and Avery, for their love and support.

brief contents

contents

foreword

It's an awesome time to learn programming. Why? Let me use an analogy to explain.

I like to make my own bread. I make it more frequently, and more reliably, when I use my stand mixer to knead the dough compared to kneading it by hand. Maybe you'd say that's lazy. I'd say it makes me more productive and more likely to actually make the bread. Maybe you have something that makes your life easier by taking over a tedious task, leaving you free to focus on more important or interesting things. Do you have a car that supports you in parallel parking? I recall when Gmail added spell and grammar checks in languages other than English. My husband's German relatives were so excited that he was writing them longer emails—because the effort of remembering little-used German language specifics went away and allowed him to spend more time on the content!

Sadly, until recently, when learning programming, you had no equivalent of a stand mixer or grammar check to support you. And there are lots of tedious things to learn and remember when you start programming.

Good news! As of spring 2023, radically new and (we think) effective support is finally here. You are about to learn programming with one of the most exciting human task supporters so far this century: artificial intelligence. Specifically, this book seeks to support you in developing your ability to program in Python to solve computational problems more easily and faster by using a tool called GitHub Copilot. GitHub Copilot is a programming support tool that uses something called a large language model (LLM) to draw "help" from a huge number of previously written programs. Once you learn how to direct it (sadly, it's more complicated than effectively using a stand mixer),

Copilot can dramatically increase your productivity and success in writing programs to solve your problem.

But should you use Copilot? Are you really learning to program if you use it? Preliminary evidence looks positive—showing that students who learned with Copilot, when assigned a programming task, did better than students assigned the task who learned without Copilot [1]. That said, compared to what we used to teach in an introductory programming class, there are different skills you will need to focus on when programming with Copilot, specifically problem decomposition and debugging (it's OK if you don't know what those are). Just know, practicing programmers need to know those skills as well, but we previously weren't able to teach them explicitly or effectively in introductory courses because students didn't have the brain space left for learning these "high-level skills" while focusing on nitpicky things like spelling and grammar (programming languages have these, just like world languages).

Leo and Dan are expert computing educators and researchers; the decisions they've made to guide your learning in this book are grounded in what we know about teaching and learning programming. With this new, updated version of the book, they are integrating up-to-date and easier-to-use tools and also improving materials based on having taught introductory programming courses using this book at both of the universities where they work. I'm excited that, with this book, they're making the new wave of programming courses accessible to readers around the world.

So, congratulations! Whether you've never done any programming or whether you started to learn before and got frustrated . . . we think you'll find learning to program with Copilot transformative, allowing you to engage your brain in more meaningful and "expert-like" programming experiences!

—Beth Simon
Professor, University of California San Diego

acknowledgments

Writing a book about technology in flux was new for us. Each day of writing started with us reading the new articles, opinion pieces, and capabilities of large language models (LLMs). Early plans had to be scrapped or revised. New ideas presented themselves for later chapters only after we'd written earlier chapters and had access to the latest LLM features. We thank the entire Manning Publications team for their agility and help throughout the process.

In particular, we thank our development editor, Rebecca Johnson, for her expertise, wisdom, and support. Rebecca provided insightful feedback, constructive criticism, and creative suggestions that have greatly improved the quality and clarity of our work.

Rebecca was supportive and encouraging, and she helped us manage book timelines and our busy schedules. Thank you, Rebecca—you went above and beyond for us.

We also thank our technical editor, Peter Morgan, who offered valuable contributions to the quality of the book. Peter Morgan is the founder of the AI consulting company Deep Learning Partnership based in London. He has been working in AI for the past 10 years and before that spent 10 years as a solutions architect for companies such as Cisco Systems and IBM. Peter has written several reports, papers, and book chapters on AI, physics, and quantum computing.

We thank Naaz Sibia for her help with the book exercises.

And many thanks to our colleagues for supporting our work and offering their ideas for what such a book should attempt to do. Many of their ideas have informed our thinking as we sought to redefine what an introductory programming course looks like. We particularly thank Brett Becker, Michelle Craig, Paul Denny, Bill Griswold, Philip Guo, and Gerald Soosai Raj.

introduction

Software is essential today. It's hard to think of any industry where software isn't changing practically everything about how work is done. Manufacturing needs software to monitor production and shipping, let alone the robots that increasingly perform the actual task. Advertising, politics, and fitness, among others, are awash in big data and they routinely use software to make sense of it. Video games and movies are created using software. We could go on and on, but you get the point.

The result has been that more people than ever want to learn how to program. We're not just talking about the computer science, computer engineering, and data science majors at universities who have been in a perpetual "enrollment crisis" for the past decade. We're also talking about the scientist who needs to write software to evaluate their data, the office worker who wants to automate some of their tedious data processing tasks, and the hobbyist who wants to create a fun video game for their friends.

Despite the desire to learn programming, there are decades of research in our field (computing education) that have identified many reasons for why learning to write software is hard. Even after you figure out how to solve the problem, you have to tell a machine how to accomplish it in a programming language whose rules are unforgiving. Granted, writing programs in a language like Python is substantially easier than in machine code using punch cards, but it's still hard. We know it's hard because we've seen the failure rates of introductory computer science courses. We've watched motivated and intelligent students fail our courses, sometimes multiple times, before they succeed or, worse, give up.

But what if we could talk to computers in a better way? A way that doesn't require us to know all the detailed syntax rules that trip up most novices. That era has just begun thanks to AI assistants such as GitHub Copilot that offer intelligent code suggestions in the same way ChatGPT can write reasonable text when prompted. This book is for everyone who wants to learn how to write software in the AI assistant era. We're excited to be on your learning journey with you.

AI assistants change how programming is done

We'll introduce you to your AI assistant, GitHub Copilot, in chapter 1, but we want to give you a brief overview now. If you read the news headlines or even opinion pieces by lauded software engineering professionals talking about GitHub Copilot or ChatGPT, you've seen that opinions run the gamut. Some people say that AI assistants mean the end of all programming jobs. Others say that AI assistants are so hopelessly flawed you are better off without them. These views of the world are at such extremes that it's easy to poke holes in either argument. AI assistants learn from existing code, so if some new tool/technology is developed, humans will need to write the bulk of the initial code. As a recent article well expressed, there isn't a lot (or any) code out there for quantum computers because they are still in their infancy [1]. So human programmers aren't going away, at least not any time soon. At the same time, in our time working with GitHub Copilot, we've seen how powerful it is. Both of us have written software for decades, and GitHub Copilot can often give us correct code much faster than we could write it on our own. To ignore such a powerful tool seems analogous to a carpenter refusing to use power tools.

As educators, the opportunity to help people learn to write software is instantly apparent. Why should learners spend so much time fighting with syntax when the code suggested by an AI assistant is almost always syntactically correct? Why should learners have to reach out to professors, instructional staff, friends, or internet forums for help explaining what a section of code is doing when AI assistants are really good at explaining code (particularly for questions asked by novices)? And if AI assistants often write correct code when solving common programming problems (by learning from huge volumes of code written in the past), why shouldn't learners be using it to help them program?

Be warned that this doesn't mean that writing software is now just easy and that we can entirely offload the skill of programming onto the AI. Instead, the skills to write good software are evolving. Skills such as problem decomposition, code specification, code reading, and code testing have become even more important than they were in the past; skills such as knowing library semantics and syntax become less important. We'll say more about this in the next chapters, but this book will teach you the skills that matter going forward. These skills will be valuable whether you dabble in writing software from time to time or you are starting a career in software engineering.

Audience

We have two primary audiences for the book. The first is everyone who has thought about writing software (and even tried and failed before) to make their lives better in some way. This includes the accountant who gets frustrated that their software can't do what they want so they are left solving problems by hand, or scientists who want to analyze their data quickly, but existing tools aren't capable of doing what they want. We also imagine the office manager who feels limited by what their spreadsheet software can do and wants a better way to gain insight from their data. Additionally, we imagine the exec at a small company who wants to be notified when something is said publicly on social media about their company but can't afford to pay a software engineering team to write the tool for them. And, we imagine the hobbyist of any age who just wants to write software for fun—whether it be for making their own small video games, storytelling with pictures, or creating fun family photo collages. These are just some of the people who want to write software to improve some element of their professional or personal lives.

The second audience is the learner who is considering a career in software engineering or programming and wants to learn how to write software. They want to learn the basics and start creating interesting software, without the trappings of a classic computer science class. Certainly, there will be more courses or books that will follow this first book on the road to becoming a professional software developer, but this will hopefully be a fun and rewarding first step.

What we expect from you

This book requires no background whatsoever in programming. If you learned some programming and forgotten it, or it didn't go well the first time, we think this is a great place to resume your learning.

This book does require basic computer literacy. This means you should be comfortable installing software, copying files between folders, and opening files on your computer. If you don't have those skills, you could still start this book, but realize there may be moments when you need to look to outside resources (e.g., YouTube videos on how to copy a file from one folder to another).

You'll also need a computer where you have permission to install software so you can follow along and apply the ideas we're learning. Any Windows, Mac, or Linux personal computer or laptop will work.

What you will be able to do after reading this book

In this book, we're going to teach you how to use GitHub Copilot to write Python code. We'll teach you how to identify whether that code does what you want, and what to do when it doesn't. We'll teach you enough about Python to be able to read it for a general understanding of what it does and whether it's doing something potentially meaningful.

We won't, however, teach you how to program in Python entirely from scratch. You'll be in a good position to learn to do that with other resources following this book if you like, but for many tasks, as we will show you, it may not be necessary.

We don't know exactly what it will look like to be a professional programmer or software engineer in light of AI coding assistants. That role is already changing and will change further as the AI technology improves. For now, you need more than this book to be a professional programmer or software engineer. You'll need to know a great deal more about Python and other computer science topics to get there.

The good news is that learning how to program using GitHub Copilot will make you capable of writing basic software to address common needs. The software will be more complex than what we typically teach in an introductory course, and you'll be able to write these useful programs without banging your head on syntax or spending months learning just Python. If you want to continue learning about writing professional software, this will be your first step toward mastery. By the end of this book, you'll be able to write basic software capable of data analysis, automating repetitive tasks, and creating simple games, among many others.

The challenge in working with AI assistants

We expect you're ready to jump into a technology that is maturing and changing quickly. What you see from GitHub Copilot may *not* match what you see in this book. GitHub Copilot is advancing and changing daily, and we can't possibly keep up to the minute with such a moving target. More than that, GitHub Copilot is nondeterministic, which means that if you ask it to solve the same task multiple times, it may not give you the same code each time. Sometimes you'll get correct code for a task, but then if you ask again, you get code that isn't correct. So even if you use the exact same prompts we do, you'll likely see different code responses than we do. Much of this book is devoted to ensuring you learn how to determine whether the answer from GitHub Copilot is right or not and, if it isn't, how to fix it. In short, we hope you're ready to learn on the leading edge of technology.

Why we wrote this book

Both of us have been professors for over a decade and programmers for a decade longer than that. Our care for our students' success led us to become researchers studying how students learn computing and how to improve their outcomes. Between the two of us, we've written nearly a hundred articles in our field exploring pedagogies, student beliefs, and assessments—all with the goal of improving the student experience.

We've also had students in our office hours who struggle to learn how to program, even when we are employing best practices in teaching computing. These are intelligent students who want to learn, but who are tripped up on some part of the programming process. The programming process has many steps, from understanding a problem, to coming up with a solution, to imparting the process of solving the problem to a computer. So, when we began working with AI assistants, specifically GitHub

Copilot, we instantly saw how it could be a game changer for students, particularly in improving that last step of "imparting the process of solving the problem to a computer." We want our students to succeed. We want you to succeed. And, we believe AI assistants can help.

Warning: Beware of elitism

One of the saddest things we see in our classes at our universities is students intimidating other students. We've heard students in our introductory Python programming courses try to show off how they already learned to program in such-and-such programming language and the effect that has on the other students in the course. Although we try to gently point these students to other, more appropriate courses, we've also seen that the students bragging in this way are often the students struggling to pass at the end of the term, having vastly overestimated their proficiency at the start. It doesn't take a licensed psychologist to see that this kind of posturing comes from a place of low self-esteem.

Beyond students in our introductory courses, we see how different kinds of programmers treat each other and their respective fields. For example, Human-Computer Interaction (HCI) professionals study how to improve the design of software to make it better for its human users. Sounds important, right? Unfortunately, that field was put down by computer scientists as merely "applied psychology" for years, and then major companies showed that maybe, just maybe, if you care about the users of your technology, those people might just appreciate it more and be inclined to buy it. It's not surprising that HCI quickly became mainstream in computer science. This snobbery isn't limited to specific fields. We even see it occurring between programmers of different languages. For example, we've seen C++ (one programming language) programmers say silly things like JavaScript (another programming language) programming isn't real programming. (It definitely is real programming, whatever that might mean!)

All of this, in our opinion, is unproductive and unfortunate posturing that pushes people away from the field. A comic we both enjoy called XKCD captured the ludicrousness of this posturing well in "Real Programmers" [2]. In the comic, programmers argue about what the best text editor app is for programming. Programmers need to use a text editor to enter their code, which is exactly what you'll start doing in chapter 2. There's been a long-standing, and mostly unserious, debate over the best editors ("emacs" is one of many editors). The comic is making light of the meaninglessness of the debate in a truly clever way.

We're talking about this unfortunate aspect of our field because we know what some people will say about learning to program with GitHub Copilot. They'll say that to learn to write software, you have to learn how to write code entirely from scratch. And, for future professional engineers, we actually agree that at some point in your career, you should learn to write code from scratch. But, for most people and even people starting their studies in software engineering, we wholeheartedly disagree that writing code entirely from scratch makes sense anymore as a starting place. So, if someone criticizes you for doing something to make yourself, your life, or the world better, we encourage you to look to the immortal wisdom of Taylor Swift and just "shake it off."

How this book is organized: A road map

This book is divided into 12 chapters. We recommend that you read this book from beginning to end, rather than skipping around, because most chapters introduce skills that will be assumed in later chapters:

- Chapter 1 describes what AI code assistants are, how they work, and why they are irrevocably changing how programming is done. It also explores the concerns we need to keep in mind when using AI coding assistants.
- Chapter 2 helps you set up your computer to be able to program with Python (that's the programming language we'll use) and GitHub Copilot (that's your AI coding assistant). Once your computer is set up, we'll use GitHub Copilot in our first programming example: doing some analysis on freely available sports data.
- Chapter 3 teaches you all about functions, which help you organize your code and make it easier for GitHub Copilot to write code for you. It also uses many examples to demonstrate the general workflow we'll use to be productive with GitHub Copilot.
- Chapter 4 is the first of two chapters that teaches you how to read Python code. It's true that GitHub Copilot will be writing code for you, but you need to be able to read that code to help you determine whether that code is going to do what you want. Don't worry, GitHub Copilot can help you read code too!
- Chapter 5 is the second of two chapters that teaches you how to read Python code.
- Chapter 6 is a primer on two critical skills that you need to hone when working with AI coding assistants: testing and prompt engineering. Testing involves checking that your code operates correctly; prompt engineering involves changing the words you use in order to communicate more effectively with your AI assistant.
- Chapter 7 is all about breaking large problems down into smaller problems that are easier for GitHub Copilot to handle. The technique is called top-down design, and, in this chapter, you'll use it to design a small but complete program that can offer spelling suggestions for misspelled words (like a spell-checker).
- Chapter 8 is a deep dive into bugs (errors in your code!), how to find them, and how to fix them. You'll learn how to step line by line through your code to pinpoint exactly what's going wrong and even how to ask GitHub Copilot to help you fix bugs.
- Chapter 9 puts GitHub Copilot to work to help you automate tedious tasks. You'll see three examples—cleaning up emails that have been forwarded many times,

adding cover pages to hundreds of PDF files, and removing duplicate images—and you'll be able to apply the principles to your own specific tasks as well.

- Chapter 10 shows you how to use GitHub Copilot to write computer games. You'll use the skills you developed throughout the book to write two games: a logic game similar to Wordle, and a two-player, press-your-luck board game.

- Chapter 11 contains an example of using top-down design to write a large program, much larger than anything to this point in the book. The program you'll write is a sophisticated one: it can guess the author of books whose authors we don't know!

- Chapter 12 delves into the fledgling field of prompt patterns, which are tools to help you get even more out of your AI assistant. It also summarizes the current limitations of AI coding assistants and looks at what may be on the horizon.

Source code downloads

For many books about programming, the reader types the code exactly as the author has written it in order to accomplish a task with code. Our book is different because, as described earlier, the code we get back from GitHub Copilot is nondeterministic; your code won't match our code. For that reason, we aren't providing all the code for download that you see in this book. We want you to focus on generating that code from GitHub Copilot, not typing it in yourself! That said, we do have some important files to share, and they are available from the publisher's website at www.manning .com/books/learn-ai-assisted-python-programming-second-edition.

This book contains many examples of source code both in numbered listings and in line with normal text. In both cases, source code is formatted in a `fixed-width font like this` to separate it from ordinary text. Comments or code we've written as prompts to be interpreted by GitHub Copilot or ChatGPT are in bold to highlight what we wrote rather than what was given to us by the large language model.

In many cases, the original source code has been reformatted; we've added line breaks and reworked indentation to accommodate the available page space in the book. In rare cases, even this wasn't enough, and listings include line-continuation markers (➡). Additionally, comments in the source code have often been removed from the listings when the code is described in the text. Code annotations accompany many of the listings, highlighting important concepts.

Software/hardware requirements

You'll need access to any Windows, Mac, or Linux computer on which you have permission to install software. As we discuss in further detail in chapter 2, you'll need to install the Python software, the Visual Studio Code (VS Code) software, as well as various extensions. You'll also need to sign up for a GitHub Copilot account, which, at the time of writing, has a free trial and is free for students and educators, but otherwise has a monthly charge.

liveBook discussion forum

Purchase of *Learn AI-Assisted Python Programming, Second Edition* includes free access to liveBook, Manning's online reading platform. Using liveBook's exclusive discussion features, you can attach comments to the book globally or to specific sections or paragraphs. It's a snap to make notes for yourself, ask and answer technical questions, and receive help from the authors and other users. To access the forum, go to https://livebook.manning.com/book/learn-ai-assisted-python-programming-second-edition/discussion. You can also learn more about Manning's forums and the rules of conduct at https://livebook.manning.com/discussion.

Manning's commitment to our readers is to provide a venue where a meaningful dialogue between individual readers and between readers and the authors can take place. It's not a commitment to any specific amount of participation on the part of the authors, whose contribution to the forum remains voluntary (and unpaid). We suggest you try asking the authors some challenging questions lest their interest stray! The forum and the archives of previous discussions will be accessible from the publisher's website as long as the book is in print.

about the authors

LEO PORTER is a professor of computer science at UC San Diego. He has more than a decade of teaching experience and is well-known for his award-winning research on effective pedagogies and assessments in computer science.

DANIEL ZINGARO is an associate teaching professor of computer science and award-winning teacher at the University of Toronto. His main area of research is computer science education research, where he studies how students learn computer science material.

about the cover illustration

The figure on the cover of *Learn AI-Assisted Python Programming, Second Edition* is "Prussien de Silésie," or "Prussian from Silesia," taken from a collection by Jacques Grasset de Saint-Sauveur, published in 1788. Each illustration is finely drawn and colored by hand. In those days, it was easy to identify where people lived and what their trade or station in life was just by their dress. Manning celebrates the inventiveness and initiative of the computer business with book covers based on the rich diversity of regional culture centuries ago, brought back to life by pictures from collections such as this one.

Introducing AI-assisted programming with GitHub Copilot

This chapter covers

- How AI assistants change how new programmers learn
- Why programming is never going to be the same
- How AI assistants such as GitHub Copilot work
- Possible perils of AI-assisted programming

Computer programming has long been the domain of professionals with special training and advanced skills. After all, you want the applications running your bank, phone, car, and so on to work exactly right every time! Just as room-sized computers with stacks of paper cards and miles of magnetic tape have been replaced by modern devices, programming languages and tools have also become easier to use. And now, artificial intelligence (AI) tools such as ChatGPT put computer programming within the reach of almost everyone. We want to help open this door for you!

Learn how to program, and you'll be able to take on new tasks at work, create your own computer games, and put the computer to work for you at your job. In this book, we'll show you how to write your own computer programs using ChatGPT and GitHub Copilot. Along the way, you'll learn some skills in Python, one of the most popular programming languages.

1.1   *Improving how we talk to computers*

Let's start by asking a computer to count from 0 to 9. Decades ago, a book about programming would have asked you to learn how to read and understand the following code (based on https://mng.bz/EOdO):

```
section .text
global _start
_start:
    mov ecx, 10
    mov eax, '0'
    l1:
    mov [num], eax
    mov eax, 4
    mov ebx, 1
    push ecx
    mov ecx, num
    mov edx, 1
    int 0x80
    mov eax, [num]
    inc eax
    pop ecx
    loop l1
    mov eax, 1
    int 0x80
section .bss
    num resb 1
```

We're glad that's not how we program anymore. That monstrosity was written using code in assembly language, a low-level programming language. Low-level programming languages, as you can see, aren't languages that humans can easily read and write. They're designed for computers, not humans.

No one wants to write programs like that, but, especially in the past, it was sometimes necessary. Programmers could use it to define exactly what they wanted the computer to do, down to individual instructions. This level of control was needed to squeeze every bit of performance out of underpowered computers. For example, the most speed-critical pieces of 1990s computer games, such as Doom and Quake, were written in assembly language like the previous code example. It wouldn't have been possible to make those games otherwise.

1.1.1   *Making it a little easier*

Okay, let's move on. Here's a more modern computer program that also prints numbers.

```
for num in range(0, 9):
    print(num)
```

This code is in the Python language, which is what many programmers use these days. Unlike assembly language, which is a low-level language, Python is considered a high-level language because it's much closer to natural language. Even though you don't know about Python code yet, you might be able to guess what this program is trying to do. The first line looks like it's doing something with the range of numbers from 0 to 9. The second line is printing something. It's not too hard to believe that this program, just like the assembly language monstrosity, is supposed to print the numbers 0 to 9. Unfortunately, something is wrong, and it prints the numbers 0 to 8 instead.

While this code is closer to English, it isn't English. It's a programming language that, like assembly language, has specific rules. As in the previous code, misunderstanding the details of those rules can result in a broken program. If you're curious, the misunderstood rule was that the `range` function stops one before the second number provided, so it doesn't include the number 9. If you wanted 0 through 9, you'd need to say `range(0,10)`.

The holy grail of communicating with a computer is to do so in a natural language such as English. We've been talking to computers using various programming languages over the past 80 years not because we want to but because we have to. Computers were simply not powerful enough for the vagaries and idiosyncrasies of a language like English. Our programming languages improved—from symbol-soup assembly language to Python, for example—but they are still computer languages, not natural languages. This is changing.

1.1.2 *Making it a lot easier*

Using an AI assistant, we can now ask for what we want in English and have the computer code written for us in response. To get a correct Python program that prints the numbers from 0 to 9, we can ask our AI assistant (Copilot) in normal English language like this:

```
# Output the numbers from 0 to 9
```

Copilot might respond to this prompt by generating something like this:

```
for i in range(10):
    print(i)
```

Unlike the example we showed you before, this piece of Python code actually works!

AI coding assistants can be used to help people write code. In this book, we'll learn how to use Copilot to write code for us. We'll ask for what we want in English and get the code back in Python.

More than that, we'll be able to use Copilot as a seamless part of our workflow. Without tools like Copilot, programmers routinely have two windows open: the one to write code and the other to ask Google how to write code. This second window has Google search results, Python documentation, or forums of programmers talking about how to write code to solve that particular problem. They're often pasting code from these results into their code, then tweaking it slightly for their context, trying alternatives, and so on. This has become a way of life for programmers, but you can imagine the inefficiency here. By some estimates, up to 35% of programmers' time is spent searching for code [1], and much of the code that is found isn't readily usable. Copilot greatly improves this experience by helping us write our code.

1.2 About the technology

We'll use two main technologies in this book: Python and GitHub Copilot. Python is the programming language that we'll use, and GitHub Copilot is our AI assistant that will help us work with the Python code.

1.2.1 Python, your programming language

As mentioned, Python is a programming language, which is a way to communicate with a computer. People use it to write all kinds of programs that do useful things such as data analysis, games, interactive websites, visualizations, file organization apps, automating routine tasks, and so on.

There are other programming languages as well, such as Java, C++, Rust, and many others. Copilot works with those, too, but at the time of this writing, it works really well with Python. Python code is a lot easier to write compared to many other languages (especially assembly code). Even more importantly, Python is easy to *read*. After all, we're not going to be the ones writing the Python code—our AI assistant is!

Computers don't know how to read and run Python code. The only thing computers can understand is something called *machine code*, which looks even more ridiculous than assembly code because it's the binary representation of the assembly code (yep, just a bunch of 0s and 1s!). Behind the scenes, your computer takes any Python code that you provide and converts it into machine code before it runs, as shown in figure 1.1.

So, no one is writing code from scratch in the machine code language of computers anymore. Programmers are all picking the language that's most convenient for their particular task at the time and using software to help them write, run, and debug (i.e., fix) the code, called an Integrated Development Environment (IDE). In the book, we'll be using Visual Studio Code (VS Code) as our IDE because it works exceptionally well with GitHub Copilot.

1.2.2 GitHub Copilot, your AI assistant

What is an AI assistant? An AI assistant is an AI agent that helps you get work done. Maybe you have an Amazon Alexa device at home or an iPhone with Siri—these are AI assistants. They help you order groceries, be aware of the weather, or determine that, yes, the woman who played Bellatrix in the *Harry Potter* movies really was in *Fight Club*. An AI assistant is just a computer program that responds to typical human inputs such as speech and text with human-like answers.

Copilot is an AI assistant with a specific job: it converts English into computer programs (along with a whole lot more, as we'll soon see). There are other AI assistants

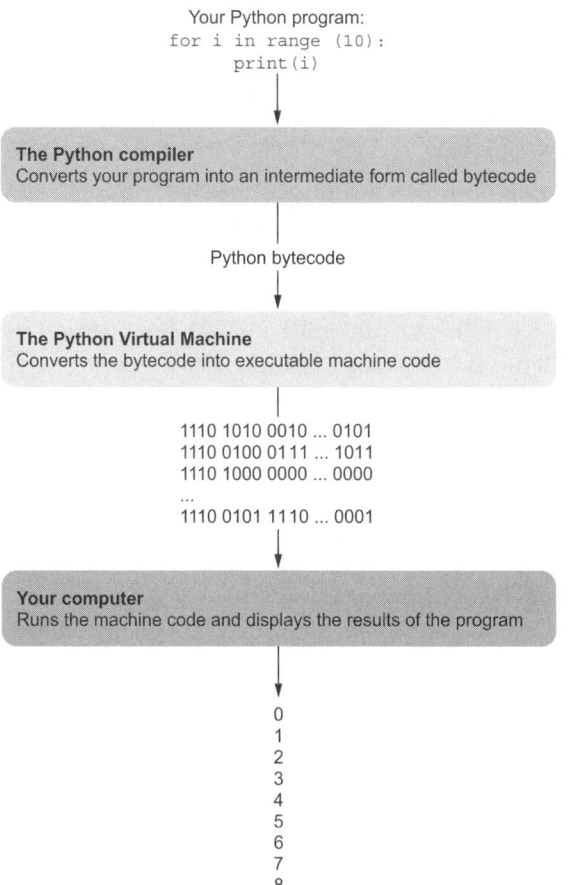

Figure 1.1   **Your Python program goes through several steps before you see the output on your screen.**

like Copilot, including Amazon Q Developer, Tabnine, and Ghostwriter. We chose Copilot for this book based on a combination of the quality of code that we've been able to produce, stability (it has never crashed for us!), and our own personal preferences. We encourage you to also check out other tools when you feel comfortable doing so.

1.2.3   *How Copilot works behind the scenes—in 30 seconds*

You can think of Copilot as a layer between you and the computer program you're writing. Instead of writing the Python directly, you simply describe the program you want in words—this is called a *prompt*—and Copilot generates the program for you.

The brain behind Copilot is a fancy computer program called a *large language model* (LLM). An LLM stores information about relationships between words, including which words make sense in certain contexts, and uses this to predict the best sequence of words to respond to a prompt.

Imagine that we asked you what the next word should be in this sentence: "The person opened the _____." There are many words that you could fill in here, like "door," "box," or "conversation," but there are also many words that wouldn't fit here, like "the," "it," or "open." An LLM takes into account the current context of words to produce the next word, and it keeps doing this until it has completed the task. It does this in a way that is *nondeterministic*, which just means that its decisions are somewhat random, meaning if you ask it to fill in that word, sometimes it will give you the word "door," and sometimes it will give you the word "box." This means that if you ask Copilot to give you code, it may give you different answers each time you ask.

In addition, notice that we didn't say anything about Copilot having an understanding of what it's doing. It just uses the current context to keep writing code. Keep this in mind throughout your journey: only we know whether the code that's generated does what we intended it to do. Very often it does, but you should always exercise healthy skepticism regardless. Figure 1.2 gives you an idea of how Copilot goes from prompt to program.

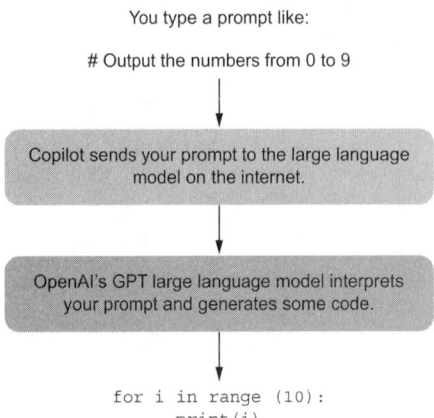

You type a prompt like:

Output the numbers from 0 to 9

Copilot sends your prompt to the large language model on the internet.

OpenAI's GPT large language model interprets your prompt and generates some code.

```
for i in range (10):
    print(i)
```

Figure 1.2 Going from prompt to program with Copilot

You might wonder why Copilot writes Python code for us and not machine code directly. Isn't Python an expendable intermediate step now? Well, no, and the reason is that Copilot is going to make mistakes. And if it's going to make mistakes that we need to fix, it's a lot easier to do that with Python than with machine code.

In fact, virtually no one checks if the machine code produced from Python is correct. This is partially because of the determinism of the Python language specification. One could imagine a future where Copilot conversations are so accurate that inspecting the Python is unnecessary, but we're a long way from that.

1.3   *How Copilot changes how we learn to program*

When learning how to program in the past, learners often spent most of their time working with the syntax and basic structure of programs. When we use the word *syntax*, we're referring to the symbols and words that are valid in a given language. Programmers would need to write all of the syntax of a program from scratch (character by character, line by line). People learning to program used to spend weeks or months to get to a point where they could write even basic programs. Now, Copilot can immediately write those same basic programs and offers code that is almost always syntactically and structurally correct. As you'll see in the rest of the book, we still need to verify that this code is correct because Copilot can make mistakes. However, we don't need to write it from scratch anymore. We believe Copilot and similar tools signal the end of the old way that people learned to program.

You, as someone interested in learning how to program, simply don't need to struggle with syntax, understanding exactly how to call a given Python function, and the host of other Python concepts needed to write code like you'd have had to in the past. Sure, we're going to learn about those concepts in this book, but not so that you can demonstrate your understanding by writing code from scratch that Copilot can produce easily. No, we'll learn those concepts only because they help us solve meaningful problems and interact productively with Copilot. Instead, you get to learn how to write larger, more meaningful software faster because of how an AI assistant fundamentally changes the skills needed to learn programming.

1.4 *What else can Copilot do for us?*

As we've seen, we can use Copilot to write Python code for us starting from an English description of what we want. So, we can say that Copilot takes a description in English syntax and gives us back code in Python syntax. That's a big win because learning programming syntax has historically been a major stumbling block for new programmers. What kind of bracket—[, (, or {—am I supposed to use here? Do I need indentation here? What order are we supposed to write these things in: x and then y, or y and then x?

Such questions abound, and—let's be honest—it's uninteresting stuff. Who cares about this when all we want to do is write a program to make something happen? Copilot can help free us from the tedium of syntax. We see this as an important step to help more people successfully write programs, and we look forward to the day when this artificial barrier is completely removed. For now, we still need Python syntax, but at least Copilot helps us with it.

But that's not all Copilot can do. Here are some associated—and no less important—tasks Copilot can help us with:

- *Explaining code*—When Copilot generates Python code for us, we'll need to determine whether that code does what we want. Again, as we said previously, Copilot is going to make mistakes. Although we're not interested in teaching you every nuance of how Python works (that's the old model of programming), we'll teach you how to read Python code to gain an overall understanding of what it does. We'll also use the Copilot feature that explains code to you in English. When you finish with this book and our explanations, you'll still have

Copilot available to help you understand that next bit of gnarly code that it gives you.

- *Making code easier to understand*—There are different ways to write code to accomplish the same task. Some may be easier to understand than others. You can ask Copilot to reorganize your code to make it easier to work with. Code that's easier to read is often easier to enhance or fix when needed.

- *Fixing bugs*—A *bug* is a mistake made when writing a program that can result in the program doing the wrong thing. Sometimes, your Python code almost works or works almost always but not in one specific circumstance. If you've listened to programmers talk, you may have heard the common story where a programmer would spend hours only to finally remove one = symbol that was making their program fail. That's not a fun few hours! In these cases, you can try the Copilot feature that helps to automatically find and fix the bug in the program.

- *Explaining errors*—If your code isn't working correctly, you'll often get an error report back from the Python runtime environment. Those errors can be fairly cryptic at times, but Copilot can help you interpret the error and guide you on how to fix it.

- *Finding Python libraries*—Python is a mature language with many modules (libraries) that can aid particular tasks, such as data analysis, writing games, working with different image file formats, and so on. A quick conversation with Copilot can often help you find modules that will make your work easier and give you examples to get you started.

1.5   *Risks and challenges when using Copilot*

Now that we're all pumped up about getting Copilot to write code for us, we need to talk about the dangers inherent in using AI assistants (see references [2] and [3] for elaboration on some of these points):

- *Copyright*—Copilot learned how to program using human-written code. (You'll hear people use the word "train" when talking about AI tools like Copilot. In this context, training is another word for learning.) More specifically, it was trained using millions of GitHub repositories containing open-source code. One worry is that Copilot will "steal" that code and give it to us. In our experience, Copilot doesn't often suggest a large chunk of someone else's code, but that possibility is there. Even if the code that Copilot gives us is a melding and transformation of various bits of other people's code, there may still be licensing problems. For example, who owns the code produced by Copilot? There is currently no consensus on the answer. The Copilot team is adding features to help; for example, Copilot can tell you whether the code that it produced is similar to already-existing code and what the license is on that code [4]. Learning and experimenting on your own is great, and we encourage that—but take care if you intend to use this code for purposes beyond your home. We're intentionally a bit vague here because it may take some time for laws to catch up to this new technology. It's best to play it safe while these debates are had within society.

- *Education*—As instructors of introductory programming courses ourselves, we've seen firsthand how well Copilot does on the types of assignments we've given our students in the past. In one study [5], Copilot was asked to solve 166 common introductory programming tasks. How well did it do? On its first attempt, it solved almost 50% of these problems. Give Copilot a little more information, and that number goes up to 80%. Education needs to change in light of tools like Copilot, and instructors are currently discussing how these changes may look. At some schools, students are allowed to use Copilot to aid in their learning and on their assignments. At other schools, Copilot isn't allowed in some contexts (i.e., exams) or for some students (computer science majors). At many schools, LLMs are being allowed to act as tutors for students. In some cases, the LLM tutors are just regular LLMs like Copilot or ChatGPT, but, in other cases, the LLM interface has been changed to restrict the kind of answers students receive. It's still too early to know how LLMs will affect computing education, but trends like these have already started to emerge.

- *Code quality*—We need to be careful not to trust Copilot, especially with sensitive code or code that needs to be secure. Code written for medical devices, for example, or code that handles sensitive user data must always be thoroughly understood. It's tempting to ask Copilot for code, marvel at the code that it produces, and accept that code without scrutiny. But that code might be plain wrong. In this book, we'll work on code that won't be deployed at large, so, while we'll focus on getting the correct code, we won't worry about the implications of using this code for broader purposes. We'll also build the foundations you'll need to independently determine whether code is correct.

- *Code security*—As with code quality, code security is absolutely not assured when we get code from Copilot. For example, if we're working with user data, getting code from Copilot isn't enough. We would need to perform security audits and have expertise to determine that the code is secure. Again, though, we won't be using code from Copilot in real-world scenarios, so we won't focus on security concerns.

- *Not an expert*—One of the markers of being an expert is awareness of what one knows and, equally important, what one doesn't. Experts are also often able to state how confident they are in their response, and if they aren't confident enough, they will learn further until they know that they know. Copilot and, more generally, LLMs, don't do this. You ask them a question, and they answer, plain as that. They will confabulate if necessary: they will mix bits of truth with bits of garbage into a plausible-sounding but overall nonsensical response. For example, we've seen LLMs fabricate obituaries for people who are alive, which doesn't make any sense, yet the "obituaries" do contain elements of truth about people's lives. When asked why an abacus can perform math faster than a computer, we've seen LLMs come up with confident-sounding responses—including something about abacuses being mechanical and therefore necessarily the fastest. There is ongoing work in this area for LLMs to be able to say, "Sorry, no, I don't know this," but we're not there yet. They don't know what they don't know, and that means they need supervision.

- *Bias*—LLMs will reproduce the same biases present in the data on which they were trained. If you ask Copilot to generate a list of names, it will generate primarily English names. If you ask for a graph, it may produce a graph that doesn't consider perceptual differences among humans. And, if you ask for code, it may produce code in a style reminiscent of how particular groups write code. (After all, the demographic groups that are well represented in computing wrote most of the code in the world, and Copilot is trained on that code.) Computer science and software engineering have long suffered from a lack of diversity. We can't afford to stifle diversity further, and we need to reverse the trend. We need to let more people in and allow them to express themselves in their own ways. How this will be handled with tools like Copilot is currently being worked out and is crucially important to the future of programming. However, we believe Copilot has the potential to improve diversity by lowering barriers to entry into the field.

1.6   *The skills we need*

If Copilot can write our code, explain it, and fix bugs in it, are we just done? Do we just tell Copilot what to do and celebrate our pure awesomeness?

No. First, Copilot can make mistakes. The code it gives us might be syntactically correct, but sometimes it doesn't do what we want it to do. We need to be vigilant to catch when Copilot makes these mistakes. Second, although some of the skills that programmers rely on (e.g., writing correct syntax) will decrease in importance, other skills remain critical. For example, you can't throw a huge task at Copilot like, "Make a video game. Oh, and make it fun." Copilot will fail. Instead, we need to break down such a large problem into smaller tasks that Copilot can help us with. How do we break a problem down like that? Not easily, it turns out. Humans need to develop this key skill when engaging in conversations with tools like Copilot, and we teach this skill throughout the book.

Other skills, believe it or not, may take on even more importance with Copilot. Testing code has always been a critical task in creating high-quality code. We know a lot about testing code written by humans because we know where to look for typical problems. We know that humans often make programming errors at the boundaries of values. For example, if we wrote a program to multiply two numbers, we'd likely get most values right but maybe not when one value is 0. What about code written by AI, where 20 lines of flawless code could hide 1 line so absurd that we likely wouldn't expect it there? We don't have experience with that. We need to test even more carefully than before.

We also need to know how to fix mistakes when the code is wrong. This process is called *debugging* and is still essential, particularly when Copilot gives you code that is close to correct but not quite there yet.

Finally, some required skills are entirely new. The main one here is called *prompt engineering*, which involves how to tell Copilot what to do. As mentioned earlier, when we're asking Copilot to write some code, we're using a prompt to make the request. Although we can use English to write that prompt and ask for what we want, it's not enough. We need to be very precise if we want Copilot to have any chance of doing the right thing. And, even when we're precise, Copilot may still do the wrong thing. In that case, we need to first identify that Copilot has indeed made a mistake. Then, we can try to tweak our description to hopefully nudge it in the right direction. In our experience, seemingly minor changes to the prompt can have outsized effects on what Copilot produces. In this book, we'll teach you all of these skills.

1.7 Societal concerns about AI code assistants like Copilot

There's societal uncertainty right now about AI code assistants like Copilot. We thought we'd end the chapter with a few questions and our current answers. Perhaps you've been wondering about some of these questions yourself! Our answers may turn out to be hilariously incorrect, but they do capture our current thoughts as two professors and researchers who have dedicated their careers to teaching programming:

Q: Are there going to be fewer tech and programming jobs now that we have Copilot?

A: Probably not. What we do expect to change is the nature of these jobs. For example, we see Copilot as being able to help with many tasks typically associated with entry-level programming jobs. This doesn't mean that entry-level programming jobs go away, only that they change as programmers are able to get more done given increasingly sophisticated tools.

Q: Will Copilot stifle human creativity? Will it just keep swirling around and recycling the same code that humans have already written, limiting the introduction of new ideas?

A: We suspect not. Copilot helps us work at a higher level, further removed from the underlying machine code, assembly code, or Python code. Computer scientists use the term abstraction *to refer to the extent that we can disconnect ourselves from the low-level details of computers. Abstraction has been happening since the dawn of computer science, and we don't seem to have suffered for it. On the contrary, it enables us to ignore problems that have already been solved and focus on solving broader and broader problems. Indeed, it's been the advent of better programming languages that have facilitated better software—software that powers Google search, Amazon shopping carts, and macOS weren't written (and likely couldn't have been written) when we only had assembly!*

Q: I keep hearing about ChatGPT. What is it? Is it the same as Copilot?

A: It's not the same as Copilot, but it's built on the same technology. Rather than focus on code, though, ChatGPT focuses on knowledge in general. As a result, it has insinuated itself into a wider variety of tasks than Copilot. For example, it can answer questions, write essays, and even do well on a Wharton MBA exam [6]. Education will need to change as a result: we can't have people ChatGPTing their way to MBAs! The worthwhile ways in which we spend our time may change. Will humans keep writing books and, if so, in what ways? Will people want to read books knowing they were partially or fully written by AI? There will be effects across industries, including finance, health care, and publishing [7]. At the same time, there is unfettered hype right now, so it can be difficult to separate truth from fiction. This problem is compounded by the simple truth that no one knows what's going to happen here in the long term. There's an old adage coined by Roy Amara (known as Amara's law) that says, "We tend to overestimate the effect of a technology in the short run and underestimate the effect in the long run." As such, we need to do our best to be tuned into the discussion so that we can adapt accordingly.

In the next chapter, we'll get you started using Copilot on your computer so you can get up and running writing software.

Summary

- Copilot is an AI assistant, which is an AI agent that helps you get work done.
- Copilot changes how humans interact with computers, as well as the way we write programs.
- Copilot changes the focus of skills we need to hone (less focus on syntax, more focus on problem decomposition and testing).
- Copilot is nondeterministic; sometimes it produces correct code, and sometimes it doesn't. We need to be vigilant.
- Problems around copyright of code, education and job training, and bias in Copilot results still need to be worked out.

Getting started with Copilot

This chapter covers

- Setting up Python, Visual Studio Code, and Copilot on your system
- Introducing the Copilot design process
- Understanding Copilot's value for a data processing task

We want you to be able to create software yourself right from the start. To do this, we'll guide you through setting up Visual Studio Code (VS Code), Python, and Copilot on your machine and familiarize you with how to interact with these tools. After you've set up the tools, you'll be able to follow along with our examples and start creating software yourself. There's no substitute for practice, and we believe you can learn right alongside us for the remainder of the book.

Once you've set up Copilot, we'll walk through a fun example that showcases the power of Copilot in solving standard tasks. You'll see how to interact with Copilot, and you'll learn how you can write software without writing any actual code. Keep in mind that Copilot isn't perfect, and you need to be able to read and understand a little Python to get what you want, but it gives you a big head start. Let's get started creating your first computer program.

2.1   *Setting up your computer to start learning*

Learning how to write software requires that you go beyond just reading about it and actually perform the task of writing software. If this were a book on how to play guitar, would you keep reading it without ever trying to play the guitar? We thought not. Reading this book without following along and trying it out yourself would be like watching a marathon runner finish the race and thinking you're ready to go run one yourself. We'll stop with the analogies, but seriously, you need to get your software installed and running before we go farther.

What scares us the most right now is that we just hit the most common point where novices, even those eager to learn programming, tend to fail, and we *really* want to see you succeed. Now, you might be thinking, "Wait, really? We're just getting started." Yes, that's exactly the point. In Leo's popular Coursera course about learning Java programming [1], can you guess the point when most new learners leave? Is it the challenging assignment at the end of the course that involves plotting earthquake markers on the globe in real time? No. It's actually the warmup assignment where learners must set up their programming environment. As such, we understand this could be a hurdle for you. We hope that with this not-so-subtle nudge, we can help you achieve all the goals you had in mind when you bought this book. It all starts with installing the software.

2.2   *The software we'll be using*

To set up and use Copilot easily, we'll install the software editing tools used by novices and software engineers alike. The tools you'll use are Python, VS Code, GitHub, and Copilot. Of course, if you already have all of these tools installed, jump to section 2.6.1.

2.2.1   *Python*

Any programming language would have worked for this book, but we picked Python because it's one of the most popular programming languages in the world and is the language we teach in our introductory courses at our universities. As we said in chapter 1, compared to other languages, Python is easier to read, easier to understand, and easier to write. For this book, Copilot will primarily generate the code, not you. However, you'll want to read and understand the code generated by Copilot, and Python is great for that.

2.2.2   *Visual Studio Code*

You can use any text editor to program. However, if you want a nice programming environment where you can write code, easily get suggestions from Copilot, and run your code, VS Code is our preferred tool. VS Code is used by novices learning software and is well liked by students [2]. It's also used globally by professional software engineers, which means you can work and learn while using this environment after finishing the book. For VS Code to work for this book, you'll need to install a few extensions that enable working with Python and using Copilot, but one of the great things about VS Code is that it's easy to install those extensions.

2.2.3   *GitHub account*

GitHub is an industry-standard tool for developing, maintaining, and storing software. We won't use GitHub in this book, however. We're signing up for GitHub simply because you'll need an account to access Copilot. Signing up for a GitHub account is free, but, at the time of writing, they charge for Copilot. If you're a student, they will waive that fee. If you aren't a student, as of writing, you can get a 30-day free trial.

You might ask why they charge for the service, and there's a good answer. It's expensive to build the GPT models (imagine thousands of computers running for a year to build the model), and GitHub incurs costs by providing predictions from the model (many machines are receiving your input, running it through the model, and generating your output). If you're not ready to commit to using Copilot, you could make a calendar note for roughly 25 days from the day you sign up, and if you aren't using Copilot at that time, just cancel. If, on the other hand, you've succeeded in learning how to write software with Copilot and are using it to improve your productivity at work or as a hobby, it may make sense to keep it.

Over the course of this chapter, we'll install all of these tools, but we're going to do this in two parts. The first part, coming up next, will get you set up to write and run code on your own so you become familiar with that process. The second part will set you up to use Copilot to assist you in the process of writing code.

2.3   *Getting your system set up: Part 1*

In this first part of our installation guide, we'll install Python and VS Code. To streamline this section, we're just outlining the main steps that you should follow. However, there are more detailed instructions available in the following locations:

- VS Code maintains a tutorial for getting started writing code in Python at https://mng.bz/znjQ.
- The website for this book (https://mng.bz/0M46) provides detailed instructions for setting up both PC and macOS systems. Because the websites for these tools might change after we write this book, we encourage you to use a combination of the GitHub link and the book website together.
- In the online book forum (https://mng.bz/NBK1), you can ask for help and see the answers to a list of frequently asked questions.

The primary steps you'll need to accomplish are as follows:

1 Install Python:
   - Go to www.python.org/downloads/.
   - Download and install the latest version of Python (3.12.3 at the time of writing).
2 Install VS Code:
   - Go to https://code.visualstudio.com/download, and select the main download for your operating system (e.g., Windows or Mac).
   - Download and install the latest version of VS Code.

  3 Install a VS Code Extension: (for details, see https://mng.bz/9o01).
     – *Python (by Microsoft)*—Follow the instructions at https://mng.bz/j0gP to set up
       the Python extension correctly (specifically, selecting the correct interpreter).

Although the instructions here are brief, we know in reality they can take some time.
If you encounter any problems, consult the resources mentioned earlier for more
detailed setup instructions.

2.4   *Working with Python in Visual Studio Code*

Now that your system is set up, let's get acquainted with the VS Code interface shown
in figure 2.1. (You may need to click the Explorer icon in the middle/top left to get
this same view.) The following regions are identified in figure 2.1:

- *Activity Bar*—On the far left is the Activity Bar where we can open file folders
  (also known as directories) or install extensions (as you did to install the Python
  extension in the previous section).
- *Side Bar*—The Side Bar shows what is presently open in the Activity Bar. In figure 2.1, the Activity Bar shows the Explorer selected, so the Side Bar is showing
  the files in the current folder.
- *Editor Pane(s)*—These are the primary areas we'll use to create our software. The
  editor in the Editor Pane is similar to any other text editor in that you can write,
  edit, copy, and paste text using the clipboard. The editor is special, however,
  because it's designed to work well with code. At this point, we'll be writing code
  in this window, but later in this chapter, you'll primarily work in this window by
  asking Copilot to generate code, and then you'll test that code.

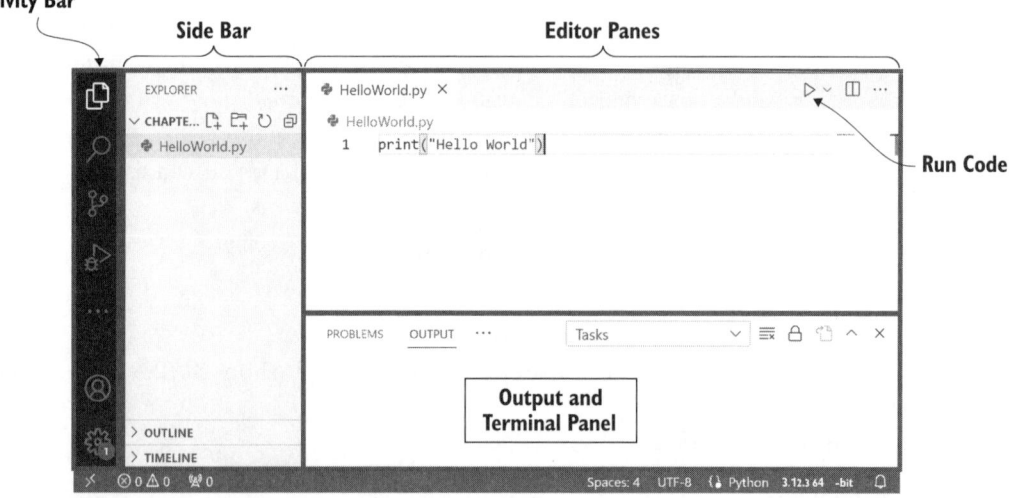

Figure 2.1   The VS Code interface [3]

- *Output and Terminal Panel*—In this area of the interface, you'll see the output of your code or any errors that have occurred in the following tabs: Problems, Output, Debug Console, and Terminal. We'll primarily use the Problems tab, where we can see potential errors in our code, and the Terminal tab, which allows us to interact with Python and see the output of our code.

VS Code has many different color schemes, so you can use any color scheme you like as the functionality is the same.

2.4.1 Set up your working folder

In the top of the Activity Bar on the left in VS Code, you'll find Explorer as the top icon. After you click Explorer, you should see a No Folder Open message. Click the button to open a folder, and select a folder on your computer (or make a new one—we like the folder name fun_with_Copilot). Once you've opened this folder, your workspace will be the folder you opened, which means you should have your code and any data files, like the one we'll use later in this chapter, in that folder.

File not found or file missing errors

If you ever receive an error that says you're missing a file, take heart: these are the kinds of errors that everyone makes. They can be really annoying when writing software. Perhaps you just didn't put the file in your working folder—this happens—but it's an easy fix by copying or moving the file into the correct folder. However, sometimes, you'll see the file in the folder, but when you run your code in VS Code, Python can't seem to find it. If this happens to you (it happened to us when writing the book!), be sure to have the folder with the code and the desired file open using Explorer in VS Code (as shown in the Side Bar in figure 2.1).

2.4.2 Check to see if your setup is working properly

Let's check to see if we've set up everything properly. To do this, we start by creating a new file to hold our program. You do this by going to File > New File (figure 2.2), and then selecting Python File (figure 2.3).

After creating the file, we like to make sure we've saved the file. Go to File > Save As, and name this file first_program.py. Next, in the text editor, type the following exactly as it appears here:

```
print("Hello World")
```

You might already be guessing what will happen when we run this program. It should print "Hello World" to the screen. Let's run it and see! First, you'll want to save your file by going to File > Save.

> **WARNING** Be sure to save your file before you run it! We're embarrassed to admit the amount of time we've spent trying to fix code that was correct but hadn't been saved.

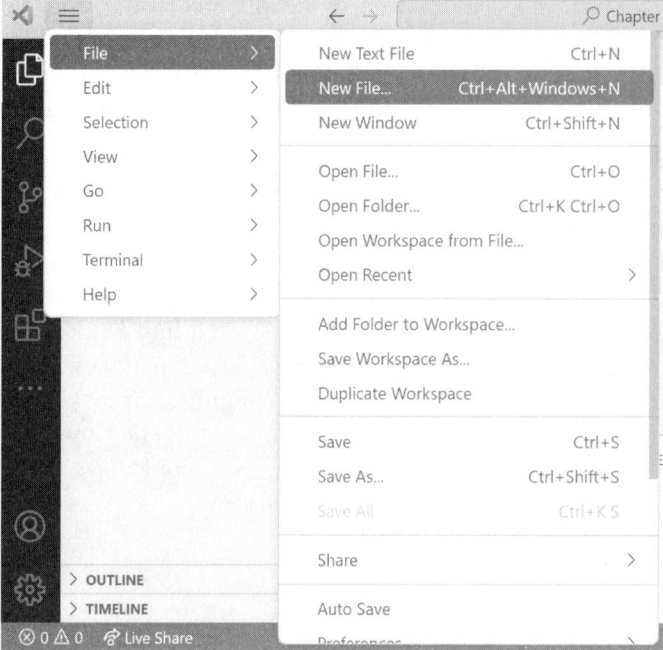

Figure 2.2   How to create a new file in VS Code

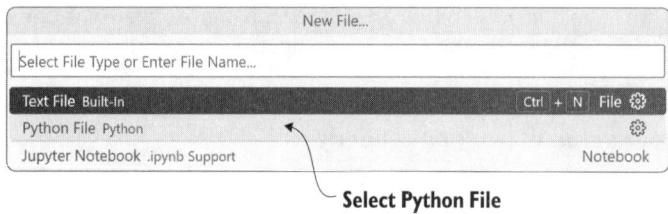

Figure 2.3   Select Python File to create the new file as a Python file.

To run your program, go to the top-right corner of the text editor, and click the Run Code icon, as shown earlier in figure 2.1. After clicking the icon, in the Terminal section at the bottom, you should see something like this:

```
> & C:/Users/<YOUR_NAME>/AppData/Local/Programs/Python/Python312/python.exe
➥ c:/Users/<YOUR_NAME>/Copilot/first_program.py
Hello World
```

The top line starting with > is the command for the computer to run your code, and all it says is to run your first_program.py using Python. The second line is the output from running the command, and it says, "Hello World," which is what we'd hoped to see.

Congratulations! You've written your first program! We now know that your programming environment is set up correctly. Let's get started with writing just a couple more small pieces of code to get familiar with this workflow, and then we'll move on to the workflow with Copilot.

2.5 *Writing and running some small programs*

You've just finished the major step of installing Python and VS Code and getting it working. Before we start working with our AI assistant, Copilot, let's write a few more small programs so you get a feel for typing and running code.

Let's start with writing a small program that involves adding numbers. Go ahead and delete the line you wrote that prints Hello World, and replace it with the following:

```
a = 10
b = 20
print(a + b)
```

What do you think that code will print? Will it print "a + b", or will it print 30? Go ahead and run it and see.

The computer calculated the sum of 10 and 20 and printed 30. This is pretty neat, right? We've used the computer to do some small calculations. If you change the value for a or b, what do you think will happen? Feel free to play with this on your own.

We'll spend a lot more time later in this book talking about the details of how to read code, but if you're curious, here's how to read that code:

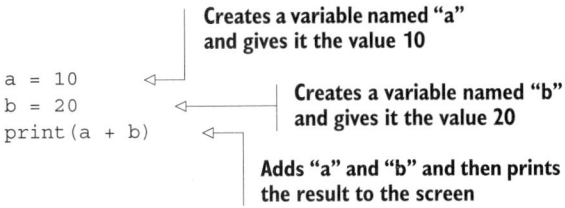

The key piece right now is that you become comfortable with the idea of typing code in the Editor Pane and running it using the Run button.

Let's do just one more small example. Suppose you want to calculate the area of a square. Recalling our formulas for shapes, the area of a square whose sides are length *s* is as follows:

$$\text{Area} = s^2$$

Let's start with defining a side to be a certain length and then printing the area:

```
side = 5
area = side * side
print("Side length:", side, " Square area is:", area)
```

We encourage you to type and run that code. When you run it, you should get the following:

```
Side length: 5 Square area is: 25
```

Did you run into any problems typing in that code? We suspect many of you did. If you missed a quotation mark, a comma, or a parenthesis, you probably got some kind of unpleasant error like this (here, if you forgot a comma) when you ran the code:

```
File "c:\Users\Leo\Copilot\first_program.py", line 7
    print("Side length:" side, " Square area is:", area)
          ^^^^^^^^^^^^^^^^^^^^^
SyntaxError: invalid syntax. Perhaps you forgot a comma?
```

In the old way of learning programming, you'd spend a lot of time making sure you understood the exact characters to write to make the programming language, Python, happy. We'll reiterate the good news: with an AI assistant like Copilot, syntax becomes much, much less important. Let's get Copilot installed so you can learn how to work with that tool.

2.6   Getting your system set up: Part 2

Now we're ready for the second part of our installation guide. There are some new steps here beyond what you did earlier. Again, feel free to refer to the following resources for more details on the installation process:

- Visit GitHub's documentation at https://mng.bz/WVP1.
- The website for this book (https://mng.bz/0M46) provides detailed instructions for setting up both PC and macOS systems. Because the websites for these tools might change after we write this book, we encourage you to use a combination of the GitHub link and the book website together.
- In the online book forum (https://mng.bz/NBK1), you can ask for help and see the answers to a list of frequently asked questions.

The primary steps you'll need to accomplish this time are as follows:

1 Set up your GitHub account, and sign up for Copilot:
   - Go to https://github.com/signup, and sign up for a GitHub account.
   - Go into your settings in GitHub and enable Copilot. This is the point where you'll either need to verify that you're a student or sign up for the 30-day free trial (available at the time of this writing).
2 Install the following VS Code extension(s) (for details, see https://mng.bz/9o01):
   - *GitHub Copilot (by GitHub)*—At the time of writing, installing GitHub Copilot automatically installs the GitHub Copilot Chat. Please check that GitHub Copilot Chat (by GitHub) has also been installed by checking your installed extensions. If it hasn't, you'll need to add this extension as well.

We know that the steps here are brief. If you encounter any problems, we encourage you to consult the resources mentioned earlier for more detailed setup instructions.

2.6.1 Check to see if Copilot is working properly

If your installation worked properly, you should see the Copilot icon (highlighted in figure 2.4) in the bottom-right corner of the VS Code interface.

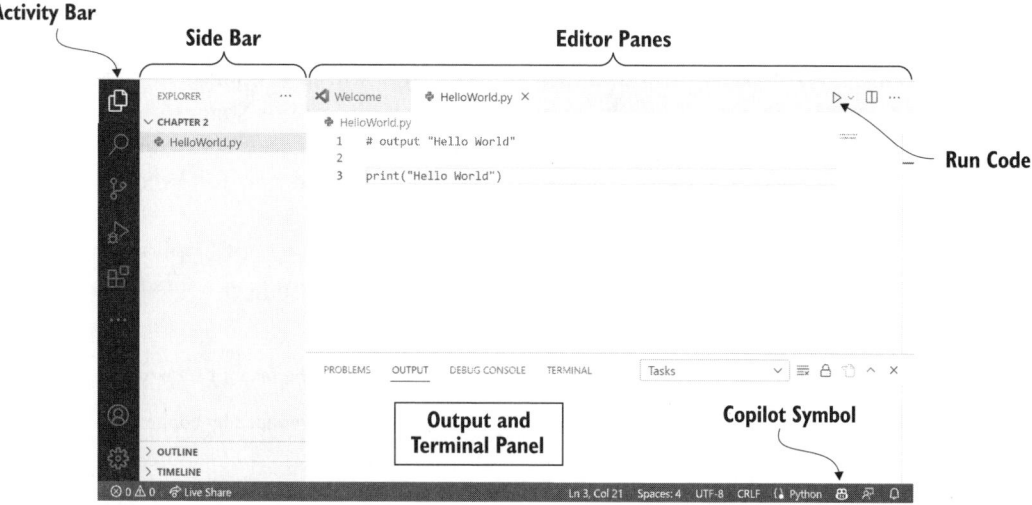

Figure 2.4 VS Code interface with Copilot running

Let's check to see that Copilot is working correctly by editing the first_program.py file. Feel free to delete whatever code you have in there now and start fresh or create a new .py file—it's up to you. In the text editor, type the following:

```
# output "Hello Copilot" to the screen
```

The prompts and code we write will be in bold font to help distinguish between what we write, and the code and comments Copilot may give us. The # sign at the start is important (and you should include it in what you typed). It means that what you wrote is a comment (depending on your VS Code color palette, it may be a different color than the code we're about to produce). Comments are *not* code: the computer executes code and doesn't execute comments. Comments are used by programmers to provide a human-readable summary of what the code did to help other software engineers read the code. Today, its purpose has expanded to also prompt Copilot. After writing a comment (and sometimes even while writing comments), Copilot will attempt to give us suggestions. You can think of this as a much more sophisticated autocomplete, like when you type "New York T" in your search engine, and it autocompletes with "New York Times."

To trigger Copilot to start giving us code (or more comments), press Enter at the end of the line, and you'll be at the start of a new line. Pause for a moment, and you should see something appear. Until accepted, Copilot's suggestions are in light gray italics. If you don't get a suggestion yet, you may need to press Enter a second time to trigger Copilot to suggest the code. Here's what happened for us:

```
# output "Hello Copilot" to the screen
print("Hello Copilot")
```

If you still don't see a suggestion from Copilot, try pressing Ctrl-Enter (hold Ctrl while pressing Enter). When you press Ctrl-Enter, a new window will appear to the right of your editor window with the program called GitHub Copilot Suggestions. If that window doesn't appear, there may be something wrong with your setup, and we encourage you to go to the book website to double-check that you followed all the steps correctly or to find (or ask for) help.

If you saw the suggestion from Copilot, press Tab to accept Copilot's suggestion. Once you do this, the suggestion that was previously in light gray italics should now be in a standard font:

```
# output "Hello Copilot" to the screen          ◁——— The prompt we wrote
print("Hello Copilot")                           ◁
                                                     The code produced by Copilot
```

If you're seeing different code than this, it's because of something we mentioned earlier: Copilot is nondeterministic so you may see different code than we do. We mention this because sometimes Copilot makes a minor mistake with the code here and may give you code similar to this:

```
print "Hello Copilot"
```

You might think this slight difference (no parentheses around `"Hello Copilot"`) wouldn't matter, but it does. Before Python 3, this was the correct syntax for a print statement, and when Python 3 was introduced, it switched to the code with parentheses. Because we're running Python 3, you need to have the parentheses for the code to work. You might ask why Copilot gets this wrong. The problem is Copilot was trained on some old Python code as part of its training. If this seems annoying, we agree. But it's another hint of the frustration novice programmers went through before Copilot. Most of what Copilot suggests is syntactically correct. But if you're a novice writing the code from scratch, missing parentheses or a missing colon somewhere might cost you a lot of time. Now we have the correct code as

```
# output "Hello Copilot" to the screen
print("Hello Copilot")
```

which is similar to the "Hello World" code we produced manually earlier. We hope you're encouraged to see that Copilot can generate code like this!

Now, let's see how it does in the example of determining the area of a square from the previous section. Go ahead and enter the following code with the prompt (again, shown in bold):

```
side = 5
area = side * side
# Print the side length is *** and the area is ***
```

We received the following response from Copilot:

```
print("The side length is", side, "and the area is", area)
```

Notice how Copilot handled that piece of code well. For humans, especially learners new to programming, it's easy to make a mistake, but Copilot rarely does. We hope Copilot gave you a similar response. Feel free to play around with Copilot for a bit if you'd like to become more comfortable with the interface.

We now know that your programming environment and Copilot are set up correctly, so we can move into a larger programming task. But before we do, we'd like to go over tips for how to deal with some common problems we've encountered when working with Copilot, so you have these tips available to you when working through the next example.

2.7 *Addressing common Copilot challenges*

It may seem early to start talking about common challenges with Copilot, but you may have already run into challenges when writing your first program. You'll certainly encounter some of these when working through our next example and in the next chapters, so we wanted to give these to you now.

In our time working with Copilot, we've run into a few common challenges. These challenges will likely decrease with time as Copilot improves, but they were still problems at the time of this writing. Although the challenges in table 2.1 aren't the only ones you might encounter, we hope our tips on how to address these common challenges will help you get up and running quickly. We'll keep a running list at our book's website, so feel free to reach out to us on the forums if you feel we've missed something.

Table 2.1   Common challenges working with Copilot

Challenge	Description	Remedies

Comments only	If you give Copilot a prompt using the comment symbol (#), when you start a new line, it wants to just give you more comments rather than code. For example:
	
	`# output "Hello Copilot"`
	`to the screen`
	`# print "Hello world" to`
	`the screen`
	
	We've seen Copilot generate line after line of comments, sometimes repeating itself! When this happens, remedy 3 in the column to the right (use docstrings) is sometimes the most effective.
		1. Add a newline (press Enter) between your comment and Copilot's suggestion to help it switch from comments to code.
		
		2. If a newline doesn't work, you can type a letter or two of code (no comment symbol). A couple letters from a keyword in your prompt usually works. For example:
		
		`# output "Hello Copilot" to the`
		`screen`
		`pr`
		
		A couple letters from a keyword typically causes Copilot to give a code suggestion.
		
		3. Switch from using # comments to docstring comments like this:
		
		`"""`
		`output "Hello Copilot" to the`
		`screen`
		`"""`
		
		4. Use Ctrl-Enter to see if Copilot will give you suggestions that are code rather than comments.

Wrong code	Sometimes Copilot just gives you obviously wrong code from the start. (You'll learn throughout this book how to identify incorrect code!) In addition, sometimes Copilot seems to get stuck down wrong paths. For example, it might seem to be trying to solve a different problem than what you've asked it to solve. (Remedy 3, in particular, can help with getting Copilot to go down a new path.)	Much of this book is about how to address this problem, but here are some quick tips to get Copilot to help: 1. Change your prompt to see if you can better describe what you need. 2. Try using Ctrl-Enter to find a suggestion from Copilot that is the correct code. 3. Close the VS Code program, wait a little bit, and restart it. This can help clear the Copilot cache to get new suggestions. 4. Try breaking down the problem into smaller steps (see chapter 7 for more details). 5. Debug the code (see chapter 8). 6. Try asking ChatGPT for the code, and paste its suggestions into VS Code. A different large language model (LLM) can sometimes give suggestions that help the other LLM to get unstuck.

Table 2.1 **Common challenges working with Copilot** *(continued)*

Challenge	Description	Remedies
Copilot gives you `# YOUR CODE HERE`	We've had Copilot seem to tell us to write our own code by generating this (or similar text) after a prompt: `# YOUR CODE HERE`	We believe this is happening when we ask Copilot to solve a problem that has been given by an instructor to students to solve in the past. Why? Well, when we write our assignments for our students, we (as instructors) often write some code and then tell our students to write the rest by writing `# YOUR CODE HERE` where we want students to write their code. Students tend to leave that comment in their solution code, which means Copilot was trained to think this comment is an important part of the solution (it's not). Often, we're able to solve this problem by finding reasonable solutions in the Copilot suggestions with Ctrl-Enter, but please see the remedies for Wrong Code if that doesn't work.
Missing modules	Copilot gives you code, but it won't work because there are modules missing. (*Modules* are additional libraries that can be added to Python to provide prebuilt functionality.)	In section 2.8.2, see the "Python Modules" sidebar for a description of modules, and see chapter 5 for instructions on how to use modules.

2.8 Our path forward

You've already seen that Copilot can generate code for you. So, can we just ask Copilot to solve our tasks for us? We're afraid not. We still need to learn some essential skills to be able to work effectively with Copilot and to design software that's meaningful to us.

To help you appreciate the skills you'll need to learn and to get you excited about where you're headed, we'll give you a larger example that represents what we hope you'll be able to do on your own about halfway through reading and working through this book.

2.8.1 How we'll be working with Copilot throughout the book

We'll expand on this workflow in later chapters, but the core elements will be the same:

1　Write a prompt to Copilot using comments (#) or docstrings (`"""`).
2　Let Copilot generate code for you.
3　Check to see whether the code is correct by reading through it and by testing:
  – If it works, move to step 1 for the next thing you'd like it to do.
  – If it doesn't work, delete the code from Copilot, go back to step 1, and modify the prompt (and see the remedies shown previously in table 2.1).

2.8.2   *Showcasing Copilot's value in a data processing task*

For this bigger example, we want you to focus on how we're interacting with the tools and the skills we need. We don't expect you to understand the code until much later in the book. We provide the code solely so you can see what Copilot gave us, but you don't need to try to understand the code in this chapter.

You're welcome to follow through this example with us or just read through it. We haven't given you the skills yet to progress if you get stuck, so feel free to wait to work through an example like this until a later chapter. We'll assume for the rest of this section that you'll just be reading along.

We want to start with some data processing as this is something that many of you have likely done in your personal or professional lives. To find a dataset, we went to a great website called Kaggle [4], which has tons of datasets freely available for use. Many of them include important data such as health statistics for different countries, information to help track the spread of disease, and so on. We're not going to use those because we'd like to have something lighter for our first program. Because both of us are American football fans, we'll play with the National Football League (NFL) offensive stats database. Here's the link to the dataset we found if you want to look into it yourself: https://mng.bz/86pw. The dataset has NFL information from 2019 to 2022 (figure 2.5).

```
nfl_offensive_stats.csv  ✕

nfl_offensive_stats.csv
   1   game_id,player_id,position ,player,team,pass_cmp,pass_att,pass_yds,p
   2   201909050chi,RodgAa00,QB,Aaron Rodgers,GNB,18,30,203,1,0,5,37,47,91.
   3   201909050chi,JoneAa00,RB,Aaron Jones,GNB,0,0,0,0,0,0,0,0,0,13,39,0,9
   4   201909050chi,ValdMa00,WR,Marquez Valdes-Scantling,GNB,0,0,0,0,0,0,0,
   5   201909050chi,AdamDa01,WR,Davante Adams,GNB,0,0,0,0,0,0,0,0,0,0,0,0,6
   6   201909050chi,GrahJi00,TE,Jimmy Graham,GNB,0,0,0,0,0,0,0,0,0,0,0,0,0,
   7   201909050chi,DaviTr03,WR,Trevor Davis,GNB,0,0,0,0,0,0,0,0,0,0,0,0,0,
   8   201909050chi,TonyRo00,TE,Robert Tonyan,GNB,0,0,0,0,0,0,0,0,0,0,0,0,6
   9   201909050chi,WillJa06,RB,Jamaal Williams,GNB,0,0,0,0,0,0,0,0,0,5,0,6
  10   201909050chi,LewiMa00,TE,Marcedes Lewis,GNB,0,0,0,0,0,0,0,0,0,0,0,0,
  11   201909050chi,TrubMi00,QB,Mitchell Trubisky,CHI,26,45,228,0,1,5,20,27
  12   201909050chi,DaviMi01,RB,Mike Davis,CHI,0,0,0,0,0,0,0,0,0,5,19,0,8,7
  13   201909050chi,MontDa01,RB,David Montgomery,CHI,0,0,0,0,0,0,0,0,0,6,18
```

Figure 2.5   The first few columns and rows of the nfl_offensive_stats.csv dataset

STEP 1: UNDERSTANDING OUR DATASET

The nfl_offensive_stats.csv file is a comma-separated values (CSV) text file (refer to figure 2.5 for a portion of the file). This is a standard format for storing data. It has a header row at the top that explains what's in every column. The way that we (or a computer) know the boundaries between columns is to use commas between cells. Also notice that each row is placed on its own line. Good news: Python has a bunch of tools for reading in CSV files.

Let's start by exploring what is stored in this file. To preview the file's contents, you can look at it on the Kaggle webpage under Detail or download and open it in either VS Code or in spreadsheet software such as Microsoft Excel. Don't worry about downloading and using this file just yet, that's for later in the book. However, if you were to download and open it, here's the start of the header (top) row (also shown earlier in figure 2.5):

```
game_id,player_id,position ,player,team,pass_cmp,pass_att,pass_yds,…
```

There are more columns, but these are enough for our first task. We'd like to know which quarterback has done the best over this time period.

STEP 2: HOW WELL DID ALL THE QUARTERBACKS DO OVER THAT TIME PERIOD?

If you don't follow American football, that's okay. You don't need to know the game to follow along. Quarterbacks are responsible for throwing the football. We'll start then with looking at how many yards they passed for in that time period. We only want to compare against other quarterbacks because they are the players whose job is to throw the ball. Sure, a running back might throw the ball once a season, and it's often fun when they do, but it's not really their job. To include only the quarterbacks, we'll need to tell Copilot to limit our results to just players whose *Position* (the third column) is *QB* (stands for Quarterback). To solve this task, we created a new Python file called nfl_stats.py and had a conversation with Copilot that you can see in listing 2.1.

Listing 2.1 Copilot's code to analyze the top quarterbacks

```
"""
open the csv file called "nfl_offensive_stats.csv" and
read in the csv data from the file
"""
```

Our first prompt to read in the data

```
# import the csv module
import csv
```

Copilot's responses sometimes include comments. Comments that we get from Copilot won't be in bold, unlike our prompts, which are in bold.

```
# open the csv file
with open('nfl_offensive_stats.csv', 'r') as f:
    # read the csv data
    data = list(csv.reader(f))
```

```
"""
the 3rd column in data is player position, the fourth
column is the player, and the 8th column is the
passing yards. For each player whose position in
column 3 is "QB", determine the sum of yards from
column 8
"""
```

Our second prompt to analyze the data

```
# create a dictionary to hold the player name and passing yards
passing_yards = {}
```

```
# loop through the data
for row in data:
    # check if the player is a quarterback
    if row[2] == 'QB':
        # check if the player is already in the dictionary
        if row[3] in passing_yards:
            # add the passing yards to the existing value
            passing_yards[row[3]] += int(row[7])
        else:
            # add the player to the dictionary
            passing_yards[row[3]] = int(row[7])

"""
print the sum of the passing yards sorted by sum
of passing yards in descending order
"""
for player in sorted(passing_yards, key=passing_yards.get, reverse=True):
    print(player, passing_yards[player])
```

Our third prompt to print the results

Notice that we gave Copilot three prompts. The first was to handle the input data, the second was to process the data, and the third was to output the response. This cycle of input data, process data, and output data is exceptionally common in programming tasks.

If you chose to follow along with us and gave these prompts to Copilot, you might have gotten back different code. That's okay because Copilot is nondeterministic, so it won't always give the same result. However, if it gave you different code, we haven't equipped you with the tools to know if it's correct yet. As such, feel free to just use our code if you'd like to follow along.

Reminder: Copilot is nondeterministic

As mentioned in both chapter 1 and this chapter, Copilot is nondeterministic, so what Copilot gives you may not match what it gives us. This is going to be a challenge for the rest of the book: What do you do if you get a wrong result when we get a right result? We're fairly confident that Copilot will give you a correct answer here, but if you get a *wrong answer* from Copilot, go ahead and read the remainder of this section rather than working along with Copilot in VS Code. We'll absolutely give you all the tools you need to fix the code when Copilot gives you a wrong answer, but that skill will be taught over the remainder of the book, so we don't want you to get stuck on this now.

Looking at the results from Copilot, we have to say this is quite impressive. You don't need to worry about the code yet, but note that writing this code from scratch would be difficult for many new learners. The good news is that anyone can use this powerful tool to do so much more than is possible to do without it.

STEP 3: USING COPILOT TO MODIFY THE CODE TO EXCLUDE ONE PLAYER

We can use Copilot not just to generate new code but to modify it as well. If we run that code from listing 2.1 on the dataset, here are the first five lines from the output:

```
Patrick Mahomes 16132
Tom Brady 15876
Aaron Rodgers 13852
Josh Allen 13758
Derek Carr 13271
```

If you follow football, these results shouldn't be a surprise to you. Just to see how well Copilot can adapt to our wishes, let's try to make a minor change. Suppose that because Tom Brady is already recognized as one of the best QBs of all time, you would rather omit him from this comparison.

To make this change, we're just going to modify the prompt at the bottom. We went to the point in the code where it says the following:

```
"""
print the sum of the passing yards sorted by sum
of passing yards in descending order
"""
for player in sorted(passing_yards, key=passing_yards.get, reverse=True):
    print(player, passing_yards[player])
```

We deleted the code, leaving just the comment, and added another line to the docstring:

```
"""
print the sum of the passing yards sorted by sum
of passing yards in descending order
Do not include Tom Brady because he wins too much
"""
```

Copilot then suggested the following to us:

```
for player in sorted(passing_yards, key=passing_yards.get, reverse=True):
    if player != "Tom Brady":                      ◁───┐  Code that excludes Tom
        print(player, passing_yards[player])            Brady from the data
```

That's exactly what we'd like to see changed in the code. (Thanks, Tom Brady, for being a good sport in this example.) The code excluded all data for Tom Brady at the point of printing the results. When we save the file and run it again, the first five lines now appear like this:

```
Patrick Mahomes 16132
Aaron Rodgers 13852
Josh Allen 13758
Derek Carr 13271
Matt Ryan 13015
```

REFLECTING ON THE EXAMPLE AND THE SKILLS WE NEED TO WRITE CODE WITH COPILOT

Without writing any code ourselves, we were able to solve a large real-world task. However, you still need to learn some essential programming skills. We'll teach you those skills in the upcoming chapters by solving a variety of tasks. By the end of chapter 7, you'll be able to solve large tasks like these. We want you to take away the following from this example:

- *Copilot is a powerful tool.* We didn't write any code ourselves, but we were able to get Copilot to generate the code needed to perform some initial analysis of the data. If you've used spreadsheets, you can probably think of a way to do this using spreadsheet applications such as Microsoft Excel, but it likely wouldn't be as easy as writing code like this. Even if you haven't used spreadsheets before, you've got to admit that it's amazing that writing basic, human-readable prompts can produce correct code and output like this.
- *Breaking problems into small tasks is important.* For this example, we tried writing this code with just a single large prompt (not shown) or by breaking it into smaller tasks. We found that Copilot was more apt to make mistakes when given one large task rather than multiple smaller tasks. In general, breaking the problem into smaller tasks significantly increases the likelihood of Copilot generating the right code. You'll see how to break down larger problems into smaller tasks throughout the remainder of this book because this is one of the most important skills you'll need. In fact, the upcoming chapter 3 will help you start understanding what are considered reasonable tasks to give to Copilot, and chapter 7 will be dedicated entirely to learning how to break down larger programs into smaller pieces.
- *We still need to understand code to some degree.* This is true for several reasons. One is that writing good prompts requires a basic understanding of what computers know and what they don't. We can't just give a prompt to Copilot that says, "Give me the number of passing yards for Tom Brady." Copilot likely wouldn't be able to figure out where the data is stored, the format of the data, which columns correspond to players and passing yards, or that Tom Brady is a player. We had to spell details like that out to Copilot for it to be successful. Another reason has to do with determining whether code from Copilot is reasonable. When the two of us read the response from Copilot, we could determine what the code is doing because we know how to read code. You'll need to be able to do this to some degree, which is why chapters 4 and 5 are dedicated to reading code.
- *Testing is important.* We need to know if the code Copilot gave us is correct or not! When programmers talk about testing, they're referring to the practice of making sure that their code works correctly, even in possibly unexpected circumstances. We didn't spend much time on this piece, other than checking whether Copilot's answer is plausible using estimates on just one dataset, but, in

general, we'll need to spend more time on testing because this is a critical part of the code-writing process. It likely goes without saying, but errors in code range from embarrassing (if you tell your hard-core NFL fan friend the wrong number of passing yards for a player) to dangerous (if software in a car behaves incorrectly) to costly (if businesses make decisions on wrong analyses). After you've learned how to read code, we have first-hand experience that even if the code looks correct, it might not be! To address this, we must test every piece of code created by Copilot to ensure it does what it should. You'll learn how to rigorously test Copilot's code in later chapters, especially chapter 6, which is dedicated to the skill.

- *Python is powerful.* It's okay if you missed this, but in listing 2.1, the code imported a module from Python's libraries (`import csv`). Python has many built-in tools (called libraries) to help people accomplish their tasks. In this case, it was importing a library to make it easier to read and modify CSV files. We'll harness more of these libraries in later chapters.

> **Python modules**
>
> Python modules expand the capability of the programming language. There are many modules in Python, and they can help you do anything from data analysis to creating websites to writing video games. You can recognize when code wants to use a Python module by the `import` statement in the code. Some modules are built-in to Python, but there are thousands more that aren't and that you need to manually install if you want to use them. Chapter 5 will show you how to use modules.

In this chapter, we've accomplished a great deal! If you've finished setting up your programming environment and gotten started writing code with Copilot, you should be proud. You've taken a huge step toward writing software! Beyond the details of setting up your environment, you've seen where we're headed by working through an example together.

In the examples in this chapter, Copilot gave us the code we wanted without us needing to change the prompt or debug the code to figure out why it's not working properly. That was a nice way to showcase the power of using an AI assistant to program, but you'll often find yourself having to test the code, change the prompts, and sometimes try to understand why the code is wrong. This is the AI assistant programming process that you'll learn more about in upcoming chapters.

Summary

- You installed Python and VS Code and set up Copilot so you can work along with the book and start writing code yourself.
- The VS Code interface has areas for file management, code editing, and running code that will be used throughout the book.

- Prompts are how we tell Copilot to generate code, which, when written carefully, can be a highly effective way of creating software.
- Data analysis is a common programming task, and using CSV files is a common way to store data to be processed by computers.
- Copilot is a powerful tool that can produce sophisticated code under the proper human supervision.

Designing functions 3

This chapter covers

- Functions in Python and their role in designing software
- The standard workflow when interacting with Copilot
- Examples of writing good functions using Copilot
- Reasonable tasks for Copilot to solve

One of the hardest challenges for programming novices is to know what a reasonable task is to give to Copilot so that it finds a good solution. If you give Copilot too big of a task, it will often fail in spectacular ways that can be extremely difficult to fix. What, then, is a reasonable task?

This question is important for our use of Copilot but goes far beyond it. Human programmers struggle with complexity too. If experienced software engineers try to write code to solve a problem that's too complex without breaking it down into smaller, more solvable subparts, they often have trouble as well. The solution for humans has been to use something called a *function*, whose job is to perform one task. Functions help us organize our code and make it easier to think about and fix any bugs. There are various rules of thumb for how to write a reasonable function in terms of number of lines of code, but, fundamentally, these rules try to capture writing something that (1) performs a single task and (2) isn't so complex that it's hard to get right.

For people who learned to program the old-fashioned way, without Copilot, they may have struggled with syntax in code that's 5–10 lines long before being introduced to functions. At that point, it's natural for them to understand through experience that they shouldn't write more code in a single function than they can handle testing and debugging. Because you're learning to work with Copilot rather than syntax directly, our job in this chapter is to teach you about functions and what are considered reasonable and unreasonable tasks to ask Copilot to solve in a single function.

To help you gain perspective on functions, we'll provide you with a number of examples in this chapter. Those examples employ the central workflow of interacting with Copilot—specifically, the cycle of writing prompts, receiving code from Copilot, and testing to see whether that code is correct. In the functions produced by Copilot, you'll begin to see the core programming tools, such as loops, conditionals, and lists, which we'll expand on in the next two chapters.

3.1 Functions

Before we can learn about the details of writing a function, we need some insight into their purpose in software. Functions are small tasks that help accomplish larger tasks, which, in turn, help solve larger tasks, and so forth. You probably already have a lot of intuition about breaking apart large tasks into smaller tasks. Let's make that intuition concrete with an example.

Suppose you've found a word search puzzle in the newspaper that you'd like to solve (see figure 3.1 for an example puzzle). In these kinds of puzzles, you're looking for each word in the word list. The words can be found going from left to right, right to left, top to bottom, or bottom to top.

```
R  M  E  L  L  L  D  I  L  A  Z  K
B  F  W  H  F  M  O  Z  G  L  Z  C
B  D  T  U  C  N  G  S  L  S  H  A
Y  Y  O  F  U  N  C  T  I  O  N  T
F  A  H  S  I  L  T  A  S  K  O  C
H  N  H  J  O  H  E  L  L  O  C  A
Y  F  M  P  I  P  W  L  B  T  R  J
L  N  S  J  N  E  Z  Y  Z  Z  I  T
```

Find the following hidden words in the puzzle:

CAT   FUNCTION   TASK

DOG   HELLO

Figure 3.1 Example word search puzzle

At a high level, your task is "find all the words in the word search." Unfortunately, that description of the task isn't helpful on its own. It doesn't tell us what steps we need to take to solve the problem.

Try working on the problem right now for a couple minutes. How did you start? How did you break down the overall task to make it more achievable?

One thing you might do is say, "OK, finding every word is a big task, but a smaller task is just finding the first word (CAT). Let me work on that first!" This is an example of taking a large task and breaking it into smaller tasks. To solve the entire puzzle, then, you could repeat that smaller task for each word that you need to find.

Now, how would we find an individual word, such as CAT? Even this task can be broken down further to make it easier to accomplish. For example, we could break it into four tasks: search for CAT from left to right, search for CAT from right to left, search for CAT from top to bottom, and search for CAT from bottom to top. Not only are we making simpler and simpler tasks, but we're also organizing our work into logical pieces. Most importantly, as we'll see throughout the chapter, it's these simpler tasks whose code we're going to ask Copilot to write and ultimately assemble into our complete programs.

Taking a large problem and dividing it into smaller tasks is called *problem decomposition,* which is such an important skill in software design that we've dedicated all of chapter 7 to it. For now, it's essential to know when a task is too big to ask Copilot to complete it. Asking Copilot to make a new video game that's a combination of Wordscapes meets Wordle isn't going to work at all. However, you can get Copilot to write a function that's important to solve a larger problem; for example, you might have a function that checks whether the word provided by the player is present in a list of valid words. Copilot can solve that problem well, and that function would help Copilot get closer to solving the larger problem.

3.1.1 *The components of a function*

The origin of the name *function* goes back to math where functions define the output of something based on an input. For example, in high school math, you probably learned to recognize the common way to write a function as follows:

$$f(x) = x^2$$

This is a function that is given a value for the variable x and computes the square of that value. So, we can say that when x is 6, $f(x)$ is 36. As programming functions also have expected output for a particular input, the name is apt for programming as well.

As programmers, we also like to think of functions as promises or contracts. If there is a function called `larger`, and we're told that it takes two numbers and gives us the larger of the two, we have faith that when we give the function the numbers 2 and 5, it will return the answer of 5. We don't need to see how that function works to use it, any more than we need to know how the mechanics of a car works to use the brake pedal. Press the brake pedal, and the car slows down. Give the `larger` function two numbers, and it gives us back the larger of the two.

Every function in Python has a *function header* (also called a *function signature*), which is the first line of code of the function. Given their ubiquitous nature, we'll want to read and write function headers. The function header describes the name of the function and its inputs. In some other languages, the function header sometimes includes information about what the output looks like, but in Python, you have to find that elsewhere in the code.

In chapter 2, we wrote # comments to tell Copilot what to do. We can continue to use that approach if we want Copilot to generate a function. For example, we can use comments to ask Copilot to write a function that tells us which of two numbers is larger:

```
# write a function that returns the larger of two numbers
# input is two numbers
# output is the larger of the two numbers
def larger(num1, num2):
    if num1 > num2:
        return num1
    else:
        return num2
```

Function body

◁——— This function header defines a function called "larger" that accepts two inputs called num1 and num2.

As with the code in the previous chapter, we just wrote the comments to prompt Copilot to give us the code. The function header has three main components: the `def` keyword, which tells Python that this is a function; the name of the function; and the inputs to the function. There's also a colon at the end of the line—be sure to include that or the code won't be valid Python code. The word `def` denotes that it's creating (defining) a function. After `def` is the name of the function; that name should describe the behavior of the function as well as possible. The name of this function is `larger`. If it's hard to name a function because it does a bunch of different things, that's usually a clue that it's too big of a task for a single function (more on that later).

In the parentheses of the function declaration, you'll find the parameters. *Parameters* are how you provide information to a function that it needs to run. A function can have any number of parameters, and some functions have no parameters. This function has two parameters named `num1` and `num2`; there are two parameters because it needs to know the two numbers it's comparing.

There can be only one output of a function; the keyword to look for when determining what the function is outputting is *return*. Whatever follows `return` is the output of the function. In this code, either `num1` or `num2` will be returned. Functions aren't required to return anything (e.g., a function that prints a list to the screen has no reason to return anything), so if you don't see a return statement, it isn't necessarily a problem because the function may be doing something else (interacting with the user, for example) rather than returning something. Functions must also either return something or not return something: they can't return something in some cases and nothing in other cases.

Although we had Copilot generate this function using # comments, this approach is actually a lot of work for Copilot. It first must get the header right, including figuring out how many parameters you need. Then, it must get the actual code of the function right. In this example, Copilot also provided the code for the function (also known as the function's body).

There's an alternate way to prompt Copilot to write the code for a function that may help it generate code more accurately and may help us better understand exactly what we want our function to do. It involves writing a docstring, and we'll use docstrings to write functions for the majority of the book.

Docstrings explain function behavior

Docstrings are how Python functions are described by programmers. They follow the function header and begin and end with three double quotation marks, as shown in the upcoming code function for `larger`.

By writing the header and docstring, you'll make it easier for Copilot to generate the right code. In the header, you'll be the one deciding on the name of the function and providing the names of each parameter that you want the function to use. After the function header, you'll provide a docstring that tells Copilot what the function does. Then, just as before, Copilot will generate the code for the function. Because we gave Copilot the function header, it will be able to learn from the header and is less likely to make mistakes. Here's what the alternate approach would look like when writing that same `larger` function:

```
def larger(num1, num2):
    """
    num1 and num2 are two numbers.

    Return the larger of the two numbers.
    """
    if num1 > num2:
        return num1
    else:
        return num2
```

Docstring description of the function

Notice that we wrote the function header as well as the docstring, and Copilot supplied the body of the function.

3.1.2 Using a function

Once we have a function, how do we use it? Thinking back to our $f(x) = x^2$ analogy, how do we give the function a value of 6 for x so that it returns 36? Let's see how to do this with code by using that `larger` function we just wrote.

The way to use a function is to *call* it. Calling a function means to invoke the function on specific values of parameters. These parameter values are called arguments.

Each value in Python has a *type*, and we need to take care to give values of the proper type. For example, that `larger` function is expecting two numbers; it might not work as expected if we supply inputs that aren't numbers. When we call a function, it runs its code and returns its result. We need to capture that result so that we can use it later; otherwise, it will be lost. To capture a result, we use a *variable*, which is just a name that refers to a value.

Here, we ask Copilot to call the function, store the result in a variable, and then print the result:

```
# call the larger function with the values 3 and 5
# store the result in a variable called result
# then print result
result = larger(3, 5)          ⟵            Calls the larger function with the values 3
print(result)                               and 5 as inputs and stores the result
```

The code correctly calls `larger`. Notice that it puts the two values we want compared after the opening parenthesis. When the function finishes, it returns a value that we assign to result. Then we print the result. If you run this program, you'll see that the output 5 gets produced because 5 is the larger of the two values that we asked about.

It's okay if you aren't comfortable with all the details here, but what we want you to recognize is when a function is being called, as in the following:

```
larger(3, 5)
```

The general format for a function call is

```
function_name(argument1, argument2, argument3,... )
```

So, when you see those parentheses right after a name, it means there's a function call. Calling functions as we did here will be important to our workflow with Copilot, particularly in how we test functions to see if they are working properly. We'll also need to call functions to get work done because functions don't do anything until we call them.

3.2   *The design cycle of functions with Copilot*

Let's introduce you to the workflow we'll use for the next few chapters. Designing functions with Copilot involves the following cycle of steps (see figure 3.2):

1   Determine the desired behavior of the function.
2   Write a prompt that describes the function as clearly as possible.
3   Allow Copilot to generate the code.
4   Read through the code to see if it seems reasonable.
5   Test the code to see if it's correct:
     – If the code is correct after multiple tests, move on.
     – If the code is incorrect, move to step 2, and edit the prompt.

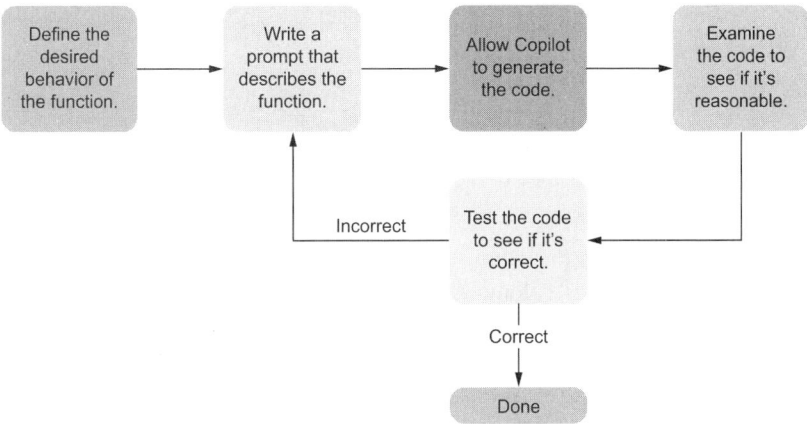

Figure 3.2 General editing cycle with Copilot. This assumes you define a reasonable function.

We won't learn how to do step 4 until the next chapter, but we bet you can already recognize when the code is blatantly wrong. For example, Copilot might give you only comments to fill the body of the function. Comments don't do anything—they aren't code—so a bunch of comments with no other code is clearly not the right thing to do. Or, Copilot might just write a single line such as return -1, or, our personal favorite, Your code here. Copilot learned that one from us professors when we provide students partial code and ask them to write the rest with "Your code here." Those are all obviously incorrect, but in the next chapter, we'll go over how to read code so you can more quickly spot when more complicated code is incorrect and, perhaps more importantly, see where and how to fix it. In later chapters, we'll keep expanding on this cycle to include effective debugging practices, and we'll keep practicing how to improve prompts.

3.3 Examples of creating good functions with Copilot

In this section, we're going to write a bunch of functions with Copilot. We think you'll get a much better feel for functions by seeing concrete examples, and we'll code them entirely in Copilot to help you see the cycle of function design we just described. Although our goal in this chapter isn't to help you read code just yet, we'll see programming features (sometimes called *constructs*) in the solutions that are very common in code (e.g., if statements, loops), so we'll point those out when we see them. Then, in chapter 4, we'll say more about how to read this code in more detail.

Many of the functions we're about to work on are unrelated to each other. For example, we'll start with a function about stock share prices and move to functions about strong passwords. You typically wouldn't store unrelated stuff like this in the same Python file. Because we're just exploring different examples of good functions, feel free to store all functions in the same Python file, perhaps named function ch3.py or function_practice.py.

3.3.1   *Dan's stock pick*

Dan is an investor in a stock called AAAPL. He purchased 10 shares for $15 each. Now, each of those shares is worth $17. Dan would like to know how much money he has made on the stock.

Remember that we want to make our function as general as possible. If the only thing our function does is calculate this exact AAAPL situation, it wouldn't be that useful in general. Sure, it would help Dan right now, but what about when AAAPL's share price changes again or when he is interested in another stock entirely?

A useful general function here would take three parameters, all of which are numbers. The first parameter is the number of shares purchased, the second is the share price when the shares were purchased, and the third is the current share price. Let's call this function money_made, because it's going to determine how much money we've made or lost on the stock. In general, you want to name your function as an action word or words that describe what your function is doing. With that, we have enough to write the function header:

```
def money_made(num_shares, purchase_share_price, current_share_price):
```

Now, we need a docstring. In the docstring, we need to explain what each parameter is for by using its name in a sentence. We also need to include what the function is supposed to do. Adding our docstring, here is the full prompt we provide to Copilot:

```
def money_made(num_shares, purchase_share_price, current_share_price):
    """
    num_shares is the number of shares of a stock that we purchased.
    purchase_share_price is the price of each of those shares.
    current_share_price is the current share price.

    Return the amount of money we have earned on the stock.
    """
```

After typing that prompt, go to the next line, and press the Tab key. Copilot will fill in the code for the function. Don't worry that the code gets indented: the code of functions is supposed to be indented, and, in fact, it's an error if it isn't! Here's what we got from Copilot:

```
    return num_shares * (current_share_price - purchase_share_price)
```

This code seems sensible. In the parentheses, it figures out the difference between the current price and the purchase price (the - is used for subtraction), and then it multiplies that by the number of shares that we have (the * is used for multiplication). Inspecting code like this is a useful skill, and we'll get serious about it in the next chapter. Another useful skill is testing the function.

To test the `money_made` function, we call it using various inputs and observe the output in each case. We could do this by asking Copilot to call the function, and then we run our program, much as we did with our `larger` function. We could then ask Copilot to change the function call by asking it to call the function with a different input, and then we would run our program again, repeating as many times as needed. However, we find it easier and more convenient to call the function ourselves from an interactive window. This way, we can call the function as many times as we like without going through Copilot at all and without cluttering up our program with stuff we're going to delete anyway.

To try this interactive approach, select/highlight all the code of the function, and then press Shift-Enter (you can access a similar interactive session by selecting the text, right-clicking, and choosing Run Selection/Line in the Python window, but the guidance here is if you use Shift-Enter). Figure 3.3 shows what this looks like if you select the text of the function and press Shift-Enter.

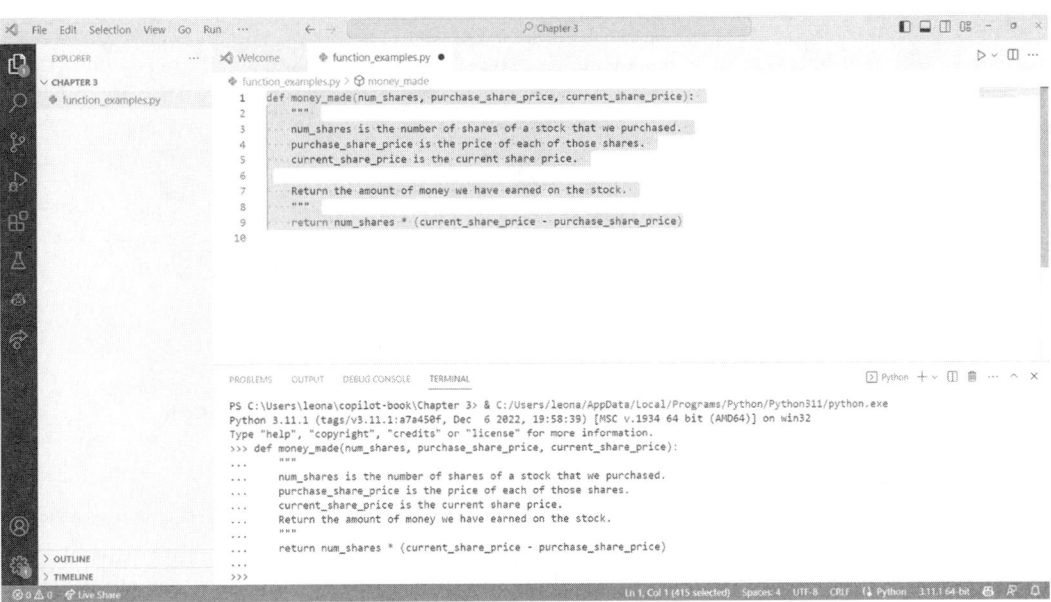

Figure 3.3 Running Python in an interactive session in VS Code. Note the >>> at the bottom of the TERMINAL tab.

At the bottom of the resulting window, you'll see three greater-than symbols >>>. This is called a *prompt*, and you're allowed to type Python code here. (This prompt has nothing to do with the kind of prompt that we use when interacting with Copilot.) It will show us right away the result of the code that we type, which is convenient and fast.

To call our `money_made` function, we need to provide three arguments, and they will be assigned left to right to the parameters. Whatever we put first will be assigned to num_shares, whatever we put second will be assigned to purchase_share_price, and whatever we put third will be assigned to current_share_price.

Let's try this! At the prompt, type the following, and press Enter (or Shift-Enter). Don't type the >>>, as that's already there; we're including it throughout the book to make it clear where we're typing. Figure 3.4 shows an example of running the function in the terminal at the Python prompt:

```
>>> money_made(10, 15, 17)
```

You'll see the following output:

```
20
```

Is 20 correct? Well, we bought 10 shares, and each of them went up $2 (from $15 to $17), so we did make $20. Looks good!

```
PROBLEMS    OUTPUT    DEBUG CONSOLE    TERMINAL

Type "help", "copyright", "credits" or "license" for more information.
>>> def money_made(num_shares, purchase_share_price, current_share_price):
...        """
...        num_shares is the number of shares of a stock that we purchased.
...        purchase_share_price is the price of each of those shares.
...        current_share_price is the current share price.
...        Return the amount of money we have earned on the stock.
...        """
...        return num_shares * (current_share_price - purchase_share_price)
...
>>> money_made(10, 15, 17)
20
>>> []
```

Figure 3.4   Calling the money_made function from the Python prompt in the VS Code terminal

We're not done testing, though. When testing a function, you want to test it in various ways, not just once. All one test case tells you is that it happened to work with the particular input values that you provided. The more test cases we try, each testing the function in a different way, the more confident we are that our function is correct.

How do we test this function in a different way? We're looking for inputs that are somehow a different *category* of input. One not-so-good test right now would be to say, "What if our stock went from $15 to $18, instead of $15 to $17?" This is pretty much the same test as before, and chances are that it will work just fine.

A good idea is to test what happens when the stock actually *loses* money. We expect to get a negative return value in this case. And it appears that our function works just fine with this category of test. Here's our function call and the output returned to us:

```
>>> money_made(10, 17, 15)
-20
```

What other tests can we do? Well, sometimes a stock price doesn't change at all. We expect 0 in this case. Let's verify it:

```
>>> money_made(10, 15, 15)
0
```

Looks good! Testing is a combination of science and art. How many categories of things are there to test? Are these two calls really two different categories? Have we missed any categories? You'll improve your testing ability through practice, and we'll spend all of chapter 6 talking about testing. For now, it looks like our money_made function is doing its job.

It's possible for a function to use variables (rather than just its parameters) in its code, and we want to show you an example of that now so that you're ready when you see Copilot doing it. Here's an equivalent way to write the code for our money_made function:

```
price_difference = current_share_price - purchase_share_price
return num_shares * price_difference
```

This code may even be easier to read for you: it first figures out the difference in share price, and then it multiplies that by the number of shares. We encourage you to test this version to help convince yourself that it's still correct.

3.3.2   *Leo's password*

Leo is signing up for a new social network website called ProgrammerBook. He wants to make sure that his password is strong.

Leo starts with a modest definition of what it means for a password to be strong: it's strong if it's not the word *password* and not the word *qwerty*. Those are terrible passwords, for sure, but in reality, we have to do way better than this definition to ensure that our password is strong! A helpful function would be one that takes a proposed password and tells us whether it's strong or not.

Unlike our previous functions in this chapter, we're not dealing with numbers here. The parameter, the password to check, is text. And the return value is supposed to indicate some yes/no result. We need new types!

The Python type for text is called a *string*. There are zillions of possible strings because we can use a string to store whatever text we want. The Python type for a yes/no result is called a *Boolean* or *bool*. A bool has only two values: True or False.

Alright! We're ready to prompt Copilot. For functions that return bool (True/False) values, we usually name the function as has_x, is_x, or similar using some other verb that implies a true/false result:

```
def is_strong_password(password):
    """
    A strong password is not the word 'password'
    and is not the word 'qwerty'.
```

```
Return True if the password is a strong password, False if not.
"""
```

In response, here's what Copilot wrote for us:

```
return password != 'password' and password != 'qwerty'
```

Look over that code for a moment. That != operator is the "not equal" operator, and each string that doesn't count as a strong password is in single quotation marks. We're going to use quotation marks every time we need to specify a specific string value. Again, we'll talk more about how to read code in the next chapter, but for now, we hope that the code makes a fuzzy sort of sense: it looks like it's checking that the password isn't password and isn't qwerty, which matches our definition of a strong password.

Now let's make sure that this function does indeed work by making a few test calls. We'll start by testing the passwords that aren't strong. We had better get back False for each of these—and we do:

```
>>> is_strong_password('password')
False

>>> is_strong_password('qwerty')
False
```

Good! Now, let's try a strong password. We need to see True here:

```
>>> is_strong_password('N3w Y0rk J375')
True
```

Good stuff! We now see that the function sometimes returns False and other times returns True, so at least it's not always returning False. Let's try one more:

```
>>> is_strong_password('Leo')
True
```

Well, technically True is correct, but, wow, is Leo a bad password. We should really have done better with our definition of a strong password. Let's change our prompt to give a more reasonable definition of what it means for a password to be strong. Here's our next prompt and what Copilot gave us:

```
def is_strong_password(password):
    """
    A strong password has at least one uppercase character,
    at least one number, and at least one special symbol.

    Return True if the password is a strong password, False if not.
    """
    return any(char.isupper() for char in password) and \
           any(char.isdigit() for char in password) and \
           any(not char.isalnum() for char in password)
```

That `for char in password` that shows up a few times here is a way for Python to consider each character of the password. It enables something called a *loop*, which is a key topic that we'll study in chapter 5.

Of course, it's possible that you didn't get the same code from Copilot as we did. But based on the code that we got, it looks like the first piece is looking for any uppercase character, the second piece is looking for any digit, and the third is looking for something that's not an `isalnum`.

Maybe `isalnum` means "is alphanumeric." Does that include special symbols, and, if so, which ones? Let's test this function to see how well we're doing:

```
>>> is_strong_password('Leo')
False

>>> is_strong_password('N3w Y0rk J37$')
True

>>> is_strong_password('N3w Y0rk J375')
True
```

Uh-oh! We got the wrong answer for that third password. It looks pretty strong, but it's not, because it lacks a special symbol. Our function returned `True`, but that's the wrong return value: it was supposed to return `False`.

The code that Copilot gave us is wrong. Maybe the code that you got worked fine, but we didn't get so lucky, and it's important we know how to identify (like we just did) when the code is wrong and then fix it. It's not important to know why it's wrong right now, but if you're curious about why our prompt may have given us the wrong behavior, it's because we didn't specify what we meant by a special character, and the code it gave us counts spaces as special characters.

At this point, as we begin to troubleshoot our wrong code, we have two options. One option is to press Ctrl-Enter and look through the other suggestions that Copilot gives us. Maybe one of those suggestions will have something to do with special symbols that looks different from the one that didn't work?

Indeed, on our computer here, we see such options, including this one:

```
num_upper = 0
num_num = 0
num_special = 0
for char in password:
    if char.isupper():
        num_upper += 1
    elif char.isnumeric():
        num_num += 1
    elif char in '!@#$%^&*':          ← Specific choice of
        num_special += 1                 special symbols
if num_upper >= 1 and num_num >= 1 and num_special >= 1:
    return True
else:
    return False
```

Test this function with strings such as Leo, N3w Y0rk J375, and N3w Y0rk J375$ and you should see that the function works well.

Our second option is to do some prompt engineering, which means adjusting our prompt to influence what Copilot gives us. In our original prompt, we talked about special symbols. This, in retrospect, is vague. We probably meant something more specific, such as punctuation. If we specifically talk about punctuation in our prompt, we get this interaction with Copilot:

```python
def is_strong_password(password):
    """
    A strong password has at least one uppercase character,
    at least one number, and at least one punctuation.

    Return True if the password is a strong password, False if not.
    """
    return any(char.isupper() for char in password) and \
           any(char.isdigit() for char in password) and \
           any(char in string.punctuation for char in password)
```

Looks good! That last line is talking about punctuation, which is hopeful. Let's test it here:

```
>>> is_strong_password('Leo')
False

>>> is_strong_password('N3w Y0rk J375')
 Traceback (most recent call last):
  File "<stdin>", line 1, in <module>
  File "ch2.py", line 44, in is_strong_password
    any(char in string.punctuation for char in password)
  File "ch2.py", line 44, in <genexpr>
    any(char in string.punctuation for char in password)
                 ^^^^^^
NameError: name 'string' is not defined
```

Looking at the bottom of that error message, you'll see that 'string' isn't defined. Copilot wants to use a module, called string, but it's a module that needs to be imported before we can use it. This "not defined" result can happen for various types of errors related to names not being found, and oftentimes the culprit is a module that hasn't been imported. There are a lot of modules in Python, but the string module is well known. As you work with Copilot more, you'll learn which modules are commonly used so you know to import them. You could also do a quick internet search to ask, "Is string a Python module," and the results would confirm that it is. What we need to do is import the module.

Note that this is similar to what happened in the code that Copilot generated for us in chapter 2. Back then, Copilot was using the csv module, which is a module already installed with Python. The string module is similarly included with Python; Copilot just forgot to import it. As we discussed in chapter 2, some modules do need to be manually installed, but the string module isn't one of them. So, we don't need to install string; we just have to import it.

Importing modules

There are a number of useful modules available in Python. In chapter 2, Copilot used the csv module to make it easier to deal with comma-separated values (CSV) files. But for Python code to take advantage of a module, we have to import that module. You might ask why we don't have modules available to us without importing them, but that would massively increase the complexity of the code and what Python has to do to run code behind the scenes. Instead, the model is to include modules if you want to use them, and they aren't included by default.

Let's add `import string` at the top of our code:

```python
import string

def is_strong_password(password):
    """
    A strong password has at least one uppercase character,
    at least one number, and at least one punctuation.

    Return True if the password is a strong password, False if not.
    """
    return any(char.isupper() for char in password) and \
           any(char.isdigit() for char in password) and \
           any(char in string.punctuation for char in password)
```

Now we're in good shape:

```python
>>> is_strong_password('Leo')
False

>>> is_strong_password('N3w Y0rk J375')
False

>>> is_strong_password('N3w Y0rk J375$')
True
```

That last one is `True`. It's a strong password because it has the $ punctuation added to it.

We hope that you're now convinced of the value of testing. Sometimes, new programmers don't test their code. They assume that the code they write is correct because it made sense to them. An interesting difference between novice and experienced programmers is that novices often assume their code is right, whereas experienced programmers assume their code is wrong until thoroughly tested and proved otherwise. Beyond this, we find that new programmers sometimes fail to test well because it's disheartening to learn that the code is wrong. But it's better to know now rather than later when others are using your code in a serious application. Finding errors through testing is actually a good thing.

3.3.3   *Getting a strong password*

Now that we have a function that tells us whether a password is strong or not, let's write a function that obtains a strong password from the user. It will ask again and again for a password until the user types a strong one. This is the kind of code that websites use when they tell you, "Sorry, your password is too weak, try again."

What should the header for such a function look like? Well, it's going to ask the user for a password, but we won't have a password parameter. In fact, we won't have any parameters at all because the function doesn't need any information to do its job—it just has to prompt the user, and the user will type the password at the keyboard. When the function has done its work, it will return the strong password, so it will continue to return a string as the output. Let's try this prompt:

```
def get_strong_password():
    """
    Keep asking the user for a password until it's a strong
    password, and return that strong password.
    """
```

We get the following code from Copilot as a result:

```
password = input("Enter a strong password: ")
while not is_strong_password(password):
    password = input("Enter a strong password: ")
return password
```

> It's calling our earlier
> is_strong_password
> function!

That `while` keyword creates another kind of loop, this one continuing as long as the entered password isn't strong. Copilot is also smart enough to call our earlier `is_strong_password` function to determine what counts as a strong password. As you'll see in future chapters, using functions as building blocks in this way is precisely how large programs are built. You'll often notice Copilot calling your earlier functions to solve later ones, much as we observed here.

Let's test this! Highlight all the code from our two password functions, and press Shift-Enter. We'll call the function that we want to test. Then, try typing passwords, pressing Enter after each one. You'll notice that it keeps asking until you finally provide a strong password:

```
>>> get_strong_password()
Enter a strong password: Leo
Enter a strong password: N3w Y0rk J375
Enter a strong password: N3w Y0rk J375$
'N3w Y0rk J375$'
```

Notice that it stops asking us for a password when we finally provide a strong password. Then, we see the string in quotes that it returned, which is, indeed, our strong password.

3.3.4 *Scrabble scoring*

One of Dan's favorite board games is Scrabble. Have you played it? If not, all you need to know is that you have some tiles in your hand, each with a letter on it, and your goal is to form a word using any combination of those letters. You don't need to form the word exclusively with your tiles—you can attach those letters to existing letters on the board to create longer words—but we're not going to worry about that here. The important thing for us is that different letters are worth different numbers of points. For example, an *a* is worth only 1 point because *a* is such a common letter. But *q* and *z*? Those doozies are each worth 10 points because they're so tough to use—or should we say *puzzling* to use. Yeah, that's better.

To calculate the score for a word, we add up the scores for each of its letters. For example, the score for *zap* would be 14. That's because *z* is worth 10, *a* is worth 1, and *p* is worth 3.

Dan would like a function that, given a word, tells him how many points that word is worth. OK, so we need a function that takes a word (which is just one parameter). Let's try this prompt, where we've included the number of points that each letter is worth per official Scrabble rules:

```
def num_points(word):
    """
    Each letter is worth the following points:
    a, e, i, o, u, l, n, s, t, r: 1 point
    d, g: 2 points
    b, c, m, p: 3 points
    f, h, v, w, y: 4 points
    k: 5 points
    j, x: 8 points
    q, z: 10 points

    word is a word consisting of lowercase characters.
    Return the sum of points for each letter in word.
    """
```

For this function, Copilot isn't filling in the whole body for us with one press of the Tab key. Tab is also used to indent the code, which we also need to do here before Copilot will present us with code. So, we're having to press Tab (sometimes once for the indentation and then again for Copilot), wait for the code to appear, then press Tab to accept that code, then press Enter again for more code to be presented, and repeat the process.

> ### Getting Copilot to suggest code may require pressing Tab or Enter
> We find that Copilot will sometimes pause in giving suggestions until you press a key to help prompt it. As mentioned in table 2.1, if you're giving it comments, Copilot will sometimes just want to give you more comments as suggestions. Pressing Enter another time can often trigger it to start generating code instead. Other times, pressing Tab will cause it to continue providing suggestions. Refer to table 2.1 if Copilot isn't generating code for you.

Finally, after doing that a few times, the entire code unfurls, and we get the following:

```python
points = 0
for char in word:
    if char in "aeioulnstr":
        points += 1
    elif char in "dg":
        points += 2
    elif char in "bcmp":
        points += 3
    elif char in "fhvwy":
        points += 4
    elif char == "k":
        points += 5
    elif char in "jx":
        points += 8
    elif char in "qz":
        points += 10
return points
```

Notice that all the letters of the alphabet are accounted for here, and the number of points that each category is worth is on the following line. We'll discuss this overall kind of decision structure in the next chapter, but, at a high level, it's walking through the word character by character and, for each character, figuring out which letter it is and adding the appropriate number of points for that letter.

Let's test this to make sure our code is performing the way we want. We know that the word *zap* should be worth 14 points, and it is:

```python
>>> num_points('zap')
14
```

Let's try a couple more. In each case, calculate by hand what you expect the answer to be—that way, you'll know if the code is doing the right thing:

```python
>>> num_points('pack')
12
```

```python
>>> num_points('quack')
20
```

There are many ways to write correct code for a function. If you press Ctrl-Enter and look at the Copilot suggestions, you may see different types of code. It doesn't necessarily mean that one of these types is right and the others are wrong. For example, here's another solution for num_points that we got from the other Copilot suggestions:

```python
points = {'a': 1, 'e': 1, 'i': 1, 'o': 1, 'u': 1, 'l': 1,
          'n': 1, 's': 1, 't': 1, 'r': 1,
          'd': 2, 'g': 2,
          'b': 3, 'c': 3, 'm': 3, 'p': 3,
          'f': 4, 'h': 4, 'v': 4, 'w': 4, 'y': 4,
          'k': 5,
```

```
            'j': 8, 'x': 8,
            'q': 10, 'z': 10}
    return sum(points[char] for char in word)
```

Notice here that each letter is listed individually along with its number of points. This structure with the letters and points is called a *dictionary*, and again, you'll learn about dictionaries properly in a later chapter. The point for now is just that there are often multiple, equivalently good ways for Copilot to write the code for a function. Give this one a try with some test cases before you continue!

3.3.5 *The best word*

Let's continue with the Scrabble theme. Suppose that Dan has a bunch of words that he can make right now, but he doesn't know which one will give him the most points. Should he make the word *zap*, *pack*, or *quack*? It would be nice if we had a function that could take a bunch of words and tell us which is the best one.

How many parameters should we have in such a function? Your first instinct may be three parameters, one for each of the 3 words in our options. But that wouldn't be very flexible. After all, what if we want to know the best of 5 words, 10 words, or 50 words? We would like our function to work no matter how many words we're considering.

The trick is to use a function with one (yes, just one!) parameter, which is a *list* of words. Just like numbers, strings, and dictionaries, a list is a type supported by Python. It's incredibly useful because it allows us to collect as many values into one place as we like. We can prompt Copilot like this to get the function that we want:

```
def best_word(word_list):
    """
    word_list is a list of words.

    Return the word worth the most points.
    """
```

How will Copilot know how many points each word is worth? Well, it can call that num_points function that we wrote in the previous section! Here's the code that Copilot gives us:

```
    best_word = ""
    best_points = 0
    for word in word_list:
        points = num_points(word)
        if points > best_points:
            best_word = word
            best_points = points
    return best_word
```

We need to be careful to call this function correctly when testing. Using

```
>>> best_word('zap', 'pack', 'quack')
```

won't work because that's passing values for three parameters, not one. The right way to call it is to put the words inside square brackets, like this (we'll see more about lists in the next chapter):

```
>>> best_word(['zap', 'pack', 'quack'])
'quack'
```

But, as usual, you shouldn't be content with just one test case. This function should work in other valid but perhaps strange cases too, such as when we have only one word in the list:

```
>>> best_word(['zap'])
'zap'
```

However, we wouldn't test this function on a list that has no words in it. What would it even make sense to do in that case? Regardless of what the function does, it'd be hard to say one way or the other whether it was doing the correct thing in a situation where there really is no correct behavior!

3.4   Benefits of functions

Now that you've seen a number of functions, we hope you're starting to get a feel for how functions are used in software. We already mentioned that functions are critical in performing problem decomposition. Beyond problem decomposition, functions are valuable in software for a number of other reasons, including the following:

- *Cognitive load*—You may have heard of cognitive load [1] before. It's the amount of information your brain can handle at any given time and still be effective. If you're given four random words and asked to repeat them back, you might be able to do that. If you're given the same task with 20 words, most of us would fail because it's too much information to handle at once. Similarly, if you've ever been on a road trip with your family and are trying to optimize the travel time, combined with stops for the kids, lunch breaks, bathroom stops, gas station stops, good locations for hotels, and so on, you might have felt your head swimming to manage all those constraints at once. That point when you can't handle it all at once is when you've exceeded your own brain's processing power. Programmers have the same problem. If they are trying to do too much at once or solve too complex a problem in one piece of code, they struggle to do it correctly. Functions are designed to help programmers avoid doing too much work at once.
- *Avoid repetition*—Programmers (and, we'd argue, humans in general) aren't very excited about solving the same problem over and over. If I write a function that can correctly compute the area of a circle once, I don't need to write that code ever again. That means if I have two sections of my code that need to compute the area of a circle, I'd write one function that computes the area of the circle, and then I'd have my code call that function in each of those two places.

- *Improve testing*—It's a lot harder to test a section of code that does multiple things compared to code that does one thing. Programmers use a variety of testing techniques, but a key technique is known as *unit testing*. Every function takes some input and produces some output. For a function that computes the area of a circle, for example, the input would be the circle's radius, and the output would be its area. Unit tests give a function an input and then compare that input to the desired result. For the area-of-a-circle function, we might test it by giving it varying inputs (e.g., some small positive numbers, some large positive numbers, and 0) and compare the result of the function against the values we know to be correct. If the answers from the function match what we expect, we have a higher degree of confidence that the code is correct. If the code produces a mistake, we won't have much code to check to find and fix the problem. But if a function does more than one task, it vastly complicates the testing process because you need to test each task and the interaction of those tasks.

- *Improve reliability*—When we write code as experienced software engineers, we know we make mistakes. We also know Copilot makes mistakes. If you imagine you're an amazing programmer and each line of code you write is 95% likely to be correct, how many lines of code do you think you can write before at least one of those lines is likely to be incorrect? The answer is only 14. We think 95% correctness per line is probably a high bar for even experienced programmers and is likely a higher bar than what Copilot produces. By keeping the tasks small, tasks solvable in 12–20 lines of code, we reduce the likelihood that there's an error in the code. If combined with good testing as noted previously, we can feel even more confident that the code is correct. Last, nothing is worse than code that has multiple mistakes that interact together, and the likelihood of multiple mistakes grows the more code you write. Both of us have been on multi-hour debugging expeditions because our code had more than one mistake, and we both became a lot better at frequent testing of short pieces of code as a result!

- *Improve code readability*—In this book, we mostly use Copilot to write code from scratch, but that's not the only way to use Copilot. If you have a larger piece of software that you or your coworkers are all editing and using, Copilot can jump in to help write code for that too. It's in everyone's interest to understand the code, whether most of it is written by humans or by Copilot. That way, we can find bugs more easily, determine what code to start modifying when we want to add new features, and understand at a high level what would be easy or difficult to achieve with our overall program design. Having tasks broken down into functions helps us understand what each part of the code is doing so we can gain better insight into how it all works together. It also helps divide up the work and responsibility for ensuring the code is correct.

These benefits are huge for programmers. Programming languages haven't always had functions. But even before they did, programmers did their best to use other features to mimic functions. They were ugly hacks (google "goto statements" if you're interested), and all programmers are happy that we have proper functions now.

You may be asking, "I see how these advantages matter to humans, but how do they affect Copilot?" In general, we believe all the principles that apply to humans apply to Copilot, albeit sometimes for different reasons. Copilot may not have cognitive load, but it's going to do better when we ask it to solve problems similar to what's been done by humans before. Because humans write functions to solve tasks, Copilot will mimic that and write functions as well. Once we've written and tested a function, whether by hand or by Copilot, we don't want to write it again. Knowing how to test if your program is working properly is just as essential for code produced by humans as it is by Copilot. Copilot is as likely to make mistakes when it generates code, so we want to catch those mistakes quickly, just as we do with human-written code. Even if you only work on your own code and never have anyone else read it, you'll often have to go back years later to edit what you've written. Having done this ourselves, we can attest that it's important for your code to be readable for your future self!

3.5   *Roles of functions*

Functions are used in many different roles in programming. At a high level, programs are functions that (often) call other functions. Critically, all programs, including Python programs, originate with a single function (named `main` in languages such as Java, C, and C++). Python's `main` function is essentially the first line of code that isn't in a function. But if every program starts with a single function and trying to solve a large problem with a single function is a mistake, how does that work? Well, `main` will call other functions, which, in turn, will call other functions, and so forth. The code will still execute (mostly) sequentially in each function, so it may start in `main` but then move to another function, and so on.

As an example, let's use the code in the following listing. We wrote this code, not Copilot, because no one would ever want to write this code for anything useful outside of teaching. It's just for demonstrating how function calls work.

Listing 3.1   Code to demonstrate how Python handles function calls

```python
def funct1():
    print("there")
    funct2()
    print("friend")
    funct3()
    print("")

def funct2():
    print("my")

def funct3():
    print(".")

def funct4():
    print("well")
```

```
print("Hi")
funct1()
print("I'm")
funct4()
funct3()
print("")
print("Bye.")
```

This is the start of the program. We'll call this "main" after the main function in other languages.

If we ran this program, the output would be (we'll explain why next):

```
Hi
there
my
friend
.

I'm
well
.

Bye.
```

In figure 3.5, we provide a diagram of how the code in listing 3.1 would be executed by the computer. We've intentionally provided an example that has many function calls to tie together what we just learned. Again, this is *not* practical code; it's just for learning purposes. Let's trace through the code execution together. It may be easier to refer to figure 3.5 than listing 3.1 as you follow along, but either will work.

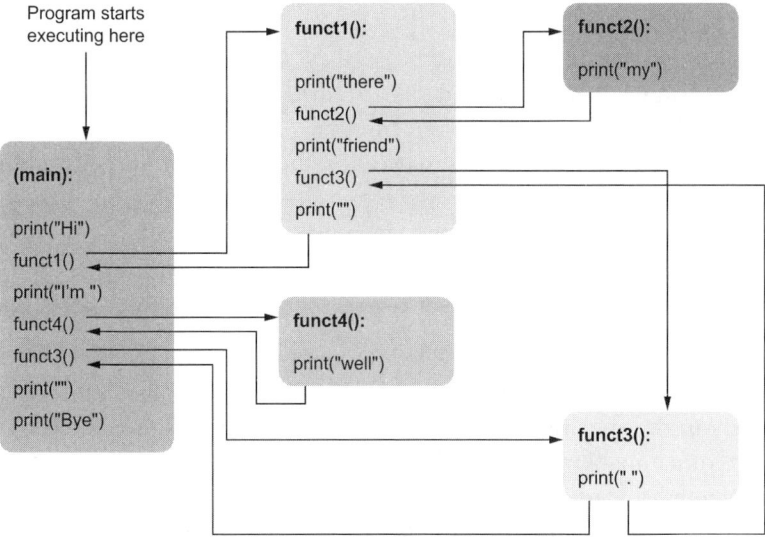

Figure 3.5   Flow of function execution in our example from listing 3.1

The program will start execution with the first line in the Python code that isn't a function (print("Hi")). Although Python doesn't have a main function per se, we'll refer to the block of code after the functions as main to help with this explanation. Code executes sequentially unless it encounters commands that tell it to execute code somewhere else. So, after executing print("Hi"), it will go to the next line, which is the call to funct1: funct1(). The call to funct1 changes where the code is executing to the start of that function, which is the following statement: print("there"). The next line of funct1 calls funct2, so the program will execute the first line of funct2: print("my"). What gets interesting is what happens when funct2 finishes. There are no more lines of code to execute, so it automatically moves execution back to the first line following the call to funct2 in funct1. (If the function call is in the middle of another statement, that statement resumes execution, but for this example, the function calls are each on their own line.) You may be curious why it goes to the next line after the call to funct2 rather than back to the call of funct2. The problem is if it returned back to the call to funct2, it would be trapped calling funct2 forever. As a result, functions always return back to the next piece of code to execute (in this example, the next line) after they are called.

Continuing this example, the next line of the code executed will be the line that prints friend. The next line calls funct3, which prints a period (.) and then returns back to its caller.

So, we're back in funct1, on the line print(""). Printing an empty piece of text causes a new line. Now funct1 is finished, so it transfers execution back to the next line in main after it was called. We suspect you're getting the idea by now, so let's move a bit more quickly:

- main next prints I'm and then calls funct4.
- funct4 prints well and then returns to main where the next line of code calls funct3.
- funct3 prints a period (.) and then returns to main. Notice that funct3 was called both by funct1 and by main, but that's okay because functions remember how to return to the function that called them. In fact, having multiple functions calling the same function is a sign that the function being called multiple times is a good function because of its reuse.
- After funct3 returns to main, it will print "", which causes a new line to be started, and then it prints the word Bye.

That was a long example, but we provided it to give you an idea of how functions execute and how programs consist of defining and calling functions. In any software you use, think about the specific tasks that it performs: the programmers probably wrote one or more functions for each one. The button in a text editor that changes the text to bold probably calls a function to change the text to bold. That function might change the editor's internal idea of the text (the editor likely stores your text in a different format than how you view it), and then it might call another function that updates the user's (your) view of the text.

We'd also like to use this example to discuss the different roles that functions play. A *helper* function is a function whose job is to make another function's job easier. In a sense, every function that isn't `main` is a helper function. The best helper functions are those that carry out some small, well-defined part of some other task, such as our `is_strong_password` function in section 3.3.2 serving as a helper function for our `get_strong_password` function in section 3.3.3.

Some functions simply call a bunch of other functions without doing any of their own work. There aren't any of these in our example. However, if you removed the three `print` statements from `funct1`, it becomes this type of coordinating function. Others may call helper function(s) and then do some work on their own. `funct1` is a great example of a function that calls other functions but also does work on its own.

Another type of function—which we call a *leaf* function—stands on its own without calling other functions for help (except perhaps functions that already come with Python). Why leaf? If you imagine all the function calls as a big tree, these functions are the leaves of the tree because they have nothing coming out of them. `funct2`, `funct3`, and `funct4` are all leaf functions in our example. We're primarily concerned with leaf functions in this chapter, but you'll see examples of other kinds of functions here and especially in later chapters.

3.6 What's a reasonable task for a function?

There's no clear rule for what makes a good function, but there are some intuitions and recommendations we can share. Make no mistake, though—identifying good functions is a skill that takes time and practice. To help you with this, we gave you some examples of good functions in section 3.3. In this section, we'll outline our recommendations and provide you with some additional good and bad examples to help build that intuition.

3.6.1 Attributes of good functions

Here are some guidelines that we believe will help you see what makes a good function:

- *One clear task to perform*—A leaf function might be something like "compute the volume of a sphere," "find the largest number in a list," or "check to see if a list contains a specific value." Nonleaf functions can achieve broader goals, like "update the game graphics" or "collect and sanitize input from the user." Nonleaf functions should still have a particular goal in mind, but they are designed knowing that they will likely call other functions to achieve their goal.
- *Clearly defined behavior*—The task "find the largest number in a list" is clearly defined. If I gave you a list of numbers and asked you for the largest number, you know what you should do. In contrast, the task "find the best word in the list" is poorly defined as stated. You need more information: What is the "best" word? Is it the longest, the one that uses the fewest vowels, or the one that doesn't share any of the same letters as "Leo" or "Dan"? You get the point; subjective tasks aren't great for computers. Instead, we could write the function

"find the word in the list that has the most characters" because what is expected is well defined. Often, programmers can't put all the particulars of a function just in the name, so they fill in the details in the docstring to clarify its use. If you find yourself having to write more than a few sentences to describe the function's behavior, the task is probably too much for a single function.

- *Short in number of lines of code*—We've heard different rules over the years for the length of functions, informed by different company style guidelines. The lengths we've heard vary from 12 to 20 lines of Python code as the maximum number of lines. In these rules, the number of lines is being used as a proxy for code complexity, and it's not a bad rule of thumb. As programmers ourselves, we both apply similar rules to our code to ensure the complexity doesn't get out of hand. With Copilot, we can use this as a guide as well. If you ask Copilot for a function, and it gives you back 50 lines of code, this probably isn't a good function name or task. As we discussed earlier, that many lines of code are likely to have errors anyway.

- *General value over specific use*—A function that returns the number of values in a list that are greater than 1 might be a specific need for a part of your program, but there's a way to make this better. The function should be rewritten to return the number of values in the list that are greater than another parameter. The new function would work for your use case (give the function 1 for the second parameter) and for any value other than 1. We strive to have functions be as simple but as powerful as possible. This is why we wrote our function in section 3.3.1 to work for any stock, not just AAAPL.

- *Clear input and output*—You generally don't want a lot of parameters. That doesn't mean you can't have a lot of input, though. A single parameter could be a list of items, as in our `best_word` function in section 3.3.5. It does mean that you want to find ways to keep the number of inputs to a minimum. You can only return one thing, but again, you can return a list so you aren't as limited as it may appear. But if you find yourself writing a function that sometimes returns a list, sometimes returns a single value, and sometimes returns nothing, that's probably not a good function.

3.6.2   *Examples of good (and bad) leaf functions*

Here are examples of good leaf functions (the function is on the left in italics, and the goal of that function is described on the right):

- *Compute the volume of a sphere*—Given the sphere's radius, return its volume.
- *Find the largest number in a list*—Given a list, return the largest value.
- *Check whether a list contains a specific value*—Given a list and a value, return True if the list contains the value and False if it does not.
- *Print the state of the checkers game*—Given a 2D list representing the game board, output the game board to the screen in text.

- *Insert a value in a list*—Given a list, a new value, and a location in the list, return a new list that is the old list with the new value inserted at the desired location.

Here are examples of bad leaf functions and our reasons for why they are bad:

- *Request a user's tax information and return the amount they owe this year*—Perhaps in some countries this wouldn't be too bad, but we can't imagine this as a single function in either the United States or Canada given the complexity of the tax rules!
- *Identify the largest value in the list and remove that value from the list*—This might not seem so bad, but it's really doing two things. The first is to find the largest value in the list. The second is to remove a value from the list. We'd recommend two leaf functions, one that finds the largest and one that removes the value from the list. However, this might make a good nonleaf function if your program needs to perform this task frequently.
- (Thinking of our dataset from chapter 2.) *Return the names of the quarterbacks with more than 4,000 yards of passing in the dataset*—This has too much specificity. Without a doubt, the number 4,000 should be a parameter. But it's likely better to make a function that takes as input the position (quarterback, running back), the statistic (passing yards, games played), and the cutoff that we care about (4,000, 8,000) as parameters. This new function provides far more capability than the original, allowing a user to call the function to determine not only the names of particular quarterbacks who threw for more than 4,000 yards but also, for example, running backs who had more than 12 rushing touchdowns.
- *Determine the best movie of all time*—This function is too vague. Best movie by what definition? What movies should be considered? A better version of this might be a function that determines the highest-rated movie by users given at least a minimum number of ratings. This function would likely be part of a larger program where the function would have data from a movie database (say, IMDB) and minimum number of user ratings as inputs. The output of the function would be the highest-rated movie that has at least as many ratings as specified.
- *Play Call of Duty*—This might be the `main` function in the large code base for the Call of Duty game, but it's definitely not a leaf function.

Overall, in this chapter, you've learned about functions in Python and how you can use Copilot to help write them. You've also learned about the characteristics of good functions and how important it is to make sure your functions are solving tasks that can be managed well by Copilot.

Our next steps in this book all revolve around understanding whether the code produced by Copilot is correct and how to fix it when it isn't. In the next chapter, we'll start by explaining the basics of being able to read the code produced by Copilot because this gives us the first sanity check for whether Copilot is doing what we think it should be. Then, in later chapters, we'll dig deeper into how to carefully test the code and what to do when it's wrong.

3.7   *Exercises*

1 Review the following function descriptions, and determine if each is a leaf function. Provide reasons for your answers based on the complexity of the tasks the functions perform and whether they are likely to require calling additional custom functions.

   a *Scrape data.* Given a list of URLs, scrape data from each page, parse the content to extract specific information, and save the extracted data to a database.

   b *Process customer orders.* Given a list of customer orders, process each order by checking inventory, calculating total price with discounts and taxes, updating inventory, and generating an order summary.

   c *Find the largest number in a list.* Given a list, return the largest value.

   d *Check whether a list contains a specific value.* Given a list and a value, return `True` if the list contains the value, and `False` if it does not.

   e *Generate student report cards.* Given a list of students and their grades, calculate the final grades, assign letter grades, determine class rank, and generate a formatted report card for each student.

2 Review the cycle of designing functions with Copilot as outlined in this chapter. This cycle includes steps from determining the function's behavior to testing the generated code. Based on general programming practices, identify which of the following steps is *not* included in the cycle described but is commonly part of a software development process:

   a Verifying the logical correctness of the generated code by running unit tests

   b Editing the function's code manually to simplify complex logic after Copilot generation

   c Conducting performance benchmarks on the generated code to ensure efficiency

   d Consulting documentation or external resources to refine the function's prompt

3 Based on the problem description provided, write a clear and concise prompt for Copilot that specifies the task to be completed. Ensure your prompt includes all necessary details such as expected inputs, the processing to be performed, and the expected output:

   a In a quaint little town, there was a humble shopkeeper who, every so often, would delight his customers with discounts on his goods. To streamline this process, he sought to create a magical formula. This formula would take the original price of any item in his store and the special discount he wished to offer. With these two pieces of information, the formula would then reveal the final price the customer needed to pay after the discount was woven into the original tag, making both the shopkeeper and his customers very happy with the ease of their transactions.

Can you think of two or three input examples to verify the correctness of the function generated by Copilot based on your prompts? Include some scenarios to ensure the function handles different types of input correctly and calculates the correct output.

4   Review the function description and the provided test cases for calculating the total cost of a meal, including tax and tip. Based on the scenario and typical requirements of such a function, can you think of inputs where the function doesn't work correctly? Explain why handling this input is necessary to ensure the function's reliability and correctness across all potential use cases.

Problem description: Create a function that calculates the total cost of a meal, including tax and tip. The function should take three inputs: the base price of the meal, the tax rate as a percentage, and the tip rate as a percentage. The function should calculate and return the total cost of the meal.

Test cases:

a   *Standard Case*—Calculate the total price of a $50 meal with a 10% tax and a 15% tip:
  - Input: `base_price = 50`, `tax_rate = 10`, `tip_rate = 15`
  - Expected output: $62.50 (calculated as $50 + $5 tax + $7.50 tip)

b   *Zero Tip Case*—Calculate the total price of a $30 meal with a 5% tax and no tip:
  - Input: `base_price = 30`, `tax_rate = 5`, `tip_rate = 0`
  - Expected output: $31.50 (calculated as $30 + $1.50 tax + $0 tip)

c   *High Tax and Tip Case*—Calculate the total price of a $100 meal with a 20% tax and a 25% tip:
  - Input: `base_price = 100`, `tax_rate = 20`, `tip_rate = 25`
  - Expected output: $145 (calculated as $100 + $20 tax + $25 tip)

5   Review the initial prompt provided to Copilot and the resulting Python function. The code doesn't fulfill the requirements as it only converts from Fahrenheit to Celsius and lacks the capability to convert in both directions based on a user-specified mode. How would you improve the prompt to ensure that the generated code meets the full requirements of the problem description?

```
Prompt: Write a Python function to convert temperature between
    Fahrenheit and Celsius.

def convert_temperature(temp):
    celsius = (temp - 32) * 5.0/9.0
    return celsius
```

Summary

- Problem decomposition involves breaking a large problem into smaller tasks.
- We use functions to perform problem decomposition in our programs.
- Each function must solve one small, well-defined task.

- A function header or signature is the first line of code of the function.
- Parameters are used to provide information to functions.
- The function header indicates the name of the function and names of its parameters.
- We use `return` to pass a value from a function to its caller.
- A docstring uses the names of each function parameter to describe the purpose of the function.
- To ask Copilot to write a function, we provide it the function header and docstring.
- We get a function to do its work by calling it with values (also called arguments) for its parameters.
- To test whether a function is correct, we call it with different types of inputs.
- A variable is a name that refers to a value.
- Every Python value has a type, such as a number, text (string), true/false value (bool), or collection of values (list or dictionary).
- Prompt engineering involves modifying our prompt for Copilot to influence the code that we get back.
- We need to ensure that we import any module (e.g., string) our code is using.
- Functions reduce duplication, make it easier to test our code, and reduce the likelihood of bugs.
- Unit testing involves checking that the function does what we expect on a variety of different inputs.
- A helper function is a small function written to make it easier to write a bigger function.
- A leaf function doesn't call any other function to do its job.

Reading Python code: Part 1

In chapter 3, we used Copilot to write several functions for us. What are they good for? Maybe our `money_made` function could be part of a stock trading system, our `is_strong_password` function could be used as part of a social networking website, or our `best_word` function could be used as part of some Scrabble AI. Overall, we've written some useful functions that could be part of larger programs. And, we did this without writing much code ourselves or, indeed, understanding what the code even does.

However, we believe that you need to understand at a high level what code does. Because this will require some time to learn, we've split this discussion over two chapters. In this chapter, we'll explain why reading code is important and introduce you to a Copilot feature that can help you understand the code. After that, we'll dive into the top 10 programming features you'll need to recognize to read most basic code produced by Copilot. We'll do the first five in this chapter and the remaining five in the next chapter. Don't worry: you've actually been informally introduced to all 10 already—we're just going to deepen your understanding of each one.

4.1 Why we need to read code

When we talk about reading code, what we mean is understanding what code does by looking at it. There are two such levels of understanding, and they're both important.

The first level is being able to understand, line by line, what a program will do. This often involves tracing the values of variables as the code runs to determine exactly what the code is doing at each step. This is useful, but isn't the whole story. It's like following a cooking recipe step-by-step without knowing what the recipe is making or how its ingredients fit together. At the end, you might have a cake, but you might not be able to grasp why the cake turned out so well or how you could come up with such a recipe yourself. You need to understand why the recipe, as a whole, is effective.

So, that's the second level: determining the overall purpose of a program. That is, you need to be able to zoom out, away from each line, and understand what the program is doing at a high level.

At the end of these two chapters, we want you to be able to begin to understand code from Copilot at both of these levels. We'll start focusing on that line-by-line understanding, but toward the end of this chapter and through the rest of the book, you'll start being able to look at a small chunk of code and determine its overall purpose.

We can illustrate the difference between the two levels of reading code by referring back to our `best_word` function from chapter 3, reprinted in the following listing.

Listing 4.1 `best_word` function for Scrabble

```
def best_word(word_list):
    """
    word_list is a list of words.

    Return the word worth the most points.
    """
    best_word = ""
    best_points = 0
    for word in word_list:
        points = num_points(word)
        if points > best_points:
            best_word = word
            best_points = points
    return best_word
```

A *tracing description* of what this program does is a description of each line. For example, we would say that we're defining a function called `best_word` that takes one parameter called `word_list`. We have a variable called `best_word` that we start off as a string with no characters, otherwise known as the empty string. (It's unfortunate that the function and this variable are both called best_word because it makes it trickier to refer to one or the other, but that's what Copilot gave us.) We also have another variable, best_points, that we start at 0. Then, we have a for loop over each word in the word_list. Inside the for loop, we call our num_points helper function and store its return value in the points variable, and so on. (We'll explain how we know what each line of code does over this chapter and the next.)

In contrast, a *description of the overall purpose* would be something like our docstring description: "Return the word with the highest Scrabble point value from a list of words." Rather than refer to each line, this description refers to the code's purpose as a whole, explaining what it does at a high level.

You'll come to an overall-purpose level of understanding through a combination of practice with tracing and testing, and we hope you arrive there in full glory by the end of the book. Working at a tracing level generally precedes the ability to work at an overall-purpose level [1], so in this chapter and the next, we're going to focus on the tracing level by understanding what each line of code does. There are three reasons why we want you to be able to read code:

1 *To help determine whether code is correct*—In chapter 3, we practiced how to test the code that Copilot gives us. Testing is a powerful skill for determining whether code does the right thing, and we'll continue to use it throughout the book. But many programmers, the two of us included, will only test something if it seems plausibly correct. If we can determine by inspection that the code is wrong, then we won't bother to test it: we'll try to fix the code first. Similarly, we want you to identify when code is simply wrong without having to spend time testing it. The more code that you can identify as wrong (through quick tracing or honing your overall-purpose skills), the more time you save testing broken code.

2 *To inform testing*—Understanding what the code is doing line by line is useful on its own, but it also helps turbocharge your ability to test effectively. For example, in the next chapter, you'll learn about loops—that they can cause your code to repeat zero times, one time, two times, or as many times as needed. You'll be able to combine that knowledge with what you already know about testing to help you identify important categories of cases to test.

3 *To help you write code*—We know, you want Copilot to write all of your code! We want that too. But inevitably, there will be code that Copilot just doesn't get right, no matter how much prompt engineering you do. Or maybe enough prompt engineering could finally cajole Copilot to write the correct code, but it would be simpler and faster to just do it ourselves. In writing this book, the two of us strive to have Copilot write as much code as possible. But, because of our knowledge of Python programming, we're often able to see a mistake and just fix it without going through any hoops to have Copilot fix it for us. Longer term, we want you to be empowered to learn more programming on your own, and having an understanding of Python is our way to provide a bridge for you

from this book to other resources later. There is research evidence that being able to trace and explain code is prerequisite to being able to write code [1].

Before we get to it, we need to be clear about the level of depth that we're striving for. We're not going to teach you every nuance of every line of code. Doing so would revert us back to the traditional way programming was taught prior to tools like Copilot. Rather, through a combination of Copilot tools and our own explanations, we're going to help you understand the gist or overall goal of each line of code. You'll need more than this if you endeavor to write large portions of programs in the future. We're trying to target the sweet spot between "this code is magic" and "I know exactly how every line of the code works."

4.2   Asking Copilot to explain code

To this point, we've used Copilot to generate code for us. That's its most well-known feature, but it's not the only one. We're going to show you another of its best features right now: explaining what Python code does!

The Copilot extension is always changing. The specific steps we give here may vary somewhat, and, in that case, we encourage you to consult more general GitHub Copilot documentation.

To try the Explain feature, you need to highlight some code that you want Copilot to describe to you. Let's try this with our `best_word` function (listing 4.1). If you don't have this code typed in from chapter 3, please enter it now.

```
def best_word(word_list):
    """
    word_list is a list of words.

    Return the word worth the most points.
    """
    best_word = ""
    best_points = 0
    for word in word_list:
        points = num_points(word)
        if points > best_points:
            best_word = word
            best_points = points
    return best_word
```

Figure 4.1   The code from the best_word function highlighted in the editor

Highlight the code as in figure 4.1. After this, we have a few options. The first is to click the Chat icon in the Activity Bar (on the left-hand side of VS Code), or press Ctrl-Alt-I. This will open the Copilot Chat interface, as in figure 4.2. (There are other interfaces for Chat, including a Quick Chat that you can open with Ctrl-Shift-I—it doesn't matter which chat interface you use.) Copilot Chat is able to respond to your questions not only with natural language but also with blocks of code, buttons/links that you can click to invoke commands, and more. It also suggests questions that you may wish to ask and, of course, allows you to type whatever code-related questions you like.

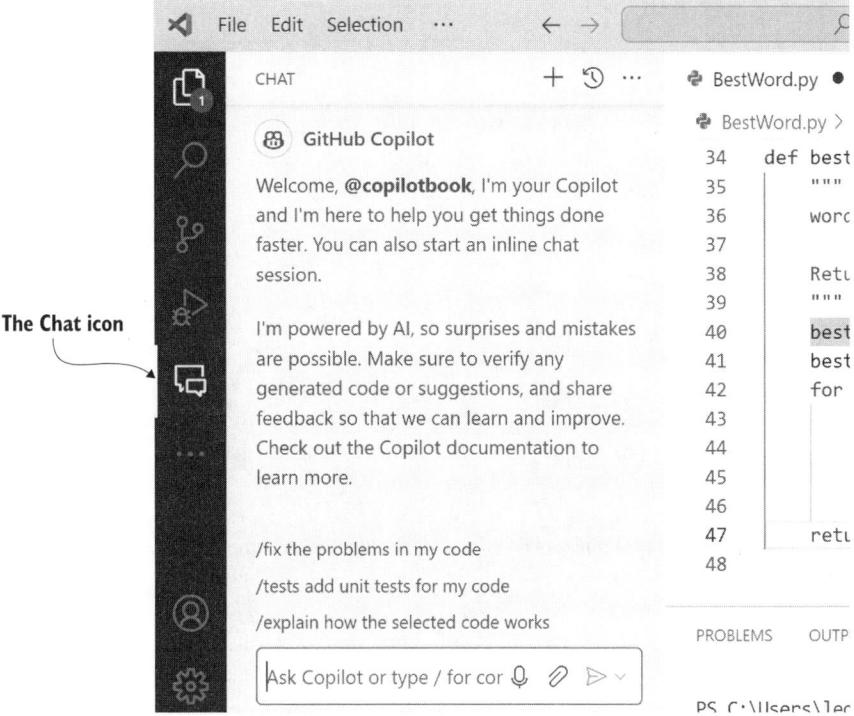

Figure 4.2   Copilot Chat interface in VS Code

For now, we'll use Copilot Chat to explain the code. In the text box, type the following command:

```
/explain
```

If Copilot asks, you want the @workspace option. If this doesn't work for you, you can also try this command:

```
/explain how the selected code works
```

Typing a forward slash (/) is how you tell Copilot Chat that you're specifying a command (Copilot documentation refers to these as slash commands), rather than natural language. In this case, we're asking for the /explain command to be run by Copilot for the selected text.

Alternatively, you could ask Copilot to explain the code by highlighting the code in the function just like in figure 4.1. Then, right-click the code in the function, and you'll see the menu that appears in figure 4.3.

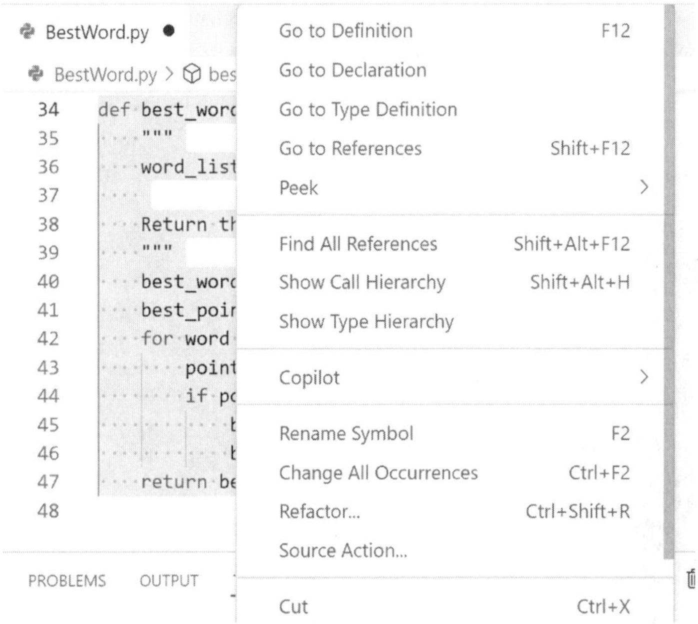

**Figure 4.3   The menu that appears when you right-click the selected
`best_word` function**

In this menu, highlight Copilot, and you'll see the list of options shown in figure 4.4. These options are the more commonly used features with Copilot.

The last step is to select the Explain This option. The Copilot Chat window will open (as shown earlier in figure 4.2), and you'll get an explanation of the code. As usual, Copilot is nondeterministic, so your results will likely differ from ours. In fact, if an explanation is confusing you, you might try the `/explain` command again or writing your own prompt to get a different explanation. As educators, this is the start of a dream come true, where learners will be able to ask for as many explanations as they need to fully understand how code works.

Copilot explanations can be wrong

As with the code produced by Copilot, the explanations from Copilot can be wrong too. You might be thinking, "Wait, what's the value of a tool to understand code if it can be wrong?!" First, we agree that this can be really frustrating. However, Copilot's explanations are right often enough in our experience that they can be really helpful, particularly for understanding code basics such as the things we're teaching in these two chapters. Moreover, what learners historically did when they were confused about their code was to ask friends or websites about the code, which can lead to mistakes too. A way to help mitigate the potential for error is to ask Copilot for its explanation a couple of times because you're less likely to get grossly incorrect answers across multiple tries.

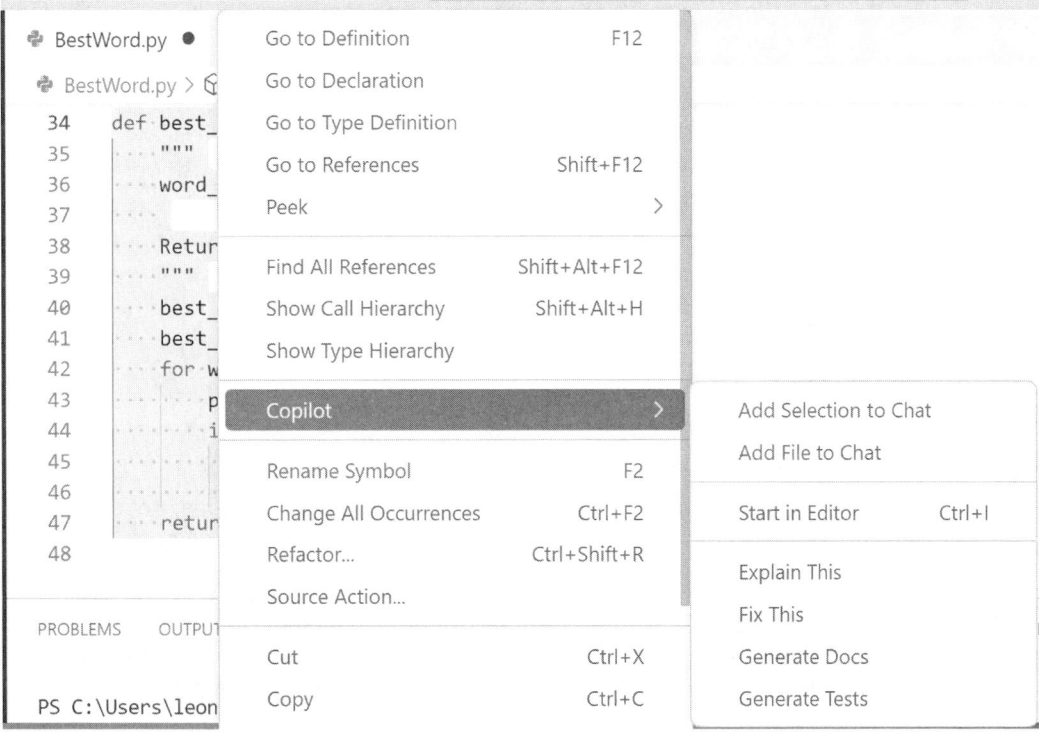

Figure 4.4   A list of options that you can use with Copilot

Here's what Copilot gave us the first time we asked:

> The provided Python code defines a function named `best_word` that takes a list of words as an argument (`word_list`). The purpose of this function is to determine and return the word from the list that is worth the most points.
>
> The function starts by initializing two variables: `best_word` and `best_points`. `best_word` is an empty string that will eventually hold the word with the highest point value, while `best_points` is set to 0 and will hold the highest point value found.
>
> The function then enters a loop where it iterates over each word in the `word_list`. For each word, it calculates the point value of the word by calling the `num_points` function (not shown in the provided code). The `num_points` function presumably takes a word as an argument and returns its point value.
>
> If the point value of the current word is greater than the current `best_points`, the function updates `best_word` to be the current word and `best_points` to be the points of the current word. This way, the function always keeps track of the word with the highest point value.
>
> After the loop has iterated over all the words in the list, the function returns `best_word`, which at this point should be the word with the highest point value from

the list. If the list is empty or all words have a point value of 0, the function will return an empty string.

To us, this is an excellent description of what the code does. It starts with an overall explanation of the code, and then proceeds to give more of a line-by-line explanation. Notice, however, to make full sense of it, you need to know important Python terminology and features. The explanation from Copilot refers to functions, arguments, variables, strings, loops, making decisions ("If the point value"), and returning. This explanation is quite useful if you understand the terminology, but much less useful if you don't. By the end of this and the next chapter, you'll know the main terminology and features of Python that you need to interpret a typical explanation from Copilot.

Asking for explanations

The type of explanation that you get from the `/explain` command may not meet your requirements. For example, suppose that you want Copilot to explicitly give you each line of code and explain what it does, so that you can more easily connect the code to its specific explanation. You can make that happen! Try this prompt: "Explain that code again, but do it line by line. Give each line of code and the explanation of what it does." Doing so gave us a very detailed breakdown of each line of code, followed by its explanation. We encourage you to craft your own prompts if built-in commands aren't giving you the level of detail that you want.

4.3   Top 10 programming features you need to know: Part 1

We're going to give you a whirlwind tour of the 10 Python features that you'll need for the rest of your programming journey, starting with the first five of those in this chapter. Python is an interactive language, which makes it easier than other languages for us to play around with and see what stuff does. We'll take advantage of that here as we explore programming features. This is how the two of us learned Python and how many thousands of programmers have done so. Don't hesitate to experiment! To get started, press Ctrl–Shift–P and type REPL, and then select Python: Start REPL. This should result in the situation shown in figure 4.5. (REPL stands for read-execute-print-loop. It's called that because Python reads what you type, executes/runs it, prints the results back to you, and does all of this over and over in a loop.)

This will put you back at the same Python prompt as in chapter 3 (as shown in figure 4.6), except with none of your functions loaded.

Then, we can start typing Python code. For example, type

```
>>> 5 * 4
```

and press Enter. You'll see the response of 20. We won't spend time on simple math here, but the way you interact with Python to learn how it works is exactly the same:

Figure 4.5   Starting REPL from VS Code

```
PROBLEMS    OUTPUT    DEBUG CONSOLE    TERMINAL

PS C:\Users\leona\copilot-book> & C:/Users/leona/AppData/Local/Programs/Python/Python3
11/python.exe
Python 3.11.1 (tags/v3.11.1:a7a450f, Dec  6 2022, 19:58:39) [MSC v.1934 64 bit (AMD64)
] on win32
Type "help", "copyright", "credits" or "license" for more information.
>>>
```

Figure 4.6   REPL running in VS Code

you type some code, and Python responds. Now, let's jump into the first five of those 10 Python features we mentioned.

4.3.1   #1. Functions

You learned all about functions in chapter 3, so let's just summarize what we learned. You use functions to break a large problem into smaller pieces. In retrospect, that best_word function we wrote in chapter 3 is a pretty big task: it has to figure out which word in a list of words is worth the most points. How many points is a word worth? Aha—that's a subtask that we can carve out from this function, which we did in our earlier num_points function.

We design a function to take parameters, one parameter for each piece or collection of data that the function needs to do its job. After doing their work, most functions use return to send the answer back to the line of code that called them. When we call a function, we pass values, known as arguments, with one value for each parameter, and we often store that return value using a variable.

For each program we write, we'll likely need to design a few functions, but there are also some functions that are built-in to Python that we get for free. We can call those like we call our own functions. For example, there's a built-in max function that takes one or more arguments and tells us the largest:

```
>>> max(5, 2, 8, 1)
8
```

There's also the `input` function, which we used in our `get_strong_password` function from chapter 3. It takes an argument that becomes the prompt to the user, and it returns whatever the user types at the keyboard:

```
>>> name = input("What is your name? ")
What is your name? Dan
>>> name
'Dan'
```

If `input` is the function to receive input from the keyboard, is there an `output` function to output a message to the screen? Well, yes, but it's called `print`, not `output`:

```
>>> print('Hello', name)
Hello Dan
```

4.3.2   *#2. Variables*

A variable is a name that refers to a value. We used variables in chapter 3 to keep track of `return` values from functions. We also just used a variable here to hold the user's name. Whenever we need to remember a value for later, we use a variable.

To assign a value to a variable, we use the = (equals sign) symbol, which is called the *assignment* symbol. It figures out the value of whatever is on the right and then assigns that to the variable:

```
>>> age = 20 + 4
>>> age
24
```
The right-hand side of the = symbol is evaluated, which means 20 + 4 is evaluated to be 24. Then, the variable age is assigned the value of 24.

The = symbol is different in Python than in math

The = sign is used in Python and other programming languages to denote *assignment*. The variable on the left side of the = symbol is given the value of the calculation performed on the right side of the = symbol. This is *not* a permanent relationship as the variable can have its value changed. People new to programming who are strong in math can find this confusing, but just remember that the = sign in Python means assignment, not equality.

We can use the variable in a larger context, called an *expression*. The value that the variable refers to gets substituted for its name:

```
>>> age + 3
27
>>> age
24
```
Age is still available in the Python prompt and has the value 24. 24 + 3 is evaluated to be 27.

The expression of age + 3 doesn't change age because we didn't reassign age.

> **Variables persist in the Python prompt**
>
> We assigned `age` in the earlier batch of code. Why can we keep referring to it? Any variable declared during a session of programming with your Python prompt will stick around until you quit. That's just how variables work in programs too. They're available as soon as you assign a value to them.

But notice that the variable `age` didn't change when we said `age + 3`! To change it, we need another = assignment statement:

```
>>> age = age + 5
>>> age
29
```
We've changed age by doing an assignment (the = symbol).

Let's see a few more ways to change what a variable refers to. We'll include some explanations as annotations with the code:

```
>>> age += 5
>>> age
34
```
A shortcut way to add. age += 5 is equivalent to age = age + 5.

```
>>> age *= 2
>>> age
68
```
A shortcut way to multiply by 2. age *= 2 is equivalent to age = age * 2.

4.3.3 #3. Conditionals

Whenever our program has to make a decision, we need a conditional statement. For example, in chapter 2, we needed to make a decision about which players to include in our data (we wanted only quarterbacks). To do so, we used `if` statements.

Remember our larger function from chapter 3? We've reproduced it here in the following listing.

Listing 4.2 Function to determine the larger of two values

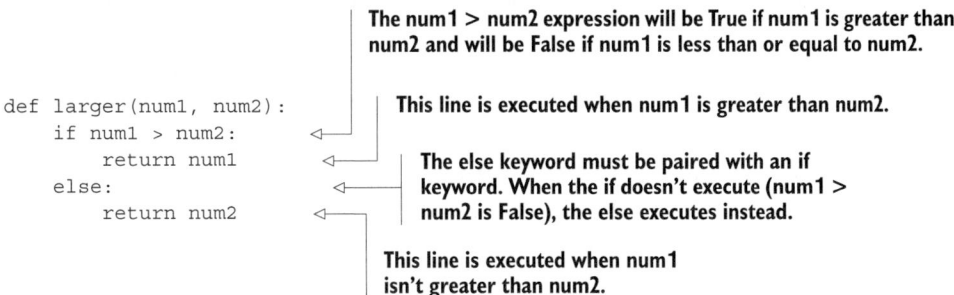

The num1 > num2 expression will be True if num1 is greater than num2 and will be False if num1 is less than or equal to num2.

```
def larger(num1, num2):
    if num1 > num2:
        return num1
    else:
        return num2
```

This line is executed when num1 is greater than num2.

The else keyword must be paired with an if keyword. When the if doesn't execute (num1 > num2 is False), the else executes instead.

This line is executed when num1 isn't greater than num2.

The `if-else` structure in listing 4.2 is known as a *conditional* statement, and it allows our program to make decisions. Here, if `num1` is greater than `num2`, then `num1` is returned; otherwise, `num2` is returned. That's how it returns the larger one!

After `if`, we put a Boolean condition (`num1 > num2`). A Boolean condition is an expression that tests a condition where the result would either be `True` or `False`. If it's `True`, then the code under the `if` runs; if it's `False`, then the code under the `else` runs. We create Boolean expressions using comparison symbols such as `>=` for greater than or equal to, `<` for less than, `>` for greater than, `==` for equal to, and `!=` for not equal to. Notice that we're using indentation not only for the code of the function but also for the code of the `if` and `else` parts of the `if-else` statement. Indentation is necessary for the code to function properly, so it's worth paying attention to (we talk more about indentation in the next chapter). This is how Python knows which lines of code belong to the function and which additionally belong to the `if` or `else`.

We can play around with conditional statements at the Python prompt too—we don't need to be writing code inside of a function. Here's an example:

```
>>> age = 40          ⟵⎤  We assign 40 to age.
>>> if age < 40:                    ⟵
...      print("Binging Friends")       Because age is 40, this code is asking
... else:                           ⟵   whether 40 < 40. It's not, so the if
...      print("What's binging?")        part of the code is skipped.
...
What's binging?                         The else portion runs because
                                        the if condition is False.
```

You'll notice that the prompt changes from `>>>` to `...` when you're typing inside the `if` statement. The change of prompt lets you know that you're in the middle of typing code that you need to complete. You need an extra press of Enter when you're done with the `else` code to get out of the `...` prompt and back to the `>>>` prompt.

We set the age variable to 40. As `40 < 40` is `False`, the `else` runs. Let's try again, this time making the `if` run:

```
>>> age = 25          ⟵⎤  We assign 25 to age.
>>> if age < 40:                    ⟵
...      print("Binging Friends")       Because age is 25, this is asking
... else:                           ⟵   whether 25 < 40. It is, so the if
...      print("What's binging?")        part of the code runs.
...
Binging Friends                         The else portion doesn't run (we
                                        already ran the if part of the code).
```

You might see some `if` statements with no `else` part, and that's okay: the `else` part is optional. In that case, if the condition is `False`, then the `if` statement won't do anything:

```
>>> age = 25          ⟵⎤  We assign 25 to age.
>>> if age == 30:                   ⟵   == tests to see if the
...      print("You are exactly 30!")    two values are equal.
...
```

Notice that the way to test whether two values are equal is to use two equals signs, (==), not one equals sign. (We already know that one equals sign is for the assignment statement to assign a value to a variable.)

What do you do if you have more than two possible outcomes? For example, let's say that a person's age determines the show they'll likely binge, as shown in table 4.1.

Table 4.1 Possible favorite TV shows by age

Age	Show
30–39	*Friends*
20–29	*The Office*
10–19	*Pretty Little Liars*
0–9	*Chi's Sweet Home*

We can't capture all of these outcomes with just an `if-else`, so the `elif` (short for `else-if`) allows us to capture the logic for more than two possible outcomes, as shown in the following code. We're presenting this code without the Python prompts (>>> and . . .) because this would be a lot to type:

```
if age >= 30 and age <= 39:
    print("Binging Friends")
elif age >= 20 and age <= 29:
    print("Binging The Office")
elif age >= 10 and age <= 19:
    print("Binging Pretty Little Liars")
elif age >= 0 and age <= 9:
    print("Binging Chi's Sweet Home")
else:
    print("What's binging?")
```

This is True if both age > = 30 and age < = 39 are true; for example, if age were 35.

This condition is checked if the above condition is False.

This code runs if all conditions above are False.

We're using `and` to capture a complex condition. For example, in the first line, we want age to be greater than or equal to 30 and less than or equal to 39. Python works from top to bottom, and when it finds a condition that's true, it runs the corresponding indented code. Then, it stops checking the remaining `elif`s or `else`—so if two conditions happened to be true, only the code for the first one would run.

Try experimenting with various values for the age variable to observe that the correct code runs in each case. In fact, if we were serious about testing this code, we could use the `if` statement structure for a good sense of the values we'd want to test. It's all about testing the boundaries of values. For example, we definitely want to test the ages 30 and 39 to make sure, for example, that we're correctly capturing the full 30–39 range with the first condition. Similarly, we'd want to test 20, 29, 10, 19, 0, 9, and then something larger than 39 to test the `else` way at the bottom.

If you use additional `if`s rather than `elif`s, then they become separate `if` statements, rather than a single `if` statement. This matters because Python always checks each independent `if` statement on its own, regardless of what may have happened in previous `if` statements.

For example, let's change the `elif`s to `if`s in our age code. That gives us the following:

```
if age >= 30 and age <= 39:
    print("Binging Friends")
if age >= 20 and age <= 29:               ◁
    print("Binging The Office")
if age >= 10 and age <= 19:               ◁     This condition is
    print("Binging Pretty Little Liars")        always checked.
if age >= 0 and age <= 9:                 ◁
    print("Binging Chi's Sweet Home")
else:                                     ◁     This else goes with the
    print("What's binging?")                    most recent if statement.
```

Suppose that you put `age = 25` above this code and run it. What do you think will happen? Well, the second `if` condition `age >= 20 and age <= 29` is `True`, so we'll certainly output `Binging The Office`. But that's not all that happens! Remember, because we're using `if`s here, each of the remaining ones is going to be checked. (If they were `elif`s, we'd be done.) `age >= 10 and age <= 19` is `False`, so we're not going to output `Binging Pretty Little Liars`.

The final `if` condition `age >= 0 and age <= 9` is also `False`, so we're not going to output `Binging Chi's Sweet Home`. But this `if` has an `else`! So, we *are* going to output `What's binging?` We didn't intend this! We only wanted `What's binging?` for people whose age is at least 40. This is all to say that `if` and `elif` behave differently and that we need to be using the one that matches the behavior that we want (`if` if we want multiple chunks of code to potentially run, and `elif` if we want only one).

4.3.4   #4. Strings

As we learned in chapter 3, a string is the type we use whenever we want to store text. Text is everywhere—stats like in chapter 2, passwords, books—so strings show up in almost every Python program.

We use quotation marks to indicate the beginning and end of the string. You'll see Copilot use double quotes or single quotes. It doesn't matter which you use; just be sure to start and end the string with the same type of quote.

Strings come with a powerful set of methods. A *method* is a function that's associated with a particular type—in this case, strings. The way you call a method is a little different from how you call a function. When you call a function, you put the argument values in parentheses. With methods, we still put values in parentheses, but we need to put the value on which we're calling the method first, outside of the parentheses, followed by a dot. We'll see an example of that next!

In chapter 3, Copilot used some string methods to implement `is_strong_password`. Let's try using those methods here to gain a better understanding of how they work:

```
>>> 'abc'.isupper()
False
>>> 'Abc'.isupper()
False
>>> 'ABC'.isupper()
True
>>> 'abc'.isdigit()
False
>>> '345bc'.isdigit()
False
>>> '345'.isdigit()
True

>>> 'abc6'.isalnum()
True
>>> 'abc def'.isalnum()
False
>>> 'abcdef#'.isalnum()
False
```

isupper needs all characters to be uppercase for it to return True.

isdigit needs all characters to be numbers for it to return True.

isalnum needs all characters to be alphanumeric to return True (a space isn't considered alphanumeric).

There are many other string methods as well. Some help you convert strings between lowercase and uppercase, others help you search a string, and still others help you format a string (e.g., centering or right-justifying it).

Copilot's Explain feature can often be helpful if you're not sure what a given string method does. For example, what does this function do:

```
def clean_number(phone_number):
    phone_number = phone_number.replace('(', '')
    phone_number = phone_number.replace(')', '')
    phone_number = phone_number.replace('-', '')
    return phone_number
```

Removes all (characters from phone number

Removes all) characters from phone number

Removes all – characters from phone number

Remember that we can ask Copilot to explain code, as we demonstrated in section 4.2. Here's what we got when we asked Copilot to explain this code:

> The provided Python code defines a function named `clean_number`. This function is designed to take a single argument, `phone_number`, which is expected to be a string representing a phone number. The purpose of this function is to remove certain characters from the phone number string, specifically parentheses "(" and ")" and hyphens "-".
>
> The function uses the `replace()` method, which is a built-in method in Python for strings. The `replace()` method replaces a specified phrase with another specified phrase. It takes two arguments: the first is the substring that needs to be replaced, and the second is the substring that will replace the first substring.
>
> In this function, the `replace()` method is called three times on `phone_number`. Each call to `replace()` is used to remove one type of character: first the open parenthesis "(", then the close parenthesis ")", and finally the hyphen "-". It does this by replacing these characters with an empty string "", effectively removing them.

After all replacements are done, the cleaned `phone_number` is returned by the function. This will be a string containing the digits of the phone number without any parentheses or hyphens.

This function could be useful in situations where you need to process or store phone numbers in a consistent, character-free format. For example, you might want to remove these characters when storing phone numbers in a database, or when comparing phone numbers for equality.

That confirms what this function does: removes parentheses and hyphens from a phone number string. And it uses the `replace` method to do so.

Wait—"replace" sounds like we're changing some characters to some other characters (replacing them), not removing them. How is `replace` able to remove characters for us, then? The explanation said, "It does this by replacing these characters with an empty string "", effectively removing them." That's a clue to how `replace` is doing this, but we might want to know more. We therefore next used the prompt "How does the replace method use the empty string to remove characters?" and received the following explanation from Copilot:

The `replace()` method in Python replaces all occurrences of a specified substring in the string it's called on with another specified substring.

In this case, the specified substrings are the characters "(", ")", and "-". The method is called on the `phone_number` string, and the second argument to `replace()` is an empty string "".

So, what happens is that every occurrence of the specified character in `phone_number` is replaced with an empty string. This effectively removes that character from the string, because replacing something with nothing is equivalent to removing it.

This is done three times in the `clean_number` function, once for each character that needs to be removed. After all three characters have been removed, the cleaned `phone_number` is returned.

And if you wanted to learn even more, you could continue asking Copilot questions or do your own testing at the Python prompt. For example, you could verify that `replace` removes all (,), and - characters, even if there are multiples of each. And you could explore using `replace` to actually replace characters (its typical use case), rather than removing them. This kind of exploration is also helpful if we need to separate truth from bits of incorrect information that Copilot may provide. This is why we need a baseline of our own Python knowledge!

You'll also often see what look like mathematical operators being used on strings. They are the same as math symbols, but they do different things on strings. The + operator is used to put two strings together, and the * operator is used to repeat a string a specific number of times. Examples are shown here:

```
>>> first = 'This is a '
>>> second = 'sentence.'
>>> sentence = first + second
>>> print(sentence)
This is a sentence.
>>> print('-=' * 5)
-=-=-=-=-=
```

Combines first and second strings and assigns result to sentence

Repeats the -= string five times

4.3.5   #5. Lists

A string is great when we have a sequence of characters, such as a password or a single Scrabble word. But sometimes, we need to store many words or many numbers. For that, we need a list. We used a list in chapter 3 for the best_word function because that function needed to work with a list of individual words.

Whereas we use quotation marks to start and end a string, we use opening and closing square brackets to start and end a list. And, as for strings, there are many methods available on lists. To give you an idea of the kinds of list methods available and what they do, let's explore some of these:

```
>>> books = ['The Invasion', 'The Encounter', 'The Message']
>>> books
['The Invasion', 'The Encounter', 'The Message']
>>> books.append('The Predator')
>>> books
['The Invasion', 'The Encounter', 'The Message', 'The Predator']
>>> books.reverse()
>>> books
['The Predator', 'The Message', 'The Encounter', 'The Invasion']
```

A list with three string values in it

Adds a new string value to the end of the list

Reverses the list (now the values are in the opposite order)

Many Python types, including strings and lists, allow you to work with particular values using an *index*. You need to use indices whenever you want to work with part of a string or list rather than the whole thing. An index is just a number that identifies an element. Indices start at 0 for the first element and go up to, but not including, the number of values. The first value has index 0 (not index 1!), the second has index 1, the third has index 2, and so on. The last value in the list is at the index, which is the length of the list minus 1. The length of the list can be determined by using the len function. For example, if we do len(books), we'll get a value of 4 (so the valid indices are from 0 up to and including 3). People also often use negative indices, which provides another way to index each value: the rightmost value has index –1, the value to its left has index –2, and so on. Figure 4.7 depicts this example with both positive and negative indexing.

Positive Index	Negative Index	books
0	-4	"The Predator"
1	-3	"The Message"
2	-2	"The Encounter"
3	-1	"The Invasion"

Figure 4.7   List elements can be accessed through either positive or negative indices.

Let's practice indexing on the current books list:

```
>>> books
['The Predator', 'The Message', 'The Encounter', 'The Invasion']
>>> books[0]
'The Predator'
>>> books[1]
'The Message'
>>> books[2]
'The Encounter'
>>> books[3]
'The Invasion'
>>> books[4]
Traceback (most recent call last):
  File "<stdin>", line 1, in <module>
IndexError: list index out of range
>>> books[-1]
'The Invasion'
>>> books[-2]
'The Encounter'
```

books[0] corresponds to the first element.

Error because index 3 is the last book!

books[-1] refers to the last element in the list.

There's also a way to pull multiple values out of a string or list, rather than just one. It's called *slicing*. We specify the index of the first value, a colon, and the index to the right of the value, like this:

```
>>> books[1:3]
['The Message', 'The Encounter']
```

Starts at index 1, ends at index 2 (not 3!)

We specified 1:3, so you might expect to get the values including index 3. But the value at the second index (the one after the colon) isn't included. It's counterintuitive but true!

If we leave out the starting or ending index, Python uses the start or end as appropriate:

```
>>> books[:3]
['The Predator', 'The Message', 'The Encounter']
>>> books[1:]
['The Message', 'The Encounter', 'The Invasion']
```

Same as using books[0:3]

Same as using books[1:4]

We can also use indexing to change a specific value in a list, for example:

```
>>> books
['The Predator', 'The Message', 'The Encounter', 'The Invasion']
>>> books[0] = 'The Android'
>>> books[0]
'The Android'
>>> books[1] = books[1].upper()
>>> books[1]
'THE MESSAGE'
>>> books
['The Android', 'THE MESSAGE', 'The Encounter', 'The Invasion']
```

Changes books[0] to refer to the string value "The Android"

Changes books[1] to be in all uppercase

If we try that on a string, though, we get an error:

```
>>> title = 'The Invasion'
>>> title[0]
'T'
>>> title[1]
'h'
>>> title[-1]
'n'
>>> title[0] = 't'
Traceback (most recent call last):
  File "<stdin>", line 1, in <module>
TypeError: 'str' object does not support item assignment
```

Looking up a char works fine.

But assigning doesn't!

A string is known as an *immutable* value, which means that you can't change its characters. You can only create an entirely new string. By contrast, a list is known as a *mutable* value, which means that you can change it. If you get errors about a type not supporting item assignment, you're likely trying to change a value that can't be changed.

In this chapter, we introduced you to five of the most common code features in Python. We'll continue with five more in the next chapter. We also showed you how you can use the Copilot explanation tool to help you understand what the code is doing and offered guidance for verifying the veracity of these explanations. Table 4.2 provides a summary of the features we covered in this chapter.

Table 4.2 Summary of Python code features from this chapter

Code Element	Example	Brief Description
Functions	`def larger(num1, num2)`	Code feature that allows us to manage code complexity. Functions take in inputs, process those inputs, and possibly return an output.
Variables	`age = 25`	A human-readable name that refers to a stored value. It can be assigned using the = assignment statement.

Conditionals	`if age < 18:    print("Can't vote")`
	`else:`
	`    print("Can vote")`
		Conditionals allow the code to make decisions. In Python, we have three keywords associated with conditionals: `if`, `elif`, and `else`.

Table 4.2   Summary of Python code features from this chapter (continued)

Code Element	Example	Brief Description
Strings	`name = 'Dan'`	Strings store a sequence of characters (text). There are many powerful methods available for modifying strings.
Lists	`list = ['Leo', 'Dan']`	A sequence of values of any type. There are many powerful methods available for modifying lists.

4.4   Exercises

1   Recall the conditionals code we looked at in listing 4.2 (section 4.3.3). How does the behavior of this program differ from the original?

```python
def larger(num1, num2):
    if num1 < num2:
        return num1
    else:
        return num2
```

2   In the following code, what gets printed if age is 32? What would be printed if you change every `if`, except for the first, to an `elif` instead?

```python
if age >= 30 and age <= 39:
    print("Binging Friends")
if age >= 25 and age <= 34:
    print("Binging The Office")
if age >= 15 and age <= 24:
    print("Binging Pretty Little Liars")
if age >= 0 and age <= 14:
    print("Binging Chi's Sweet Home")
else:
    print("What's binging?")
```

3   What Python data type would you use to hold a series of temperature readings from a sensor that records data every minute? What would this data type store?

4   Arrange the following blocks of Python code to create a program that calculates the sum of all even numbers in a provided list.

```python
for number in numbers:
total += number
if number % 2 == 0:
numbers = [1, 2, 3, 4, 5, 6, 7, 8, 9, 10]
total = 0
print(f"The sum of all even numbers is: {total}")
```

5   (Recall section 4.3.1.) Consider the Python function call `min(input("Enter a number: "), input("Enter another number: "))`. Before running this code,

think about what this line is supposed to do, and then answer the following questions:

a   What do you expect to happen when this code is run? Describe each step of the execution process.

b   How does Python handle the inputs and the `min` function together in this scenario?

c   If the inputs aren't numbers but strings that are numeric (e.g., 5 or 2), how might Python's behavior change, if at all?

d   What would be the outcome if one or both inputs aren't numeric? Test your hypothesis by trying different inputs.

6   In section 4.3.2, we talked about how variables persist in Python. How does this property of variables influence the way you might structure your code? Think of an example scenario where maintaining variable states across different parts of a program would be beneficial.

7   We ask Copilot to explain how the following code works:

```
age = int(input("Enter your age: "))

if age < 13:
    print("You are a child.")
elif age < 20:
    print("You are a teenager.")
elif age < 60:
    print("You are an adult.")
else:
    print("You are a senior.")
```

Copilot provides the following explanation:

This Python code is a simple program that asks the user for their age and then prints out a message based on the age range they fall into.

The first line of the code uses the `input()` function to prompt the user to enter their age. The `input()` function reads a line from input (usually from the user's keyboard), converts it into a string, and returns that string. In this case, the prompt is "Enter your age: ". The returned string is then converted into an integer using the `int()` function and stored in the variable age.

The rest of the code is a series of conditional statements that check the value of age and print out a corresponding message. The `if` statement checks if the age is less than 13, and if so, it prints "You are a child." If the age is not less than 13, the program moves to the next condition, the `elif` (short for `else if`) statement, which checks if the age is less than 20. If so, it prints "You are a teenager." If the age is not less than 20, it moves to the next `elif` statement, which checks if the age is less than 60. If so, it prints "You are an adult."

It turns out that the explanation from Copilot is incomplete as it doesn't describe the code for *all inputs*. Determine what the explanation is missing, and add your answer to the explanation.

8 Review the Python code provided and the initial prompt to Copilot. The explanation returned was too vague and didn't help you understand the string methods used in the code.

```python
text = "Hello, World! Programming is fun."
index = text.find("World")
new_text = text[index:].replace("World", "Everyone")

print(new_text)
```

Prompt given to Copilot:

Can you explain what this code does?

Copilot explanation given back:

The code involves manipulating a string stored in text by finding a specific word and replacing it with another word. It uses methods to locate where the word starts and then constructs a new string where the word has been replaced. Finally, it prints out the modified string.

Your task is to do the following:

a Identify why the initial prompt might lead to a vague or unhelpful explanation.

b Improve the prompt to ensure a more detailed and specific explanation from Copilot. Consider what you specifically don't understand about the string methods and how the code uses them.

c Write the revised prompt to Copilot, and discuss how your changes will lead to a better explanation.

Summary

- We need to be able to read code to determine whether it's correct, test it effectively, and write our own code when needed.
- Copilot can provide line-by-line explanations of code to explain what the code is doing, and you can use your own prompt to influence the type of explanation you get.
- Python has built-in functions such as `max`, `input`, and `print` that we call just like we call our own functions.
- A variable is a name that refers to a value.
- An assignment statement makes a variable refer to a specific value.
- An `if` statement is used to have our programs make decisions and proceed down one of multiple paths.

- A string is used to store and manipulate text.
- A method is a function associated with a particular type.
- A list is used to store and manipulate a general sequence of values (e.g., a sequence of numbers or a sequence of strings).
- Each value in a string or list has an index; indexing starts at 0, not 1.
- Strings are immutable (not changeable); lists are mutable (changeable).

Reading Python code: Part 2

This chapter covers

- Repeating code the required number of times using loops
- Using indentation to tell Python which code goes together
- Building dictionaries to store pairs of associated values
- Setting up files to read and process data
- Using modules to work in new domains

In chapter 4, we explored five Python features that you're going to see all the time as you continue in your programming journey: functions, variables, conditionals (`if` statements), strings, and lists. You need to know those features to read code, and we explained why being able to read code is important whether or not we're using Copilot.

We'll continue in this chapter with five more Python features, which will round out our top 10. As in chapter 4, we'll do this through a combination of our own explanations, explanations from Copilot, and experimenting at the Python prompt.

5.1   Top 10 programming features you need to know: Part 2

This section details the next five of the top 10 programming features you need to know. Let's continue where we left off in the previous chapter with feature number 6: loops.

5.1.1   #6. Loops

A loop allows the computer to repeat the same block of code as many times as needed. If a single one of our top 10 programming features exemplifies why computers are so useful for helping us get work done, it's this one. Without the ability to loop, our programs would generally execute in order, line by line. Sure, they could still call functions and use `if` statements to make decisions, but the amount of work a program does would be proportional to the amount of code we write. Not so with loops: a single loop can process thousands or millions of values with ease.

There are two types of loops: `for` loops and `while` loops. Generally speaking, we use a `for` loop whenever we know how many times we need the loop to run, and we use a `while` loop when we don't. For example, in chapter 3, our `best_word` function (reproduced as listing 5.1) used a `for` loop because we know how many times we want the loop to run: once for each word in `word_list`! But in `get_strong_password`, which we'll see again in listing 5.4, we used a `while` loop, because we have no idea how many bad passwords the user is going to type before they type a strong one. We'll start with `for` loops and then move on to `while` loops.

Listing 5.1   `best_word` function from chapter 3

```
def best_word(word_list):
    """
    word_list is a list of words.

    Return the word worth the most points.
    """
    best_word = ""
    best_points = 0
    for word in word_list:            ◁──┐  This is an
        points = num_points(word)         example of a
        if points > best_points:          for loop.
            best_word = word
            best_points = points
    return best_word
```

A `for` loop allows us to access each value in a string or list. Let's try it with a string first:

```
>>> s = 'vacation'
>>> for char in s:                 ◁──┐  This repeats the indented code one
...     print('Next letter is', char)   time for each character of string s.
...     .                          ◁──┐  Because "vacation" has
Next letter is v                         eight letters, this code
Next letter is a                         will run eight times.
```

```
Next letter is c
Next letter is a
Next letter is t
Next letter is i
Next letter is o
Next letter is n
```

Notice that we don't need an assignment statement for `char`. That's because it's a special variable called a loop variable that's automatically managed by the `for` loop. `char` stands for character, and it's an extremely popular name that people use for the loop variable. The `char` variable automatically gets assigned each character of the string. When talking about a loop, we often use the word *iteration* to refer to the code that executes each time through the loop. Here, for example, we would say that on the first iteration, `char` refers to v; on the second iteration, it refers to a; and so on. Notice also, just like for functions and `if` statements, we have indentation for the code that makes up the loop. We have only one line of code in the body of this loop, but just like for functions and `if` statements, we could have more.

Let's see an example of a `for` loop on a list this time (listing 5.2), demonstrating that we can process each value of a list like we process each value of a string. We'll also throw two lines of code into the loop instead of just one, to demonstrate how that works too.

Listing 5.2   Example using a `for` loop

```
>>> lst = ['cat', 'dog', 'bird', 'fish']       1st is a list, so this is
>>> for animal in lst:                          a for loop on a list.
...       print('Got', animal)                This code runs on
...       print('Hello,', animal)             each iteration.
...
Got cat
Hello, cat
Got dog
Hello, dog
Got bird
Hello, bird
Got fish
Hello, fish
```

The code in listing 5.2 is just one way to loop through a list. The approach of `for animal in lst` assigns the variable `animal` to the next value in the list each time through the loop. Alternatively, you could use an index to access each element of the list. To do that, we need to learn about the built-in `range` function.

The `range` function gives you numbers within a range. We can provide a starting number and an ending number, and it will produce the range that goes from the starting number up to, but not including, the ending number. To see the numbers that `range` produces, we need to put the `list` function around it. Here's an example of using `range`:

```
>>> list(range(3, 9))
[3, 4, 5, 6, 7, 8]
```
◁— **Produces the range**
from 3 to 8 (not 3 to 9!)

Notice that it starts with the value 3 and includes all values between 3 and 8. That is, it includes all numbers from the starting value 3 up to, but not including, the ending value 9.

Now, how is range going to help us write a loop? Well, rather than hard-coding numbers like 3 and 9 in the range, we can include the length of a string or list, like this:

```
>>> lst
['cat', 'dog', 'bird', 'fish']
>>> list(range(0, len(lst)))
[0, 1, 2, 3]
```
Start at 0 and go up
to, but not including,
the length of 1st.
◁—

Notice that the range values here are 0, 1, 2, 3, which are the valid indices of our lst list! We can therefore use range to control a for loop, and that will give us access to each valid index from the string or list.

We can use range to perform the same task in listing 5.2. See listing 5.3 for the new code.

Listing 5.3   Loop example using for loop and range

```
>>> for index in range(0, len(lst)):
...     print('Got', lst[index])
...     print('Hello,', lst[index])
...
Got cat
Hello, cat
Got dog
Hello, dog
Got bird
Hello, bird
Got fish
Hello, fish
```
◁— **for loop using the**
range function

Indexing into the list
using the index variable

We've used a variable named index here, but you'll also often see people use just i for simplicity. That variable will be given the value 0 for the first iteration of the loop, 1 for the second, 2 for the third, and 3 for the last iteration. It stops at 3 because the length of the list is 4, and range stops one before that. Using indexing into the list, the code grabs the first element, then the second, then the third, and then the fourth, using the increasing indices. We could have also written the for loop without the 0; range will assume we want the values between 0 and the value provided, like this:

```
for index in range(len(lst)):
    print('Got', lst[index])
    print('Hello,', lst[index])
```
◁— **With one argument,**
range assumes that we
want to start at 0.

We'll stop here with `for` loops. But we're not done with loops yet because there's another type of loop that we need to talk about: the `while` loop.

We use a `while` loop when we don't know how many times to loop. A nice example of this situation is in our `get_strong_password` function from chapter 3. We've reproduced that code here as listing 5.4.

Listing 5.4   `get_strong_password` function from chapter 3

```
def get_strong_password():
    """
    Keep asking the user for a password until it's a strong password,
    and return that strong password.
    """
    password = input("Enter a strong password: ")
    while not is_strong_password(password):
        password = input("Enter a strong password: ")
    return password
```

Keeps looping while
the password isn't
strong

We have no idea how many passwords the user is going to type until they type a strong one. Will it be on the 1st try, 2nd try, or 50th try? Who knows. That's why we need a `while` loop: it ensures that the user is asked again and again until they provide a strong password.

To write a `while` loop, we follow `while` with a Boolean condition. If it's `True`, Python runs one iteration of the loop. If, after that iteration, that Boolean condition is still `True`, then it runs another iteration. It keeps doing that until the condition is `False`, at which point the loop terminates.

Now, we have enough information to make sense of the code for our `get_strong_password` function. By looking at the code, we can see that it begins by using the `input` function to ask the user for a password. Then, there's a `while` loop. This loop continues as long as the password isn't a strong password. The Boolean condition `not is_strong_password(password)` is equivalent to writing it as `is_strong_password (password) == False`. To avoid an infinite loop and to ask the user to try again, we have another use of `input` inside of the loop. We need the call of `input` above the loop to get the first try from the user. Without that, the `password` variable wouldn't exist, and the `while` loop line would give an error because it wouldn't have a `password` value to pass to the `is_strong_password` function.

Don't forget that we can ask Copilot for an explanation of this code, using what we learned in chapter 4, section 4.2. This is useful whenever you're feeling that you aren't quite understanding what the code is doing or how it works. Here's the explanation we received from Copilot:

> This Python code defines a function named `get_strong_password`. The purpose of this function is to interactively prompt the user to enter a password and keep asking until the user provides a password that is considered strong. The criteria for what constitutes a strong password is not defined in this function but is determined by another function named `is_strong_password`.

The function begins by asking the user to enter a password using Python's built-in `input` function. The entered password is then stored in the variable `password`.

Next, the function enters a `while` loop. The condition for this loop is `not is_strong_password(password)`. This means that the loop will continue to execute as long as the `is_strong_password` function returns `False` when called with the current password. In other words, the loop will keep running until the user enters a password that is considered strong.

Inside the loop, the function again prompts the user to enter a password. The new password replaces the previous one stored in the `password` variable. If this new password is still not strong, the loop will continue to prompt the user.

Once the user enters a password that is considered strong (i.e., `is_strong_password(password)` returns `True`), the `while` loop condition becomes `False` and the loop ends. The function then returns the strong password entered by the user.

This function is a good example of using a `while` loop to repeatedly prompt the user for input until the input meets certain criteria. However, the actual criteria for a strong password are not defined in this function and would need to be implemented in the `is_strong_password` function.

This explanation is a very good description of the function and matches the description that we just gave! It contains useful general Python information as well, including a reminder in the final paragraph of why exactly we're using a `while` loop. The explanation also mentions that we need the `is_strong_password` function to tell us whether a password is strong or not; we didn't highlight that function, which is why Copilot is telling us that we need to implement it.

Copilot explanations can be wrong

We chose the previous Copilot explanation because it was the best answer from Copilot after we asked it to explain the code three times. One of the answers it gave us sounded quite plausible, until it started talking about functions that didn't exist. We believe the explanations can be helpful as a learning aid if you run it multiple times and look for common ideas, but a principal goal of this chapter is to give you the tools you need to understand when it makes mistakes.

We encourage you to use Copilot explanations going forward and, if you're interested, ask Copilot to explain any code from prior chapters that you're still curious about. Again, these explanations can be wrong, so you should ask Copilot for several explanations to limit your reliance on a single erroneous explanation.

As with anything related to AI coding assistants right now, they're going to mess up. But we've given the explanation here because we see this Copilot feature as a potentially powerful teaching resource now and that will become even more true as Copilot improves.

We're supposed to use a `while` loop in these kinds of situations where we don't know how many iterations there will be. But we *can* use a `while` loop even when we know how many iterations there are. For example, we can use a `while` loop to process the characters in a string or the values in a list. We sometimes see Copilot do this in the code that it generates, even though a `for` loop would have been a better choice. For example, we can use a `while` loop to process the animals in our earlier `animals` list, as in the following listing. It's more work, though!

Listing 5.5   Loop example using a `while` loop

```
>>> lst
['cat', 'dog', 'bird', 'fish']
>>> index = 0
>>> while index < len(lst):          ◁──┐  len tells us the length of the
...        print('Got', lst[index])        string and is the number of
...        print('Hello,', lst[index])     iterations we want.
...        index += 1               ◁──┐
...                                     │  It's a common
Got cat                                 │  human error to
Hello, cat                              │  leave this out!
Got dog
Hello, dog
Got bird
Hello, bird
Got fish
Hello, fish
```

Without the `index += 1`, we would never increase the index through the string, and we'd print out the information for the first value over and over. That's called an *infinite loop*. If you think back to how we wrote `for` loops, you'll find that we didn't have to manually increase any index variables. For such reasons, many programmers prefer to use `for` loops when they can. We don't have to manually keep track of any index in a `for` loop, so we automatically avoid certain kinds of indexing problems and infinite loops.

5.1.2   *#7. Indentation*

Indentation is critical in Python code, because Python uses it to determine which lines of code go together. That's why, for example, we always indent all the lines of code inside a function, the various portions of an `if` statement, and the code for a `for` or `while` loop. It's not just nice formatting: if we get the indentation wrong, then we get the code wrong. For example, let's say that we want to ask the user for the current hour and then output some text based on whether it's morning, afternoon, or evening:

- If it's morning, we want to output "Good morning!" and "Have a nice day."
- If it's afternoon, we want to output "Good afternoon!"
- If it's evening, we want to output "Good evening!" and "Have a good night."

Take a look at the following code we've written and try to spot the problem with the indentation:

```
hour = int(input('Please enter the current hour from 0 to 23: '))

if hour < 12:
    print('Good morning!')
    print('Have a nice day.')
elif hour < 18:
    print('Good afternoon!')
else:
    print('Good evening!')
print('Have a good night.')
```

This line is not indented.

The problem is the last line: it's not indented, but it should be! Because it's not indented, we'll output Have a good night. regardless of which hour the user types in. We need to indent it so that it's part of the else portion of the if statement, ensuring that it only executes when it's evening.

Whenever we write code, we need to use multiple levels of indentation to express which pieces of code are associated with functions, if statements, loops, and so on. For example, when we write a function header, we need to indent all the code associated with that function below the function header. Some languages use brackets (e.g., {}) to show this, but Python just indents. If you're already in the body of a function (one indent) and write a loop, then you'll have to indent again (two indents) for the body of the loop, and so forth.

Looking back at our functions from chapter 3, we can see this in action. For example, in our larger function (reprinted as listing 5.6), the whole body of the function is indented, but there's further indentation on the if portion and the else portion of the if statement.

Listing 5.6 Function to determine the larger of two values

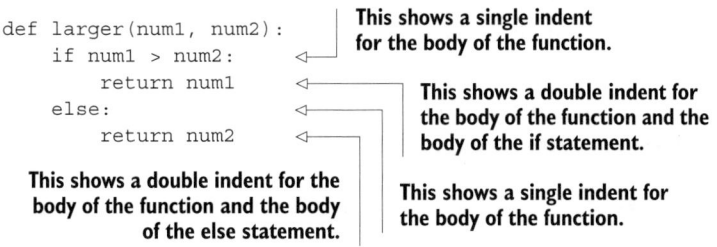

```
def larger(num1, num2):
    if num1 > num2:
        return num1
    else:
        return num2
```

This shows a single indent for the body of the function.

This shows a double indent for the body of the function and the body of the if statement.

This shows a single indent for the body of the function.

This shows a double indent for the body of the function and the body of the else statement.

Next, consider our get_strong_password function that we looked at in listing 5.4 earlier: as usual, everything in the function is indented, but there's further indentation for the body of the while loop.

There are even more levels of indentation in the first version of our num_points function (reproduced here from chapter 3 as listing 5.7). That's because, inside of the for loop through each character of the word, we have an if statement. Each piece of the `if` statement, as we've learned, needs to be indented, leading to the extra level of indentation.

Listing 5.7   `num_points` function

```python
def num_points(word):
    """
    Each letter is worth the following points:
    a, e, i, o, u, l, n, s, t, r: 1 point
    d, g: 2 points
    b, c, m, p: 3 points
    f, h, v, w, y: 4 points
    k: 5 points
    j, x: 8 points
    q, z: 10 points

    word is a word consisting of lowercase characters.
    Return the sum of points for each letter in word.
    """
    points = 0
    for char in word:
        if char in "aeioulnstr":
            points += 1
        elif char in "dg":
            points += 2
        elif char in "bcmp":
            points += 3
        elif char in "fhvwy":
            points += 4
        elif char == "k":
            points += 5
        elif char in "jx":
            points += 8
        elif char in "qz":
            points += 10
    return points
```

This is indented to be inside the function.

This is indented again to be inside the for loop.

This is indented yet again to be inside the if statement.

There's additional indentation in `is_strong_password` too (reproduced from chapter 3 as listing 5.8), but that's only to spread out one super-long line of code across multiple lines. Notice that the lines end with \, which is the character that allows us to continue a line of code on the next line.

Listing 5.8   `is_strong_password` function

```python
def is_strong_password(password):
    """
    A strong password has at least one uppercase character,
    at least one number, and at least one punctuation.

    Return True if the password is a strong password,
    False if not.
    """
    return any(char.isupper() for char in password) and \
```

The line ends with a backslash to continue the statement.

```
any(char.isdigit() for char in password) and \
any(char in string.punctuation for char in password)
```

The indent isn't required but is useful for visually laying out the single return statement.

Similarly, there's some further indentation in our second version of num_points (reproduced from chapter 3 as listing 5.9), but that's just to spread the dictionary out over multiple lines to make it more readable.

Listing 5.9 num_points alternative solution

```
def num_points(word):
    """
Each letter is worth the following points:
a, e, i, o, u, l, n, s, t, r: 1 point
d, g: 2 points
b, c, m, p: 3 points
f, h, v, w, y: 4 points
k: 5 points
j, x: 8 points
q, z: 10 points

word is a word consisting of lowercase characters.
Return the sum of points for each letter in word.
    """
    points = {'a': 1, 'e': 1, 'i': 1, 'o': 1, 'u': 1, 'l': 1,
              'n': 1, 's': 1, 't': 1, 'r': 1,
              'd': 2, 'g': 2,
              'b': 3, 'c': 3, 'm': 3, 'p': 3,
              'f': 4, 'h': 4, 'v': 4, 'w': 4, 'y': 4,
              'k': 5,
              'j': 8, 'x': 8,
              'q': 10, 'z': 10}
    return sum(points[char] for char in word)
```

We're allowed to write a dictionary value over multiple lines.

The indent isn't required but is useful for visually laying out the dictionary.

Indentation makes a huge difference on what our programs ultimately do. For example, let's compare putting two consecutive loops versus nesting one in the other using indentation. Here are two loops in a row:

```
>>> countries = ['Canada', 'USA', 'Japan']
>>> for country in countries:
...     print(country)
...
Canada
USA
Japan
>>> for country in countries:
...     print(country)
...
Canada
USA
Japan
```

This is the first loop.

This is the second loop (happens after the first loop).

That caused us to get the same output twice because we looped two separate times through the countries list. Now, if instead we nest the loops, this happens:

```
>>> for country1 in countries:
...      for country2 in countries:
...          print(country1, country2)
...
Canada Canada
Canada USA
Canada Japan
USA Canada
USA USA
USA Japan
Japan Canada
Japan USA
Japan Japan
```

This is the first loop.

This is the nested loop inside of the first loop.

print is nested in the second loop, which is nested in the first loop.

We've used different variable names, `country1` and `country2`, for each `for` loop, so that we can refer to both. On the first iteration of the `country1` loop, `country1` refers to `Canada`. On the first iteration of the `country2` loop, `country2` refers to `Canada` as well. That's why the first line of output is `Canada Canada`. Did you expect the next line of output after that to be `USA USA`? That isn't what happens! Instead, the `country2` loop moves on to its next iteration, but the `country1` loop doesn't move yet. The `country1` loop only moves ahead when the `country2` loop is complete. That's why we get `Canada USA` and `Canada Japan` before the `country1` loop finally moves on to its second iteration. When one loop is inside of another loop, this is called *nested loops*. In general, when there's nesting, the inner loop (`for country2 in countries`) will complete all of its steps before the outer loop (`for country1 in countries`) moves on to its next step, which, in turn, will restart the inner loop.

If you see a loop nested inside another loop, chances are good that the loops are being used to process two-dimensional data. Two-dimensional data is organized into rows and columns, of the kind you might see in a table (e.g., table 5.1). This kind of data is really common in computing because it includes basic spreadsheet data such as CSV files, images such as photos or a single frame of video, or the computer screen.

In Python, we can store two-dimensional data using a list where the values themselves are other lists. Each sublist in the overall list is one row of data, and each row has a value for each column. For example, say we had some data about the figure skating medals won at the 2018 Winter Olympics, as shown in table 5.1.

Table 5.1   Medals in the 2018 Winter Olympics

Nation	Gold	Silver	Bronze
Canada	2	0	2
OAR	1	2	0
Japan	1	1	0

Table 5.1 Medals in the 2018 Winter Olympics *(continued)*

Nation	Gold	Silver	Bronze
China	0	1	0
Germany	1	0	0

We could store this as a list, with one country per row:

```
>>> medals = [[2, 0, 2],
...           [1, 2, 0],
...           [1, 1, 0],
...           [0, 1, 0],
...           [1, 0, 0]]
```

Notice that our list of lists is just storing the numeric values, and we can find a value in the list of lists by referring to its row and column (e.g., Japan's gold medal corresponds to the row at index 2 and the column at index 0). We can use an index to get a complete row of data:

```
>>> medals[0]        ◁──┘  This is row 0 (first row).
[2, 0, 2]
>>> medals[1]        ◁───  This is row 1 (second row).
[1, 2, 0]
>>> medals[-1]       ◁──┐  This is the last row.
[1, 0, 0]
```

If we do a `for` loop on this list, we get each complete row, one row at a time:

```
>>> for country_medals in medals:      ◁──┐  The for loop gives us one
...         print(country_medals)            value of the list at a time
...                                           (i.e., one sublist at a time).
[2, 0, 2]
[1, 2, 0]
[1, 1, 0]
[0, 1, 0]
[1, 0, 0]
```

If we want just a specific value from the medals list (not a whole row), we have to index twice:

```
>>> medals[0][0]     ◁──┘  This is row 0, column 0.
2
>>> medals[0][1]     ◁───  This is row 0, column 1.
0
>>> medals[1][0]     ◁──┐  This is row 1, column 0.
1
```

Suppose we want to loop through each value individually. To do that, we can use nested `for` loops. To help us keep track of exactly where we are, we'll use `range` for loops so that we can print out the current row and column numbers in addition to the value stored there.

The outer loop will go through the rows, so we need to control it using `range (len(medals))`. The inner loop will go through the columns. How many columns are there? Well, the number of columns is the number of values in one of the rows, so we can use `range(len(medals[0]))` to control this loop.

Each line of output will provide three numbers: the row coordinate, the column coordinate, and the value (number of medals) at that row and column. Here's the code and output:

```
>>> for i in range(len(medals)):          ◁──────── Loops through the rows
...     for j in range(len(medals[i])):   ◁──┐
...         print(i, j, medals[i][j])         │  Loops through
...                                            │  the columns for
0 0 2                                          │  the current row
0 1 0
0 2 2
1 0 1
1 1 2
1 2 0
2 0 1
2 1 1
2 2 0
3 0 0
3 1 1
3 2 0
4 0 1
4 1 0
4 2 0
```

Notice how the row stays constant for the first three lines of output, during which the column varies from 0 to 2. That's how we work our way through the first row. Only then does the row increase to 1, at which point we complete the work for columns 0 to 2 on this new row.

Nested loops give us a systematic way to loop through each value in a two-dimensional list. You'll see them frequently when dealing with two-dimensional data in general, such as images, board games, and spreadsheets.

5.1.3   *#8. Dictionaries*

Remember that each value in Python has a specific type. There are a lot of different types because there are many kinds of values that we might want to use! We've talked about using numbers to work with numeric values, Booleans to work with `True`/`False` values, strings to work with text, and lists to work with a sequence of other values such as numbers or strings.

There's one more Python type that shows up often, and it's called a *dictionary*. When we talk about a dictionary in Python, we don't mean a list of words and their definitions. In Python, a dictionary is a useful way of storing data whenever you need to keep track of associations between data. For example, imagine that you wanted to know which words are used most often in your favorite book. You could use a dictionary to map each word to the number of times it's used. That dictionary would probably be huge, but a small version of such a dictionary might look like this:

```
>>> freq = {'DNA': 11, 'acquire': 11, 'Taxxon': 13, \
... 'Controller': 20, 'morph': 41}
```

Each entry in the dictionary maps a word to its frequency. For example, we can tell from this dictionary that the word *DNA* shows up 11 times and that the word *Taxxon* shows up 13 times. The words here (*DNA, acquire, Taxxon,* etc.) are referred to as *keys,* and the frequencies (11, 11, 13, etc.) are referred to as *values.* So, a dictionary maps each key to its value. We're not allowed to have duplicate keys, but as shown here with the two 11 values, having duplicate values is no problem.

We saw a dictionary in chapter 2 (listing 2.1) that stored each quarterback's name and their associated number of passing yards. In chapter 3, we saw a dictionary again in our second solution for num_points (reproduced earlier in listing 5.9). There, the dictionary mapped each letter to the number of points awarded for using that letter.

Just like for strings and lists, dictionaries have methods that you can use to interact with them. Here are some methods operating on our freq dictionary:

```
>>> freq
{'DNA': 11, 'acquire': 11, 'Taxxon': 13, 'Controller': 20, 'morph': 41}
>>> freq.keys()
dict_keys(['DNA', 'acquire', 'Taxxon', 'Controller', 'morph'])          ◁──┐  Gets all
>>> freq.values()                                                ◁──┐        the keys
dict_values([11, 11, 13, 20, 41])                                   │
>>> freq.pop('Controller')        ◁──┐  Gets rid of key and          │  Gets all the
20                                      associated value              │  values
>>> freq
{'DNA': 11, 'acquire': 11, 'Taxxon': 13, 'morph': 41}
```

You can also use the index notation to access the value for a given key:

```
>>> freq['dna']  # Oops, wrong key name because it is case sensitive
Traceback (most recent call last):
  File "<stdin>", line 1, in <module>
KeyError: 'dna'
>>> freq['DNA']      ◁──┐  Gets values
11                        associated with
>>> freq['morph']         the key "DNA"
41
```

Dictionaries, like lists, are mutable. This means that we can change the keys and values in a dictionary, which is useful for modeling data that changes over time. We can use indexing to change a value. The value associated with 'morph' is currently 41. Let's change it to 6:

```
>>> freq['morph'] = 6
>>> freq
{'DNA': 11, 'acquire': 11, 'Taxxon': 13, 'morph': 6}
```
⟵──────────── **Changes value associated with key "morph" to 6**

Our `freq` dictionary allows us to start from whatever word we want and find its frequency. More generally, a dictionary allows us to go from *key to value*. However, it doesn't allow us to easily go in the opposite direction, from value to key. If we wanted to do that, we'd need to produce the opposite dictionary—for example, one whose keys are frequencies and whose values are lists of words with those frequencies. That would enable us to answer questions such as the following: which words have a frequency of exactly 5? Which words have the minimum or maximum frequency of all?

As with strings and lists, we can use a loop to process the information in a dictionary as well. A `for` loop gives us the dictionary keys, and we can use indexing to get the associated value for each key:

```
>>> for word in freq:
...     print('Word', word, 'has frequency', freq[word])
...
Word DNA has frequency 11
Word acquire has frequency 11
Word Taxxon has frequency 13
Word morph has frequency 6
```
⟵ **Loops through each key in the freq dictionary**

⟵ **Uses the key (word) and associated value (freq[word])**

5.1.4   *#9. Files*

It's often the case that we'll want to work with datasets that exist in files. For example, in chapter 2, we worked with a file of NFL stats to determine the most effective quarterbacks. Using files is common for other data science tasks as well. For example, if you're plotting information about earthquakes around the world or determining whether two books are written by the same author, you'll need to work with those datasets, and typically those datasets will be stored in files.

In chapter 2, we worked with a file called nfl_offensive_stats.csv. Make sure that this file is in your current program directory because we'll use that file now to further understand some of the code we used in chapter 2.

The first step in working with data from a file is to use Python's `open` function to open the file:

```
>>> nfl_file = open('nfl_offensive_stats.csv')
```

You'll sometimes see Copilot add an `r` as a second argument here:

```
>>> nfl_file = open('nfl_offensive_stats.csv', 'r')
```

But we don't need the `r`; the `r` just means that we want to read from the file, but that's the default anyway if we don't specify it.

We've used an assignment statement to assign that open file to a variable named `nfl_file`. Now, we can use `nfl_file` to access the contents of the file. An open file is a Python type, just like numbers and strings and all of the other types you've seen to this point. As such, there are methods that we can call to interact with the file. One method is `readline`, which gives us the next line of the file as a string. We'll use it now to get the first line of our open file, but don't worry about the line itself because it's super long with tons of information about columns we won't end up using:

```
>>> line = nfl_file.readline()        ⟵— Reads the line from the file
>>> line
'game_id,player_id,position,player,team,pass_cmp,pass_att,pass_yds,pass_td,pa
    ss_int,pass_sacked,pass_sacked_yds,pass_long,pass_rating,rush_att,
rush_yds,rush_td,rush_long,targets,rec,rec_yds,rec_td,rec_long,
fumbles_lost,rush_scrambles,designed_rush_att,comb_pass_rush_play,
comb_pass_play,comb_rush_play,Team_abbrev,Opponent_abbrev,two_point_conv,
total_ret_td,offensive_fumble_recovery_td,pass_yds_bonus,rush_yds_bonus,
rec_yds_bonus,Total_DKP,Off_DKP,Total_FDP,Off_FDP,Total_SDP,Off_SDP,
pass_target_yds,pass_poor_throws,pass_blitzed,pass_hurried,
rush_yds_before_contact,rush_yac,rush_broken_tackles,rec_air_yds,rec_yac,
rec_drops,offense,off_pct,vis_team,home_team,vis_score,home_score,OT,Roof,
Surface,Temperature,Humidity,Wind_Speed,Vegas_Line,Vegas_Favorite,
Over_Under,game_date\n'
```

It's not easy to pull individual values out of a messy string like that. So, one of the first things we tend to do with such a line is split it up into its individual column data. We can do that using the string `split` method. That method takes a separator as an argument and splits the string into a list by using that separator:

```
>>> lst = line.split(',')          ⟵┐  Splits the string using a
>>> len(lst)                          │  comma (,) as a separator
69
```

Now we can look at individual column names:

```
>>> lst[0]
'game_id'
>>> lst[1]
'player_id'                    The space at the end of the
>>> lst[2]                     word is in the original dataset,
'position '                    but no other column headers
          ⟵┘                   have a space.
>>> lst[3]
'player'
>>> lst[7]
'pass_yds'
```

That first line of the file that we're looking at isn't a real data line—it's just the header that tells us the name of each column. The next time we do `readline`, we get the first real line of data:

```
>>> line = nfl_file.readline()
>>> lst = line.split(',')
>>> lst[3]
'Aaron Rodgers'
>>> lst[7]
'203'
```

Moving one line at a time like this is fine for exploring what's in a file, but eventually, we'll probably want to process the whole thing. To do so, we can use a `for` loop on the file. It'll give us back one line on each iteration, which we can process in any way we like. Once we're finished with a file, we should call `close` on it:

```
>>> nfl_file.close()
```

After closing, we aren't allowed to use the file anymore. Now that we've discussed how to read, process, and close a file, let's see a full example. In listing 5.10, we provide a new version of our program from chapter 2 that sorts quarterbacks by their total passing yards. In addition to showcasing files, we're also using many of the Python features that we've seen in chapter 4 and the current chapter, including conditionals, strings, lists, loops, and dictionaries.

Listing 5.10 Alternative NFL statistics code without the csv module

```
nfl_file = open('nfl_offensive_stats.csv')          This dictionary maps quarterback
passing_yards = {}                                   names to their passing yards.

for line in nfl_file:           ◁——— Loops through each line of the file
    lst = line.split(',')
    if lst[2] == 'QB':          ◁——— Focuses only on the quarterbacks
        if lst[3] in passing_yards:              ◁
            passing_yards[lst[3]] += int(lst[7])  ◁      Quarterback is
        else:                                    ◁      already in our
            passing_yards[lst[3]] = int(lst[7])   ◁      dictionary.

nfl_file.close()                                         Add to quarterback's
                                                         total; int converts
for player in sorted(passing_yards,                      string like '203' to
                key=passing_yards.get,                   integer.
                reverse=True):   ◁————————
    print(player, passing_yards[player])                 Quarterback isn't yet
                                                         in our dictionary.

         Loops through quarterbacks from          Sets initial
         highest to lowest passing yards          quarterback's total
```

That loop at the bottom, `for player in sorted(passing_yards, key=passing_yards .get, reverse=True):`, has a lot going on. We explained this line in the annotations as looping through the quarterbacks from highest to lowest. The `reverse=True` makes us sort from highest to lowest rather than the default of lowest to highest. The `key=passing_yards.get` focuses the sort on the number of passing yards (rather than, e.g., the player's names). If you'd like to break down this line of code further, feel free to ask Copilot for further explanation. This highlights the balancing act that we're trying to maintain here: to know enough to be able to get the gist of code without necessarily needing to understand every nuance.

This program works just fine; if you run it, you would see the same output as if you ran the code from chapter 2. Sometimes, though, it's possible to write a program more easily using modules (we cover modules in more depth in the next section), and that's what the program from chapter 2 did. Because CSV files are so common, Python comes with a module to make it easier to process them. In chapter 2, the solution that we were given used the csv module. So, let's discuss the main differences between our code in listing 5.10 that doesn't use the module and our code from chapter 2, reprinted here in the following listing (our prompts given to Copilot aren't shown).

Listing 5.11 NFL statistics code using the csv module

```
# import the csv module
import csv

# open the csv file
with open('nfl_offensive_stats.csv', 'r') as f:      ←── Shows the
                                                          alternate syntax
    # read the csv data                                   for opening a file
    data = list(csv.reader(f))      ←── Uses a special csv module;
                                          reads all data from the file
# create a dictionary to hold the player name and passing yards
passing_yards = {}

# loop through the data                    Loops through
for row in data:                     ←──   each line of data
    # check if the player is a quarterback
    if row[2] == 'QB':
        # check if the player is already in the dictionary
        if row[3] in passing_yards:
            # add the passing yards to the existing value
            passing_yards[row[3]] += int(row[7])
        else:
            # add the player to the dictionary
            passing_yards[row[3]] = int(row[7])

for player in sorted(passing_yards, key=passing_yards.get, reverse=True):
    print(player, passing_yards[player])
```

First, listing 5.11 uses the csv module to make dealing with CSV files easier. The csv module knows how to manipulate CSV files, so, for example, we don't have to worry about breaking a line into its columns. Second, listing 5.11 uses the `with` keyword, which results in the file automatically being closed when the program is done with it. Third, listing 5.11 reads the entire file first before doing any processing. By contrast, in listing 5.10, we read and process each line as soon as we read it.

More than one way to solve a programming problem

There are always many different programs that can be written to solve the same task. Some may be easier to read than others. The most important criterion for code is that it does the correct thing. After that, we care most about readability and efficiency. So, if you find yourself struggling to understand how some code works, it may be worth some time looking at other code from Copilot in case there's a simpler or more understandable solution available there.

Files are used commonly in computing tasks because they are a common source of data to be processed. This includes CSV files like the one from this section, log files that keep track of events on computers or websites, and files that store data for graphics you might see in video games, among others. Because files are so commonly used, it's no surprise there are many modules that help us read various file formats. That leads us to the larger topic of modules.

5.1.5   #10. Modules

People use Python to make all kinds of things—games, websites, and apps for analyzing data, automating repetitive tasks, controlling robots, you name it. You might be wondering how Python can possibly let you create so many different types of programs. Surely, the creators of Python couldn't have anticipated or created all the needed support!

   The truth is that, by default, your Python program has access only to some core Python features (such as those we've showed you in the previous and current chapter). To get any more than that, we need to use modules. And, to use a module, you need to import it.

Modules in Python

A *module* is a collection of code designed for a specific purpose. Recall that we don't need to know how a function works to use it. It's the same with modules: we don't need to know how modules work to be able to use them, much as we don't need to know how a light switch works internally to use it. As users of modules, we just need to know what a module will help us do and how to write the code to correctly call its functions. Of course, Copilot can help us write that kind of code.

Some modules come with Python when you install it, but we still need to import them. Other modules we first have to install before we can import them. Trust us, if there's a specific kind of task you want to do with Python, someone's probably already written a module to help you out.

   You might be wondering how to determine which Python modules you should use. How do you know which ones exist? A simple chat with Copilot or Google search is often helpful. For example, if we google "Python module to create a zip file," the first result tells us that the module we need is part of the Python standard library, which means that it comes with Python. If we google "Python module for visualization," we learn about modules named matplotlib, plotly, seaborn, and more. Searching for each of these should lead you to galleries of visualizations showing you their capabilities and what each is typically used for. Most modules are free to download and use, although your search results can help you confirm whether a module is free and its specific usage license. We're going to hold off on installing and using newly installed modules until chapter 9, but, at that time, you'll see this process of finding, installing, and using relevant modules to help us complete our tasks.

Table 5.2 has a list of some of the commonly used Python modules and whether they are built-in or not. If a module is built-in, you can import the module and start using it right away; if not, you need to install it first.

Table 5.2   Summary of commonly used Python modules

Module	Built-In	Description
csv	Yes	Aids in the reading, writing, and analysis of CSV files
zipfile	Yes	Aids in the creation and extraction of compressed zip archive files
matplotlib	No	Graphics library for plotting that serves as the basis of other graphics libraries and can offer high levels of customization
plotly	No	A graphics library used for creating interactive plots for the web
seaborn	No	A graphics library built on top of matplotlib that aids in creating high-quality plots more easily than matplotlib
pandas	No	A data processing library that specializes in data frames, which are analogous to spreadsheets
scikit-learn	No	Contains basic tools for machine learning (i.e., helping to learn from data and make predictions)
numpy	No	Offers highly efficient data processing
pygame	No	A game programming library that helps to build interactive, graphical games in Python
django	No	Web development library that aids in designing websites and web applications

In chapter 2, our code used the csv module that comes with Python. Let's continue here by learning about a different module that comes with Python.

When people want to organize their files, perhaps prior to backing them up or uploading them, they often archive them first into a .zip file. Then they can pass around that single .zip file, rather than potentially hundreds or thousands of individual files. Python comes with a module called zipfile that can help you create a .zip file.

To try this, create a few files in your programming directory, and make them all end with .csv. You could start with your nfl_offensive_stats.csv file and then add a few more. For example, you could add one called actors.csv with the names of a few actors and their ages, such as

```
Actor Name, Age
Anne Hathaway, 40
Daniel Radcliffe, 33
```

and you could add one called chores.csv with a list of chores and whether you've finished each one:

```
Chore, Finished?
Clean dishes, Yes
Read Chapter 6, No
```

The contents don't matter as long as you have a few .csv files to test with. Now we can use the zipfile module to add them all to a new .zip file!

```
>>> import zipfile
>>> zf = zipfile.ZipFile('my_stuff.zip', 'w',          Creates the
    ➥ zipfile.ZIP_DEFLATED)                            new .zip file
>>> zf.write('nfl_offensive_stats.csv')        ◁──── Adds the first file
>>> zf.write('actors.csv')          ◁─┐  Adds the second file
>>> zf.write('chores.csv')          ◁─┘
>>> zf.close()                        │  Adds the third file
```

If you run that code, you'll find a new file called my_stuff.zip that contains your three .csv files. Working with .zip files directly used to be a very specialized, error-prone task with other earlier programming languages, but that's not so with Python. Python comes with modules that are helpful for data science, making games, dealing with various file formats, and so on, but again, Python can't come with everything. When we need more, we turn to downloadable modules as we'll see in chapter 9.

In this chapter, we introduced you to the second half of our top 10 Python features, as summarized in table 5.3. We've covered a lot about reading code in the previous chapter and this chapter. Although we haven't covered everything you might see Copilot produce, you're in a good position to spot-check Copilot code to determine whether it's given a good attempt at producing the code you requested. We also showed more examples of using the Copilot explanation tool to help you understand new code. In the next chapters, we'll see how to test the code from Copilot to determine whether it's correct, and what you can do when it's not.

Table 5.3   Summary of Python code features from this chapter

Code Element	Example	Brief Description

Loops	for loop:
	`for country in countries:`
	`    print(country)`
	while loop:
	`index = 0`
	`while index < 4:`
	`    print(index)`
	`    index = index + 1`
		Loops allow us to run the same code as many times as needed. We use a for loop when we know how many iterations there will be (e.g., number of characters in a string) and a while loop when we don't (e.g., asking the user for a strong password).

Indentation	`for country in countries:` `    print(country)`	Indentation tells Python when a piece of code belongs as part of another body of code (e.g., that the print call is within the for loop).

Table 5.3 Summary of Python code features from this chapter *(continued)*

Code Element	Example	Brief Description
Dictionaries	`points = {'a': 1, 'b': 3}`	Dictionaries allow us to associate a key with a value. For example, the key `'a'` is associated with the value `1`.

Files	`file = open('chores.csv')`
	`first_line =`
	`file.readline()`
		Files contain data and are stored on your computer. Python can be used to open many types of files and read their contents, allowing you to process the data in the file.

Modules	`import csv`	Modules are already-existing libraries that provide additional functionality. Commonly used modules include csv, numpy, matplotlib, pandas, and scikit-learn. Some modules come with the standard Python distribution; others need to be installed separately.

5.2   Exercises

1 Recall the `for` loop code we looked at in listing 5.3 to print animals in a list. What does this modified code do differently compared to the original example in the chapter? Specifically, what additional output does it produce?

```
lst = ['cat', 'dog', 'bird', 'fish']

for index in range(len(lst)):
    print('Got', lst[index])
    if lst[index] == 'bird':
        print('Found the bird!')
    print('Hello,', lst[index])
```

2 Consider the following `while` loop code that seeks to repeat what we did using a `for` loop in listing 5.3. When we run the code, we notice that it runs indefinitely. Can you identify and fix the error that would cause it to run indefinitely?

```
lst = ['cat', 'dog', 'bird', 'fish']

index = 0
while index < len(lst):
    print('Got', lst[index])
    print('Hello,', lst[index])
```

3 Arrange the following lines of code to create a `while` loop that prints each number in the list until it encounters the number 7. Be careful about indentation!

```
index += 1
while index < len(numbers) and numbers[index] != 7:
index = 0
numbers = [1, 2, 3, 4, 5, 6, 7, 8, 9]
print(numbers[index])
```

4   Think of a real-world scenario where a `while` loop would be more appropriate than a `for` loop. Describe the scenario and explain why a `while` loop is the better choice.

5   Modify the `get_strong_password` function (or the `is_strong_password` function that it calls) to provide specific feedback on why the entered password isn't strong enough. For instance, if the password doesn't have an uppercase character, print "Password must include an uppercase character," and if it doesn't contain a digit, print "Password must contain at least one digit."

6   Given the following `print_quarterbacks` function, can you rewrite it to use the "with" statement to open and close the file? Why is it important to close the file?

```
def print_quarterbacks():
    nfl_file = open('nfl_offensive_stats.csv')
    for line in nfl_file:
        lst = line.split(',')
        if lst[2] == 'QB':
            print(f"{lst[3]}: {lst[7]} passing yards")
    nfl_file.close()
```

7   In this exercise, we'll further practice working with the zipfile module to create a .zip file containing multiple CSV files. Follow these steps to complete the task and answer the questions:

a   First, create three CSV files in your current directory:
   –   nfl_offensive_stats.csv (you should already have this file)
   –   actors.csv with the following content:

```
Actor Name, Age
Anne Hathaway, 40
Daniel Radcliffe, 33
```

   –   chores.csv with the following content:

```
Chore, Finished?
Clean dishes, Yes
Read Chapter 6, No
```

b   Using Copilot (don't type the code directly as we did in the chapter), write a Python script that uses the zipfile module to add these three CSV files to a .zip file named my_stuff.zip.

c   What are some of the other functions provided by the zipfile module that Copilot suggests? How can they be useful?

Summary

- A loop is used to repeat code as many times as needed.
- We use a `for` loop when we know how many iterations the loop will do; we use a `while` loop when we don't know how many iterations a loop will do.
- Python uses indentation to determine which lines of code go together.
- A dictionary is a mapping from keys (e.g., words in a book) to values (e.g., their frequencies).
- We need to open a file before we can read from it.
- Once a file is open, we can use methods (e.g., readline) or a loop to read its lines.
- Some modules, such as csv and zipfile, come with Python and can be used by importing them.
- Other modules, such as matplotlib, need to be installed first before they can be imported and used.

Testing and prompt engineering

This chapter covers

- Understanding the importance of testing Copilot code
- Using closed-box versus open-box testing
- Addressing errors by Copilot by modifying prompts
- Working through examples of testing Copilot-generated code

In chapter 3, we first started to see the importance of testing the code produced by Copilot. Testing is an essential skill for anyone writing software because it gives you confidence that the code is functioning properly. In this chapter, we'll learn how to test our code thoroughly and how to help Copilot fix code that doesn't work by modifying our prompts.

Testing is an essential skill that you'll need to learn how to do well on your own, so that you're able to check that the code works correctly. Copilot can generate tests and has been improving in the quality of tests it produces, but we encourage you to hold off on using Copilot to generate tests just yet because you need to learn to do this well enough on your own to be able to verify that the tests Copilot produces are reasonable. This will be true of the next few chapters as well—problem decomposition, testing, and debugging are all skills that are essential to learn how to do on your own, before asking for Copilot's help, as you need to know how to do it on your own to know if Copilot is doing something reasonable.

6.1 Why it's crucial to test code

Back in chapter 3, we mentioned that you should test code to make sure it's correct. Unfortunately, in our experience, beginning programmers seem to have an aversion to testing! Why? We think a couple of things are at play. The first is that there's this well-documented problem nicknamed the *Superbug*, which is that humans, when first learning to code, think the computer can understand the intent of the code and respond accordingly [1]. Because they wrote the code and the code made sense to them, they find it hard to even imagine that the code might not work. The second problem is compounded on the first: if you think your code is right, testing can only bring you bad news. If you don't test, you can't find out if the code is wrong. It's like the old saying about putting your head in the sand.

Professional software engineers take a completely different approach than new programmers. They take testing extremely seriously because a mistake in the code can have significant consequences for their company. No one wants to be the person whose code causes the company to lose tons of revenue, lets hackers gain access to confidential user data, or has the self-driving car cause an accident. Given the cost of a mistake, it makes more sense to assume the code is wrong until proven otherwise. Only after testing it extensively should we trust that it's working correctly. And, companies don't just test the code once, they keep the tests in their system so every time someone changes code, tests are run not just on the changed code but also on any code that the changed code might affect (this is called regression testing).

Companies take this so seriously that they often write their tests *before* writing their code in a process called test-driven development (TDD). This ensures everyone agrees on what the code should or shouldn't do. We don't think you (as readers) need to take this approach for the programs you're writing with this book, but we mention it here to convey how crucial it is to test. Thinking about testing before writing code can help you understand what the code should do and that will help you write better prompts. In fact, you can include test cases directly in your prompts!

Finally, let's remember what we know about Copilot: it makes mistakes. We shouldn't assume anything about the correctness of any code given to us by Copilot. All this is to say that any code you're given by Copilot should be tested before you trust it.

6.2 Closed-box and open-box testing

There are two ways that software engineers commonly test their code. The first is called closed-box testing, and this approach assumes you know nothing about how the code works. As such, this kind of testing involves varying the inputs and observing the outputs. We often see closed-box testing applied to functions or entire programs. The advantage of closed-box testing is that you don't need to look at the code to perform the tests and can therefore focus simply on the desired behavior.

The second approach to testing is called open-box testing, and in this approach, we look at the code to see where the errors might occur. The advantage of open-box testing is that by looking at the particular structure of the code, we may see where the code is likely to fail and can design additional tests specific to that code. We'll use both closed-box and open-box testing to come up with test cases that combine to strengthen our testing. A brief summary of closed-box and open-box testing appears in table 6.1. In this section, let's look at how we might test some functions using these approaches.

Table 6.1   Brief overview of closed-box and open-box testing

Closed-box testing	Open-box testing
Requires understanding the function specification to test	Requires both the function specification and the code that implements the function to test
Tests don't require an understanding of what the code does.	Tests should be tailored based on how the code was written.
Testers need not have technical expertise about the code they're testing.	Testers need to be able to understand the code sufficiently well to determine which tests may be more important.
Tests the function by varying inputs and checking against expected results	Can test the function in the same way as closed-box testing but can also have more granular tests within a function

6.2.1   Closed-box testing

Let's imagine we're trying to test a function that takes in a list of words (strings) and returns the longest word. To be more precise, the function signature would be

```
def longest_word(words):
```

The expected input is a list of words. The expected output is the word in that list with the most characters. In the event that multiple words are tied for the most characters, it should return the first word of that length.

Shorthand for expressing test cases

When writing tests for a function, the standard format is to write the function name and its input along with the desired outcome. For example, the call

```
>>> longest_word(['a', 'bb', 'ccc'])
'ccc'
```

means that if we call the function `longest_word` with the input list `['a', 'bb', 'ccc']`, then the value returned from the function should be `'ccc'`.

There are two categories for which we typically think about writing test cases:

- *Common use cases*—These cases include some standard inputs you could imagine the function receiving and the corresponding result.
- *Edge cases*—These cases are uncommon but possible cases that might break the code. These are inputs that might test some of the rules for the function in more depth or contain unexpected inputs (e.g., a list with all empty strings).

Looking back at our `longest_word` function signature in the previous example, let's think about some test cases we might use to test it. Later in the chapter, we'll see how to actually run these test cases to determine whether our code is working correctly. Let's start with *common use cases*. We would likely want to include a test with just a few words where one word is longer than the others:

```
>>> longest_word(['cat', 'dog', 'bird'])
'bird'
```

Here's another test with more words with the longest word appearing elsewhere in the list:

```
>>> longest_word(['happy', 'birthday', 'my', 'cat'])
'birthday'
```

And last, let's have a test with just one word:

```
>>> longest_word(['happy'])
'happy'
```

If the program is working for these common uses, our next step would be to think about some *edge cases*. Let's consider some edge cases.

Say we want to check whether the function conforms to our description by returning the first word when there are multiple words of the same length. This test may be considered a common case or an edge case, depending on whom you ask:

```
>>> longest_word(['cat', 'dog', 'me'])
'cat'
```

What do we do if all the words in the list have no characters? A string with no characters is called an *empty string* and is written as just an empty pair of quotes. If all we have is a list of empty strings, then the longest word is just the empty string! So, a test with all empty strings should just give us back an empty string:

```
>>> longest_word(['', ''])
''
```

The term *edge case* comes from the fact that errors often happen at the "edge" of execution, meaning either the first or last element. In many loops, mistakes can be made when the loop is starting (e.g., forgetting or mishandling the first element in the list) or at the end (e.g., forgetting the last element or going past the end of the list and trying to access an element that doesn't exist). Especially when the code is likely to have loops processing many elements, you'll want to watch the behavior at the start and end of the loop.

> ### Incorrect input testing
>
> Another category of tests will test the function on how it responds when given incorrect input. We won't talk about this much in our book because we're assuming you're correctly calling your own functions, but in production code, this kind of testing can be common. A few examples of calling this function with incorrect inputs might be to give the function a nonexisting list by using the value None instead of an actual list (e.g., `longest_word(None)`), to give the function an empty list (e.g., `longest_word([])`), to give the function a list with integers as input (e.g., `longest_word([1,2])`), or to provide a list of strings but have the strings contain spaces or more than single words (e.g., `longest_word(['hi there', ' my ', 'friend'])`). It's hard to say what the function should do when given incorrect input, and programmers need to decide whether they care about this in larger code bases, but we'll ignore this category of tests in this book because we'll assume you'll call your own functions in ways that the functions are designed to handle.

6.2.2   *How do we know which test cases to use?*

In chapter 3, we discussed that good testing involves capturing different categories of function calls. One way to find these categories is by using the types of parameters and varying their values.

For example, if the function takes a string or list as a parameter, it may make sense to test the case when that string or list is empty, has one element, and has multiple elements. If we're trying to test multiple elements, we might use four elements, for example. It likely also wouldn't make sense to test with five or six elements or more because if our code works with four elements, it's unlikely that something could suddenly go wrong when we increase to five. Sometimes, some of these test cases may not make sense for a given function; for example, it wouldn't make sense to ask for the longest word in a list that didn't have any words in it, so we wouldn't test the empty list for our `longest_word` function.

As another example, if a function takes two numbers as parameters, it may make sense to test when one number is zero, both numbers are zero, one number is negative, both numbers are negative, and both numbers are positive.

Another way to find categories is to think about the specific task of the function. For example, for our `longest_word` function, it's supposed to be finding the longest word, so we should test that it's actually doing that in a typical case. And, if multiple words are the longest, it's supposed to return the first of those, so we should have a test case where the list has multiple words that are the longest.

Finding the categories to test is a mix of science and art. We've given you some rules of thumb here, but what counts as useful test cases often depends on the specific functionality being tested. As is so often the case, practicing your testing skill is the best way to improve your ability to write useful tests that ultimately help you make your code better.

6.2.3   Open-box testing

The big difference between open-box testing and closed-box testing is that open-box testing examines the code to see if there are additional kinds of test cases to check. In theory, closed-box testing may be sufficient to fully test the function, but open-box testing tends to give you more ideas about where the code might be failing. Let's say we asked for Copilot to write our `longest_word` function and got back the code shown in the following listing.

Listing 6.1   Function to find the longest word (incorrect!)

```
def longest_word(words):
    '''
        words is a list of words

        return the word from the list with the most characters
        if multiple words are the longest, return the first
        such word
    '''
    longest = ""
    for i in range(0,len(words)):
        if len(words[i]) >= len(longest):        <--- >= is wrong.
            longest = words[i]                         It should be >.
    return longest
```

For this example, we intentionally introduced an error in the code to help explain the role of open-box testing. Let's say that when you were thinking through your test cases, you forgot to test what happens when there are two words in the list of `words` that both have the most characters. Well, reading through this code you might spot the following `if` statement:

```
    if len(words[i]) >= len(longest):
        longest = words[i]
```

When reading the `if` statement, you might notice that it's going to update the longest word in the list of words when the length of the most recent element is greater than *or equal* to the longest word we've seen so far. This is a mistake; it should be >, not >=, but suppose you aren't sure. This would motivate you to write a test case like the one we described previously that has multiple words, more than one of which is the longest:

```
>>> longest_word(['cat', 'dog', 'me'])
'cat'
```

This test will fail with the code in listing 6.1 as it would return `'dog'` rather than the correct answer of `'cat'`. The test failing is valuable information that the code in listing 6.1 is incorrect.

As we've said, open-box testing is useful because it leads to test cases that follow the structure of the code itself. For example, if our code is using a loop, we'll find that loop when doing open-box testing. The loop in listing 6.1 is correct, but by seeing the loop in our code, we'll be reminded to test the edge cases to make sure it's properly handling the first element, the last element, and an empty list. In sum, knowing how the code is processing the input often offers insight into when the program might be misfunctioning.

6.3   *How to test your code*

There are a number of good ways to test your code that vary from quick tests you might perform just to check if your code is working for yourself to tests that are built into a company's regression test suite. For production code, Python programmers typically use testing tools more powerful and full-featured than what we're about to demonstrate in this chapter. The most common of those tools is pytest, which is a module that needs to be installed before it can be used. We feel that pytest is beyond what we need here to introduce the core ideas of testing. We'll focus on more lightweight testing to help you gain confidence that the code from Copilot works properly. We can do that either by testing at the Python prompt or using a built-in Python module called doctest.

6.3.1   *Testing using the Python prompt*

The first way to test is in the Python prompt through the interactive window like we have in the previous chapters. The advantage of this testing is that it can be quick to run, and you can easily add more tests as a result of output from the previous test. The tests we've run so far are examples of testing with the Python prompt. For example,

```
>>> longest_word(['cat', 'dog', 'me'])
'cat'
```

In running that test, if you expected the result to be `'cat'`, you'd be pleased to see that result. However, if the test shows that your code was wrong, you now have the opportunity to go back to fix it.

After you fix the code, you'll want to test the new code. Here is where you may go wrong with testing using the Python prompt alone. When you come back to test the code you just changed, you might be tempted to run *just* the test case that had failed previously. However, in fixing the code to correctly address the test case that had failed, you could have introduced an error that would cause the *previous* test cases that had already passed to now fail. What you really want then is a way to run not just your current test but all previous tests as well.

6.3.2 *Testing in your Python file (we won't be doing it this way)*

It would be tempting to then put all your test cases in your Python program (outside a function, so in the equivalent of a main function) so they can all run. This solution addresses the problem with Python prompts that we just described, but it introduces a new problem. What happens when you want your Python program to perform the main task for which it was designed rather than just run tests? You could delete all the tests, but the point was running them again if so desired. You could comment them out so you can run them in the future, but that's not a very clean solution either. What we want then is a way to run all our tests on our functions when we want to but still have the ability to run the program. The way to do this is using a module called doctest.

6.3.3 *doctest*

The doctest module is built in to Python. The great thing about using doctest is that we simply add our test cases to the docstring that describes the function. This beefed-up docstring serves a dual purpose. First, we can use doctest to run all those test cases whenever we'd like. Second, it can sometimes help Copilot generate better code in the first place or fix already-written code that isn't quite working. Let's write that `longest_word` function with all the test cases included and ready to be executed with doctest (see listing 6.2).

Listing 6.2 Using doctest to test the `longest_word` function

```
def longest_word(words):
    '''
    words is a list of words

    return the word from the list with the most characters
    if multiple words are the longest, return the first
    such word

    >>> longest_word(['cat', 'dog', 'bird'])
    'bird'

    >>> longest_word(['happy', 'birthday', 'my', 'cat'])
    'birthday'

    >>> longest_word(['happy'])
    'happy'

    >>> longest_word(['cat', 'dog', 'me'])
    'cat'

    >>> longest_word(['', ''])
    ''
    '''
    longest = ''
    for i in range(0,len(words)):
        if len(words[i]) > len(longest):
            longest = words[i]
    return longest
```

Shows the test cases for doctest

Shows the correct code for the function

```
import doctest
doctest.testmod(verbose=True)
```

| **Code (in main) that calls doctest to perform the test**

In this code, we see the docstring with our test cases provided as the prompt to Copilot. Copilot generated the correct code to implement this function. We then manually wrote the last two lines of the code to perform the testing. When run, we get the output in the following listing.

Listing 6.3   Doctest output from running our program in listing 6.2

```
Trying:
    longest_word(['cat', 'dog', 'bird'])
Expecting:
    'bird'
ok                              First test in
Trying:                         longest_word passed
    longest_word(['happy', 'birthday', 'my', 'cat'])
Expecting:
    'birthday'
ok                              Second test in
Trying:                         longest_word passed
    longest_word(['happy'])
Expecting:
    'happy'
ok                              Third test in
Trying:                         longest_word passed
    longest_word(['cat', 'dog', 'me'])
Expecting:
    'cat'
ok                              Fourth test in
Trying:                         longest_word passed
    longest_word(['', ''])
Expecting:                      Fifth test in
    ''                          longest_word passed
ok
1 items had no tests:           There are no tests in main
    __main__                    (outside the function).
1 items passed all tests:
    5 tests in __main__.longest_word    longest_word
5 tests in 2 items.                     passed all tests.
5 passed and 0 failed.
Test passed.                    0 failed is what
                                you hope to see.
```

From this output, we can see that each test ran and each test passed. The reason these tests ran is because of the last two lines that we added in listing 6.2:

```
import doctest
doctest.testmod(verbose=True)
```

In the first line, we import the doctest module. That's the module that helps us test our code by automatically running the test cases when we run our program. In the second line, we're calling the `testmod` function from the doctest module. That function call tells doctest to perform all the tests; the argument `verbose=True` tells doctest to give us the outcome for all tests, whether they pass or not. If we switch to `verbose=False`, it will only give us output if test cases fail (`verbose=False` is actually the default, so you can just call the function with no arguments, and it will default to not providing output unless one or more tests fail). This can be a nice feature as we can keep the doctest running and only see the output when tests fail.

In this case, our code passed all the test cases. But let's experience what happens when our code doesn't pass.

If we find a word that's the same length as our current longest word, we should ignore it because we always want to return the first longest word if there are multiple words tied for the longest. That's why the correct thing to do is to use `>` in the `if` statement (finding a new longest word only if it's truly longer than our current longest word) rather than `>=`.

We can break the code in listing 6.2 then by changing the `>` to `>=`, which will cause it to select the last word of the longest length rather than the first. Let's change the following line from

```
if len(words[i]) > len(longest):
```

to

```
if len(words[i]) >= len(longest):
```

Now, the tests shouldn't all pass. In addition, let's change the last line to

```
doctest.testmod()
```

By providing no arguments to the `testmod` function, `verbose` is now set to `False`. When we run the code, this is the output:

```
**********************************************************************
File "c:\Users\leo\Copilot_book\Chapter6\test_longest_word.py",
line 12, in __main__.longest_word
Failed example:
    longest_word(['cat', 'dog', 'me'])
Expected:
    'cat'
Got:
    'dog'
**********************************************************************
1 items had failures:
   1 of   5 in __main__.longest_word
***Test Failed*** 1 failures.
```

Doctest conveniently tells us which test was run, what the expected output was, and what the function produced instead. This would catch the bug and allow us to go back to fix the error.

Test cases aren't automatically run by Copilot

We commonly hear the following question: Why doesn't Copilot directly incorporate the test cases when generating code? For example, if we add test cases, it would be nice if Copilot could try to generate functions and only provide us with the code that would pass those test cases. Unfortunately, there are some technical challenges in doing this, and as of the time of writing, this feature isn't yet included. So, if you add test cases, it just improves the prompt to Copilot but doesn't guarantee that the Copilot code suggestion passes those tests.

At this point, we've seen how to run our tests with both the Python prompt and doctest. Now that we know how to test our code, let's think about how this modifies our code design cycle.

6.4   *Revisiting the cycle of designing functions with Copilot*

In chapter 3, we gave you an early version of how to design functions in figure 3.3. At that point, we didn't know as much about examining our code (which we learned in chapters 4 and 5) or as much about how to test our code as we do now. As such, let's create a new version of this cycle (figure 6.1) to reflect our new understanding.

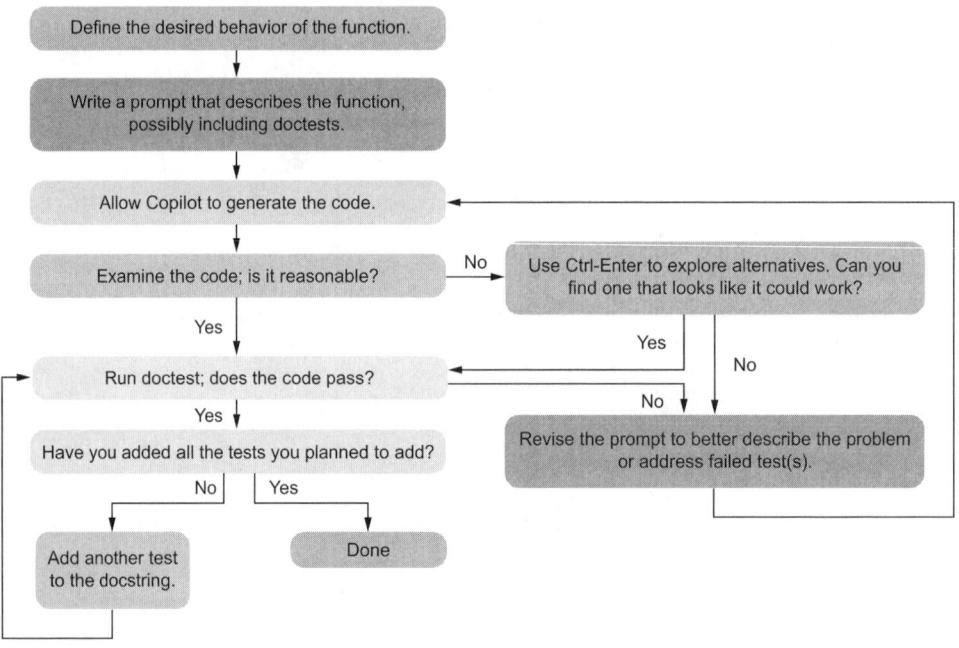

Figure 6.1   **The function design cycle with Copilot, augmented to include more about testing**

The figure is a bit more complex than before, but if we examine it closely, we can see much of the original process is retained. The things that have been added or changed include the following:

- When we write the prompt, we may include doctests as part of that initial prompt to help Copilot in generating the code.
- Having made our way through chapters 4 and 5, we're in good shape to read the code to see whether it behaves properly, so we now have an additional step to address what happens when the initial code from Copilot looks wrong. If that occurs, we'll use Ctrl-Enter to explore the Copilot suggestions to hopefully find a solution. If we can find such a solution, we'll select it and move forward. If we can't, we'll need to revise our prompt to help Copilot generate improved suggestions.
- After finding code that looks like it could be correct, we'll run doctest to see whether the code passes the doctests we included in the prompt (if we didn't include any, it will pass automatically). If doctest passes, then we can continue adding tests and checking them until we're happy that the code is functioning properly. If doctest fails, we'll need to figure out how to modify the prompt to address the failed tests. Once the prompt is modified, it will hopefully help Copilot generate new code that may be capable of passing the tests that we've provided.

With this new workflow, we're in a much better position not only to determine whether our code is working properly but also to fix the code if it isn't already working. In the next chapters, we'll give ourselves even more tools to help when the code isn't working properly, but for now, let's put this all together by solving a new problem and testing the Copilot solutions using the workflow we described here.

6.5 Full testing example

Let's try a problem that we might need to solve to help students decide where to sit in in-person classes. Although we're talking about finding empty seats in a classroom, this problem is the same as trying to find the number of empty seats in a concert hall, theater, movie theater, or office layout.

Suppose we have the classroom layout as a two-dimensional list with rows of seats. Each seat either contains a space (' ') or a student ('s') to represent an empty or occupied seat, respectively. We're going to ask Copilot to create a function to determine which row we could add the most students to, and along the way, we'll design the tests needed to check whether the code is working properly.

6.5.1 *Finding the most students we can add to a row*

We want to figure out the largest number of new students we could add in a single row in the classroom. (Equivalently, we're looking for the largest number of empty seats in any row.) For this, let's start with a somewhat ambiguous prompt and see how well Copilot does.

Listing 6.4   Largest number of students we can add to a row

```
def most_students(classroom):
    '''
    classroom is a list of lists
    Each ' ' is an empty seat
    Each 'S' is a student
    How many new students can sit in a row?
    '''
    max_students = 0
    for row in classroom:
        students = 0
        for seat in row:
            if seat == 'S':
                students += 1
            else:
                students = 0
            if students > max_students:
                max_students = students
    return max_students
```

> This is a somewhat ambiguous part of the prompt.

For the sake of this example, our prompt wasn't very good. "How many new students can sit in a row?" is a reasonable starting point to give to a human, but it's not that specific, and it's easy to imagine Copilot struggling to interpret what we mean. Copilot might get confused about whether we're counting the number of students or the number of empty seats in a row, or it might return the total number of available seats in the classroom rather than in a row. It turns out that our prompt confused Copilot, and the code isn't correct, but before we dive into the code, let's think about what tests we should run. We've come up with the following set of test cases:

- A classroom with some number of consecutive empty seats and some number of nonconsecutive empty seats to make sure it isn't just counting consecutive empty seats
- A classroom with no empty seats to make sure it returns 0 in that case
- A classroom with a row full of empty seats to make sure all are counted, including the first and last seats (edge case)
- A classroom with multiple rows with the same number of empty seats to make sure it returns just one of those values (and not, perhaps, the sum of the number of empty seats across all of these rows)

Let's start by adding the first test case and adding the doctest code to run the test, as shown in the following listing.

> **Listing 6.5   Largest number of students we can add to a row**

```
def most_students(classroom):
    '''
    classroom is a list of lists
    Each ' ' is an empty seat
    Each 'S' is a student

    How many new students can sit in a row?

    >>> most_students([['S', ' ', 'S', 'S', 'S', 'S'], \
                       ['S', 'S', 'S', 'S', 'S', 'S'], \
                       [' ', 'S', ' ', 'S', ' ', ' ']])
    4
    '''
    max_students = 0
    for row in classroom:
        students = 0
        for seat in row:
            if seat == 'S':
                students += 1
            else:
                students = 0
            if students > max_students:
                max_students = students
    return max_students

import doctest
doctest.testmod(verbose=False)
```

Doctest for a common case. The \ is necessary in docstring test cases if you need to do a newline.

When we run this code, we get this output (we cleaned up the formatting of the classroom list manually to help with the readability of the answer):

```
**********************************************************************
Failed example:
    most_students([['S', ' ', 'S', 'S', 'S', 'S'],
                   ['S', 'S', 'S', 'S', 'S', 'S'],
                   [' ', 'S', ' ', 'S', ' ', ' ']])
Expected:
    4
Got:
    6
**********************************************************************
1 items had failures:
   1 of   1 in __main__.most_students
***Test Failed*** 1 failures.
```

Although we'd prefer the code to work, we appreciate that the first test case found an error. The row with the most empty seats is the third row with four seats available. But the code from Copilot is incorrectly telling us the answer is six. That's pretty odd. Even without reading the code, you might hypothesize that it's counting either the number of seats per row or the maximum number of students seated per row. Our test case had a full row of students in the second row, so it's hard to tell. What we can do is change the classroom to be

```
>>> most_students([['S', ' ', 'S', 'S', 'S', 'S'], \
                    [' ', 'S', 'S', 'S', 'S', 'S'], \     ◁──  We removed the
                    [' ', 'S', ' ', 'S', ' ', ' ']])           first student from
4                                                              the second row.
```

So, the second row now has five students. When we run the code again, the test again fails with the code giving us an answer of five. It seems that the code isn't just telling us the number of seats per row. It must be doing something related to where students are sitting. Our next step is to improve the prompt and determine whether we can get better code from Copilot, but for completeness, let's first explain what the code was really doing in the following listing.

Listing 6.6   Walkthrough of the incorrect code from Copilot

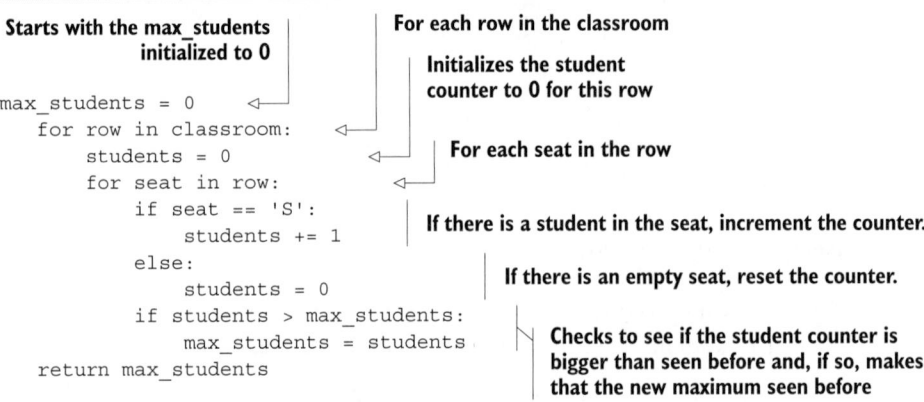

```
max_students = 0
    for row in classroom:
        students = 0
        for seat in row:
            if seat == 'S':
                students += 1
            else:
                students = 0
            if students > max_students:
                max_students = students
    return max_students
```

Starts with the max_students initialized to 0

For each row in the classroom

Initializes the student counter to 0 for this row

For each seat in the row

If there is a student in the seat, increment the counter.

If there is an empty seat, reset the counter.

Checks to see if the student counter is bigger than seen before and, if so, makes that the new maximum seen before

You can see from the code description what is happening per line, but at a high level, this code is counting the number of consecutive students in each row. It does this by initializing a counter to 0 for each row and then incrementing that counter as long as it keeps seeing a student in a seat. It also resets the counter as soon as it sees an empty seat. The `if` statement at the end of the inner loop is a pretty standard way of keeping track of the largest of something seen before, and in this case, it's keeping track of the largest number of consecutive students seen. That's not at all what we wanted, and our poor prompt is partially to blame. The key piece, though, is that our test lets us know the code is incorrect. (If you spotted the error yourself in reading the code, that's great too!)

6.5.2   *Improving the prompt to find a better solution*

Let's rewrite the prompt, keep the test case, and see whether we can do better in the following listing.

Listing 6.7 Trying again to find the largest number of students

```
def most_students(classroom):
    '''
    classroom is a list of lists
    Each ' ' is an empty seat
    Each 'S' is a student

    Return the maximum total number of ' ' characters
    In a given row.

    >>> most_students([['S', ' ', 'S', 'S', 'S', 'S'], \
                       [' ', 'S', 'S', 'S', 'S', 'S'], \
                       [' ', 'S', ' ', 'S', ' ', ' ']])
    4
    '''
    max_seats = 0
    for row in classroom:
        seats = row.count(' ')
        if seats > max_seats:
            max_seats = seats
    return max_seats
```

> The improved prompt says we specifically want the maximum number of ' ' characters in any given row.

> count is a list function that returns the number of the argument in the list.

> Code to keep track of maximum seats

```
import doctest
doctest.testmod(verbose=False)
```

To get this solution, we had to look through the possible Copilot solutions using Ctrl-Enter. Some of the solutions now counted the consecutive occurrences of ' ', whereas others, like the one in listing 6.7, passed the doctest. Oddly, the first time we tried the improved prompt, the suggested solution was correct. This is another reminder of why nondeterminism in the Copilot output makes testing so important.

Let's take a minute and look at what made this second prompt better than the first. Both prompts had

```
def most_students(classroom):
    '''
    classroom is a list of lists
    Each ' ' is an empty seat
    Each 'S' is a student
```

The part of the prompt that led to us receiving the wrong answer was

```
How many new students can sit in a row?
```

The part of the prompt that yielded a correct answer was

```
Return the maximum total number of ' ' characters in a given row.
```

You can never really know why a large language model (LLM) like Copilot produces the answer it does, but let's remember that it's trained to just make predictions of next words based on the words it's been given and words that were in its training data (i.e., lots of code in GitHub).

The first prompt asks Copilot to make some inferences, some of which it does well, and some not so well. The prompt, in a sense, is asking Copilot to know what a row is in a list of lists. Thankfully, that's really common in programming, so it had no problem there.

Then, the prompt asks Copilot to make the basic logical step of inferring that an empty seat is where a *new* student could sit. Here is where Copilot struggled. We suspect that because we're asking about new students sitting in a row, it wasn't able to make the jump to realize that "new" students would require figuring out how many students you can *add* or, in other words, how many empty seats there are. Instead, Copilot focused on the "students °.°.°. in a row" part of the prompt and started counting students in each row. It could have also used the function name (which, admittedly, could be better; i.e., `max_empty_seats_per_row`) to think it needs to count the maximum number of students. That's not what we want, but we can understand how Copilot makes this mistake.

Now let's talk about why, in response to our vague first prompt, Copilot decided to count *consecutive* students in a given row. Maybe counting consecutive students is a more common pattern in Copilot's training data. Maybe it's because "sit in a row" could be interpreted as "sit consecutively." Or maybe it's because when we were coding this example, we'd been working on another version of the problem that asked for consecutive empty seats, and Copilot remembered that conversation. We don't know why Copilot gave us this answer, but we know that our prompt was too vague.

In contrast, our second prompt was more specific in a few ways. First, it clearly asks for the maximum. Second, it asks for the number of spaces, or empty seats, in a row. That takes away the need for Copilot to infer that an empty seat means a spot for a new student. We also used "total" and "given row" to try to get Copilot out of its current approach to counting consecutive values, but that didn't quite do the trick. Consequently, we ended up having to sift through Copilot answers (using Ctrl-Enter) that were sometimes looking for consecutive empty seats and sometimes finding the count of empty seats.

6.5.3 *Testing the new solution*

Returning to our example, because the new code passes the current test, let's give it more tests to ensure that it's behaving correctly. In the next test, we'll check that the code properly returns 0 when there are no empty seats in any rows:

```
>>> most_students([['S', 'S', 'S'], \
                   ['S', 'S', 'S'], \
                   ['S', 'S', 'S']])
0
```

The next test will ensure that the code properly counts all three empty seats in a single row (here, the second row) so there isn't an edge case problem (e.g., it fails to count

the first or last element). Admittedly, looking at the code, we can see the count function is being used, and because that function is built in to Python, we should be fairly
confident this test will pass. However, it's still safer to test it to make sure:

```
>>> most_students([['S', 'S', 'S'], \
                   [' ', ' ', ' '], \
                   ['S', 'S', 'S']])
3
```

The last test checks to see that Copilot properly handles the case that two rows have
the same number of empty seats:

```
>>> most_students([[' ', ' ', 'S'], \
                   ['S', ' ', ' '], \
                   ['S', 'S', 'S']])
2
```

After adding these test cases, we again ran the full program, shown in the following
listing, and all test cases passed.

> **Listing 6.8   Full code and doctests for largest number of students**

```
def most_students(classroom):
    '''
    classroom is a list of lists
    Each ' ' is an empty seat
    Each 'S' is a student

    Return the maximum total number of ' ' characters in a
    given row.

    >>> most_students([['S', ' ', 'S', 'S', 'S', 'S'], \
                       [' ', 'S', 'S', 'S', 'S', 'S'], \
                       [' ', 'S', ' ', 'S', ' ', ' ']])
    4
    >>> most_students([['S', 'S', 'S'], \
                       ['S', 'S', 'S'], \
                       ['S', 'S', 'S']])
    0
    >>> most_students([['S', 'S', 'S'], \
                       [' ', ' ', ' '], \
                       ['S', 'S', 'S']])
    3
    >>> most_students([[' ', ' ', 'S'], \
                       ['S', ' ', ' '], \
                       ['S', 'S', 'S']])
    2
    '''
    max_seats = 0
    for row in classroom:
        seats = row.count(' ')
        if seats > max_seats:
```

```
        max_seats = seats
    return max_seats

import doctest
doctest.testmod(verbose=False)
```

In this example, we saw how to write a function to solve a problem from start to finish. Copilot gave us the wrong answer, partially because of a difficult-to-interpret prompt. We figured out that it gave us the wrong answer because the code failed on our first test. We then improved the prompt and used the code reading skills we learned in the previous two chapters to pick out a solution that looked correct for our needs. The new code passed our initial basic test, so we added more test cases to see whether the code worked in more situations. After seeing it pass those additional tests, we have more evidence that the code is correct. At this point, we've tested the common cases and edge cases, so we're highly confident that our current code is correct. Regarding testing, this example showed us how tests can help us find mistakes *and* give us more confidence that the code will function properly.

6.6   *Another full testing example: Testing with files*

In most cases, you'll be able to test your code by adding examples to the docstring like we did in the previous example. However, there are times when testing can be a bit more challenging. This is true when you need to test your code against some kind of external input. An example is when we need to test code that interacts with external websites, but this is more common in advanced code than the kind of code you'll be creating within the scope of this book.

An example that *is* within the scope of this book is working with files. How do you write test cases when your input is a file? Python does support doing this in a way internal to the docstring here, but for continuity with what we've already done, we're not going to do it that way. Instead, we'll use external files to test our code. Let's see how to do that by revising our NFL quarterback (QB) example from chapter 2.

We could walk through an example with the entire file, but because our queries about quarterbacks were only for the first nine columns of the file, we're going to strip off the remaining columns of the file to make things more readable. After stripping off the remaining columns, table 6.2 shows the first four rows of the file.

Table 6.2   The first four lines of an abridged version of the NFL dataset

game_id	player_id	position	player	team	pass_cmp	pass_att	pass_yds	pass_td
201909050chi	RodgAa00	QB	Aaron Rodgers	GNB	18	30	203	1
201909050chi	JoneAa00	RB	Aaron Jones	GNB	0	0	0	0
201909050chi	ValdMa00	WR	Marquez Valdes-Scantling	GNB	0	0	0	0

We'll assume that each row in the dataset has just these nine columns for the remainder of the example, but we hope it's not a big stretch to imagine how to do this for the full dataset (you'd just need to add all the additional columns in each case).

Suppose we want to make a function that takes in the filename of the dataset and the name of a player as input and then outputs the total number of passing yards that player achieved in the dataset. We'll assume that the user will be providing the data as formatted in the NFL offensive stats file in chapter 2 and in table 6.2. Before we write the prompt or function, how should we test this? Well, we have some options:

- *Find tests in the larger dataset*—A solution is to give the full dataset to the function and multiple player names as inputs. The challenge is figuring out whether we're correct or not. We could open the file in software such as Google Sheets or Microsoft Excel and use spreadsheet features to figure out the answer for each player. For example, we could open the file as a sheet in Excel, sort by player, find a player, and use the sum function in Excel to add up all the passing yards for that player. This isn't a bad solution at all, but it's also a fair bit of work, and if you put enough time into finding the answer for testing, you might have already fulfilled your needs and no longer require the Python code! In other words, figuring out the answer for the test cases might just give you the answer you wanted in the first place, making the code less valuable. Another problem is in finding all the edge cases you might want to test: Will your dataset have all the edge cases you'd want to test to write a program that will work on other datasets later? Yet another drawback of this approach is determining what you do when the function is doing something considerably more complicated than just summing a value in a bunch of rows. There, figuring out the answers for some real test values might be a great deal of work.

- *Create artificial dataset(s) for testing*—Another solution is to create artificial datasets where you know the answer to a number of possible queries. Because the dataset is artificial, you can add edge cases to see how the code performs in those cases without having to find such rare examples in the real dataset. (Sometimes the real dataset won't include those edge cases, but you still want to test them, so the code behaves properly if you get an updated or new dataset.)

Given the advantages to creating test cases in an artificial dataset, we're going to proceed with that approach here.

6.6.1 What tests should we run?

Let's think through the common cases and edge cases that we would want to test. For common cases, we'd want to have a few tests:

- *A player appears multiple times in different rows of the dataset (nonconsecutively), including the last row.* This test makes sure the code iterates over all the players before returning a result (i.e., doesn't make the false assumption that the data is sorted by player name).

- *A player appears in consecutive rows of the dataset.* This test makes sure there isn't some kind of error where consecutive values are somehow skipped.
- *A player appears just once in the dataset.* This test makes sure that the sum behaves properly even when it's just summing one value.
- *A non-quarterback could appear in the dataset.* For this, we ensure the code is including all players, not just quarterbacks.
- *A player has 0 total passing yards in a game.* This checks to make sure that the code behaves properly when players don't have any passing yards. This is a common case to test because players can get hurt and miss a game due to the injury.

For edge cases, we'd want to test a couple more things:

- *The player isn't in the dataset.* This is actually pretty interesting: What do we want the code to do in this case? A reasonable answer is to return that they passed for 0 yards. If we asked the dataset how many yards Lebron James (a basketball player, not a football player) passed for in the NFL from 2019 to 2022, 0 is the right answer. However, this may not be the most elegant solution for production code. For example, if we ask for the passing yards for Aron Rodgers (misspelling Aaron Rodgers), we'd rather have the code tell us he's not in the dataset than that he passed for 0 yards, which could really confuse us when he won the league MVP twice during this time frame. To signal that the name was missing, we might return a large negative value (e.g., –9999), or we might use something called exceptions, but they are beyond the scope of this book.
- *A player has a negative total number of yards across all games or a player has a single game with negative yards to ensure the code is properly handling negative values.* If you don't follow American football, this can happen if a player catches a ball and is tackled behind the starting point (line of scrimmage). It's unlikely a quarterback would have negative passing yards for an entire game, but it could happen if they throw one pass for a loss (negative yards) and get hurt at the same time, causing them to not play for the rest of the game.

Now that we have an idea of what we want to test, let's build an artificial file that captures these test cases. We could have split these tests across multiple files, which would be a reasonable choice to make as well, but an advantage of putting them all in one file is that we can keep all of our test cases together. Table 6.3 is what we built and saved as test_file.csv.

Table 6.3   Our file to test the NFL passing yards function

game_id	player_id	position	player	team	pass_cmp	pass_att	pass_yds	pass_td
201909050chi	RodgAa00	QB	Aaron Rodgers	GNB	20	30	200	1
201909080crd	JohnKe06	RB	Kerryon Johnson	DET	1	1	5	0
201909080crd	PortLe00	QB	Leo Porter	UCSD	0	1	0	0

Table 6.3 Our file to test the NFL passing yards function *(continued)*

game_id	player_id	position	player	team	pass_cmp	pass_att	pass_yds	pass_td
201909080car	GoffJa00	QB	Jared Goff	LAR	20	25	200	1
201909050chi	RodgAa00	QB	Aaron Rodgers	GNB	10	15	150	1
201909050chi	RodgAa00	QB	Aaron Rodgers	GNB	25	35	300	1
201909080car	GoffJa00	QB	Jared Goff	LAR	1	1	−10	0
201909080crd	ZingDa00	QB	Dan Zingaro	UT	1	1	−10	0
201909050chi	RodgAa00	QB	Aaron Rodgers	GNB	15	25	150	0

Notice that the data here is entirely artificial. (These aren't the real statistics for any player, as you can tell by the fact that Dan and Leo are now magically NFL quarterbacks.) We did keep the names of some real players as well as real `game_ids` and `player_ids` from the original dataset. It's generally a good idea to make your artificial data be as close to real data as possible so that the tests are genuine and more apt to be representative of what will happen with real data.

Let's look at how we incorporated all the test cases in this test file (table 6.3). Aaron Rodgers occurs multiple times in the file, both consecutively and nonconsecutively, and as the last entry. Jared Goff appears multiple times, and we gave him an artificial −10 yards in a game (as an elite NFL QB, I hope he's okay with us giving him an artificially bad single game). We kept Kerryon Johnson as a running back (RB) from the real dataset and gave him 5 passing yards to make sure the solution doesn't filter for only QBs. Kerryon Johnson also only has one entry in the data. We added Leo Porter to the dataset and gave him 0 passing yards (he's pretty sure he'd do anything to not get tackled by an NFL player). We also added Dan Zingaro and gave him a completed pass, but for −10 yards, covering the case that a single player's total is negative. Table 6.4 shows what it *should* return per player when we run the query for each player.

Table 6.4 Passing yards per player in the test case

Player	Passing yards in the test case
Aaron Rodgers	800
Kerryon Johnson	5
Leo Porter	0
Jared Goff	190
Dan Zingaro	−10

6.6.2   *Creating the function*

Let's start with the function name and describe the problem in the docstring. This problem may be complicated enough that we'll need to offer prompts within the function to help it know to open the file, process the data, and close the file, but let's try to just describe the function first and see how Copilot does.

Listing 6.9   Function to find total passing yards per player

```
def tot_pass_yds_player(input_file, player):      ◁──   We abbreviated the
    """                                                 function name.

    input_file is a string that is the name of a file
    player is the name of a player

    The file is a csv file with a header row
    Column 4 is the player's name and column
    8 is the number of passing yards for that player

    return the total number of passing yards for the player
    """
    import csv
    with open(input_file, 'r') as csvfile:
        reader = csv.reader(csvfile)
        next(reader)
        total = 0
        for row in reader:
            if row[3] == player:
                total += int(row[7])
        return total
```

Before looking at the code produced, we want to point out that we didn't include the test cases for this example because they likely wouldn't help Copilot. We recommend having Copilot generate code prior to you adding test cases if your test cases will simply open and use artificial files. Each test case will just be a filename, a player, and the expected output. Copilot likely can't read the file that corresponds to that filename and figure out that we're summing the eighth column to get the desired result. This means that giving Copilot the test cases isn't going to add to the quality of the prompt. In fact, the artificial nature of our data might even confuse it (e.g., in what scenario does a real NFL player have a negative total for passing yards?).

Now looking at the code that Copilot gave us, we can see that it's quite reasonable and almost identical to the code we saw in chapter 2. Given that it seems reasonable when we read it, let's see how to test it.

6.6.3   *Testing the function*

To test the function, we'll augment the docstring to include our test cases for the full piece of code, as shown in the following listing.

Listing 6.10 Testing the function to find player passing yards

```
def tot_pass_yds_player(input_file, player):
    """
    input_file is a string that is the name of a file
    player is the name of a player

    The file is a csv file with a header row
    Column 4 is the player's name and column
    8 is the number of passing yards for that player

    return the total number of passing yards for the player

    >>> tot_pass_yds_player('test_file.csv', 'Aaron Rodgers')
    800
    >>> tot_pass_yds_player('test_file.csv', 'Kerryon Johnson')
    5
    >>> tot_pass_yds_player('test_file.csv', 'Leo Porter')
    0
    >>> tot_pass_yds_player('test_file.csv', 'Jared Goff')
    190
    >>> tot_pass_yds_player('test_file.csv', 'Dan Zingaro')
    -10
    >>> tot_pass_yds_player('test_file.csv', 'Tom Brady')
    0
    """
    import csv
    with open(input_file, 'r') as csvfile:
        reader = csv.reader(csvfile)
        next(reader)
        total = 0
        for row in reader:
            if row[3] == player:
                total += int(row[7])
        return total

import doctest
doctest.testmod(verbose=False)
```

The additional test case for a player not in the dataset

We ran this code, and all the test cases passed. (We know that all test cases passed because there was no output from doctest.) We now have additional evidence that the code is functioning properly!

6.6.4 Common challenges with doctest

Let's rewrite the previous prompt and add a really subtle error to the first test, as shown in the following listing.

Listing 6.11 Mistake in doctest

```
def tot_pass_yds_player(input_file, player):
    """
    input_file is a string that is the name of a file
    player is the name of a player
```

```
    The file is a csv file with a header row
    The 4th Column is the player's name and the 8th column
    is the number of passing yards for that player

    return the total number of passing yards for the player

    >>> tot_pass_yds_player('test_file.csv', 'Aaron Rodgers')
    800
    >>> tot_pass_yds_player('test_file.csv', 'Kerryon Johnson')
    5
    >>> tot_pass_yds_player('test_file.csv', 'Leo Porter')
    0
    >>> tot_pass_yds_player('test_file.csv', 'Jared Goff')
    190
    >>> tot_pass_yds_player('test_file.csv', 'Dan Zingaro')
    -10
    >>> tot_pass_yds_player('test_file.csv', 'Tom Brady')
    0
    """
    import csv
    with open(input_file, 'r') as csvfile:
        reader = csv.reader(csvfile)
        next(reader)
        total = 0
        for row in reader:
            if row[3] == player:
                total += int(row[7])
        return total

import doctest
doctest.testmod(verbose=False)
```

There is an extra space after the 800 that isn't visible.

When we ran this code, we received this error:

```
Failed example:
    tot_pass_yds_player('test_file.csv', 'Aaron Rodgers')
Expected:
    800
Got:
    800
```

On first glance, this seems really odd. The test case expects 800 and it got 800, but it's telling us it failed. Well, it turns out that we made a mistake in writing the test case and wrote "800 " (with a space at the end) rather than "800". This mistake causes Python to think the space is important and causes the test to fail. The bad news is that this is a really common problem working with doctest! We've made this mistake more often than we'd like to admit. The good news is it's really easy to fix by just finding and deleting the space. If a test is failing but the output from doctest suggests that it should be passing, always check ends of lines for spaces or extra or missing spaces anywhere in your output compared to exactly what doctest is expecting.

Given that all our test cases passed, we can feel confident returning to the larger dataset and using the function we just created. The key thing from this example is that we can, and should, create artificial files to test functions that work with files. Again, testing is all about gaining confidence that the code is working properly, and you want to be sure you test any code you write or given to you by Copilot.

In this chapter as a whole, we learned about the importance of testing code, how to test code, and how to do it in two detailed examples. In our examples, we wrote and tested functions. But how do we decide which functions should be written to solve even larger problems? Well, we figure that out through a process known as problem decomposition that we'll cover in detail in our next chapter.

6.7 Exercises

1 Given the following scenarios, identify whether closed-box testing or open-box testing would be more appropriate and explain why:

a A tester is given a function specification and needs to ensure that the function behaves correctly without looking at the implementation.

b A tester needs to debug a function by writing tests that specifically target edge cases revealed by understanding the code implementation.

2 Here is a function with some test cases. Identify which of the following test cases are common use cases and which are edge cases:

```
def calculate_average(numbers):
    if not numbers:
        return 0
    return sum(numbers) / len(numbers)
# Test cases:
calculate_average([1, 2, 3, 4, 5])
calculate_average([10, 20, 30])
calculate_average([])
calculate_average([-1, -2, -3, -4, -5])
calculate_average([1000000, 2000000, 3000000])
calculate_average([3.5, 4.5, 5.5])
calculate_average([1, 2, "a", 4])
calculate_average([0])
```

3 We're building a program to analyze website traffic. Website traffic is represented as a list of dictionaries. Each dictionary has two keys: `"weekday"` (a string representing the day of the week) and `"visitors"` (an integer representing the number of visitors on that day). The same day of the week can appear in multiple dictionaries. Our goal is to find the day of the week with the highest number of visitors.

Here's the initial prompt we gave to an AI code-generation tool:

```
def busiest_day(traffic_data): # traffic_data is a list of dictionaries. # Find the
busiest day.
```

The tool generated the following code, but it doesn't seem quite right.

```python
def busiest_day(traffic_data):
  most_visitors = 0
  busiest_day = None
  for day in traffic_data:
    if day["visitors"] > most_visitors:
      most_visitors = day["visitors"]
      busiest_day = day["weekday"]
  return busiest_day
```

Can you explain why and how you would improve the prompt to get the desired functionality?

4 Imagine you have a function (`find_highest_grossing_book(filename)`) that analyzes book sales data and returns information about the book with the highest total revenue. Sales data is stored in a CSV file where each line represents a sale. The columns in the CSV file are as follows:

a `title`—The title of the book sold (string)

b `author`—The author of the book (string)

c `price`—The price of the book (float)

d `quantity`—The number of copies sold for that particular sale (integer)

Create a Python script containing the `find_highest_grossing_book` function (implementation not provided here). Include a docstring explaining the function's purpose, and add test cases using the doctest module.

5 Review the provided test cases for the `is_palindrome` function. Identify which test cases are incorrect, and explain why. Provide the correct version of the test cases.

```python
def is_palindrome(s):
    """
    Return True if string s reads the same forward and backward.
    >>> is_palindrome("racecar")
    True
    >>> is_palindrome("hello")
    False
    >>> is_palindrome("A man, a plan, a canal, Panama")
    True
    >>> is_palindrome("")
    True
    >>> is_palindrome("a")
    True
    >>> is_palindrome("Noon")
    True
    """
    cleaned = ''.join(char.lower() for char in s if char.isalnum())
    return cleaned == cleaned[::-1]
```

6 Analyze the test coverage of the `find_max` function. Are there any scenarios not covered by the existing test cases? Suggest additional test cases if necessary.

```
def find_max(numbers):
    """
    Returns the maximum number from a list.
    >>> find_max([1, 2, 3, 4, 5])
    5
    >>> find_max([-1, -2, -3, -4, -5])
    -1
    >>> find_max([42])
    42
    >>> find_max([])
    None
    """
    if not numbers:
        return None
    max_number = numbers[0]
    for num in numbers:
        if num > max_number:
            max_number = num
    return max_number
```

Summary

- Testing is a critical skill when writing software using Copilot.
- Closed-box and open-box testing are different approaches to ensuring the code is correct. In closed-box testing, we come up with test cases based on what we know about the problem; in open-box testing, we additionally examine the code itself.
- Doctest is a module that comes with Python that helps us test our code.
- To use doctest, we add test cases to the docstring description of a function.
- Creating artificial files is an effective way to test code that uses files.

Problem decomposition 7

This chapter covers

- Understanding problem decomposition and why we need to do it
- Using top-down design to carry out problem decomposition and write programs
- Writing a spelling suggestions program using top-down design

In chapter 3, we talked about why we shouldn't ask Copilot to solve big problems. Imagine what could happen if we asked Copilot to "Design a two-player strategy game."

In the worst case, Copilot wouldn't do anything useful. We observe this sometimes when Copilot gives us comments again and again but never provides us with real code.

In the best case, we'd get a canned program with all the decisions made for us. That program may not match what we wanted. Part of the power of being a programmer is customizing what we're creating. Even if we didn't want to customize anything, what would we do if the program from Copilot had flaws? It would be difficult for us to fix a large program that we don't understand.

For us to get a program that does what we want, we need to feed small subproblems to Copilot and assemble those solutions into our own program. The focus of this chapter is learning how to break large problems into smaller subproblems, which is essential to being able to solve the large problems we want to solve.

7.1 Problem decomposition

Problem decomposition involves starting with a large problem that may not be fully specified and breaking it down into subproblems, each of which is well-defined and useful for solving our overall problem. Our goal is then to write a function to solve each of those subproblems. We may be able to do this for some subproblems with a reasonable amount of code, but other subproblems may still be too big for us to capture in a function of reasonable size. (In chapter 3, we mentioned that we want to keep functions short—something like 12–20 lines—to give us the best chance of getting good code from Copilot, testing that code, and fixing bugs in that code if necessary.) If a subproblem is still too large to be implemented in a single function, then we further divide that subproblem into sub-subproblems of their own. Hopefully, each of those sub-subproblems will be small enough now, but if not, we'll continue dividing those too! The key reason we do this is to manage complexity. Each function should be simple enough so that we can understand its purpose and so that Copilot can solve it well. If something does go wrong, we won't have too much code to trawl through to find the problem. When we write code that is extremely complex, we're likely to make mistakes. The same goes for Copilot! And, when we have mistakes in long, complex code, they aren't easy to find and fix. It's hard to overstate the importance of problem decomposition for quality code.

The process of starting with a large problem and breaking it down is called *problem decomposition*. The way we're doing this here is synonymous with the software engineering technique known as *top-down design*. It's called top-down design because we're starting with the large task we want to complete and breaking it down into smaller tasks. Once we've completed the top-down design, we can implement the resulting functions in code. We'll have one function for our overall problem, which will call the functions for each of our subproblems. Each of those subproblem functions will further call their own functions, as needed, to solve any of their sub-subproblems, and so on.

As we discussed in chapter 3, we're looking to end up with functions that each have a small role to play in our overall program and whose behavior is clearly defined. We need those functions so that we can call them to reduce the complexity of functions that would otherwise be too complex. To improve clarity and ease of understanding, we seek to design functions that have a small number of parameters and return a small amount of highly useful information.

7.2 Small examples of top-down design

We'll soon jump into a more authentic example of how top-down design works, but we'd first like to set the stage using a couple of our earlier examples. Let's think about the design of a function we previously wrote in chapter 3: `get_strong_password`. It repeatedly prompts the user for a password until they enter a strong password. Don't go back and look at that code—we want to start fresh here.

Suppose that we want to use a top-down design to solve this task. If it were one small, well-defined task, we could implement it directly as a single function. However, for this task, we do see a subtask; namely, what's a strong password? What are the rules around that? To us, this sounds like a subtask that we can try to carve out of this function to make it simpler. Indeed, in chapter 3, when we wrote this function, we did call our earlier `is_strong_password` function, which makes the True/False decision about what it means for a password to be strong.

We can depict this top-down design as shown in figure 7.1. For ease of displaying what will ultimately be large figures later in the chapter, we're going to consistently show the design from left to right rather than top to bottom, but the same fundamental principles still apply.

Figure 7.1   Functions diagram for the `get_strong_password` function. `get_strong_password` calls `is_strong_password`.

This figure indicates that it's our goal to have `get_strong_password` call `is_strong_password` to do some of its work.

Now, for our second example, recall from chapter 3 that we also wrote a `best_word` function that takes a list of words as its parameter and returns the one worth the most points. Again, don't go back and look at that code—we want to figure it out again here. Let's think about what the code for this task might look like. It will probably use a loop to consider each word, and in that loop, it will need to keep track of the best word we've seen so far. For each word, we need to figure out how many points it's worth by adding up the number of points for each of its letters. Remember that *a* is worth 1 point, *b* is worth 3 points, *c* is worth 3 points, *d* is worth 2 points, *e* is worth 1 point, and so on.

Whoa there! We're really going in-depth on this "How many points each letter is worth" thing. This sounds like a subtask to us. If we had a function that we could call to tell us the number of points each word is worth, we wouldn't need to worry about this points business in our `best_word` function. In chapter 3, we wrote a function called `num_points` that carries out exactly this subtask: take a word as a parameter and return its total point value. We can call `num_points` from `best_word`, as depicted in figure 7.2. Again, this makes the task of `best_word` easier for us.

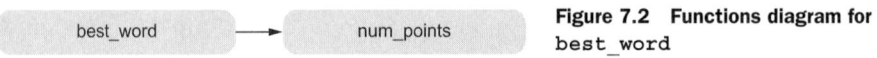

Figure 7.2   Functions diagram for `best_word`

In chapter 3, we happened to write these functions from subtask to task, from the leaf function to the parent function. We'll continue to do that in this chapter, but we'll do the top-down design first to figure out which functions we'll need.

These two examples from chapter 3 we just talked about are small, and you may indeed be able to get their code written by powering ahead with a single function. But with large examples, problem decomposition is the only way to keep the complexity under control.

We'll next dive into a larger example of top-down design. The key skill that we want you to take from this chapter is how to break a large problem down into smaller subproblems. We encourage you to read through the upcoming example multiple times. On your first read, aim for a high-level view of how the pieces fit together to solve the overall problem. On your second read, feel free to dive deeper into how each function works on its own.

7.3   Spelling suggestions

For the rest of the chapter, we're going to solve a problem from beginning to end using top-down design. We want you to be sucessful when you use this approach on your own to solve your own problems, so you'll see top-down design reappear throughout the remainder of the book.

Oops—did we have a typo there? *Sucessful?* That was supposed to be *successful.* English words can be tricky to spell sometimes! You've probably run into many such words. Is it thorough or thourough? Acceptable or acceptible? Receive or recieve? We're going to write a program that takes a word that's potentially misspelled and offers possible corrections to that misspelling. It's a basic spell-checker for individual words!

How are we supposed to come up with these possible corrections? Well, let's look at the pairs of words we just provided and discuss the types of mistakes they exemplify.

The mistake we made with the word *sucessful* is that we left out one letter—we need to add a *c* in there to get the correct word *successful.* So, in general, it seems like a good idea to consider adding a letter to a misspelled word because that might be exactly what's needed to fix it. We're going to consider adding any possible letter in any possible position, not just adding a copy of a letter that's already there. This will help us fix misspelled words such as *acknowlege* (which is missing a *d*).

There are other types of mistakes we'll want to consider too. For example, the mistake in *thourough* isn't that we're missing a letter, but that we have an extra letter—we need to delete the first *u* to get *thorough.* We're therefore going to consider removing any single letter from a misspelled word to see if that fixes it.

What other mistakes can we fix? Well, there's that misspelled word *acceptible.* That's a new type of mistake: there's no missing or extra letter, but there is a letter that should be changed to another letter. That is, if we change the *i* to an *a*, we arrive at the correctly spelled word *acceptable.* To that end, we can try changing each letter to each other letter in the alphabet to see if that fixes the misspelling.

There are many ways to fix misspelled words beyond the three that we just gave. But we'll stop here because we think that fixing three types of mistakes is sufficient for our purposes of demonstrating top-down design. This means that our program will fail to correct the misspelled word *recieve* to *receive*, because we won't be fixing the mistake of having two letters in the wrong order. We'll also fail to correct the misspelled word *camoflague* to camouflage, because we'll be fixing only one mistake in a misspelled word (*camoflague* has two different errors, one missing *u* and one added *u*). Once you finish the chapter, we encourage you to continue to improve your program and learn more about correcting misspelled words if you'd like to go further.

7.4   Spelling suggestions using top-down design

Our task is to "write a program that takes a word that's potentially misspelled and offers possible corrections to that misspelling." That's a big task that we definitely don't want to try to jam into a single function.

Many programs—whether they analyze data, provide spelling suggestions, or guess the author of an unknown text—have three distinct tasks to perform. First, there's the input task: we need to acquire the data on which our program will run. Second, there's the process task, where the program does whatever it's supposed to do with that data. Now, processing the data is all well and good, but it's useless if our users don't know what our programs discovered through that processing. That's where the third step, the output step, comes in, and it's where we communicate something to the user. Table 7.1 summarizes this process.

Table 7.1   A summary of the input, process data, and output tasks

Phase	Role	Spelling Suggestions Example
Input	Take, as input, the information needed for the function.	Provide the misspelled word *sucessful* and a collection of real words (properly spelled words).
Process data	Perform the operation specified by the function on that data.	Consider changes to that word that might result in a correctly spelled word, for example, adding a letter *c* either before or after the *c* in *sucessful* would produce the real word *successful*. Many other incorrect words (i.e., *scucessful* obtained by adding the letter *c* before the *u*) may also be attempted, but only real words should be in the result.
Output	Return the result of that data processing.	Return the suggestion "successful".

You can see this input-process-output model at work back in our data processing example from chapter 2. We needed to read the data from the CSV file (that's the input step), determine the number of passing yards for each quarterback (that's the process step), and then output the quarterbacks and their passing yards (that's the output step).

We can think about our Spelling Suggestions problem in a similar way. What's amazing here is that the input-process-output model gives us exactly the three subproblems that we'll want to solve in our top-down design. Here's what we mean (also see the example in table 7.1):

- For the input step, we need to ask the user for the word for which they want to obtain spelling suggestions.
- For the process step, we need to figure out all the possible suggestions for the user's word.
- For the output step, we need to tell the user about all the spelling suggestions that we found during the process step.

Notice that we started with one large problem to solve (the overall Spelling Suggestions problem), and now we have three smaller problems to solve. Our main or top-level function will end up calling any functions that result from this problem decomposition. We'll name this main function `spell_check`.

It's often but not always the case that we need a separate function for each of the subproblems we identify. Take a look at the input step again. We need to ask the user for a word. While we could split off a separate function for this subtask, that would be overkill. Why? This is because Python already has a built-in function for asking the user for input! The function is called `input`, and we saw it at work in chapter 3, section 3.3.7, when we were asking the user to enter passwords.

Do we need to split off a separate function for the output step? No again! The output step is just outputting stuff to the user. We know that we can do that with Python's already-existing print function. Again, it wouldn't be a mistake to split off a function for this, and you may have done so if you were doing this problem decomposition on your own. What you'd notice, though, is that the function would be very short, consisting of not much more than a call of `print`—and at that point you might think again about whether you want it as a separate function or not.

The process step, by comparison, is going to involve a lot more work. There's quite a bit that goes into figuring out all the possible spelling suggestions! We have to support deleting a letter, inserting a letter, changing one letter to another, and so on, which is way too much to keep all in our main `spell_check` function. We need a separate function for the process step. This is what we need to work on next.

7.5 *Breaking down the process subproblem*

We need a name for our function that implements the process step. We'll call it `get_spelling_suggestions` because it will be responsible for returning the spelling suggestions for what the user typed. It certainly needs to take the user's misspelled word as an argument, or it wouldn't have access to it!

Pause here for a second, though: Do you think this function needs any additional parameters? Answer: it does! Somehow the function needs to know which strings are real words in English. For example, it has to know about the words *successful, thorough, acceptable*, and thousands of other English words. We could do that in a couple of ways: we could pass a list or (Python) dictionary of real words as a parameter, or we could pass the name of a file that contains all the real words as a parameter. When you're designing your functions, you'll need to make similar decisions, focused on the inputs that the function needs to do its work and the return value that we need when it's done.

In addition to the misspelled word, we're going to have our function take a parameter giving the name of a file that contains the list of valid words. There will be one valid word per line of this file. In the resources for this book, we've included one sample word list file called wordlist.txt that you can use. (We found a list of free dictionary words online with a simple internet search.)

What do we need to do for this process step? We can think of four subtasks. This is more problem decomposition! Those subtasks are as follows:

- *Get a list of words from the word list file.* A file of words is a good start, but it's more convenient to have the words inside a Python list. That way, we can easily determine if a string is a valid word. We'll name this function `create_word_list`.
- *Generate a list of all possible words from the user's string.* We need to delete a letter, insert a letter, or change one letter to another letter. This is going to generate many strings, some of which are real words and others that aren't real words. For example, from the string `sucessful`, it would generate the real word *successful*, but also the strings `xsuccesful`, `sucxcesful`, and `succesfrl`, which are clearly not real words. But that's OK. For now, we just want to generate every possible word so that we don't miss any. We'll name this function `all_possible_words`.
- *Using the list of all possible words, generate a list of only the real words.* This is the step where we prune our full list of potential words down to those words that actually exist in English. We'll name this function `all_real_words`.
- *Return a list of the unique words.* Why unique? We don't want to return the same spelling suggestion twice, even though there may be two or more ways to arrive at that spelling suggestion from the user's string. For example, to fix the word *sucessful*, there are two ways to do it: we can add the missing *c* before the *c* that's already there, or we can add the *c* before the *e*. Both result in the correctly spelled word *successful*, but we only want to maintain that word once.

If we were to split out that final subtask—obtaining a list of unique words—into its own function, we'd call it something like `unique_words` or `only_unique_words`. While we could split out that subtask, and you'd be justified in doing so, we've decided to keep it as part of the `get_spelling_suggestions` function. The reason is that in Python, it ends up being just one line of code to remove duplicates from a list. For expediency, we're telling you this now, but again, this would be a perfectly good subtask if you were doing this top-down design on your own.

Multiple ways to break down problems

There's no single correct way to do a top-down design and no single correct way to decompose problems into subproblems. For example, you may have been surprised that we decided to first generate all possible words (including fake ones that aren't actually English words), and then prune that to the list of actual English words. Why not just check each possible word first, and only add it to our list if it's a real word? We certainly could have done it that way too! If you had this alternate decomposition in mind, or we've piqued your curiosity, we encourage you to try this alternate design on your own after you've finished with the chapter.

There's also no shame in trying a top-down design and then abandoning it if the design isn't working out. What might it mean for the design to not work out? Well, maybe you're finding it difficult to break up large functions into distinct subproblems. Or maybe you're getting dozens of tiny functions and starting to worry that your functions are too specific and not solving general problems. Or maybe you're having to pass around many parameters, perhaps some of which are only there to be passed further and further until finally a function needs them. Or maybe you just want to play out an alternate top-down design to see how it goes!

We encourage experimentation at the design phase before you settle on a final design for the code. In this experimentation, you'd try different possible functions and different inputs/outputs for functions. For example, earlier we debated whether the `get_spelling_suggestions` function should take a name of a file containing real words or a list (or dictionary) containing real words. Both options would be worth considering during your design phase.

That leaves us with three subtasks we need to solve. We're going to do our top-down design on these shortly. But first, let's take stock of where we are right now (see figure 7.3).

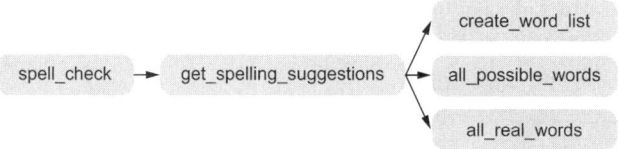

Figure 7.3 Functions diagram showing the three subtasks of
`get_spelling_suggestions`

7.5.1 *Getting the list of words from the word list file*

The function for this task is `create_word_list`. It will take one parameter, which is the name of the word list file, and will return the list of words from that file.

Do we need any further top-down design on this function? Let's imagine we thought the answer was yes. What subtasks could we split out? We could imagine the tasks of opening the file, reading its contents, and closing the file. But opening the file, as we learned in chapter 5, section 5.1.4, is done by just calling Python's `open` function. Similarly, closing the file is done by just calling Python's `close` function. What about reading the words from the file? That doesn't sound much different from reading the lines of the CSV file in chapter 5, section 5.1.4. So we feel justified in leaving this function alone, without any further subtask splitting.

7.5.2 *Generating the list of all possible words*

The function for this task is `all_possible_words`, which will take one parameter giving us the string for which we want to provide spelling suggestions. It will return the list of all possible words that can be obtained by adding one letter, deleting one letter, or changing one letter.

Adding one letter, deleting one letter, and changing one letter are three distinct types of tasks. Moreover, they don't strike us as particularly simple tasks: they're going to involve some sort of loop over the letters in the user's string. Aha! Looks like we have some further top-down design to do on this one. In particular, we're going to split three subtasks out of this function:

- `add_letter`—This function will take a string parameter and return a list of all strings that can be obtained by adding one letter anywhere in the word.
- `delete_letter`—This function will take a string parameter and return a list of all strings that can be obtained by deleting one letter.
- `change_letter`—This function will take a string parameter and return a list of all strings that can be obtained by changing one letter.

Table 7.2 provides what we expect each function will return for two different input strings. For both add_letter and change_letter, a large number of strings are returned because they will consider adding or changing every letter in English in every location in the input string.

Table 7.2 **Examples of the** `add_letter`, `delete_letter`, **and** `change_letter` **function**

Input String	Strings Returned by `add_letter`	Strings Returned by `delete_letter`	Strings Returned by `change_letter`
cu	acu, bcu, ccu, …, zcu cau, cbu, ccu, …, czu cua, cub, cuc, …, cuz	u, c	au, bu, du, …, zu, ca, cb, cc, …, cz
cad	acad, bcad, ccad, …, zcad caad, cbad, ccad, …, czad caad, cabd, cacd, …, cazd cada, cadb, cadc, …, cadz	ad, cd, ca	aad, bad, dad, …, za cbd, ccd, cdd, …, czd caa, cab, cac, …, caz

As usual, it's important to think through whether we need to split out further subtasks from these three functions. However, given that the pattern we expect to see is just a loop through the letters, we'd be comfortable pushing forward here and revisiting our top-down design if our assumption proves to be incorrect. For now, we can tell you that we'll be just fine without any further splitting.

Knowing when to stop dividing into subtasks

In general, knowing when to stop breaking a task into smaller subtasks is more art than science. It takes practice designing programs to get intuition about where to stop. Many experienced developers often pause for each subtask and consider how complex it is to program and sketch the steps of the function out in their mind. If the solution isn't straightforward, they often choose to divide it into more steps. But we don't expect you to be able to do this yet. Some companies put out guidelines to encourage simple functions by suggesting limits on the number of lines permitted (e.g., no more than 12 lines), but many feel the limit should be on the complexity moreso than the length, although length and complexity are certainly related.

When you're just getting started, a decent proxy then is to limit the number of lines per function to something like 12–20. If you later find that a function ends up being just a single line, it's still a subtask, but may not deserve its own function. (Sometimes, it's okay to keep a short function though if it's called many times by different functions or helps simplify the calling function.)

It's okay to get this wrong when you're first practicing; we certainly have. Sometimes a subtask seems like it'll make a simple function, only to end up being much more difficult than expected. In cases like that, you know to just subdivide it more. Likewise, we've had functions that were a single line and if they were used commonly or made the calling function simpler to understand, we just kept that line as a function.

7.5.3   *Generating the list of all real words*

The function for this task is `all_real_words`. It will take two parameters: the list of real words, and the list of all possible words. It will return a list consisting of only the real words from the full list of possible words. The code for this function would involve going through the list of possible words and checking whether each one shows up in the list of real words. As this task is a small, well-defined task that won't yield a lot of code, we're comfortable leaving this function alone without any further splitting.

7.6   *Summary of our top-down design*

We've reached the end of our top-down design process. You can see our final top-down design in figure 7.4.

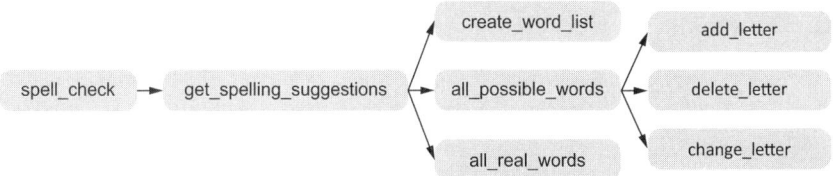

Figure 7.4   Functions diagram with the three subtasks of `all_possible_words` added

Let's not lose the forest for the trees here. If we zoom out, what we've done is break down our original big problem into several smaller problems, each of which we're going to implement as a function. Our original `spell_check` problem may have felt overwhelming. That's OK, though, because we broke it down into one primary subtask of `get_spelling_suggestions`. The `get_spelling_suggestions` function is still a big problem in its own right, but we were able to solve that through the same process: we split it into three subtasks. Two of those subtasks, `create_word_list` and `all_real_words`, felt as though they could be solved in a single function, but the other task, `all_possible_words`, was complex enough that we felt it needed three more additional subtasks (`add_letter`, `delete_letter`, and `change_letter`). The important thing we want you to take away from this is that we used the same technique of problem decomposition at every step to turn an initially daunting task into just a collection of solvable subtasks that will become functions.

Our next step is to move from design to implementation. We know which functions we need now to solve our problem. It's time for the code!

7.7   *Implementing our functions*

When you're doing a top-down design, as we just did, you start with your overall problem and break it into subproblems. That's why we started with `spell_check` (our overall problem) and eventually reached functions such as `add_letter`, which didn't need any further splitting. But when we ask Copilot to implement these functions, we're not going to work in the same order. Rather, we're going to work in the *opposite* order, doing the smallest subproblems first, then moving onto the functions that depend on those subproblems. This corresponds to moving from right to left in a figure such as figure 7.4, starting with leaf functions and continuing to nonleaf functions.

We implement functions in the opposite order like this so that Copilot knows about the smaller functions by the time we want to implement larger functions. That way, Copilot will be more likely to call our subtask functions as desired.

We want to stay squarely focused on problem decomposition here, and we've made some decisions toward that end. First, while we'll include some tests in our docstrings, we won't be pursuing full testing in this example as we would have done in chapter 6. We encourage you to use doctest to run the tests that we do provide as well as add your own tests for further confidence in the code. Second, we haven't dwelled much on our prompt engineering, instead focusing on the prompts that yielded good results. In the next chapter, we'll focus on debugging, and that's where we'll return to prompt engineering. Third, we're not focusing on reading and understanding the code in full detail. That said, we've included some annotations to explain what the code is doing and how it works.

7.7.1 create_word_list

We'll start with our `create_word_list` function. As in chapter 3, we write the function header (the `def` line) and the docstring, and Copilot fills in the code. This is how we'll have Copilot write the code for all the functions in this chapter.

We already know what our `create_word_list` function is supposed to do: read the words from the word list file and return them as a Python list of words. We carefully write what we want in the docstring, as shown in listing 7.1.

Listing 7.1 Function to read the list of words

```
def create_word_list(filename):          ◁┐  The header we wrote ourselves
    '''                                    ◁┘  The docstring we
                                                wrote ourselves
    filename is the name of a file that has one English word per line.

    Return a list of the words in the file.
    '''
    file = open(filename)          ◁──  Opens the file
    words = []
    for line in file:             ◁┐  Loops through each
        words.append(line.strip())  ◁┘  line of the file
    file.close()
    return words                    Adds each word to
                                    our list of words
```

We've used a descriptive parameter name, `filename`, which gives a good clue to the purpose of the parameter. We've also been careful to use this parameter name in the docstring. Our docstring also makes it explicit that we want to *return* the list (rather than, say, print it).

We haven't included a test in the docstring for this function, and that's because we didn't want to distract from the overall goal of implementing each of our functions. If you wanted to, though, you know how! Specifically, we did this in chapter 6 where we created a small file for purposes of testing. Here, you could create a small file with one word per line but with only a few English words, and then test that the list of words we read from the file matches the words that we put in the file. We're finished with our `create_word_list` function, so we can mark it as complete as in figure 7.5.

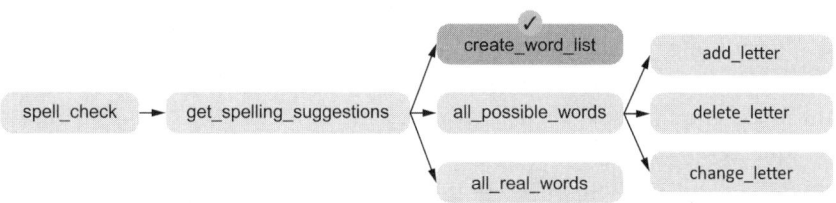

Figure 7.5 Full functions diagram with `create_word_list` finished

To save space, we won't show the updated figure after we implement each function, but we'll show it occasionally.

7.7.2   *add_letter*

Now we'll work on the functions that `all_possible_words` needs, starting with `add_letter`. The `add_letter` function takes a string as a parameter and returns the list of potential words that can be formed by adding one letter to that string. Let's think briefly about what to expect from this function with a quick example. If we gave the function the string `cu` (as in table 7.2) it's going to generate a list of words with every letter added to each possible position. This means it should include strings that have an `a` added before `cu` to make `acu`, a `b` added before `cu` to make `bcu`, and so forth for the character before `cu` stopping with `zcu`. The function should also include every letter in between `c` and `u` to form `cau`, `cbu`, `ccu`, . . . , `czu`. Lastly (as there are three possible positions to add a letter), we'd expect the function to add every possible letter after `cu` to form `cua`, `cub`, `cuc`, . . . , `cuz`. Our prompt to Copilot and the code generated by Copilot is shown in listing 7.2.

Listing 7.2   Function to add any possible letter

```
def add_letter(word):
    '''
    word is a string with at least one letter.

    Return a list of all the strings that can be obtained by
    adding one letter to word.
    '''
    words = []
    for i in range(len(word) + 1):
        for c in 'abcdefghijklmnopqrstuvwxyz':
            new_word = word[:i] + c + word[i:]
            words.append(new_word)
    return words
```

Loops through each index, from 0 to just past the final character

Loops through each lowercase letter

Forms a new word by placing character c at index i

Adds this new word to our list of words

The code here is quite subtle and deserves careful testing. For example, notice that the outer loop uses `len(word) + 1`, rather than the more standard `len(word)`. Without the `+ 1`, we would add characters at each existing index of the word string. But that would actually miss the fact that we also want to be able to add letters *past* the existing letters! The `+ 1` adds one extra iteration where we add a character to the end of the string.

For each index of the outer loop, we consider each possible lowercase letter in the inner loop. The line `new_word = word[:i] + c + word[i:]` uses string slicing, the technique of extracting letters out of a string using two indices, to add the current inner-loop character to the current outer-loop position.

Although we aren't spending much time on testing in this chapter because the focus is problem decomposition, you would want to test this function by giving it a single misspelled word (i.e., *cu*) and then printing the returned words and ensuring it includes strings such as `acu` (add at the start), `cau` (add in the middle), and `cua` (add at the end), as well as possible real words such as *cup* and *cut*.

Note that we wouldn't want to include exact tests in the docstring because the lists returned by this function are huge! For example, try typing this at the Python prompt:

```
>>> add_letter('cu')
```

You'll get a list with 78 strings in it! And that's for our tiny `'cu'` string. The number of strings returned in the list grows significantly as we increase the number of characters in the parameter string.

7.7.3 *delete_letter*

Like `add_letter`, `delete_letter` takes a string as a parameter and returns a list of potential words. The difference is that rather than adding a letter, `delete_letter` deletes each possible letter from the string to arrive at new possible words. Let's think about what we expect this function to do. If we give it the string "carf", it should try deleting each letter to produce the strings "arf" by deleting "c", "crf" by deleting "a", "caf" by deleting "r", and "car" by deleting "f". Again, we gave the prompt to Copilot for this function, as shown in listing 7.3.

Listing 7.3 Function to delete any letter

```
def delete_letter(word):
    '''
    word is a string with at least one letter.

    Return a list of all the strings that can be obtained by
    deleting one letter from word.

    >>> delete_letter('carf')          Loops through each
    ['arf', 'crf', 'caf', 'car']       index, from 0 to the
    >>> delete_letter('a')             final character
    ['']
    '''
    words = []                         Forms a new word by
    for i in range(len(word)):         deleting character at
        new_word = word[:i] + word[i + 1:]   index i
        words.append(new_word)         Adds this new word
    return words                       to our list of words
```

This code is similar to our code for `add_letter`. One difference is that we have only one loop this time, not two. The reason is that we don't need an inner loop to loop through the letters *a, b, c, d*, and so on. That's because we're deleting letters that already exist in the word, rather than figuring out which letter to add.

7.7.4   *change_letter*

Now, it's time for our third and final subtask of `all_possible_words`: `change_letter`! This function is responsible for generating words where one letter in the string is changed to some other letter. In thinking about what we'd like to see happen here, let's consider the string cu again (as in table 7.2). We want this function to replace the letter *c* with all possible letters to create the strings au, bu, du, . . . , zu and to replace the letter *u* with all possible letters to create the strings ca, cb, cc, . . . , cz. (Note that we omit trying cu as that's the initial string, we only consider changes to letters.) See listing 7.4 for our prompt and the code from Copilot.

Listing 7.4   Function to change any letter

```python
def change_letter(word):
    '''
    word is a string with at least one letter.

    Return a list of all the strings that can be obtained by
    changing one letter to another letter in word.
    '''
    words = []
    for i in range(len(word)):
        for c in 'abcdefghijklmnopqrstuvwxyz':
            if c != word[i]:
                new_word = word[:i] + c + word[i + 1:]
                words.append(new_word)
    return words
```

Loops through each index, from 0 to the final character

Loops through each lowercase letter

If c is a different letter from the letter at index i

Forms a new word by changing the character at index i to character c

Adds this new word to our list of words

This code is quite similar to our `add_letter` code! The main difference is that we use string slicing not to add a new character but to change an existing character.

At this point, we've completed the three functions we need to implement `all_possible_words`. Check out figure 7.6, where we've marked off the substantial progress that we've made! We'll next tackle `all_possible_words`.

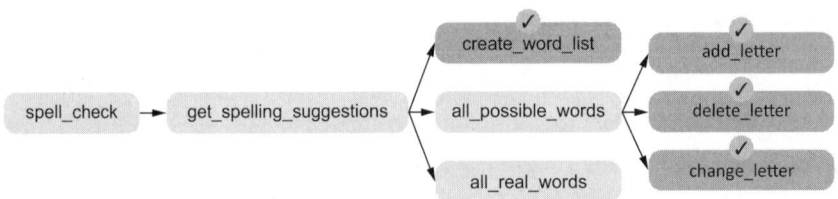

Figure 7.6   Full functions diagram with `all_possible_words` helper functions finished

7.7.5 all_possible_words

The reason we can now implement `all_possible_words` is that we've already implemented the three subtask functions that `all_possible_words` needs to do its job. When we ask Copilot to write this code, we're expecting to see calls of `add_letter`, `delete_letter`, and `change_letter`. Take a look at listing 7.5, and you'll see Copilot doing exactly this with the prompt we've given it.

Listing 7.5 Function to generate all possible words

```
def all_possible_words(word):
    '''
    word is a string with at least one letter.

    Return a list of all the strings that can be obtained by
    adding one letter to word, deleting one letter from word,
    or changing one letter in word.
    '''
    return add_letter(word) + delete_letter(word) \
            + change_letter(word)
```

Calls helper functions to add a letter and delete a letter

Calls helper function to change a letter

Generating all possible words is no easy feat. Yet, we've managed to do it with a single line of Python code here! It just calls to three helper functions and that's it. This is exactly why we're doing top-down design: to make complex functions much easier to implement by offloading much of their complexity to helper functions.

7.7.6 all_real_words

We're close to being able to implement `get_spelling_suggestions`, but not quite, because we first need to implement its subtask function `all_real_words`. The `all_real_words` function takes two parameters. The first parameter is the English word list (this will come from an English word list file). The second parameter is the list of possible words (this will come from `all_possible_words`). The function returns the list of possible words that are real words. Let's do this!

Listing 7.6 Function to generate all real words

```
def all_real_words(word_list, possible_words):
    '''
    word_list is a list of English words.
    possible_words is a list of possible words.

    Return a list of words from possible_words that are in word_list.
    >>> english_words = ['scarf', 'cat', 'card', 'cafe']
    >>> possible_words = ['carfe', 'card', 'cat', 'cafe']
    >>> all_real_words(english_words, possible_words)
    ['card', 'cat', 'cafe']
    '''
```

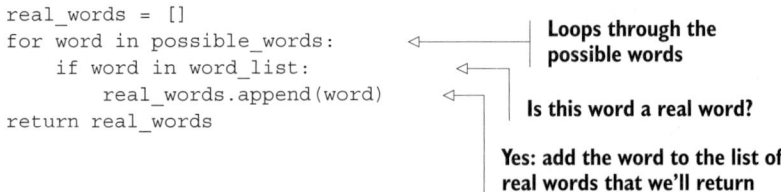

```
real_words = []
for word in possible_words:
    if word in word_list:
        real_words.append(word)
return real_words
```

Loops through the possible words

Is this word a real word?

Yes: add the word to the list of real words that we'll return

The test in the docstring is a good example of how this function works. It's using the `english_words` list for the first parameter and the `possible_words` list as the second parameter. The function will return those words from `possible_words` that are also in `english_words`. We're using this very small test case, rather than using thousands of English words, because this makes it much easier for us to determine by hand what the correct return value should be!

Let's check how well we're progressing in figure 7.7. We're getting close—just two functions to go!

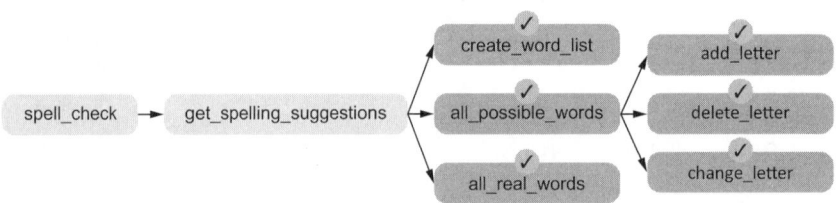

Figure 7.7   Full functions diagram with `all_possible_words` and `all_real_words` finished

7.7.7   *get_spelling_suggestions*

We've implemented `create_word_list`, `all_possible_words`, and `all_real_words`, and those are the only three subtask functions that `get_spelling_suggestions` needs. That means it's time for us to implement `get_spelling_suggestions`!

This function takes two parameters: the name of a file that contains real words (one word per line) and the string that we want to provide suggestions for. It returns the list of the unique suggestions. As always, when scrutinizing Copilot code for a non-leaf function, you want to check that it's calling the helper functions that you expect it to be calling, as shown in listing 7.7. Before you move on, convince yourself that it's calling all the helper functions that it should be calling.

Listing 7.7   Function to return spelling suggestions

```
def get_spelling_suggestions(word_file, possible_word):
    '''
    word_file is the name of a file that has one English word per line.
    possible_word is a string that may or may not be a real word.
```

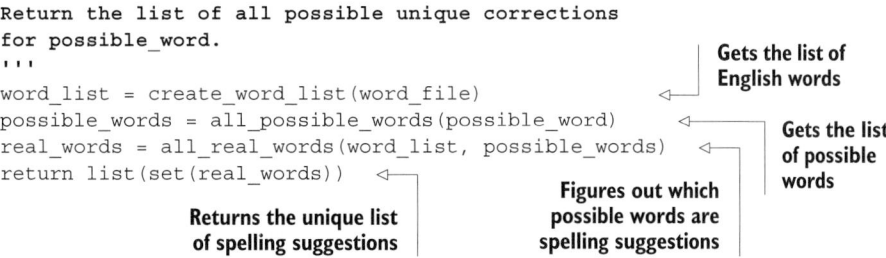

```
Return the list of all possible unique corrections
for possible_word.
'''
word_list = create_word_list(word_file)
possible_words = all_possible_words(possible_word)
real_words = all_real_words(word_list, possible_words)
return list(set(real_words))
```

Gets the list of
English words

Gets the list
of possible
words

Returns the unique list
of spelling suggestions

Figures out which
possible words are
spelling suggestions

That last line there is tricky. Apparently, it's ensuring that we return only unique words—but how? Let's ask Copilot to explain! Here's the explanation that we got when we used the /explain command to Copilot:

Copilot This line of Python code is performing two operations:

1 set(real_words): This is creating a set from the real_words list. A set in Python is an unordered collection of unique elements. So, this operation is removing any duplicate elements from the real_words list.

2 list(set(real_words)): This is converting the set back into a list. The result is a list where all elements are unique.

So, in summary, this line of code is removing any duplicate words from the real_words list.

7.7.8   spell_check

We've made it to our final function, spell_check! It takes one parameter: a string indicating the name of a word list file. It asks the user to type a string, and then shows the user all spelling corrections for that string.

Listing 7.8   Our main function that interacts with the user

```
def spell_check(word_file):
    '''
    word_file is the name of a file that has one English word per line.
    Ask user for a word.
    Print all possible corrections for the word, one per line.
    '''
    word = input('Enter a word: ')
    suggestions = get_spelling_suggestions(word_file, word)
    for suggestion in suggestions:
        print(suggestion)
```

Asks the
user to type
a string

Gets the spelling
suggestions for
the user

Loops through
the spelling
suggestions

Prints each spelling
suggestion on its own line

Consult figure 7.8 to see that we have indeed implemented all of our functions!

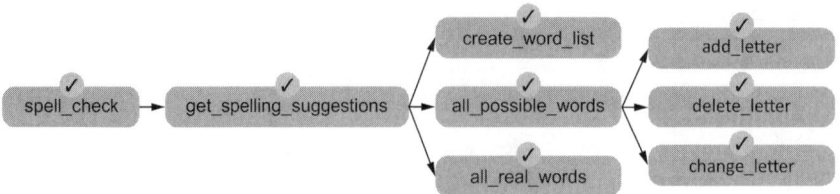

Figure 7.8   Full functions diagram with all functions complete!

You need to add one line of code at the bottom of your Python program to actually call this function. Otherwise, your program won't do anything because no function is being called! So, add this line at the bottom:

```
spell_check('wordlist.txt')
```

Now, assuming that you have the wordlist.txt file in your directory along with your Python program, you can run it! It will ask you to type a word. Try typing the misspelled word *sucessful* (the word that started it all!), and you should see the program provide the spelling suggestion of *successful*, like this:

```
Enter a word: sucessful
successful
```

Try other misspelled words too, such as *thourough* and *acceptible*. With these misspelled words so far, our program is replying with only a single spelling suggestion because there is only one real word a single edit away from the words we're trying. We encourage you to try entering the word *carf* to see that our program can provide many possible spelling suggestions.

Congratulations! You've completed your first real-world top-down design. Your program provides spelling suggestions for a word, much as a spellchecker does. We made the problem considerably easier to implement by doing some up-front design work to break down the original problem into smaller subproblems.

Many computer scientists view problem decomposition as *the* most critical skill needed to write good software [1]. We saw the value of problem decomposition in this chapter: it made a large problem solvable by breaking it into smaller steps until each step was easier to solve. We applied this skill in this chapter using top-down design (start with the large task and break it into smaller tasks) to put it in practice. This skill remains critical when working with tools such as Copilot and ChatGPT because they perform better when solving small, well-defined problems compared to large problems. As mentioned at the beginning of the chapter, problem decomposition is more of an art than a science, and it takes practice to get it right. We'll do more problem decomposition in our upcoming chapters to help give you more intuition into how to approach it yourself.

7.8   **Exercises**

1 Using the examples of `get_strong_password` and `best_word` discussed previously, let's apply the top-down design approach to a new problem. Suppose we want to write a function called `find_highest_scoring_word` that takes a list of sentences as its parameter and returns the word with the highest score from all the sentences. Each word's score is calculated the same way as in the `best_word` function:

   a Identify the subtasks needed to solve this problem. What are the individual functions you would design to break down the task into smaller, manageable pieces?

   b Draw a function diagram similar to figures 7.1 and 7.2, depicting how these functions would call each other to solve the overall problem.

2 We talked about how sometimes a task is simple enough to be kept as it is, that is, not broken down into smaller tasks. Given the following tasks, decide if you would divide them into smaller subtasks. If so, list the subtasks and explain why. If not, explain why the task is simple enough to remain a single function.

   a Reading a file and printing its contents

   b Calculating the average grade for a class of students from a list of scores

   c Finding the maximum value in a list of numbers

   d Processing an order for an online store, which includes verifying the order, calculating the total price, applying discounts, and generating an invoice

3 Why did we choose to create the `create_word_list` function as a separate function? Could this task be kept as part of a larger function? Explain your reasoning.

4 Imagine you need to change the way the spell-checker works. Specifically, you want to modify the `add_letter` function to exclude certain letters (e.g., *q, x, z*) from being added. How would you modify the program we've written?

5 The following function processes a list of orders, calculates the total price with tax, applies a discount if applicable, and generates a summary report.

```
def process_orders(orders):
    total_price = 0
    for order in orders:
        price = order['price']
        quantity = order['quantity']
        total_price += price * quantity
    tax = total_price * 0.08
    total_price_with_tax = total_price + tax
    report = f"Total price: ${total_price:.2f}\n"
    report += f"Tax: ${tax:.2f}\n"
    if total_price_with_tax > 100:
        discount = total_price_with_tax * 0.1
        total_price_with_tax -= discount
        report += f"Discount: ${discount:.2f}\n"
```

```
    report += f"Total price with tax: ${total_price_with_tax:.2f}\n"
    print(report)

a = {'price': 20, 'quantity': 5}
lst = [a]
process_orders(lst)
```

Refactor (redesign) the `process_orders` function by breaking it down into smaller subproblems. Implement each subproblem as a separate function, and ensure the overall behavior remains the same.

6 In this exercise, you're given a code snippet already broken down into two functions: a main function and a helper function. When we call the function with Test Case 2 in the following code, we get a `ZeroDivisionError`. Your task is to identify and fix the error based on the provided error message.

```
def calculate_average(numbers):
    total = sum(numbers)
    count = len(numbers)
    return total / count

def process_numbers(data):
    valid_numbers = [n for n in data if isinstance(n, int)]
    average = calculate_average(valid_numbers)
    print(f"The average of the valid numbers is: {average}")

# Test Case 1
data = [10, 20, 'a', 30, 'b', 40]
process_numbers(data)

# Test Case 2
data = ['a', 'b']
process_numbers(data)
```

Summary

- We need to divide a big programming problem into smaller subproblems before we can effectively implement it. This is known as problem decomposition.
- Top-down design is a systematic technique for breaking a problem down into small subtask functions.
- In top-down design, we seek small functions that solve well-defined tasks and that can be used by one or more other functions.
- When we're ready to implement our functions that arose from top-down design, we implement them from the bottom up; that is, we implement the leaf functions first, then functions that depend on those leaf functions, and so on until we implement the topmost function.

Debugging and better understanding your code

There will be a point in every programmer's career when their code isn't doing what they want it to do. This has likely happened to you already, and, rest assured, it's a normal part of learning to program. How do we fix the code? Sometimes, changing the prompt or better decomposing the problem like you learned in earlier chapters is sufficient to fix the problem. But what do you do when you just can't get Copilot to give you different or better code, nor can you figure out why the code you've been given doesn't work properly?

This chapter serves two purposes. The primary goal is to learn how to find errors (called bugs) in the code and fix them. To find those bugs, you'll need to fulfill the second goal, which is gaining a deeper understanding of how your code works while you're running it.

The good news is that having an error in your code is such a common occurrence for programmers that programming environments, such as Visual Studio Code (VS Code), have tools to help us uncover what's going wrong. We'll learn how to use that tool, called a debugger, in this chapter as well.

Like the past few chapters where we started small, we'll learn the concepts behind finding and fixing errors with some small examples, and then we'll more authentically showcase the process by diving into a larger example that's similar to the kind of code you're likely to write in the future.

8.1 What causes errors (bugs)?

First up is a quick terminology lesson. Many decades ago, computers used relays or vacuum tubes rather than transistors. The story goes that Dr. Grace Hopper, while programming one of these early computers, experienced an error caused by an actual bug (a moth) in a relay. Today, we use the term bug to refer to a mistake in a program, though we're not dealing with literal bugs anymore. Now, bugs are caused by mistakes by programmers; when we debug our code, we're working on removing those bugs. (There can be bugs in the implementation of Python itself or even in computer hardware, but they are so rare, it's safe to assume an error in your code is because of your code.)

No one intentionally causes bugs in their code if they are genuinely trying to solve a problem. So why do bugs happen? Well, software engineers, and Copilot, make mistakes. What kind of mistakes you might ask? There are two primary categories of bugs:

- *Syntax errors*—These errors occur when the code doesn't follow the Python syntax requirements. For example, forgetting to write a : at the end of the first line of a for loop is a syntax error. When you run Python, because it's trying to generate machine code based on your program description, it will run into a mistake, not know what to do, and give you an error. Sometimes, these error messages are more readable than others. When people learn to program in the traditional way, without Copilot, these errors are really, really common. It takes a while to learn all the rules of Python and to make those rules a habit. Even the two of us still sometimes write code with syntax errors, despite decades of writing code. The good news is that writing code with Copilot almost entirely eliminates this problem! The bad news is that of the two types of bugs, syntax errors are the easier to find and fix.

- *Logical errors*—These errors occur when there is something logically wrong with the program. For example, maybe the intent of the code is to count how many times the exact word "Dan" appears in a list of words, but the code actually counts how many words in the list contain "dan" (ignoring case) anywhere in the word. This code would be doing the wrong thing on two counts: it would count words like *dan* and *DAN* as matches even though we don't want those to be matches, and it would find *dan* as any part of a word rather than the full word. That is, it would count words like *Daniel*, *danger*, and *dan*, even though we don't want to count any of these! Somewhere, the code isn't doing what it should, and we have to figure out where and why. Often, finding the logical error is the hardest part. Once we know where the mistake is, we have to fix it, and fixing these bugs can range from changing a single character to completely rewriting the code. Logical errors can happen when a prompt isn't well described or when Copilot, for various reasons, generates the wrong code.

8.2 How to find the bug

Finding bugs can be challenging. Fundamentally, whether you or Copilot wrote the code, you thought or Copilot "thought" the code was correct when it was written. This is why it's often easier for a colleague to find a bug in the code rather than the author. The author can't see the bug because they created it!

Bugs aren't new to us in this book as we've seen mistakes in code already, and we've found those errors by reading the code and/or testing. In previous chapters, we figured out the source of the bug by reading through the code. In this chapter, we'll address the bugs that you identify when testing but can't seem to figure out why the code is wrong. Often, you can bypass the process of figuring out why the code is wrong by trying other Copilot suggestions, using new prompts to fix the error, or asking Copilot to fix the bug for you, but in our experience, these techniques don't always work. What we need then are more tools to help us figure out where the error is in the code.

8.2.1 Using print statements to learn about the code behavior

Fundamentally, a logical error means that there is a mismatch between what the author thought the code would do and what the code actually does. A common way to identify that mismatch is by using `print` statements to get insight into the behavior of the program because they tell you what the computer is actually doing. A useful practice is to print variables at various points in time to see what the values of those variables are at those points. Let's try this for that example we just gave of looking for the word *Dan* in a list of words. Here's the wrong code.

> **Listing 8.1 Incorrect function for counting matching words**

```
def count_words(words):
    count = 0
    for word in words:
        if "dan" in word.lower():        The method lower makes the
            count += 1                    word all lowercase letters.
    return count
```

You may already see what's wrong with the code, but let's assume we don't know what's going on, and we're trying to figure out where the code went wrong. Suppose we found out that our code is wrong by running the following test case:

```
>>> words = ["Dan", "danger", "Leo"]
>>> count_words(words)
2
```

We expected the answer of 1, but we got 2. Notably, including *danger* in this test case helped us catch the error in the code. Where in the code did things go wrong? To figure that out, we could add `print` statements. When you want to do this, you'll need to read the code to figure out where to put them. Looking at this code, printing the list at the start of the function might not be a bad idea depending on the bug we're seeing, but the bug here seems to have to do with the count and not specifically with the list of words. Printing each word in the list as the first line in the `for` loop may be helpful so we can check that the code is processing each word. We might print `count` right before it's returned, but we already have a good idea of the value returned. These are all reasonable ideas that will help you get closer to the bug, but it's not where we'd start. To be clear, if we started with one of these other ideas, we wouldn't be wrong; it might just take a few more steps before finding the bug.

Because the bug is counting too many words as *Dan* words, we'd put the `print` statement within the `if` statement right where `count` is incremented, as in the following listing.

Listing 8.2   Example of a print statement to find the bug

```python
def count_words(words):
    count = 0
    for word in words:
        if "dan" in word.lower():
            print(word,"is being counted")      # A print statement to
            count += 1                           #   show which words
    return count                                 #   are being counted
```

Rerunning our code with the same test case, this is what is printed now:

```
>>> words = ["Dan", "danger", "Leo"]
>>> count_words(words)
Dan is being counted
danger is being counted
2
```

Aha! This would tell us that our program is counting the word *danger* when it shouldn't be. We could then give Copilot a new prompt incorporating what we just learned to hopefully have Copilot fix the problem. Here's the prompt we added in the editor, and Copilot fixed the code in the following listing.

Listing 8.3   Using a prompt to fix a known bug

```python
def count_words(words):
    count = 0
    for word in words:
        # only count words that are exactly "Dan"    # Prompt that causes
        if word == "Dan":                            #   Copilot to generate
            count += 1                                #   the correct code
    return count
```

Code added by Copilot in response to the prompt

Once we knew the bug, it was easier to tell Copilot how to fix it. Granted, this is a basic example, but the idea applies to far more complex code. The process is often iterative. You ask the code to print something, and what it prints aligns with what you think it should be doing. You then ask the code to print something else and check it against what you expect. You keep doing this until there's a point where what the code prints doesn't align with what you wanted it to do. That's when you've found the bug and can give Copilot a prompt to help it give you better code, or if the fix is simple, you can change the code directly.

Depending on the complexity of the code, using `print` statements is often an effective way of debugging. We often use it as our first step in debugging.

> ### Debugging: An art more than a science
> The iterative process when debugging is necessary because we're genuinely confused about what the code is doing and why it isn't matching our expectations. It's okay to add a bunch of `print` statements that just tell you what you thought was happening in the first place because each of these `print` statements tells you where *not* to look for the bug and is an effective process of elimination. Figuring out where to look for bugs takes time and practice, so don't worry if you find yourself spending a fair bit of time on it when you first start.

8.2.2 Using VS Code's debugger to learn about the code behavior

VS Code is used by novices and professionals alike, so it has tools to help with the process of debugging. Because it's used by professionals, debugging tools have a large number of features. For the purpose of this book, we'll focus on a few of the most commonly used features, but feel free to look into more resources on using the VS Code debugger if you're curious (https://code.visualstudio.com/docs/editor/debugging).

To showcase these tools, we'll work through debugging the same function from the previous example (refer to listing 8.1) in a few ways. Listing 8.4 provides the code we'll be working with throughout this section. Note that we've added the test of the `count_words` function to the program.

Listing 8.4 Incorrect `count_words` function for debugging

```python
def count_words(words):
    count = 0
    for word in words:
        if "dan" in word.lower():
            count += 1
    return count

words = ["Dan", "danger", "Leo"]        Code to call the count_words
print(count_words(words))               function directly
```

GETTING STARTED WITH THE DEBUGGER AND SETTING BREAKPOINTS

To use the debugger, we need to set a *breakpoint* and start the debugger. Setting a breakpoint tells the debugger when you want to start debugging the program as it executes. Once you hit the breakpoint, you'll be able to inspect variable values and step through the program line by line. Breakpoints are extremely useful. For a large program, you wouldn't want to step line by line through the entire program because that could take a great deal of time. Instead, using a breakpoint, you can step through just the lines of code that are most relevant to you.

To set a breakpoint, hover your mouse cursor to the left of the code, and you'll see a dot appear. Click that dot, as shown in figure 8.1, and you'll have a breakpoint set. For your projects, you'll likely want to start by creating a breakpoint at the start of the function's execution and then step through it one step at a time.

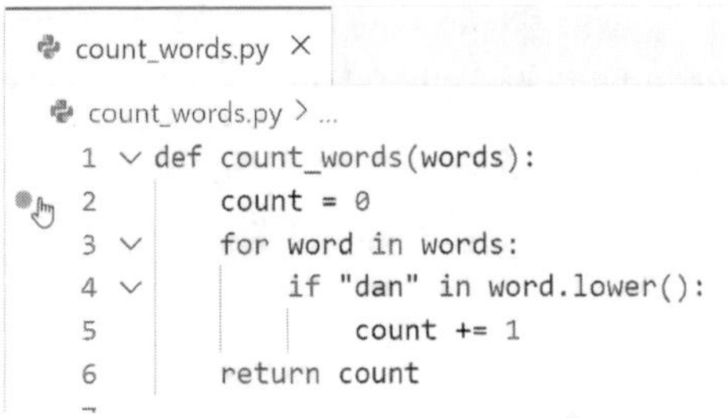

Figure 8.1 Creating a breakpoint in VS Code by clicking to the left of the line of code

If you see a red dot to the left of the breakpoint after you move your mouse away, as shown in figure 8.2, that means it's properly set.

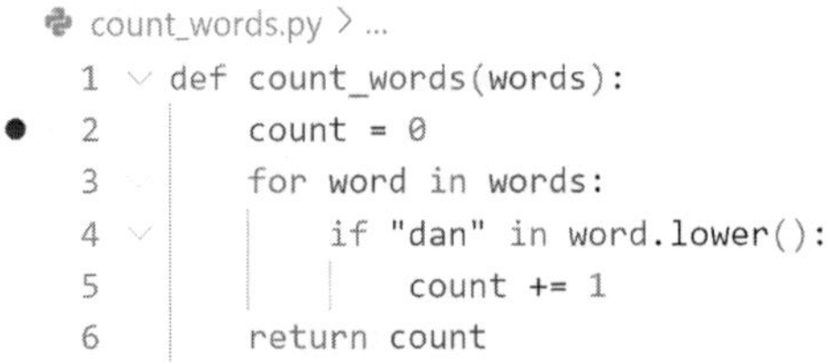

Figure 8.2 A breakpoint has been set on line 2 of our count_words.py file in VS Code.

You can have more than one breakpoint, but for this example, let's just stick with the one breakpoint on line 2. (Note that you can remove a breakpoint by clicking on that red dot again.) Next, we'll start the debugger and see how it works with the breakpoint.

HOW TO STEP THROUGH THE CODE LINE BY LINE

To start the debugger, choose Run > Start Debugging, as shown in figure 8.3.

Once the debugger is started, you should see a screen similar to figure 8.4. (If this is the first time using the debugger, it may ask you to select a debug configuration, in which case, you'll want to choose Python.)

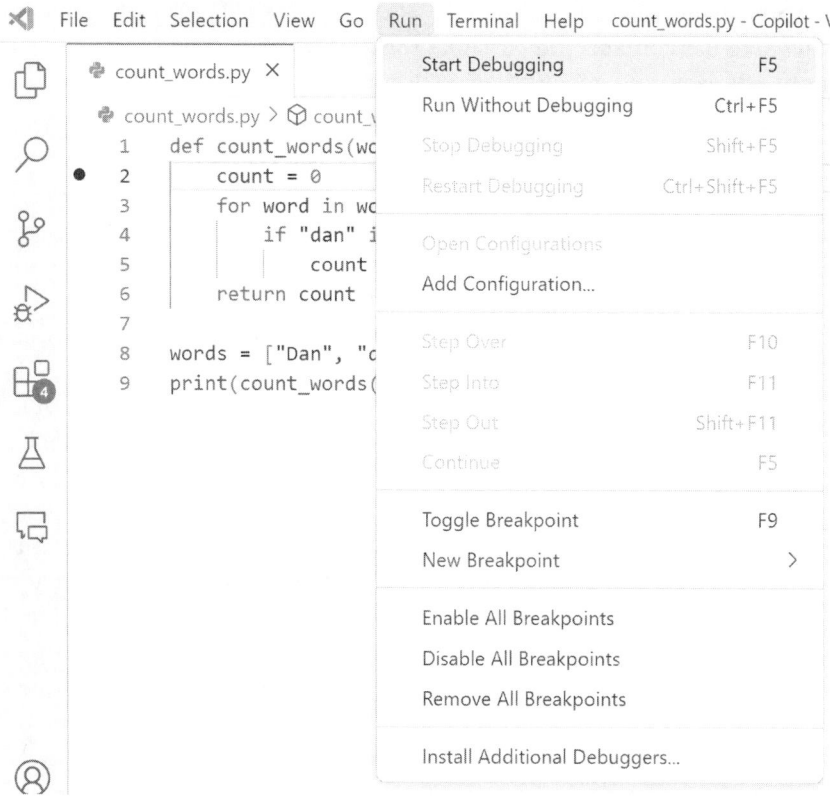

Figure 8.3   Starting the debugger in VS Code

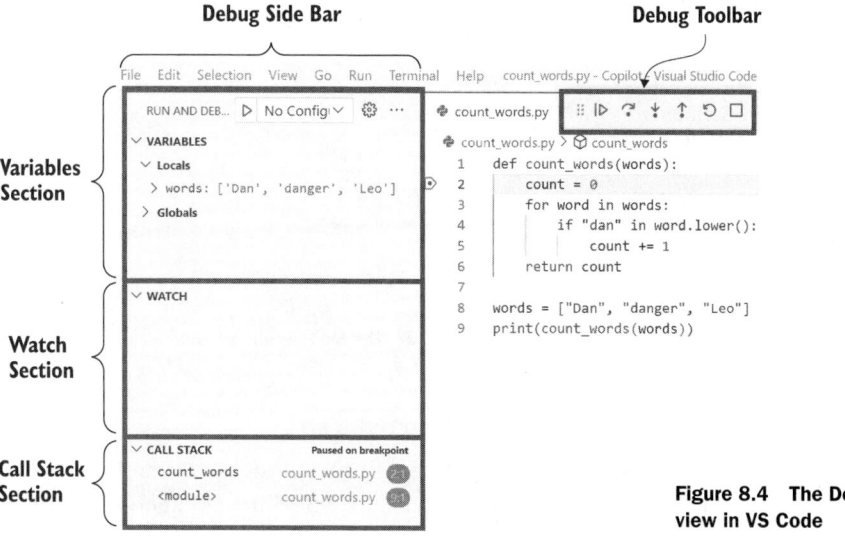

Figure 8.4   The Debugging view in VS Code

The VS Code debugger has a number of components [1]. On the left-hand side, the Debug Side Bar contains the Variables section, Watch section, and Call Stack section. Let's briefly examine each of these sections:

- The *Variables section* contains the variables that are declared within the current scope (e.g., within `count_words`) and their current values. For example, the `words` parameter is defined to be a list containing `['Dan', 'danger', 'Leo']`. You can click the arrow (>) to the left of `words` to see more details about that variable. This section is incredibly useful because you can examine the value of each variable.

- The *Watch section* contains any expressions you want to watch specifically. For example, you might add the expression: `"dan" in word.lower()` to the watched expressions, and you'd be able to see if it's `True` or `False` for each different value of `word`. To add an expression, hover over the Watch section and click the + sign.

- The *Call Stack section* contains the functions that have been called that have led to this line of code executing. Here, the main function (called `<module>` by VS Code) called the function `count_words` on line 9. Within the function `count_words`, we're presently on line 2. You can double-check that this is true by looking at the line of code presently highlighted as line 2 is highlighted in figure 8.4.

  Speaking of which, on the right-hand side, which shows our code editor, we can see the line `count = 0` highlighted. This is the current line of code that hasn't yet been executed. The reason the line hasn't been executed yet is because we set our breakpoint, shown by the arrow with a dot in it, at this line of code. When we started the debugger, it ran the code until just before executing `count = 0`.

The Debug Toolbar (figure 8.5) is critical as it drives the process once you start debugging: you can advance an instruction, restart debugging, or stop debugging.

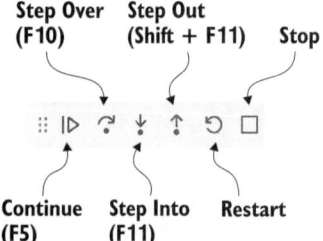

Figure 8.5   The Debugging Toolbar

The buttons on the toolbar, going left to right, are

- *Continue (F5)*—This button will advance until the next time a breakpoint is executed. In our example, line 2 of `count_words` never executes again, so clicking Continue will cause the program and debugging session to run to the end.

- *Step Over (F10)*—This button advances to the next line of code in the current function. Step Over means that if a line of code in this function calls another function (e.g., when `word.lower()` is called on line 4), the debugger will stay in the `count_words` function and will just run the called function (e.g., `word.lower()`) to its completion.

- *Step Into (F11)*—This button advances to the next line of code, including going into any functions that are called. Unlike Step Over, when you use Step Into, the debugger will go into any function called by the current function. For example, if you used Step Into on a line of code that calls another function, it would go into that function and continue debugging (line by line) from inside that function. By default, it doesn't step into library function calls (e.g., `word.lower()` is part of the Python standard library) but will step into functions you've written.

- *Step Out (Shift + F11)*—This button will execute the code until the present function ends and then continue debugging from after this function's exit.

- *Restart*—This button restarts the debugging process. It will restart the program, and the program will execute until its first breakpoint.

- *Stop*—This button stops the debugging process.

STEPPING THROUGH THE CODE LINE BY LINE

Now that we have a handle on the debugger, let's continue our example by using the Step Over button. Let's click Step Over once and see how our view changes (figure 8.6). Step Over advanced to the next line of code, line 3. This means it executed

```
count = 0
```

and is just about ready to execute

```
for word in words:
```

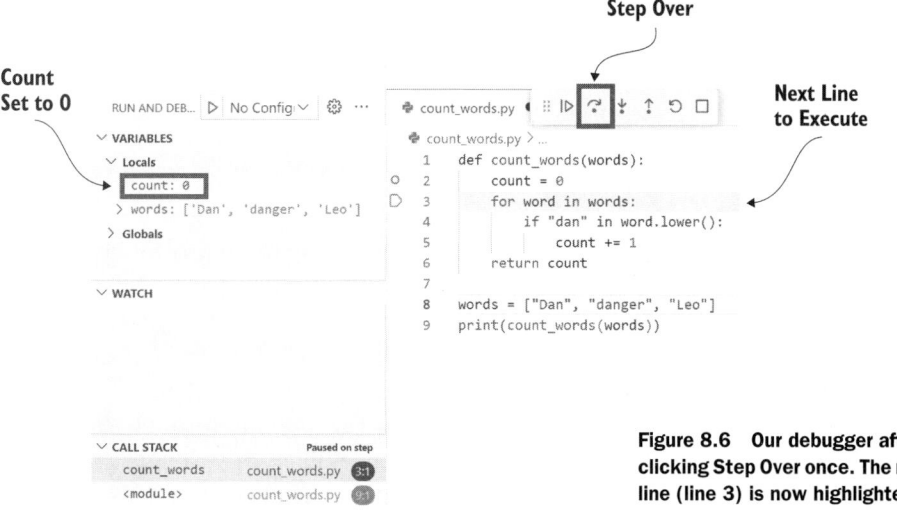

Figure 8.6   Our debugger after clicking Step Over once. The next line (line 3) is now highlighted.

We can see from various clues in the interface that the line count = 0 was executed. First, in the editor on the right, we can see the for loop is highlighted, and the arrow on the left points to this line of code. On the left, in the Call Stack section, we can see that it's now on line 3 of count_words (as shown by the line count_words being highlighted and the number in the oval on the right reading 3:1). Perhaps most importantly, on the left in the Variables section, we can now see the variable count has been added to the local variables, and it has a value of 0. This last piece is pretty amazing because if you were trying to read through the code and trace what is happening line by line, the line count = 0 on line 2 would mean that a variable count is created and assigned a value of 0. This is just what the VS Code debugger has told us as well. We hope you're starting to see how powerful this tool can be.

Let's click Step Over one more time. Now we're stopping just before the line

```
if "dan" in word.lower():
```

We can see that there is now a new variable, word, which has been assigned the value "Dan", and that's just what we'd expect: word was given the value of the first element in the list words. This is a good spot to point out that in addition to being able to read the variables values in the Variables section, you can also just hover your mouse over any variable that's been declared already to see its value as well. Pretty neat, huh?

Let's click Step Over one more time and see that the condition in the if statement, "dan" in word.lower(), evaluated to True, so we're going to execute the line

```
count += 1
```

Now that we're getting the hang of this, let's keep clicking Step Over a few more times. The first time you click Step Over, it will go back to the for loop, and you can see count has incremented to 1. The second time you click Step Over, it will stop at the if statement, and you can see that word is now "danger". We could stop here and add a watch expression to see what this if statement will do. To add a watch expression, hover your mouse over the Watch section, and click the plus arrow that appears to the right of the word Watch. This will let you type anything you want. We typed "dan" in word.lower() and pressed Enter to add this watch expression, as shown in the Debug Side Bar of figure 8.7.

If we hadn't already found the bug earlier in this chapter, this is where we'd find it. The expression "dan" in word.lower() evaluates to True, which means count will be incremented again. But we only wanted exact matches to the word "Dan" and didn't want "danger" to count!

This is a completely reasonable way to debug a function. As we noted earlier, putting a breakpoint at the start of the function's execution and then stepping through it one step at a time often is a great starting point for debugging. The only times you might struggle to use this approach is if the for loop ran through thousands of values before making a mistake. To address challenges like this, we might put a breakpoint in a specific spot to avoid spending a lot of time in the debugger. Let's stop the debugger

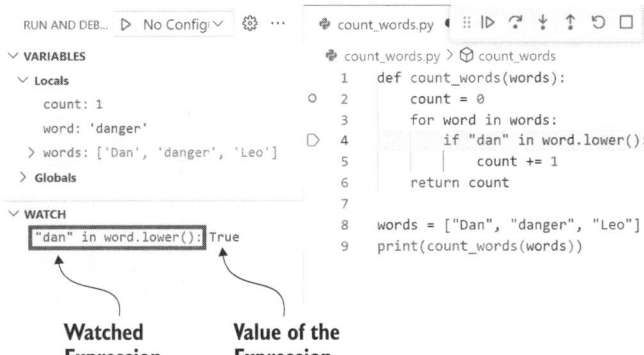

Figure 8.7 View of the debugger after adding the watch expression

(click Stop in the Debug Toolbar), remove the breakpoint from line 2 (click the red dot to the left of the line), and try a different breakpoint.

USING A BREAKPOINT TO SELECTIVELY DEBUG

This time, let's put the breakpoint at a point in the code we want to monitor more closely. Based on our test case showing that two words of the list "counted" when we expected just one to, we should try putting our breakpoint at the line where count is incremented, as we have in figure 8.8.

```
count_words.py ●

count_words.py > ...
1    def count_words(words):
2        count = 0
3        for word in words:
4            if "dan" in word.lower():
●   5                count += 1
6        return count
7
8    words = ["Dan", "danger", "Leo"]
9    print(count_words(words))
```

Figure 8.8 View of the code after placing our new breakpoint on line 5

Once we start the debugger, the code will run until the first time the if statement is evaluated to True and the line count += 1 is ready to execute. Figure 8.9 offers the view of the debugger once we start it.

We put the breakpoint at the incrementing of count because we wanted to see what item in the list is causing count to increment. Examining our local variables, we can see that word is 'Dan', and that is when we want the count variable to be incremented. Given this is what we wanted to happen, we haven't found our bug yet.

Now is when we can really take advantage of our breakpoint placement. We want the code to execute until it comes across the breakpoint again. The way to do this is to

```
RUN AND DEB...  ▷  No Config ∨  ⚙  ⋯        count_words.py  〉    ⠿ |▷ ⟳ ↡ ↑ ⟲ ☐

∨ VARIABLES                                 count_words.py 〉 ⬡ count_words
  ∨ Locals                                   1   def count_words(words):
      count: 0                               2       count = 0
      word: 'Dan'                            3       for word in words:
    〉 words: ['Dan', 'danger', 'Leo']       4           if "dan" in word.lower():
    〉 Globals                          ▷    5               count += 1
                                             6       return count
∨ WATCH                                      7
                                             8   words = ["Dan", "danger", "Leo"]
                                             9   print(count_words(words))
                                            10
```

Figure 8.9   View of the debugger when it encounters the breakpoint (line 5) for the first time

click Continue in the Debug Toolbar (refer to figure 8.5). After clicking Continue, the debugger should appear as in figure 8.10.

Highlighted Variables Changed during Continue

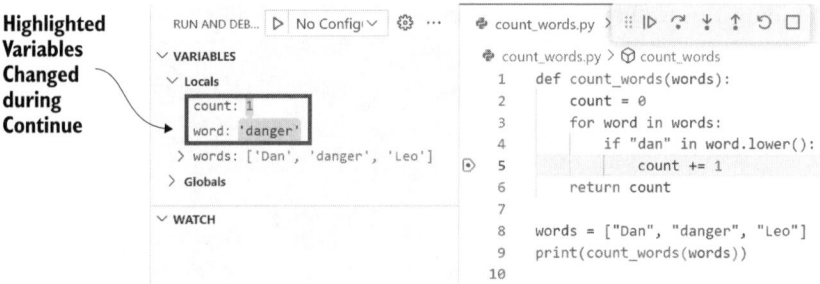

Figure 8.10   View of the debugger when it encounters the breakpoint (line 5) for the second time

In the Variables section, notice that the value of count and the value of word are highlighted. This is to tell you that because you clicked Continue, those two values have changed. The value in count increased to 1, as expected, after having found the word 'Dan'. The value in word updated to 'danger'. Although 'danger' is the next value in the list of words, we shouldn't expect to find the code incrementing count for the word 'danger'. At this point, we'd have found our bug. Notice how much quicker it can be to find a bug with a good placement of a breakpoint. But we caution that knowing the best place to put a breakpoint is a lot like knowing the best variables to print when debugging—it takes time and practice to learn how to do it well.

In this section, we've seen how powerful the debugger can be in VS Code. It's pretty easy to set a breakpoint and start a debugging session. As the debugger monitors the variables in the function, you can inspect those in the Debug Side Bar as the code executes.

8.3 How to fix a bug (once found)

In the old way of learning to program, this would be a short section that would tell you to fix the bug yourself. Although that's still an option, we have a lot of choices now with Copilot. These choices include asking Copilot to fix it, giving it a new prompt for the entire function that better describes the problem in a way to avoid the bug, giving Copilot a targeted prompt to fix the spot in the code you found that was wrong, and, if it's a small fix, making it yourself. Let's see how we could do each of these.

8.3.1 Asking Copilot to fix your bug via Copilot Chat

In the following example, we'll interact with the Copilot Chat feature. The Copilot Chat feature lets you interact with Copilot as you might with ChatGPT but is limited to questions pertaining to programming. Feel free to interact with ChatGPT instead (available via https://openai.com with free tiers at the time of writing) in the same way as we interact with Copilot in this section. We're preferential to Copilot Chat just because its interface is built in to the latest version of VS Code and the Copilot extension.

In previous chapters, we've mostly just asked Copilot Chat for single answers, whereas in this chapter and later chapters, we'll be using Copilot Chat to have a conversation with the tool. When we're having a conversation with the tool, we'll work to separate out what we write ("Human") from Copilot's responses ("GitHub Copilot"). Using the Copilot Chat feature, let's see if Copilot can help us out here:

Human I have a function, below, that is supposed to count the number of times the word "Dan" appears in the parameter list "words". Instead, it seems to be counting the number of times the characters "dan" appear anywhere in the list. Can you help fix this for me?

```
def count_words(words):
    count = 0
    for word in words:
        if "dan" in word.lower():
            count += 1
    return count
```

GitHub Copilot Certainly! To count the number of times the word "Dan" appears in the list, you can modify the `if` statement to check if the whole word is equal to "Dan" (case-insensitive). Here's the modified code:

```
def count_words(words):
    count = 0
    for word in words:
        if word.lower() == "dan":
            count += 1
    return count
```

> This code will count the number of times the word "Dan" (case-insensitive) appears in the list.

The answer back from Copilot Chat changed the line

```
if "dan" in word.lower():
```

to

```
if word.lower() == "dan":
```

Although the change may look small, it has a big effect. The original line of code searched for the string `"dan"` anywhere in `word` (after the word has been made all lowercase letters by the `.lower()` method). The new line of code checks to see whether `word` (again, made all lowercase letters by the `.lower()` method) is an exact match for the string `"dan"`.

This answer from Copilot is a step closer to a correct solution as it will only match the whole word rather than looking for an occurrence of `dan` anywhere in the word. However, the call to `.lower()` makes it case-insensitive, so it would also match `dan` rather than how our solution earlier (listing 8.3) was case-sensitive (it had to be exactly `Dan`). We'd like to be case-sensitive, so we could continue with Copilot Chat to have Copilot fix this for us.

> **Human**   Can you give me the same code but count only the word "Dan" (case-sensitive)?

> **GitHub Copilot**   Sure! Here's the modified code that counts only the word "Dan" (case-sensitive):

```
def count_words(words):
    count = 0
    for word in words:
        if word == "Dan":
            count += 1
    return count
```

> This code will count the number of times the word "Dan" (case-sensitive) appears in the list.

In this case, Copilot Chat was able to solve the problem for us when we knew how the code was misfunctioning. We didn't explicitly say what line of code was broken, but if you knew this, you could convey that to Copilot Chat as well. One advantage of knowing which line was broken, like we did here, is that we could look to make sure the fix from Copilot changes the broken line. Let's move on and examine other options for fixing the bug.

8.3.2 Giving Copilot a new prompt for the whole function

You've seen us rewrite the prompt for a function a fair number of times already in this book. It simply involves rewriting the function prompt and seeing if Copilot can do better, sometimes using Ctrl-Enter to explore Copilot's solutions. We won't repeat this here because you've already seen it many times before (e.g., in chapter 6, section 6.5.2).

8.3.3 Giving Copilot a targeted prompt for part of a function

We used this technique earlier in the chapter in listing 8.3. We've reproduced this as listing 8.5.

Listing 8.5 Using a prompt to fix a known bug (relisted)

```
def count_words(words):
    count = 0
    for word in words:
        # only count words that are exactly "Dan"    ◁──┐ Prompt that causes
        if word == "Dan":                                │ Copilot to generate
            count += 1                                    │ correct code
    return count
```

Here, we'd figured out that the previous line

```
if "dan" in word.lower():
```

wasn't doing what we wanted. So, we removed the incorrect code and specifically added a prompt to say exactly what we wanted Copilot to do, and it was able to produce the correct code.

8.3.4 Modifying the code to fix the bug yourself

This approach to fixing broken code is new to this chapter. You've seen enough code at this point in the book that you can likely fix some code by yourself by directly modifying it. For example, suppose we wrote the following code.

Listing 8.6 Function to count specified numbers in a list

```
def count_between(numbers, x, y):
    count = 0
    for number in numbers:
        if number >= x and number <= y:
            count += 1
    return count
```

We've seen functions like this earlier in the book. It iterates through all the numbers in the list of numbers and checks if each number is bigger than or equal to x and is less than or equal to y. If a number is between x and y, it increases the count. At the end of the function, it returns the count. The code isn't wrong here if the goal is to count numbers in the list that are between x and y (including x and y).

However, the term *between* can be a bit ambiguous. Do you want to include x and y or just the values between them (not including them)? Suppose that when you imagined this function, you wanted to not include x and y. For example, if the list were 2, 4, 8, and you provided x and y values of 3 and 8, you would want the count to be 1 (including 4, but not 8). You might already see how the function is wrong for this goal and how to fix it, but let's pretend you don't realize yet that the code doesn't match what you want.

As with any function that is created either by Copilot or us, we should test the function. Fortunately, when writing the first test case, we included a value in the test case (numbers) that is equal to x (the lower bound) and equal to y (the upper bound):

```
>>> numbers = [1, 2, 3, 4, 5, 6, 7, 8, 9]
>>> print(count_between(numbers, 3, 7))
5
```

Testing the code at the prompt, we found that our function returns 5 as the answer, but we thought the answer should be 3. By our definition of *between*, we felt that only the numbers 4, 5, and 6 are between 3 and 7, so the answer should be 3, that is, there are three numbers between 3 and 7. Instead, the code gave us the answer of 5. So, we know it isn't working correctly thanks to our test cases. Whether we go on to find the bug by inspecting the code or by using the debugging techniques from this chapter, we realize the statement

```
if number >= x and number <= y:
```

is the culprit. Here, the complete fix requires us to change the if statement from

```
if number >= x and number <= y:
```

to

```
if number > x and number < y:
```

This is a change we could just make directly, without asking for Copilot's help (although Copilot would likely be able to help us here as well). Listing 8.7 has the fixed function after the change.

> **Listing 8.7   Function to count specified numbers (corrected)**

```
def count_between(numbers, x, y):
    count = 0
    for number in numbers:
        if number > x and number < y:        ◁——┤  Changed the >= to >
            count += 1                              and <= to < manually
    return count
```

8.4 Modifying our workflow in light of our new skills

Now that we know how to find and fix bugs in a more deliberate manner, let's revisit the workflow we last visited in chapter 6. Note that this workflow is about how to design a single function, so it presumes you've already done the function decomposition described in chapter 7 to determine the appropriate functions. The new workflow appears in figure 8.11.

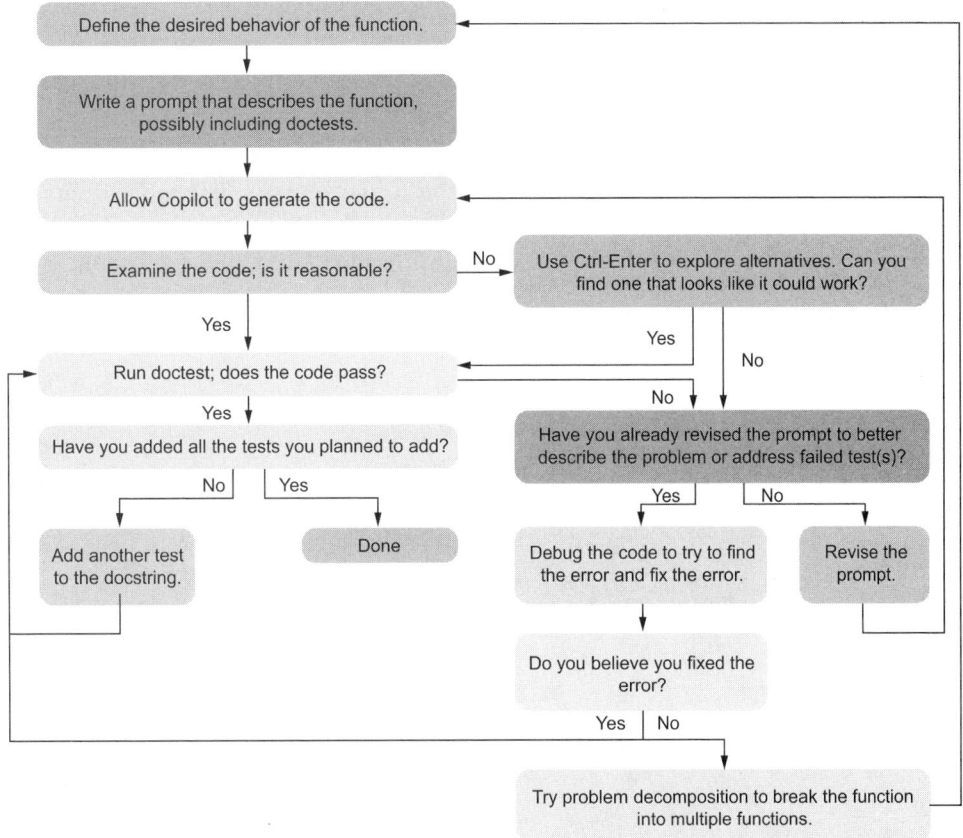

Figure 8.11 The function design cycle with Copilot, augmented to include debugging

Although the figure is starting to get a bit complicated, most of this is what you saw previously in chapter 6. The only changes here are to include debugging. Specifically, if you've already tried to revise the prompt and you still can't get code that works, then it's time to try debugging explicitly. With the tools you've gained in this chapter, you'll likely be successful at finding some bugs but not all possible bugs. If you find the bug and feel you've successfully fixed it, the flowchart sends you back to testing to make sure your fix worked (and didn't break any other test cases). On the off chance you can't get the code to work through new prompts and just can't seem to debug it, we've found that problem decomposition is often your best next step. In other words, if you can't get a function to work no matter how hard you try, the function should probably be broken into multiple functions, and you're more likely to be successful coding those smaller functions.

8.5   *Applying our debugging skills to a new problem*

With our new skills in place and a new workflow, let's try tackling a more challenging debugging problem. Remember in chapter 6 when we tried to determine the largest number of empty seats in a given row in a classroom? We're going to solve a similar problem here.

Instead of looking for empty seats, let's say that we want to count the most students seated consecutively in a row because you're trying to space them out better before an exam. You could also imagine using this to space out people more if they want more personal space or if there's a pandemic. We wrote the prompt and a basic doctest, and Copilot generated a solution. The code appears in the following listing.

Listing 8.8   First attempt to count consecutive students in a row

```
def most_students(classroom):
    '''
    classroom is a list of lists                        Our prompt
    Each ' ' is an empty seat                           to Copilot
    Each 'S' is a student

    Find the most students seated consecutively in a row

    >>> most_students([['S', ' ', 'S', ' ', 'S', 'S'],\
                       ['S', ' ', 'S', 'S', 'S', ' '],\    The first
                       [' ', 'S', ' ', 'S', ' ', ' ']])    test case
    3
    '''
    max_count = 0
    for row in classroom:
        count = 0
        for seat in row:
            if seat == 'S':                     The code
                count += 1                      from Copilot
            else:
                if count > max_count:
                    max_count = count
                count = 0
    return max_count

import doctest                      The code to run the
doctest.testmod(verbose=True)       doctest that we added
```

Given this chapter is about debugging, you can probably guess the code isn't working correctly. We caught this bug when we read the code Copilot gave us, but it's a subtle bug that we suspect could be missed fairly easily. If you see it already, great job, but pretend you didn't for the rest of the chapter. If you haven't seen it, the rest of the chapter is going to be more valuable to you.

Let's imagine then that we just wrote this prompt and test case. We read through the code, and it looks like it's probably keeping track of the most consecutive students. As long as it sees a student in a seat, it increments the count. When there isn't a student in the seat, it checks to see whether the count is bigger than any previously seen and resets the count. It seems like it's at least on the right track. We included a test case, so we ran the code, and the test case passed. We're feeling pretty good about the code but know we need to do more test cases, particularly ones to catch edge cases (remember that edge cases are uncommon cases that could break the code).

We know when we work with lists, it's good to check that the code does the right thing at the start and end of the list. To test the end of the list, let's add a test case where the largest group of consecutive students includes the last seat and then rerun the code. Here's the new test case we're adding to the docstring:

```
>>> most_students([['S', ' ', 'S', 'S', 'S', 'S'],\
                   ['S', ' ', 'S', 'S', 'S', ' '],\
                   [' ', 'S', ' ', 'S', ' ', ' ']])
4
```

◁——— **The longest group of consecutive students is 4.**

We run the code again and are surprised when the test cases fail. Here's what it told us (we reformatted the output for readability):

```
Trying:
    most_students([['S', ' ', 'S', 'S', 'S', 'S'],
                   ['S', ' ', 'S', 'S', 'S', ' '],
                   [' ', 'S', ' ', 'S', ' ', ' ']])
Expecting:
    4
**********************************************************************
File "c:\Copilot\max_consecutive.py",
line 12, in __main__.most_students

Failed example:
    most_students([['S', ' ', 'S', 'S', 'S', 'S'],
                   ['S', ' ', 'S', 'S', 'S', ' '],
                   [' ', 'S', ' ', 'S', ' ', ' ']])
Expected:
    4
Got:
    3
```

That's odd—the code seemed to be working properly. Something about this edge case has uncovered the error. At this point, we'd want to generate some hypotheses about why the code isn't working properly to help guide our debugging efforts. (If you're truly stumped, you could take the approach of just setting a breakpoint at the first line of code in the function and stepping through it rather than trying to create a hypothesis.) Here are two hypotheses that come to mind:

- The updating of count is skipping the last element in the list.
- The updating of max_count is missing the last element in the list.

To simplify the debugging process, we removed the test that is passing (just set it aside to restore later) and are only going to run the test that is failing. The following listing shows our full code before we start the debugging process.

Listing 8.9   Code that we'll debug to count consecutive students

```
def most_students(classroom):
    '''

    classroom is a list of lists
    Each ' ' is an empty seat
    Each 'S' is a student

    Find the most students seated consecutively in a row

    >>> most_students([['S', ' ', 'S', 'S', 'S', 'S'],\
                       ['S', ' ', 'S', 'S', 'S', ' '],\          Failed test case
                       [' ', 'S', ' ', 'S', ' ', ' ']])
    4
    '''
    max_count = 0
    for row in classroom:
        count = 0
        for seat in row:
            if seat == 'S':
                count += 1
            else:
                if count > max_count:
                    max_count = count
                count = 0
    return max_count

import doctest
doctest.testmod(verbose=True)
```

We'll start with the first hypothesis, that count isn't updating properly at the end of the list and set a breakpoint at the updating of count. Figure 8.12 shows the first time the debugger pauses after it's started.

From the debugger, we can see that count is still 0, so it hasn't been updated yet. We're in the first row of that first test case because row is ['S', ' ', 'S', 'S', 'S', 'S']. The seat we're looking at is an 'S', which is why the count is increasing. Let's click Continue in the Debug Toolbar to see the next update of count. The state of the debugger after clicking Continue appears in figure 8.13.

A fair bit has happened, it seems, since the last update of count because max_count is now 1. This must have happened when the empty space was processed because

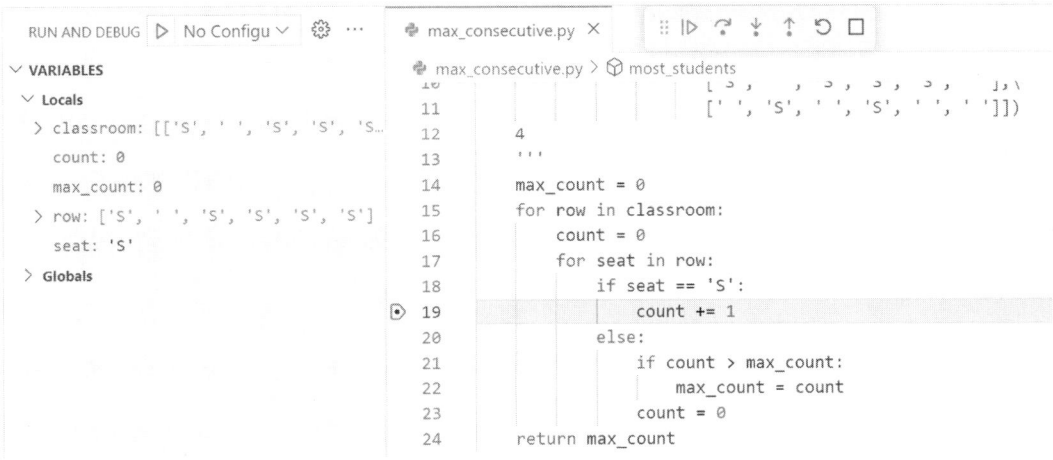

Figure 8.12   Debugger stopping before the first update of `count`

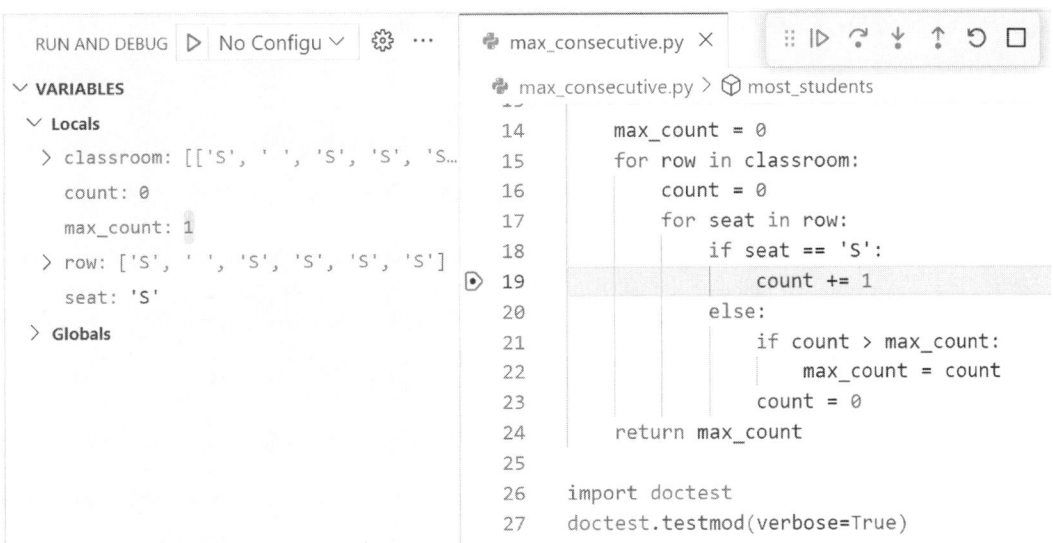

Figure 8.13   Debugger stopping before the second update of `count`

`max_count` was set to 1 and `count` was reset back to 0. At this point, we're at the third
seat in the row with a student there, and `count` is ready to update. We'll want to check
that `count` keeps updating with each new student. We clicked Continue, and `count`
increased to 1. We clicked Continue again, and the `count` increased to 2. We click
Continue once more, and the `count` increased to 3. At this point, we're at the last student in the row, and we want to check that `count` increases to 4. To check this, we

clicked Step Over once, and count indeed updates to 4. You can see the state of the debugger at this point in figure 8.14.

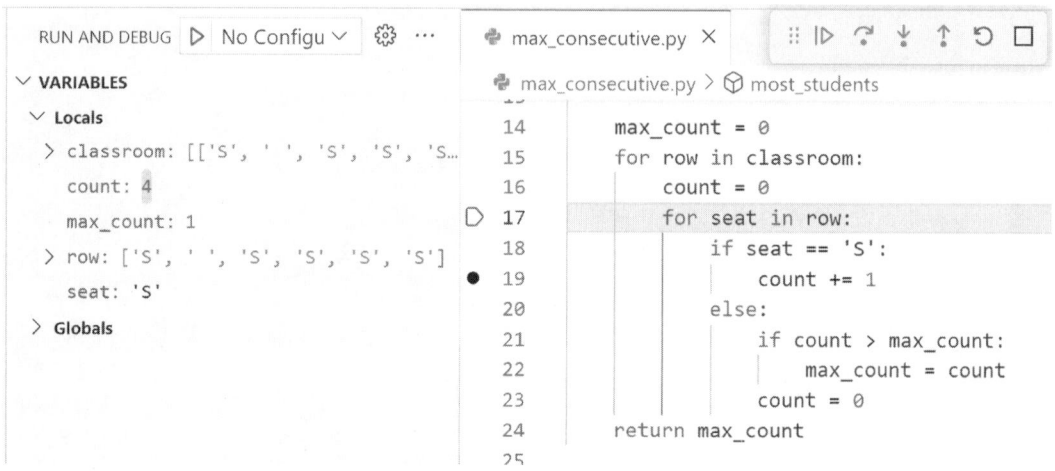

Figure 8.14   Debugger stopping right after the fourth consecutive update of count

Well, we have good news and bad news at this point. The good news is that count is properly updating. The bad news is that our first hypothesis was wrong, and we haven't found our bug yet. We could move our breakpoint to the line where max_count is updated (line 22) and then click Restart and start over the debugging process for our second hypothesis, but given that count is 4 right now in our debugger, let's just continue to trace through the code and make sure max_count gets updated. Or rather, we know it won't be, so we want to see why.

Before clicking Step Over, we've got a clue already present in the debugger. This clue comes from the fact that the next line of code to execute is for seat in row. But the student we just saw was the last student in row. This means this for loop is just about to finish (meaning we won't execute the body of the loop again, which means max_count can't get updated). Let's see whether that's what happens by clicking Step Over. The state of the debugger appears in figure 8.15.

We just finished processing the first row, but we never updated the max_count. The next line of code will pick the next row, and the line after that will set count to 0 again. We finished the loop over the row without ever updating max_count even though we found a count that's bigger than the current max_count. If you don't see the bug yet, we encourage you to step through until the next time max_count is updated, and it may be more obvious at that point.

The error in the code is that it only updates max_count when it encounters an empty seat. This means that if a row ends with a student, the code to check whether

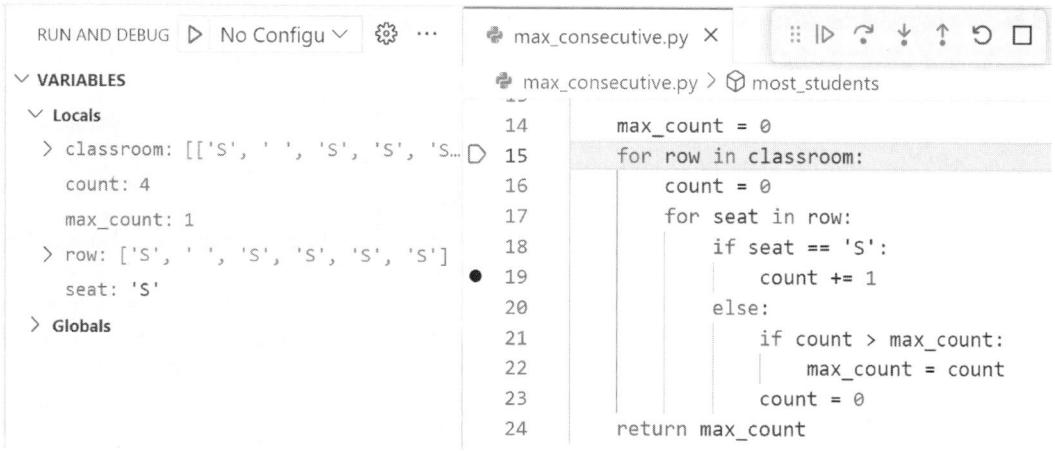

Figure 8.15   Debugger stopping after finishing the first row

`max_count` should be updated will never run for that row. Examining the code more closely, the test to see whether `max_count` should be updated and the update of `max_count` should both occur either outside the `if-else` statement or right after `count` is updated.

This is a fix we can probably just make manually because all we need to do is move two lines of code to a better location. The code in listing 8.10 is the corrected function (without the tests or prompts).

Listing 8.10   Corrected function to count consecutive students

```python
def most_students(classroom):
    max_count = 0
    for row in classroom:
        count = 0
        for seat in row:
            if seat == 'S':
                count += 1
                if count > max_count:        Moved the testing of count
                    max_count = count         against max_count to
            else:                             immediately after the
                count = 0                     updating of count
    return max_count
```

This new code does pass the test that failed with the old code and the original test. After adding another test that makes sure the code works when the longest group of consecutive students appears at the start of the row, we're more confident the code is now working properly.

8.6   *Using the debugger to better understand code*

We suspect you're already pretty impressed by the debugger. We are too. When students were taught programming in the traditional manner, a lot of time was spent making sure students could essentially trace through code like a debugger would, drawing out the state of all the variables and updating them with each new line of execution. Indeed, there's even a free tool on the web called Python Tutor [2] that creates diagrams of the state of memory that can be easier to read than a debugger, just to help new programmers learn how the code executes.

Whether you like using the debugger or want to use a tool like Python Tutor, we encourage you to play with some of the code you've written from earlier sections of the book. In our personal experience working with people learning how to program, walking through a program line by line and watching how the state of variables changes can be a truly enlightening experience, and we hope you'll appreciate it too.

8.7   *A caution about debugging*

From working with students, we've also seen that debugging can be a really frustrating experience for new learners [3]. When learning how to program, everyone wants their code to work, and finding and fixing bugs is time spent when things aren't working. There are a couple of ways to help overcome this frustration. First, problem decomposition can go a really long way to helping you get code from Copilot that is right without the need for extensive debugging. Second, remember that everyone's code doesn't work sometimes, including ours. It's just a natural part of the programming process and a part that can take some practice. Last, always, and we mean always, test every function you write. More often than not, when our students are really stuck debugging, it's because there are bugs in multiple functions interacting as a result of not testing each function. When that happens, it's exceptionally hard to find and remedy the bugs. Debugging interacting bugs is so frustrating that avoiding the experience is a big reason why both of us religiously test every function we write.

The good news is that if you test every function you write and diligently break down problems into small, manageable steps, you shouldn't find yourself debugging that often. And, if you do, you'll be debugging the error in one function, which is what essentially every programmer on the planet does. With some practice, you'll get the hang of it.

8.8   *Exercises*

1   You're given a Python function that is supposed to calculate the sum of all even numbers in a list. However, the function isn't working correctly. When you call the function with the list [1, 2, 3, 4], it returns 4 instead of 6:

```
def sum_even_numbers(numbers):
    total = 0
    for number in numbers:
        if number % 2 == 0:
```

```
            total += number
        else:
            total = 0
    return total
```

Identify the bug in the `sum_even_numbers` function, and explain how to fix it. Modify the code to correct the bug, and verify your solution with the provided test case.

2 You're given a Python function that is supposed to find the maximum number in a list of numbers. However, the function isn't working as expected. Your task is to determine why the function is working incorrectly, and how you can fix this (hint, think about the possible integer values in the input list):

```
def find_max(numbers):
    max_number = 0
    for i in range(0, len(numbers)):
        if numbers[i] > max_number:
            max_number = numbers[i]
    return max_number
```

3 You're given a Python function that is supposed to check if a string is a valid password. A valid password must meet the following criteria:

a It must be at least 8 characters long.

b It must contain at least one uppercase letter.

c It must contain at least one lowercase letter.

d It must contain at least one digit.

However, the function isn't working correctly. Determine what is wrong with the function and fix it:

```
def is_valid_password(password):
    if len(password) <= 8:
        if any(char.isupper() for char in password):
            if any(char.islower() for char in password):
                if any(char.isdigit() for char in password):
                    return True
            return False
        return False
    return False
```

4 You're writing a Python function to greet users based on the time of day. The function takes an hour (integer between 0 and 23) as input and returns a greeting message ("Good morning", "Good afternoon", or "Good evening"):

```
def greet_user(hour):
  # This code has an error!
  if hour < 12:
    greeting = "Good morning"
  else:
```

```
        greeting = "Good evening"
    return greeting
```

You're considering using this prompt to ask Copilot to help you fix the bug: "I have a function to greet users based on the time of day, but it seems to classify noon as 'Good evening'. Can you help me fix the logic?" The prompt mentions the problem but doesn't pinpoint the exact error. See if you can edit the provided prompt to make it more specific and guide Copilot toward suggesting the correct fix.

Summary

- Debugging is an important skill that includes finding errors in code and then correcting them.
- `Print` statements can be an effective way of learning about what is happening in your code.
- The VS Code debugger is another way of learning what is happening in your code that provides powerful features for monitoring how variables change as the code executes.
- Once an error is uncovered, there are multiple ways to help Copilot fix the error for you, but if that fails, you can often fix the code directly.
- Our workflow of designing functions now includes debugging, and with the skill of debugging, you're more apt to write the software you want.
- Outside of debugging, the VS Code debugger can be a powerful tool in learning more about how the code works.

Automating tedious tasks

9

This chapter covers

- Understanding why programmers write tools
- Determining which modules we need to write a given tool
- Automating cleaning up emails that have > > > symbols
- Automating manipulating PDF files
- Automating removing duplicate pictures across multiple image libraries

Suppose that you're responsible for creating 100 reports, one for each of 100 people. Perhaps you're a teacher and need to send a report to each of your students. Perhaps you work for HR and need to send an annual assessment report to each employee. Regardless of your role, you have the problem of having to create these reports, and you decided to prepare your reports as .pdf files. You need a customized cover page for each report too, and those cover pages are designed by one of your colleagues (a graphic design artist).

You and your colleague work independently, and, finally, the job is done. Or wait, not so fast. Because now you have to put each cover page at the beginning of each report.

At this point, a nonprogrammer might grit their teeth and start on the job, manually merging the cover page with the first report, the second cover page with the second report, and so on. That could take hours. Not knowing that there may be another way, a nonprogrammer may just power ahead until the job is done.

But you're a programmer now. And most programmers, the two of us included, would never power ahead with manual work like this.

In this chapter, we're going to show you how to write programs to automate tedious tasks. The second example in the chapter will automate the "merging cover pages with reports" situation. But we'll do others as well. Received an email that's been forwarded so many times

> > > > > > that it looks

like

> > > > > > this?

Or does your family have several phones, each with hundreds of images, and you just want to get the images all in the same place so that you can archive them without losing anything? In this chapter, we'll show you how to automate tasks like that.

9.1   Why programmers make tools

There's a common sentiment that programmers often express: we're lazy. This doesn't mean that we don't want to do our work. It means that we don't want to do *repetitive, boring, tedious* work because that's what computers are good at. Programmers develop a sort of spidey-sense for this kind of drudgery. Suppose Leo has a few hundred photos, and he wants to delete any photos that are duplicates. There's no way he'd do this by hand. Or suppose that Dan has to send out a customized email to each of his students. If it's more than a few students, there's no way he's doing this by hand. As soon as programmers start noticing that they're repeating the same keys on the keyboard or working through the same steps over and over, they'll stop and make a tool to automate it.

When programmers talk about tools, they're talking about programs that do something that saves them time. A tool often isn't the end goal, and writing one can itself feel tedious and not glamorous. But once we have a tool, we can use it to save us time. Sometimes, we'll use a tool once, for one specific job, and then never again. Commonly, though, a tool ends up being useful over and over, whether we use the tool exactly as we wrote it or by making some small changes. For example, after Dan finishes teaching each course, he uses a program he wrote to collate all student grades and submit them to the university. He makes small changes to the tool each time—changing the weights of each assignment, for example—but then Dan can use that slightly modified tool to do the work.

The great thing about using Copilot is that it makes cranking out these tools easier. Here's how one software engineer explains it:

We all know that tools are important, that effective tools are challenging to create, and that management doesn't care or understand the need for tools. . . . I can't express how fundamentally different programming feels now that I can build two quality tools per day, for every single itch I want to scratch. [1]

9.2   How to use Copilot to write tools

As we learned in chapter 5 when talking about modules, sometimes we need to use a module to help us write the program we want. Some modules are built into Python. For example, in chapter 5, we used the built-in zipfile module to help us create a .zip file. Other modules aren't built in, and we need to install them first before we can use them.

When writing a tool, it's often the case that we'll be working with some specialized data format (zip files, PDF files, Microsoft Excel spreadsheets, images) or performing some specialized task (sending email, interacting with a website, moving files around). For most of this, we're going to need to use a module. Which module, though? And is it built in, or do we need to install it? These are the first questions we need to get answers to.

Fortunately, we can use Copilot Chat (or ChatGPT) to help us get started. As a reminder, we're using the Copilot Chat feature because it's built into our Visual Studio Code (VS Code) IDE and because Copilot Chat has access to the very code we're currently writing so it can incorporate what we're doing into its answers.

The plan is to have a conversation with Copilot to determine which module we need to use. Once we know that and install the module, if necessary, then we can get down to the business of writing the code for our tool. We'll do that the way we've always done it: by writing the function header and a docstring and having Copilot fill in the code for us. Once Copilot starts writing code, we need to follow the same steps as in previous chapters, including checking code correctness, fixing bugs, and maybe even doing some problem decomposition. To focus our attention on writing tools to automate tasks, we'll minimize the time we spend on these additional tasks here.

It may be possible to ask Copilot or ChatGPT to write the entire tool for us, without even having to put it inside of a function. We won't do that here, though, because we still think that the benefits of functions are worthwhile. A function will help us document our code so that we know what it does, and it enables flexibility if we later decide, for example, to add additional parameters to our function to change the behavior of the tool.

9.3   Example 1: Cleaning up email text

Sometimes, an email gets replied to and forwarded so many times that it becomes a mess, with many greater than (>) signs and spaces on some of the lines. Here's a sample email of what we mean:

> > > Hi Leo,
> > >   > > Dan – any luck with your natural language research?

>>>Yes! That website you showed me

https://www.kaggle.com/

>>>is very useful. I found a dataset on there that collects
a lot

>>>of questions and answers that might be useful to my research.

>>>Thank you,

>>>Dan

Suppose that you wanted to save this email information for future use. You might like to clean up the > and space symbols at the start of lines. You could start manually deleting them—this email isn't that long, after all—but don't do that because here you have an opportunity to design a general-purpose tool that you can use whenever you need to perform this task. Whether your email has five lines, a hundred lines, or a million lines, it won't matter: just use the tool and be done.

9.3.1   *Conversing with Copilot*

We need to make the messy email available to our tool so that the tool can clean it up. One way we can do this is to first copy the text of an email to the clipboard (using your Copy to Clipboard command on your operating system, such as Ctrl-C).

Each computer operating system has a clipboard to store the last thing copied. If you've ever used Copy-Paste, you've used that clipboard. We're going to use the clipboard for temporary storage of text so we can edit the text in the clipboard and then paste it where we need it.

After copying the text from the messy email to the clipboard, we could then run the tool on the text in the clipboard, and the tool could clean up the email and replace the clipboard contents with the cleaned-up version. For the tool to do something reasonable, we assume that your clipboard has email text on it. The tool will remove the > and space characters at the start of each line so that you can paste (using your operating system Paste command, such as Ctrl-V) the newly cleaned-up email wherever you want. In terms of Python, it will need to pull the clipboard contents into a string (i.e., copy the contents of the clipboard), clean it up, and then put that new cleaned-up text back on the clipboard (i.e., paste to the clipboard), replacing the junky version of the email that was there before.

So, how do we access the clipboard in our Python program? That's what we need to figure out, so that will frame the conversation that we have with Copilot. Similar to chapter 8, we're going to use "Human" for the prompts that we type and "GitHub Copilot" for Copilot's responses. You can use the Copilot Chat feature or ChatGPT to have a similar conversation. We're typing our prompts into the Copilot Chat window.

In our chats with Copilot, we're going to explore widely before settling on a solution. We'll explain why we're doing this once we've gotten the hang of things through one example, but we note this here so that you'll be ready for this seemingly less direct approach. Copilot provides quite a bit of sample code in its responses. As we're exploring, feel free to skim that code, but don't get bogged down in it. We'll look at more particulars of the code once we finish exploring and settle on a plan. Let's start learning!

> **Human**   I would like to write a Python program that accesses the clipboard and lets me copy and paste using the clipboard. How can I do this?

> **GitHub Copilot**   You can use the pyperclip module to access the clipboard in Python. Here's an example program that lets you copy and paste using the clipboard:

```python
import pyperclip

# Copy to clipboard
pyperclip.copy('Hello, world!')

# Paste from clipboard
text = pyperclip.paste()

print(text)
```

> This program first imports the pyperclip module. It then copies the string `'Hello, world!'` to the clipboard using the `copy()` function. Finally, it pastes the contents of the clipboard into the "text" variable using the `paste()` function and prints the result.

> You can install the pyperclip module using pip by running `pip install pyperclip` in your terminal.

Copilot's response teaches us that we can use the pyperclip module to interact with the clipboard in our Python program. The sample code that it provided even showed us how to copy stuff from our program to the clipboard and paste stuff from the clipboard into a variable (`text`). We're making great progress!

The final paragraph of the response tells us how to install pyperclip. Aha! So pyperclip doesn't come with Python by default. While we'll learn how to install modules later, it might be nice to not have to worry about that. So, let's continue the conversation, asking Copilot if we can do better.

> **Human**   Is there a way I can do it without having to install a Python module?

> **GitHub Copilot**   Yes, you can use the tkinter module that comes with Python to access the clipboard. Here's an example program that lets you copy and paste using the clipboard without installing any additional modules:

```python
import tkinter as tk

# Create a Tkinter window
root = tk.Tk()
```

```
# Hide the window
root.withdraw()

# Copy to clipboard
root.clipboard_clear()
root.clipboard_append('Hello, world!')

# Paste from clipboard
text = root.clipboard_get()

print(text)
```

This program first creates a hidden Tkinter window using the `Tk()` function and hides it using the `withdraw()` method. It then clears the clipboard using the `clipboard_clear()` method and appends the string `'Hello, world!'` to the clipboard using the `clipboard_append()` method. Finally, it retrieves the contents of the clipboard using the `clipboard_get()` method and prints the result.

Note that this method only works if you have a graphical environment available, such as a desktop environment on Linux or macOS, or the Windows desktop on Windows. If you're running Python in a terminal-only environment, you'll need to use a different method to access the clipboard.

It seems that we've won something and lost something else. The win is that this tkinter module is built into Python. The loss is that "the method only works if you have a graphical environment available." Do we have a graphical environment available in our Python setup? While we could certainly try the code to find out, this requirement gives us pause. After all, the pyperclip solution didn't have that requirement, so we might not need it (whatever it happens to mean). Let's try again.

Human   Is there another way I can do it without having to install a Python module?

GitHub Copilot   Yes, you can access the clipboard using the win32clipboard module, which is included in the standard library on Windows. Here's an example program that allows you to copy and paste using the clipboard without installing any additional modules:

```python
import win32clipboard

# Copy to clipboard
text = "Hello, world!"
win32clipboard.OpenClipboard()
win32clipboard.EmptyClipboard()
win32clipboard.SetClipboardText(text)
win32clipboard.CloseClipboard()

# Paste from clipboard
win32clipboard.OpenClipboard()
pasted_text = win32clipboard.GetClipboardData()
```

```
win32clipboard.CloseClipboard()
print(pasted_text)
```

This program first imports the win32clipboard module. To copy text to the clipboard, you can call the `OpenClipboard()` function to open the clipboard, then call `Empty-Clipboard()` to clear any existing data, and finally call `SetClipboardText()` to set the text on the clipboard. After setting the text, you should call `CloseClipboard()` to close the clipboard.

To paste from the clipboard, you can call `OpenClipboard()` to open the clipboard, then call `GetClipboardData()` to get the text from the clipboard. After getting the text, you should call `CloseClipboard()` to close the clipboard. In this example, the program copies the text `"Hello, world!"` to the clipboard, then pastes it and prints it to the console.

"Standard library on Windows," eh? That's concerning because it means that our tool might not work on other operating systems. Let's see about that.

Human Does that work on Linux or macOS too?

GitHub Copilot No, the win32clipboard module is specific to Windows and won't work on Linux or macOS. On Linux, you can use the `xclip` command-line utility to access the clipboard. Here's an example program that allows you to copy and paste using the clipboard on Linux:

```python
import subprocess

# Copy to clipboard
text = "Hello, world!"
subprocess.run(['xclip', '-selection', 'clipboard'],
input=text.encode('utf-8'))

# Paste from clipboard
p = subprocess.Popen(['xclip', '-selection', 'clipboard', '-o'], std-
out=subprocess.PIPE)
pasted_text = p.stdout.read().decode('utf-8')
print(pasted_text)
```

This program uses the subprocess module to run the `xclip` command-line utility. To copy text to the clipboard, you can call `subprocess.run()` and pass in the `xclip` command with the `-selection clipboard` option to specify the clipboard selection, and the `input` parameter to pass in the text you want to copy. To paste from the clipboard, you can call `subprocess.Popen()` and pass in the `xclip` command with the `-selection clipboard -o` options to read the text from the clipboard, and then read the output of the command using the `stdout` attribute of the `Popen` object. In this example, the program copies the text `"Hello, world!"` to the clipboard, then pastes it and prints it to the console.

On macOS, you can use the `pbcopy` and `pbpaste` command-line utilities to access the clipboard. The usage is similar to `xclip`.

We've gotten some solutions that are specific to different operating systems. We don't like this! We want our tool to work no matter which operating system we're using. (Even if we're using only Windows ourselves, maybe one day, we'll share this tool with others who use different operating systems.)

We could continue our conversation, but in retrospect, having to install that single pyperclip module doesn't seem so bad. Let's go ahead with it. In general, it can be valuable to explore your options when deciding how to start writing a tool, and conversing with Copilot is helpful for carrying out this exploration.

Why we should explore and understand our options

There are several reasons why you shouldn't just use the first module that Copilot chat tells you to use:

- It may not work on all operating systems. In general, we want to find modules that work across multiple operating systems so that the tool can be used by you (if you later switch operating systems) or others with whom you've shared the tool.
- It may turn out not to work for our use case after all, or we may struggle to get the code to work. If we have other options, we can start trying those before sinking too much time into a strategy that may or may not ultimately work out.
- Modules are updated frequently. Usually this is to add new features and fix bugs, but sometimes, functions are removed or changed in this process as well. When the author of a module removes a function, it's known as *deprecating that function*. Once a function is deprecated, it may no longer work, and we need to find a replacement. Copilot is trained only every once in a while, not continuously, so if a new version of a module comes out after Copilot was trained on it, Copilot won't know about the updates. This can lead to Copilot suggesting code that depends on an older version of the module than the one you have. There are ways to address this, as we'll see later in the chapter. But if you run into trouble, having other options to explore is useful.

9.3.2 *Writing the tool to clean up email*

The first thing we need to do is to install the pyperclip module. How do we install it, though? The good news is that Python has made it easy to install new modules. Go to the Terminal at the bottom right of VS Code and type the following:

```
pip install pyperclip
```

> **NOTE** For some operating systems, you may need to use `pip3` rather than `pip`. On Windows machines, we recommend using `pip` if you followed our installation instructions from chapter 2. On Mac or Linux machines, we recommend using `pip3`.

When you run this command, you might see that other modules get installed too. Don't worry about that: sometimes modules need other modules to be able to do their work, and Python just installs them all so that you don't have to worry about installing those dependencies yourself.

Once that's installed, we can import the module and then write the header and docstring for our function that will remove the > and space characters from the start of lines. The reason we're importing the module here is to influence Copilot to use that module when writing the code for the function. Here's the prompt we used and the code that Copilot gave us.

Listing 9.1   First try: Clean up email text in the clipboard

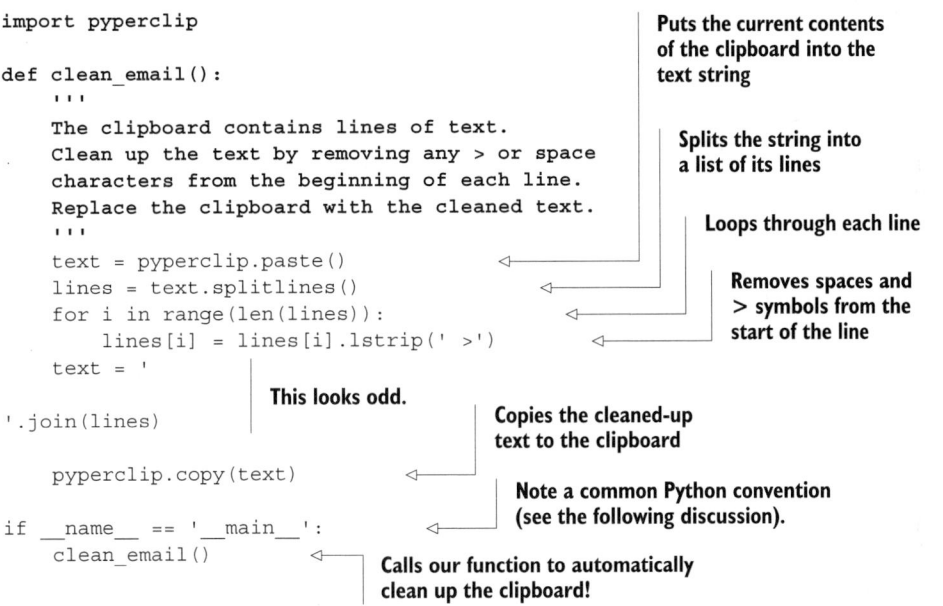

```
import pyperclip

def clean_email():
    '''
    The clipboard contains lines of text.
    Clean up the text by removing any > or space
    characters from the beginning of each line.
    Replace the clipboard with the cleaned text.
    '''
    text = pyperclip.paste()
    lines = text.splitlines()
    for i in range(len(lines)):
        lines[i] = lines[i].lstrip(' >')
    text = '
'.join(lines)

    pyperclip.copy(text)

if __name__ == '__main__':
    clean_email()
```

Puts the current contents of the clipboard into the text string

Splits the string into a list of its lines

Loops through each line

Removes spaces and > symbols from the start of the line

This looks odd.

Copies the cleaned-up text to the clipboard

Note a common Python convention (see the following discussion).

Calls our function to automatically clean up the clipboard!

We can see that the program is carrying out the correct sequence of steps: it's obtaining the clipboard contents, cleaning up that text, and then copying the cleaned-up text back to the clipboard. As we learned from our earlier chat with Copilot, we want Copilot to write code that uses the `paste` and `copy` functions of `pyperclip`, and that's exactly what it's doing. The second-to-last line of the program is something we haven't seen before in this book:

```
if __name__ == '__main__':
```

You can actually remove this line if you like (and if you do, also unindent the line below it). It ensures that the `clean_email` function is only called when you run your program, not when you import it as a module. After all, if you did want to import this as a module (to be used as part of a larger program), you would call `clean_email` whenever you needed that functionality, not necessarily as soon as the module was imported. (And, in general, whenever you're interested in understanding a line of code more fully, you can ask Copilot about it!) Unfortunately, this code doesn't work. If you run it, you'll receive this error:

```
File "C:\repos\book_code\ch9\email_cleanup.py", line 14
    text = '
           ^
SyntaxError: unterminated string literal (detected at line 14)
```

The syntax error means that we have a program that isn't written in valid Python code. We're going to fix this now! We have a couple of options for how to do so. One is to highlight your code and ask Copilot Chat to fix the bug. For us, this did fix the problem. You could also try asking ChatGPT in conversation: "Propose a fix for the bugs in my code <insert your code>." This is a useful tip to keep in mind whenever the code that you get back from Copilot doesn't work as expected.

Copilot fixed the code for us by fixing the line with the syntax error. The new code is shown in the following listing.

Listing 9.2   Second try: Clean up email text in the clipboard

```
import pyperclip

def clean_email():
    '''
    The clipboard contains lines of text.
    Clean up the text by removing any > or space
    characters from the beginning of each line.
    Replace the clipboard with the cleaned text.
    '''
    text = pyperclip.paste()
    lines = text.splitlines()
    for i in range(len(lines)):
        lines[i] = lines[i].lstrip(' >')
    text = '\n'.join(lines)       ◁────┐  Joins the individual
                                        │  lines back into one
    pyperclip.copy(text)                │  string

if __name__ == '__main__':
    clean_email()
```

The new line of code, changed from the odd line of code that we had previously, is

```
text = '\n'.join(lines)
```

The goal of this line is to join all the lines of text together into a single string that the program will later copy to the clipboard. What does that \n mean? That represents the start of a newline in code. What is the `join` method? It takes all the items in a list (lines) and joins them together into a single string.

We can understand how this works in more detail by experimenting a little with `join`. Here's an example of using `join` with an empty string rather than the `'\n'` string:

```
>>> lines = ['first line', 'second', 'the last line']
>>> print(''.join(lines))
first linesecondthe last line
```

Shows the list of three lines ←

Calls join on the empty string ←

Notice that some of the words are squished together. That's not exactly what we want—we need something between them. How about a space? Let's try using `join` again, this time with a space in the string rather than the empty string:

```
>>> print(' '.join(lines))
first line second the last line
```

Or, we could use `'*'`:

```
>>> print('*'.join(lines))
first line*second*the last line
```

That fixes our squished words. And, the `*`s tells us where each line ends, but it would be nicer to actually maintain the fact that the email is three lines.

We need a way in Python to use a line break or newline character, rather than a space or `*`. We can't just press Enter because that would split the string over two lines and that isn't valid Python syntax. The way to do it is by using `'\n'`:

```
>>> print('\n'.join(lines))
first line
second
the last line
```

Now our tool is ready to be used. If you copy some messy email text to your clipboard, run our program, and paste the clipboard, you'll see that the email has been cleaned up. For example, if we run it on our previous sample email, we get the following cleaned-up version:

> Hi Leo,
> Dan – any luck with your natural language research?
> Yes! That website you showed me
> https://www.kaggle.com/
> is very useful. I found a dataset on there that collects
> a lot
> of questions and answers that might be useful to my research.
> Thank you,
> Dan

Of course, we could still do more. The line breaks in that email aren't great (the line "a lot" is extremely and needlessly short), and you might want to clean that up as well.

You could begin to make these kinds of improvements by adding new requirements to your prompts to Copilot. We'll stop here because we've accomplished our initial goal of email cleanup, but we encourage you to continue exploring more robust solutions on your own.

9.4   Example 2: Adding cover pages to PDF files

Let's return to the scenario from the start of the chapter. We have written 100 reports that are in .pdf format. Our colleague has designed 100 covers for those reports that are also in .pdf format, and we need to merge the covers with the reports so that each finalized .pdf file starts with the cover and continues with the report. Figure 9.1 provides an illustration of the desired process.

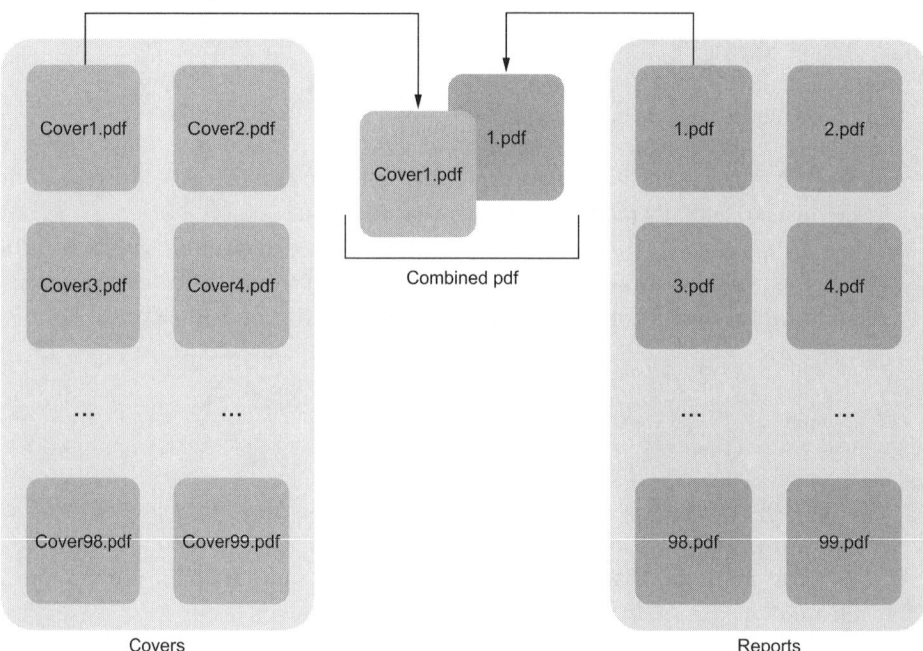

Figure 9.1   Illustration of the desired process of creating combined .pdfs by merging the report cover in the cover directory with the report in the report's directory. Note that the reports may be more than one page.

PDF files (and Microsoft Word and Excel files) aren't text files

You might wonder why we can't simply use Python methods such as `read` and `write` to manipulate .pdf files. After all, that's just what we did when working with .csv files in chapter 2.

The big difference is that .csv files are text files, which are files readable by humans with no formatting or special commands. However, many other file formats aren't text files. A .pdf file, for example, isn't human-readable and needs to be processed by code that is aware of the .pdf format. This is true of Microsoft Word files and Microsoft Excel files as well: they're not text files, so we need specialized tools to work with them.

In the resources for this book, in the ch9 folder, you'll find two subfolders: the reports subfolder contains 100 reports as .pdf files, and the covers subfolder contains 100 covers as .pdf files, one for each report. The reports are named 1.pdf, 2.pdf, 3.pdf, and so on; the respective covers are named cover1.pdf, cover2.pdf, cover3.pdf, and so on. We'll merge these reports and covers together in this section.

Open some of the cover .pdf files and some of the report .pdf files. You can do that using a program such as Adobe Acrobat or however you typically open .pdf files on your computer. You'll notice that the covers are always exactly one page, but the reports can be more than one page. When we get to the code, we should take care to tell Copilot that reports can be more than one page; otherwise, Copilot might write code assuming that the reports, like the covers, are only one page.

You might be wondering how we created these 100 covers and reports. You'd be disappointed if we made them manually, one at a time, right? Don't worry. We automated that creation process in much the same way we'll automate the merging process next.

9.4.1   Conversing with Copilot

We need our tool to find all reports and covers, add the cover to the front of each report, and produce a finalized .pdf for each report that contains both the cover page and report pages. How do we merge .pdf files using Python? Let's find out.

Human   I need to write a Python program that merges .pdf files. How do I do this?

GitHub Copilot   You can use the PyPDF2 library to merge PDF files in Python. Here is an example code snippet that shows how to merge two PDF files:

```python
import PyPDF2

# Open the PDF files to be merged
pdf1 = open('file1.pdf', 'rb')
pdf2 = open('file2.pdf', 'rb')

# Create a PDF reader object for each file
reader1 = PyPDF2.PdfFileReader(pdf1)
reader2 = PyPDF2.PdfFileReader(pdf2)
```

```python
# Create a PDF writer object
writer = PyPDF2.PdfFileWriter()

# Loop through the pages of each PDF and add them to the writer object
for i in range(reader1.getNumPages()):
    page = reader1.getPage(i)
    writer.addPage(page)

for i in range(reader2.getNumPages()):
    page = reader2.getPage(i)
    writer.addPage(page)

# Write the merged PDF to a file
output = open('merged.pdf', 'wb')
writer.write(output)

# Close the input and output files
pdf1.close()
pdf2.close()
output.close()
```

In this example, we first open the two PDF files to be merged using the `open()` function. We then create a PDF reader object for each file using the `PdfFileReader()` function from PyPDF2.

Next, we create a PDF writer object using the `PdfFileWriter()` function. We then loop through the pages of each PDF file using the `getNumPages()` and `getPage()` methods of the reader objects and add each page to the writer object using the `addPage()` method.

Finally, we write the merged PDF to a file using the `write()` method of the writer object and close all the input and output files using the `close()` method.

We have a lead! This PyPDF2 module seems to do what we need. It looks like it gives us `PdfFileReader` to read an existing .pdf file and `PdfFileWriter` to create a new .pdf file. We see the code using `getPage` to get a page from an existing .pdf file and `addPage` to write it to the new .pdf file—very promising. Is there something built-in to Python that we could use, so that we don't have to worry about installing PyPDF2?

Human   Is there a way I can do it without having to install a Python module?

GitHub Copilot   Yes, you can use the subprocess module to call a command-line tool like `pdftk` to merge PDF files. Here is an example code snippet that shows how to merge two PDF files using `pdftk`:

```python
import subprocess

# Call pdftk to merge the PDF files
subprocess.call(['pdftk', 'file1.pdf', 'file2.pdf',
                 'cat', 'output', 'merged.pdf'])
```

In this example, we use the `subprocess.call()` function to call `pdftk` with the appropriate arguments to merge the two PDF files `file1.pdf` and `file2.pdf`. The `cat` argument tells `pdftk` to concatenate the input files, and the `output` argument specifies the output file name as `merged.pdf`.

Note that you will need to have `pdftk` installed on your system for this code to work. If you don't have `pdftk` installed, you can download it from the official website: https://www.pdflabs.com/tools/pdftk-the-pdf-toolkit/.

This approach may ultimately end up being valuable, but it's not exactly a built-in solution. After all, the final paragraph talks about us having to install some new software called `pdftk`!

At this point, we'd probably go with the first option of using PyPDF2. But let's press forward once more with Copilot to make sure we don't miss any good options.

Human Are there other Python .pdf libraries that I should consider?

GitHub Copilot Yes, there are several other Python libraries that you can use to work with PDF files. Here are some popular ones:

1 ReportLab—a library for creating PDF documents from scratch, with support for text, graphics, and images.

2 FPDF—a library for creating PDF documents from scratch, with support for text, graphics, and images.

3 PDFMiner—a library for extracting text and metadata from PDF files.

4 PyMuPDF—a library for working with PDF files, with support for text, graphics, and images.

5 pdfrw—a library for reading and writing PDF files, with support for text, graphics, and images.

Each library has its own strengths and weaknesses, so you should choose the one that best fits your needs. If you only need to merge PDF files, then PyPDF2 or pdftk may be sufficient. However, if you need to create or manipulate PDF files in more complex ways, then one of the other libraries may be a better choice.

The last paragraph tells us that we're probably in good shape using PyPDF2 if all we need to do is merge .pdf files. But let's finish our conversation here by understanding the pros and cons of all of these tools. That way, if we get stuck with PyPDF2, we know where to turn to next.

Human Can you summarize the strengths and weaknesses of these libraries?

GitHub Copilot Certainly! Here is a summary of the strengths and weaknesses of the libraries I mentioned:

PyPDF2—a library for working with PDF files, with support for text, graphics, and images.

Strengths:

1 Easy to use for simple tasks like merging PDF files.

2 Good documentation and examples available.

3 Supports a wide range of PDF features.

Weaknesses:

1 Limited support for advanced PDF features like forms and annotations.

2 Can be slow for large PDF files.

ReportLab—a library for creating PDF documents from scratch, with support for text, graphics, and images.

Strengths:

1 Very powerful and flexible for creating complex PDF documents.

2 Supports a wide range of PDF features.

3 Good documentation and examples available.

Weaknesses:

1 Steep learning curve for beginners.

2 Can be slow for large PDF files.

FPDF—a library for creating PDF documents from scratch, with support for text, graphics, and images.

Strengths:

1 Lightweight and easy to use.

2 Good documentation and examples available.

3 Supports a wide range of PDF features.

Weaknesses:

1 Limited support for advanced PDF features like forms and annotations.

2 Can be slow for large PDF files.

PDFMiner—a library for extracting text and metadata from PDF files.

Strengths:

1 Very powerful and flexible for extracting text and metadata from PDF files.

2 Supports a wide range of PDF features.

3 Good documentation and examples available.

Weaknesses:

1 Steep learning curve for beginners.

2 Limited support for creating or manipulating PDF files.

PyMuPDF—a library for working with PDF files, with support for text, graphics, and images.

Strengths:

1 Very fast and efficient for working with PDF files.

2 Supports a wide range of PDF features.

3 Good documentation and examples available.

Weaknesses:

1 Steep learning curve for beginners.

2 Limited support for creating or manipulating PDF files.

pdfrw—a library for reading and writing PDF files, with support for text, graphics, and images.

Strengths:

1 Very powerful and flexible for reading and writing PDF files.

2 Supports a wide range of PDF features.

3 Good documentation and examples available.

Weaknesses:

1 Steep learning curve for beginners.

2 Can be slow for large PDF files.

Don't be too intimidated by the "Steep learning curve for beginners" cautions in there. If Copilot has been trained on the library, then you may still be successful.

Based on what we've learned here, we might eliminate PDFMiner because it apparently has "limited support for creating or manipulating PDF files," but we'd keep all others in contention just in case we need them. For now, we're going to proceed with PyPDF2 and see how it goes.

9.4.2 *Writing the tool*

Go ahead and install the PyPDF2 module. Be careful with the capitalization: the module is called exactly PyPDF2, not pypdf2, pyPDF2, or any other capitalization.

In our previous example, we wrote a function to clean up an email that was on the clipboard. We didn't need to pass any information to that function, so the function had no parameters. Here, our function will need three parameters: the name of the directory with the reports, the name of the directory with the covers, and the name of the directory where we want to write our finalized (merged) .pdf files.

In our docstring, we need to explain what each of these directories is for and also the pattern of the filenames in the directories. After all, Copilot will need to know how the reports match up with the cover pages.

TRYING PYPDF2

We're going to use the PyPDF2 Python library to try to get the job done. Look back to what Copilot Chat told us about the PyPDF2 library. The sample code it gave us used `PdfFileReader` to read existing .pdf files and `PdfFileWriter` to create a new .pdf file. It also used `getPage` and `addPage` to manipulate pages. Look out for these in the code that Copilot produces—they're telltale signs that Copilot is generating code that's on the right track. Here's the prompt that we used and the code that Copilot gave us.

Listing 9.3   Function to add covers to .pdf documents

```python
import PyPDF2

def add_covers(report_dir, cover_dir, final_dir):
    '''
    report_dir is a directory of reports named 1.pdf, 2.pdf, and so on.
    These files may be one page or more than one page.

    cover_dir is a directory of covers, with one cover per report.
    The filenames in this directory are cover1.pdf, cover2.pdf, and
    so on. Each of these files is one page.

    Add the cover to the beginning of each report,
    and store all resulting pdfs in final_dir.
    '''
    report_files = os.listdir(report_dir)
    for report_file in report_files:
        report = open(os.path.join(report_dir, report_file), 'rb')
        report_reader = PyPDF2.PdfFileReader(report)
        report_writer = PyPDF2.PdfFileWriter()
        for page_num in range(report_reader.numPages):
            report_writer.addPage( \
            report_reader.getPage(page_num))
        cover = open(os.path.join(cover_dir,
                    'cover' + report_file), 'rb')
        cover_reader = PyPDF2.PdfFileReader(cover)
        report_writer.insertPage( \
                    cover_reader.getPage(0), 0)
        result = open(os.path.join(final_dir, report_file), 'wb')
        report_writer.write(result)
        report.close()
        cover.close()
        result.close()

if __name__ == '__main__':
    add_covers('reports', 'covers', 'final')
```

Gets list of the .pdf reports

Loops through the .pdf reports

Adds the cover to the start of our new .pdf file

We can use cover_reader to read the cover.

Opens the cover associated with this report

Adds the page to our new .pdf file

Loops through each page of the report

We can use report_writer to write pages into a new .pdf file

Calls our function to do all the merging!

Saves our new .pdf file

We can use report_reader to read the pages of the report.

Be careful with automation programs

Programs like the one we've written to merge .pdf files can rip through hundreds or thousands of files very quickly. If they aren't operating correctly, they can easily result in damaged or lost files. Any time we use `open` with `'w'` or `'wb'` as the second parameter, it means that we're overwriting a file.

Let's focus on this line from our program in listing 9.3:

```
result = open(os.path.join(final_dir, report_file), 'wb')
```

It's using the `open` function to open a file. Specifically, it's opening the current `report_file` file in the `final_dir` directory. The second argument to `open` here, `'wb'`, means that we want to open the file so we can write to it (that's the `'w'`) and that the file we're writing is a binary file (that's the `'b'`), not a text file. If the file doesn't already exist, then the `'w'` we've included will result in the file being created. That's not the dangerous part. The dangerous part is what happens when the file already exists. In that case, `'w'` wipes out its contents and gives us an empty file that we can start writing to. Now, if our program is working correctly and only doing this in our `final_dir`, then we're OK. But this is what we need to carefully verify before letting our program loose.

We highly recommend that you first test on a small directory of files that you don't care about. Further, we recommend changing lines of code that open files using `'w'` or `'wb'` to print a harmless output message instead, so that you can see exactly which files are going to be overwritten or created. For example, in our program here, we need to comment out these two lines:

```
result = open(os.path.join(final_dir, report_file), 'wb')
report_writer.write(result)
```

Instead, we'll use `print` to print out the file that we would have created or overwritten:

```
print('Will write', os.path.join(final_dir, report_file))
```

Then, when you run your program, you'll see the names of files that the program *intended* to write. If the output looks good—that is, the program is operating exactly on the files that you wanted it to operate on—then you can uncomment the code that actually does the work.

Exercise caution, and *always* keep backups of your important files!

The last line of the program in listing 9.3 makes the assumption that the directory of reports is called `reports`, the directory of cover pages is called `covers`, and the directory where the final .pdf files should go is called `final`.

Now, create the `final` directory. It should be there along with your `reports` and `covers` directories.

The overall structure of the code looks promising to us: it's getting a list of the .pdf reports, and then, for each one, it's merging those pages with the cover page. It's using a `for` loop to loop through the pages of the report, which is good because it can grab all the pages that way. By contrast, it's *not* using a `for` loop on the cover .pdf file, which again is good because we know that the cover has only one page anyway.

However, the first line of code it gave us looks like it's using a function called `listdir` in a module called `os`. There are other lines that use this module as well. Do we need to be importing that os module? Indeed, we do! And we can prove it by running the code. If you run the code, you'll get an error:

```
Traceback (most recent call last):
  File "merge_pdfs.py", …
    add_covers('reports', 'covers', 'final')
  File " merge_pdfs.py",  …
    report_files = os.listdir(report_dir)
                   ^^
NameError: name 'os' is not defined
```

We need to add `import os` at the start of our program to fix this. The updated code is in the following listing.

Listing 9.4 Improved function to add covers to .pdf documents

```
import os              ⊲——| We were missing
import PyPDF2                this import before.

def add_covers(report_dir, cover_dir, final_dir):
    '''
    report_dir is a directory of reports named 1.pdf, 2.pdf, and so on.
    These files may be one page or more than one page.

    cover_dir is a directory of covers, with one cover per report.
       The filenames in this directory are cover1.pdf, cover2.pdf, and so on.
    Each of these files is one page.

    Add the cover to the beginning of each report,
    and store all resulting pdfs in final_dir.
    '''
    report_files = os.listdir(report_dir)
    for report_file in report_files:
        report = open(os.path.join(report_dir, report_file), 'rb')
        report_reader = PyPDF2.PdfFileReader(report)
        report_writer = PyPDF2.PdfFileWriter()
        for page_num in range(report_reader.numPages):
            report_writer.addPage(report_reader.getPage(page_num))
        cover = open(os.path.join(cover_dir, 'cover' + report_file), 'rb')
        cover_reader = PyPDF2.PdfFileReader(cover)
        report_writer.insertPage(cover_reader.getPage(0), 0)
        result = open(os.path.join(final_dir, report_file), 'wb')
        report_writer.write(result)
        report.close()
        cover.close()
        result.close()
```

```
if __name__ == '__main__':
    add_covers('reports', 'covers', 'final')
```

We're not out of the woods yet, though. Our updated program still doesn't work. Here's the error we get when we run our program:

```
Traceback (most recent call last):
  File "merge_pdfs.py", line 34, in <module>
    add_covers('reports', 'covers', 'final')
  File "merge_pdfs.py", line 20, in add_covers
    report_reader = PyPDF2.PdfFileReader(report)
                    ^^^^^^^^^^^^^^^^^^^^^^^^^^^^^

  File "...\PyPDF2\_reader.py", line 1974, in __init__
    deprecation_with_replacement("PdfFileReader", "PdfReader", "3.0.0")
  File "...\PyPDF2\_utils.py", line 369, in deprecation_with_replacement
    deprecation(DEPR_MSG_HAPPENED.format(old_name, removed_in, new_name))
  File "...\PyPDF2\_utils.py", line 351, in deprecation
    raise DeprecationError(msg)
PyPDF2.errors.DeprecationError: PdfFileReader is
deprecated and was removed in PyPDF2 3.0.0. Use
PdfReader instead.
```

The line in our code that's causing an error

We can't use PdfFileReader anymore—it's gone!

We've run into the problem where Copilot thinks, "Hey, let's use `PdfFileReader`, since I've been trained that this is part of PyPDF2," but between Copilot being trained and the time of our writing, the PyPDF2 maintainers have removed `PdfFileReader` and replaced it with something else (`PdfReader`, according to the final line of the error message). This discrepancy may very well be fixed for you by the time you read this book, but we want to pretend it's still messed up so that we can teach you what to do if this does happen to you in the future. At this point, we have three options:

- *Install an earlier version of PyPDF2.* The last two lines of the error message tell us that `PdfFileReader`, the function we need from PyPDF2, was removed in PyPDF2 3.0.0. As a result, if we install a version of PyPDF2 earlier than 3.0.0, we should have our function back. In general, installing earlier versions of libraries isn't advisable because security concerns may be present in those versions that have since been fixed in more recent versions. In addition, there may be bugs present in the older versions that have since been fixed. It's worth googling what has been changed in the library recently to determine whether using an older version is safe. In this case, we have done that homework and see no obvious risk in using an older version of PyPDF2.

- *Fix the code ourselves using the suggestion in the error message.* That is, we would replace `PdfFileReader` with `PdfReader` and run the program again. In this case, we would be told about other deprecations, and we'd need to fix those following the same process. It's very nice of the authors of PyPDF2 to tell us what to do inside the error messages. For practice, you might like to work through this, making each update suggested by the error message. We wish all error messages were so useful, but this won't always be the case. Sometimes, a function will be removed without giving us any recourse. In that case, it may be easier to consider our next option.

- *Use a different library.* Earlier, we asked Copilot for other possible .pdf Python libraries we could use, and we received many suggestions. If the first two of our options here aren't satisfactory, we could jump to trying one of those.

We're going to illustrate how to solve the problem and get our code running with the first option (using an earlier version of PyPDF2) and the third option (using a different library entirely).

USING AN EARLIER VERSION OF PYPDF2

When using `pip install` to install a Python library, by default, we get the most current version of the library. That's usually what we want—the latest and greatest—but it's also possible to explicitly request an older version of the library.

Here, we need a version of PyPDF2 prior to version 3.0.0. Rather than the standard usage of pip,

```
pip install PyPDF2
```

we can instead use

```
pip install "PyPDF2 < 3.0.0"
```

The `< 3.0.0` is what we use to ask for the most recent version of the library that's less than version 3.0.0. The command should result in output like the following:

```
Collecting PyPDF2<3.0.0
  Installing collected packages: PyPDF2
  Attempting uninstall: PyPDF2
    Found existing installation: PyPDF2 3.0.1
    Uninstalling PyPDF2-3.0.1:
      Successfully uninstalled PyPDF2-3.0.1
Successfully installed PyPDF2-2.12.1
```

We had an existing version that is >= 3.0.0.

That version is being removed . . .

. . . and version 2.12.1 is being installed.

Now we have an older version of PyPDF2 installed. At this point, you should be able to run our program. It'll take a few seconds, and then the job will be done. You can check your final directory for the newly created .pdf files. Open a few of them to make sure that our program has done the right thing: each .pdf file should start with a cover page and contain all the pages of the report (not just the first page if the report has multiple pages).

Think of how tedious this would have been by hand, and we've gotten the computer to do it for us. Moreover, the next time we have to do the same thing at work (more reports for more people), we've got a tool all set to help us get it done quickly.

USING A DIFFERENT .PDF LIBRARY

Now let's try solving our problem with PyPDF2 by using another library—one of those that Copilot told us about in our initial conversation about .pdf libraries.

We won't go through all the gory details with you on how we decided which library to try next, but we'll walk through the highlights of our journey. We started by asking Copilot Chat how we can use the ReportLab Python module to merge .pdf files, but that redirected us back to using PyPDF2. We received the same response for FPDF: we were told that FPDF can't merge .pdf files but that PyPDF2 can. We then moved on to asking about PyMuPDF, and this part of the conversation was productive:

Human   How can I use the Python PyMuPDF library to merge .pdf files?

GitHub Copilot   You can use the fitz module from the PyMuPDF library to merge PDF files. Here's an example code snippet that shows how to merge two PDF files using PyMuPDF:

```python
import fitz

# Merge the two PDF files
pdf_files = ['file1.pdf', 'file2.pdf']
pdf_writer = fitz.Document()
for pdf_file in pdf_files:
    pdf_reader = fitz.open(pdf_file)
    for page in pdf_reader:
        pdf_writer.insert_pdf(page)
pdf_writer.save('merged.pdf')
pdf_writer.close()
```

This code first creates a list of PDF files to merge (file1.pdf and file2.pdf). It then creates a new Document object using fitz, which represents the merged PDF. It loops through each PDF file in the list, opens it using fitz, and inserts each page of the PDF file into the pdf_writer object using the insert_pdf() method. Finally, it saves the merged PDF to a new file called merged.pdf using the save() method.

You can modify this code to add any additional content to the merged PDF using PyMuPDF. Just create a new Page object, add the content to the page, and insert the page into the pdf_writer object using the insert_page() method.

The sample code here is using insert_pdf to add each .pdf file to the merged .pdf file. We should be on the lookout for our code using insert_pdf as well. The library is called PyMuPDF, so we need to install it with

```
pip install PyMuPDF
```

But then we have to use import fitz? Why import fitz and not import PyMuPDF? Apparently, the designers of this library liked fitz more than PyMuPDF, so we'll need to go with it. It's rare indeed, but occasionally we use one name to install the library and another to import it!

If you encounter NameError when you import

If Python gives you a `NameError` referring to the library that you're trying to import, it's a good bet that you haven't successfully imported that library. It could be that the library isn't in fact installed, or that you need to use a different name to import it. Use Copilot Chat to have a conversation if you ever find that you've installed a library but can't seem to import it.

Now we're ready to generate some code. The following listing shows the prompt that we used and the code that Copilot gave us.

Listing 9.5   Improved function to add covers to .pdf documents

```python
import os
import fitz

def add_covers(report_dir, cover_dir, final_dir):
    '''
    report_dir is a directory of reports named 1.pdf, 2.pdf, and so on.
    These files may be one page or more than one page.

    cover_dir is a directory of covers, with one cover per report.
    The filenames in this directory are cover1.pdf, cover2.pdf, and so on.
    Each of these files is one page.

    Add the cover to the beginning of each report,
    and store all resulting pdfs in final_dir.
    '''
    if not os.path.exists(final_dir):
        os.mkdir(final_dir)
    for report in os.listdir(report_dir):
        report_path = os.path.join(report_dir, report)
        cover_path = os.path.join(cover_dir, f'cover{report}')
        final_path = os.path.join(final_dir, report)
        cover_doc = fitz.open(cover_path)
        report_doc = fitz.open(report_path)
        final_doc = fitz.open()
        final_doc.insert_pdf(cover_doc)
        final_doc.insert_pdf(report_doc)
        final_doc.save(final_path)

if __name__ == '__main__':
    add_covers('reports', 'covers', 'final')
```

Annotations:
- If the final_dir directory doesn't exist, ... create the final_dir directory.
- Loops through the .pdf reports
- Used to read the cover
- Used to read the report
- Used as our new output file
- Adds the cover to our new .pdf file
- Adds the report to our new .pdf file
- Saves our new .pdf file

This program happens to start with some code that creates the output directory if it doesn't already exist. After that, the steps are similar to those in our earlier program that used PyPDF2, although the functions called by each program are different. (That makes sense because PyPDF2 and PyMuPDF are different libraries, with different features and functions.) In both cases, we're using `listdir` to get a list of the report .pdf filenames. In the `for` loop, we go through each of those reports; the code in the loop is responsible for creating a new .pdf file that contains the cover followed by the report. In our PyPDF2 code, there was an inner `for` loop that we needed to loop through all the pages of the report. In our current program, we don't need that because Copilot used the `insert_pdf` function, which inserts a .pdf file into another .pdf file in one shot (not page by page). Whether you took the approach of installing the older library or you chose to use a different library, we've solved our problem and automated what would have been an unpleasantly tedious task.

Notice that we've slightly altered the workflow that we described in the previous chapter to take into account handling the different Python modules that could aid you with your task. A modified workflow is provided in figure 9.2.

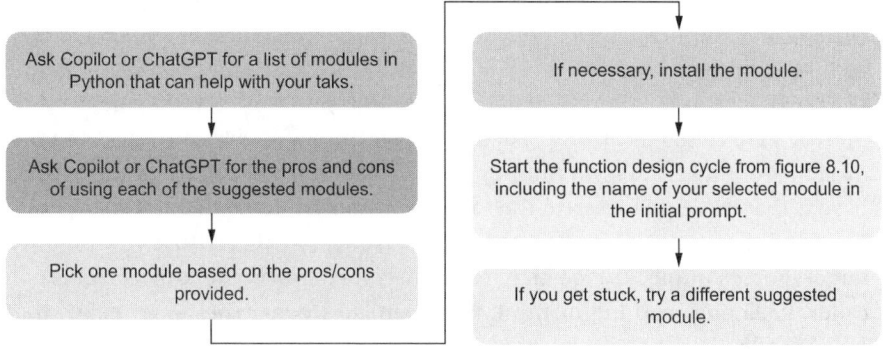

Figure 9.2   Additions to our workflow to account for working with different Python modules

9.5   *Example 3: Merging phone picture libraries*

Now suppose that you take a lot of pictures on your phone. Your partner (or sibling, parent, or child) also takes a lot of pictures on their phone. You each have hundreds or thousands of pictures! Sometimes you send pictures to your partner, and they send pictures to you, so that you and your partner have some but not all of each other's pictures.

You live life like this for a while, but honestly, it's becoming a mess. Half the time when you want a picture, you can't find it because it's a picture that your partner took on their phone that they didn't send you. And, you're starting to have many duplicate pictures all over the place.

You then have an idea: "What if we take all the pictures from my phone and all the pictures from your phone, and we create a combined library of all the pictures! Then we'll have all the pictures in one place!" Remember that both of your phones may have hundreds of pictures, so doing this manually is out of the question. We're going to automate this!

To specify our task more precisely, we'll say that we have two directories of pictures (think of each directory as the contents of a phone) that we want to combine into a new directory. A common file format for pictures is a .png file, so we'll work with those files here. Your actual phone might use .jpg files rather than .png files, but don't worry. You can adapt what we do here to that picture file format (or any other picture file format) if you like.

In the resources for this book, in the ch9 directory, you'll find two subdirectories of picture files. These subdirectories are named pictures1 and pictures2. You can imagine that pictures1 has the pictures from your phone (98 pictures) and pictures2 has the pictures from your partner's phone (112 pictures). We're going to combine these two phone directories into a new directory.

Open some of the .png files in the same way that you open pictures or photos on your computer. The pictures we've generated are just some random shapes, but the program we write here will work no matter what's inside the pictures.

At the outset, we said that the same picture might be on both phones, so we've generated some duplicate files in our pictures. (We have a total of 210 picture files, but 10 of them are duplicates, so there are only 200 unique pictures.) For example, in the pictures1 directory, there's a file called 1566.png, and in the pictures2 directory, there's a file called 2471.png. These two files are identical, and when we generate our directory of files from both phones, we'll only want to keep one of these. What's tricky here is that these pictures are the same even though their filenames are not.

What if two filenames are the same? Does that mean that the pictures are the same? For example, notice that each directory, pictures1 and pictures2, has a file called 9595.png. You might think that filenames being the same means that the pictures inside will be the same too. But no, if you open these pictures, you'll see that they're different! This could happen in real life too: you and your partner could both take different pictures, and, however remote, it's possible that the filenames your phones choose for those pictures just happen to be the same.

If we're not careful, we'll end up copying 9595.png from pictures1 into our new directory and then overwriting it later by copying 9595.png from pictures2 into our new directory. We need to be sure that when we copy a file, we're not overwriting a different picture that may already be there with the same filename. We provide an example of this process in figure 9.3.

We're working with directories, not actual phones

We're assuming here that you have two directories of pictures already on your computer. These directories could have come from anywhere, and nothing we do here has anything specific to do with cell phones.

But if you wanted to do this task for real, with pictures on your phones, you'd need to get those pictures onto your computer first. You could use ChatGPT to have that discussion! As the details are specific to different phones and go beyond what we want to use Copilot to automate, we won't go further into this here.

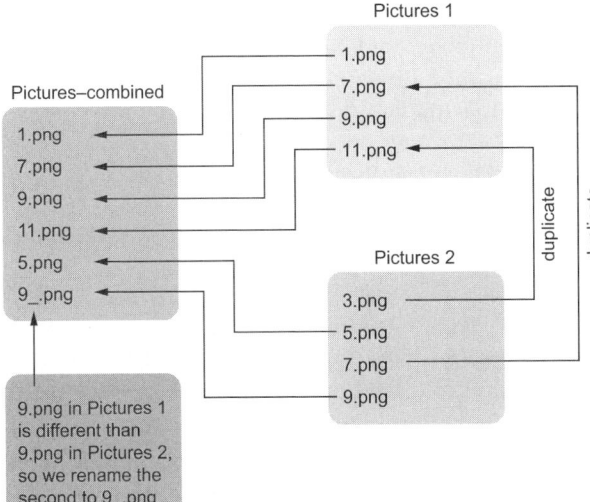

Figure 9.3 Example of merging the photos in the pictures1 and pictures2 folders into the pictures–combined folder and managing the removal of duplicates

9.5.1 Conversing with Copilot

Our tool is going to create a combined directory of pictures from pictures1 and pictures2, but without duplicate pictures. If our combined original picture directories have the same picture multiple times, we want only one of those copies of the picture to survive in our new directory.

At this point, there are at least two things we might like to know: How do we copy a file using Python, and how do we know whether two files are the same picture? Let's start by asking Copilot Chat how we can copy a file:

> **Human** I need to write a Python program that copies files. How do I do this?

> **GitHub Copilot** You can use the shutil module in Python to copy files. Here's an example:

```python
import shutil

# Replace the source and destination paths with your own
source = '/path/to/source/file'
destination = '/path/to/destination/file'

# Copy the file
shutil.copy(source, destination)
```

> This will copy the file from the source path to the destination path. If the destination file already exists, it will be overwritten.

Excellent. We can use that shutil module to copy a file; we'll need to remember to import that module. The final sentence that Copilot gave us is an important warning. We should be careful to avoid copying a file over the top of another file that already exists. Next, let's determine whether this shutil module is built-in to Python.

Human   Is this shutil module built into Python?

GitHub Copilot   Yes, the shutil module is a built-in module in Python, so you don't need to install anything extra to use it.

You might wonder why we're focusing on making copies of files and putting them into our new directory, rather than moving them from our original directories into the new directory. The reason is that we want to leave our original directories alone just in case we have a bug and fail to get all the files into our new directory. If anything goes wrong in our new directory, it won't matter because our original directories will still be intact.

That wraps up what we need to know about copying files. Now let's move on to learn how we can determine whether two files are the same picture.

As we've already said, it's not sufficient to use filenames to determine whether pictures are the same. How can we do it, then?

Human   Using Python, how can I determine whether .png files are the same?

GitHub Copilot   You can use the filecmp module in Python to compare two files and check if they are the same. Here's an example code snippet that compares two .png files:

```python
import filecmp

# Replace these file paths with the actual file paths of the .png files
# you want to compare
file1 = '/path/to/file1.png'
file2 = '/path/to/file2.png'

if filecmp.cmp(file1, file2):
    print('The files are the same.')
else:
    print('The files are different.')
```

This code will compare the contents of the two files and return `True` if they are the same, and `False` if they are different.

As a quick aside, the last sentence from Copilot is wrong. That code isn't returning `True` or `False` anywhere. Just like Copilot can generate faulty code for us in our Python file, Copilot Chat can produce faulty explanations.

Our prompt wasn't precise about the number of files that we need to compare. Do we want to compare two files? Hundreds of files? Our prompt doesn't say. Copilot has told us what to do if we want to compare two files, which is a reasonable thing to tell us. But that's not quite what we need. We need to be able to determine, among hundreds of files, which files are duplicates of other files. That way, we can detect a duplicate file and not copy it into our new directory. Let's try again.

Human   What if I have hundreds of .png files and I want to find duplicates—is that approach you gave me still good?

GitHub Copilot   If you have hundreds of .png files and you want to find duplicates, you can use the os module to iterate over all the files in a directory and compare each file to every other file in the directory. Here's an example code snippet that does that:

```python
import os
import filecmp

# Replace this with the actual directory path where your .png
# files are located
directory = '/path/to/directory'

# Iterate over all the files in the directory
for filename1 in os.listdir(directory):
    if filename1.endswith('.png'):
        for filename2 in os.listdir(directory):
            if filename2.endswith('.png') and filename1 != filename2:
                file1 = os.path.join(directory, filename1)
                file2 = os.path.join(directory, filename2)
                if filecmp.cmp(file1, file2):
                    print(f'{filename1} and {filename2} are dupli-
cates.')
```

This code will iterate over all the files in the directory and compare each .png file to every other .png file in the directory. If two files are the same, it will print a message indicating that they are duplicates. Note that this approach can be slow for large directories with many files.

The outer for loop goes through each file in the directory. How do we know whether the current file has a duplicate? Well, we can go through each other file in the directory and compare it to the current file. That's the role of the inner for loop: it uses filecmp.cmp to compare the current file (file1) to each other file (file2).

We didn't mention in our prompt that we care about finding duplicates across multiple directories, so Copilot has focused on a single directory here. If that difference turns out to be a roadblock, we could make our prompt more precise.

Copilot is using two other modules here, os and filecmp. We could ask Copilot if these are built-in Python modules or not, but we'll save a little time and just tell you here that they are built-in.

We now want you to focus on the final sentence from Copilot: "Note that this approach can be slow for large directories with many files." How slow is "slow"? How many is "many"? We don't know.

You might be tempted to ask Copilot for a better solution, one that isn't "slow for large directories with many files." But many programmers wouldn't do that. It's often a mistake to optimize our solution before we have even tried out our (unoptimized, apparently slow) approach for two reasons. First, maybe our "slow" program turns out to be fast enough! We may as well try it. Second, more optimized programs are often more sophisticated programs, and they may be more difficult for us to get right. That isn't always the case, but it can be. And again, if our unoptimized program gets the job done, we don't even have to worry about a more optimized version at all.

Now, if it turns out that our program really is too slow or you find yourself using the program repeatedly, then it may be worth the extra investment in continuing to work with Copilot on a faster solution. For now, though, we're good.

9.5.2   *Top-down design*

There's a little more going on in this task than in our prior two tasks. For one, we need to be careful not to overwrite a file that already exists in our new directory. For another, we need to determine which files to copy in the first place (remember that we only want to copy files that don't already match a file in our new directory). Compare this to the .pdf merging task we just accomplished, where we didn't have these extra concerns.

To that end, we're going to use top-down design and problem decomposition here. Don't worry, it won't be a full-on top-down design example like we did in chapter 7. Our task here is much smaller than our spelling suggestions task from that chapter. We'll just do a little top-down design and that will help Copilot get us what we want.

Our top-level function will be responsible for solving our overall task: taking the pictures1 and pictures2 directories and putting all unique pictures into a target directory. Back in chapter 3, we learned that we should make functions as general as we can, to make them more useful or generalizable to other tasks. Here, we've been thinking about combining two picture directories together. But why not 3, 5, or 50 directories? Who cares how many directories we have; we should be able to just combine as many directories as we want.

So, instead of designing our top-level function to take two strings (directory names) as parameters, we'll have the function take a list of strings. That way, we can use it on as many picture directories as we want. And, we can still readily use it on two picture directories—we'll just pass a list containing the names of the two directories.

We'll name our top-level function `make_copies`. We'll need two parameters: the list of directory names that we just discussed, and the name of our target directory where we want all the files to go.

What's this function going to do? It's going to loop through each directory in the list of directories, and then, for each directory, it's going to loop through each file.

For each file, we need to determine whether to copy it or not and, if we need to copy it, to do the actual copying.

Determining whether to copy the file, and then possibly copying it, is a subtask that we can split out of make_copies. We'll name our function for this subtask make_copy. Our make_copy function will take two parameters: the name of a file and the target directory. If the file isn't identical to any file in the target directory, then the function will copy the file into the target directory.

Say we want to copy a file called 9595.png from one of our picture directories into our target directory but that file already exists in the target directory. We don't want to overwrite the file that's already there, so we'll need to come up with a new filename. We might try adding an _ (underscore) character prior to the .png part of the filename. That would give us 9595_.png. That one probably wouldn't exist in the target directory, but if it did, we could then try 9595__.png, 9595___.png, and so on, until we find a filename that doesn't already exist in there.

Generating a unique filename is a task that we can split out of our make_copy function. We'll call it get_good_filename. It will take a filename as a parameter and return a version of that filename that doesn't already exist.

And with that, our top-down design is done. Figure 9.4 depicts our work as a tree (well, at least the trunk of a tree), showing which function is called by which other function.

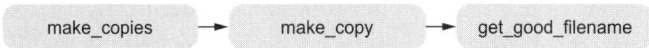

Figure 9.4 Top-down design for image merging. The top-most (left-most) function is make_copies, **the child of that is** make_copy, **and the child of that is** get_good_filename.

9.5.3 Writing the tool

We don't have any modules to install this time around. We do know from our Copilot conversation that we'll use the built-in shutil module to copy files. We'll also use the built-in filecmp module to compare files and the built-in os module to get a list of the files in a directory. We'll therefore import these three modules at the top of our Python program.

As in chapter 7, we're going to solve our problem by starting at the bottom of our function tree and working toward the top. We do that so Copilot can call our already-written functions when writing code for a parent function. For each function, we provide the def line and docstring, and Copilot writes the code. We've also provided some annotations to explain how the code works.

Looking again at figure 9.4, we see that the first function we need to implement is get_good_filename. Let's get that one done now in the following listing.

Listing 9.6 `get_good_filename` **function for our picture merge task**

```
import shutil
import filecmp
import os

def get_good_filename(fname):
    '''
    fname is the name of a png file.

    While the file fname exists, add an _ character
    right before the .png part of the filename;
    e.g. 9595.png becomes 9595_.png.

    Return the resulting filename.
    '''
    while os.path.exists(fname):
        fname = fname.replace('.png', '_.png')
    return fname
```

While the filename exists . . .

. . . insert an _ prior to .png by replacing .png with _.png.

Returns the filename that we know now doesn't exist

The next function we need to write is `make_copy`. This is the function that copies a file into a target directory but only if the file isn't identical to a file that we've already copied. We're looking for Copilot to do several things in its code here:

- Use `os.listdir` to get a list of files in the target directory.
- Use `filecmp.cmp` to determine whether two files are identical.
- Use `shutil.copy` to copy the file if there was no identical file.
- Call the function `get_good_filename` that we just wrote.

The following listing shows our prompt and the code that Copilot provided. Notice that the code is doing everything that we wanted it to do.

Listing 9.7 `make_copy` **function for our pictures merge task**

```
def make_copy(fname, target_dir):
    '''
    fname is a filename like pictures1/1262.png.
    target_dir is the name of a directory.

    Compare the file fname to all files in target_dir.
    If fname is not identical to any file in
    target_dir, copy it to target_dir
    '''
    for target_fname in os.listdir(target_dir):
        if filecmp.cmp(fname, os.path.join( \
                target_dir, target_fname)):
            return
    shutil.copy(fname, get_good_filename(
            os.path.join(target_dir, \
                os.path.basename(fname))))
```

Loops through the files in the target directory

If the file is the same as one of the files in the target directory, . . .

. . . returns from the function without having copied the file.

Otherwise, copies the file and uses a good filename that doesn't already exist.

There's only one function to go, and it's our top-level `make_copies` function. For each file in each of our picture directories, we're expecting the code to call `make_copy` to copy the file if needed, as shown in the following listing.

Listing 9.8 `make_copies` function for our picture merge task

```
def make_copies(dirs, target_dir):
    '''
    dirs is a list of directory names.
    target_dir is the name of a directory.

    Check each file in the directories and compare it to all files
    in target_dir. If a file is not identical to any file in
    target_dir, copy it to target_dir
    '''
    for dir in dirs:
        for fname in os.listdir(dir):
            make_copy(os.path.join(dir, fname), \
                    target_dir)

make_copies(['pictures1', 'pictures2'],
            'pictures_combined')
```

Loops through our picture directories

Loops through the files in the current picture directory

Copies the current file into the target directory, if needed

Runs our program on our two picture directories and the given target directory

The final line of code from Copilot, beneath the `make_copies` function, makes the assumption that our target directory will be named pictures_combined. Create that directory now so that it sits alongside your pictures1 and pictures2 directories of pictures.

As we discussed when working with .pdf files earlier in the chapter, it's important that you first test the program on sample directories that you don't care about. Your sample directories should have only a few files in them, so that you can manually determine whether the program is working as expected. You should also include important edge cases, such as having the same filename in each directory.

Once you have your sample directories, you should create a "harmless" version of the program that simply outputs messages rather than actually copying files. For our program here, you would change the line in `make_copy` to use `print` rather than `shutil.copy`.

If the output looks good after you check the results carefully, only then should you run the real program on your real directories. Remember that our program is copying (rather than moving) files, so even in our real directories, if something goes wrong, there's a good chance that the problem will be in our new directory and not the original directories that we actually care about.

We'll assume that you're now ready to run the program on the pictures1 and pictures2 directories. Once you run it, you can check your pictures_combined directory for the results. You should see that the directory has 200 files, which is exactly the number of unique pictures that we had across our two picture directories. Did we correctly handle the situation where the same filename existed in both picture directories but were different pictures? Yes, you can see that we have files named 9595.png and 9595_.png and that we therefore haven't overwritten one with the other.

Oh, and how long did the program take to run on your computer? At most a few seconds, right? It turns out that Copilot's warning that "this approach can be slow for large directories with many files" didn't matter for us.

Now, we all know that people tend to have thousands of pictures on their phones, not hundreds. If you ran this program on two real phone picture libraries, you would again need to determine whether it completes in an acceptable amount of time. You could run the program and let it run for a minute or two or however long you're willing to wait. For fun, we also tested our program on a total of 10,000 small image files (a more realistic scenario than the 210 pictures across our pictures1 and pictures2 directories that we used in this chapter), and we found that it only took 1 minute to complete. At some point, our program will become too slow to be practical, and that's when you'd need to do further research with Copilot Chat to arrive at a more efficient program.

In this chapter, we succeeded in automating three tedious tasks: cleaning up an email, adding covers to hundreds of .pdf files, and wrangling multiple picture libraries into one. The approach in each case was the same: use Copilot Chat to determine which module(s) to use, then follow the approach that we've honed throughout the book to have Copilot write the required code.

Remember, whenever you find yourself repeating the same task, it's worth trying to automate it using Copilot and Python. There are many helpful Python modules for doing so, beyond what we showed in this chapter. For example, there are modules to manipulate images, work with Microsoft Excel or Microsoft Word files, send email, scrape data from websites, and more. If it's a tedious task, chances are that someone has made a Python module to help with it and that Copilot will be able to help you use that module effectively.

9.6   Exercises

1   You already have a tool that cleans up email text by removing any > or space characters from the beginning of each line. What steps will you take to enhance this tool to also remove lines that are excessively short (e.g., lines with fewer than five characters, excluding spaces)?

2   You're writing a Python program to clean up a bunch of images that you have stored on your computer, and you've decided to use the Pillow library (a fork of the Python Image Library [PIL]). After installing the latest version of Pillow, you run your program but encounter the following error:

```
Traceback (most recent call last):
  File "image_cleanup.py", line 4, in <module>
    resized_image = image.resize((new_width, new_height), Image.ANTIALIAS)
                                                          ^^^^^^^^^^^^^^^^
AttributeError: module 'PIL.Image' has no attribute 'ANTIALIAS'
```

What steps can you take to fix this problem?

3 You've been given an Excel file named sales_data.xlsx that contains monthly sales data for different products. Your task is to write a Python program that reads the sales data, calculates the total sales for each product, and writes the results to a new Excel file named total_sales.xlsx. The sales_data.xlsx file has columns for each month (January, February, etc.).

Your program should do the following:

a Read the data from sales_data.xlsx.

b Calculate the total sales for each product across all months.

c Write the product names and their total sales to total_sales.xlsx.

Hints: make reasonable assumptions about the input file and you may need to import libraries to help you work with the .xlsx files. If you don't have Excel or OpenOffice to read/write .xlsx files, feel free to do the task with .csv files instead.

4 It can be tedious to find news articles from different sources to read every day. Your task is to write a webscraper in Python that extracts and display the titles and URLs of the latest articles from a news website. You'll need the beautiful-soup4 and requests modules.

Summary

- Programmers often make tools to automate tedious tasks.
- It's often necessary to use a Python module to help us write our tool.
- We can use Copilot Chat to determine which Python modules we should be using.
- It's helpful to converse with Copilot to understand the pros and cons of various Python modules that may be available to us.
- There are Python modules for working with the clipboard, working with .pdf files and other file formats, copying files, and more.

Making some games

This chapter covers

- Adding randomness to our programs
- Designing and programming a code-breaking logic game
- Designing and programming a press-your-luck dice game

People learn to program for many reasons. Some people want to automate tedious tasks as we did in the previous chapter. Some people want to work with artificial intelligence (AI; you'll get a taste of that in chapter 11). Other people want to make interactive websites, Android or iOS apps, or Alexa skills. There's an endless amount of stuff that programmers can make.

Another popular reason to learn programming is to create games. For that reason, we thought we'd continue our Copilot programming journey with you by designing two small computer games. The first is a code-breaking game where you use clues to identify the computer's secret code. The second is a two-player dice game where each player needs to balance risk and luck to reach the required number of points before the other player does. Instead of using graphics and animation, these games use text. We've made this decision to help us stay focused on the game logic, rather than the way that the game is represented or the way that the player interacts with the games. Along the way, we offer some next steps if you're interested in taking your game-making abilities further. And don't worry, your current skills are a great start to that!

10.1 Game programs

If you think about playing a board game with your family or friends, you can break down what happens in two major phases. The first phase is game setup. This will include setting up the game board, giving each player starting funds or cards, and so on. The second phase is the playing of the game. In a board game, the game typically includes a person taking a turn and, assuming no one has won yet, another person taking a turn. With each turn, the game state (board, players' funds, etc.) all change. We need to take care to implement each of these phases when programming a computer game as well.

In many programming environments catered to video game design, the two phases are often separate standard functions. There's a setup function for what is done to set up the game and an update function to change the state of the game either because a player has taken an action or because time has passed. Figure 10.1 shows the basic flow for video games.

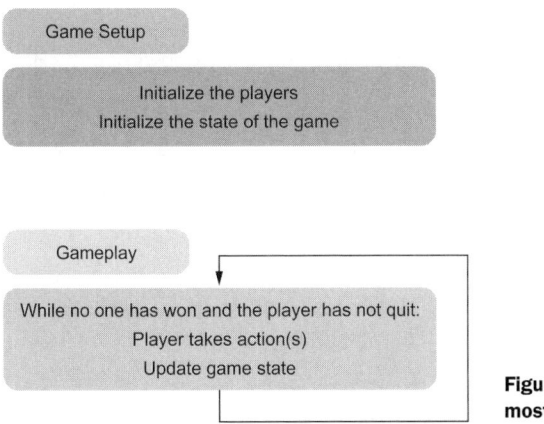

Figure 10.1   Basic flow of most video games

Let's focus on the update part of the game for a moment. Suppose a player can press a button on their keyboard to move forward in a 2D game. The update function will cause the player's character to move forward and also check to see if the player's movement caused the player to interact with something in the game world. Some games also change state based on time, regardless of a player's actions. In those games, the update function would also update the state of the game itself (e.g., move the ghosts in a game of Pac-Man). At the end of every time step or user action, the game will check for end conditions. End conditions typically include the following:

- A player won the game by achieving an objective.
- A player lost the game by falling off a cliff, running into a monster, and so on.
- A player chose to quit the game.

There are many programming environments that cater to game design, and we recommend the Python pygame module [1] as a good starting place. If you continue pursuing game design beyond that, we recommend checking out Unity [2] for 3D game design. In this chapter though, we'll be working with just standard Python to show you how to design a basic game without having to dive into these new environments.

10.2   *Adding randomness*

Many games, including the two that we'll build in this chapter, rely on randomness to make them fun. In our first game, we'll need the computer to generate the random digits of the number that we'll be deducing. In the second game, we'll need to roll dice, which just amounts to generating random numbers between one and six. Enemy behavior, initial orientation of a puzzle, or amount of damage caused by attacks, that is, randomness, is typically involved in all of these and many other aspects of game design.

We'll therefore need to be able to generate random numbers in our Python programs. To learn how to do that, let's use Copilot Chat, much as we did in the previous chapter.

> **Human**   I need to generate random numbers in my Python program. How can I do this?

> **GitHub Copilot**   You can use the random module in Python to generate random numbers. Here's an example:

```python
import random

# Generate a random integer between 1 and 10 (inclusive)
random_number = random.randint(1, 10)
print(random_number)

# Generate a random float between 0 and 1
random_float = random.random()
print(random_float)
```

> This code imports the random module and then uses the `randint` function to generate a random integer between 1 and 10 (inclusive), and the `random` function to generate a random float between 0 and 1.

Copilot suggests using functions inside of a module called random to generate the random numbers. Let's check whether the random module is built into Python.

Human   Is this random module built into Python?

GitHub Copilot   Yes, the random module is a built-in module in Python, so you don't need to install any additional modules to use it. You can simply import it in your Python code and start using its functions.

We'll follow Copilot's suggestion and import this module to test the two functions that we just learned. We'll do this at the Python >>> prompt, which we've used in previous chapters to explore how Python features work. To get to the Python prompt, press Ctrl-Shift-P, type REPL, and then select Python: Start REPL.

Based on Copilot's response to our first question, we know that we can use the randint function to generate a random integer in a range from the lowest allowed number to the highest allowed number. We might use this function to generate individual digits that could be assembled into a larger number. Each digit is between 0 and 9, so we'll ask randint for some random numbers between 0 and 9:

```
>>> import random
>>> random.randint(0, 9)
5
>>> random.randint(0, 9)
1
>>> random.randint(0, 9)       We happened to
9                              get the maximum
>>> random.randint(0, 9)       value.
9
>>> random.randint(0, 9)
5                              We happened to
>>> random.randint(0, 9)       get the minimum
0                              value.
>>> random.randint(0, 9)
4
```

Or, we might want to generate rolls of a die. Each roll is between 1 and 6, so we can ask randint for some random numbers between 1 and 6:

```
>>> random.randint(1, 6)
2
>>> random.randint(1, 6)
2
>>> random.randint(1, 6)
4
>>> random.randint(1, 6)
1
>>> random.randint(1, 6)
5
```

The other function that Copilot told us about is called random. (Yes, both the module and this function are called random! So, we'll need to use random.random() to call this function.) This one doesn't generate a random integer; rather, it generates a random fractional number between 0 and 1 (not including 1). For example, rather than a random number like 5, you'll get a random number like 0.1926502. These kinds of numbers, with decimals, are referred to as floats (or floating-point numbers). Here are a few calls of this function:

```
>>> random.random()
0.03853937835258148
>>> random.random()
0.44152027974631813
>>> random.random()
0.774000627219771
>>> random.random()
0.4388949032154501
```

We can imagine this function being useful for games as well. For example, you can think of these float values as probabilities that an event occurs, with higher numbers corresponding to higher probabilities. You could then use these floats to determine whether an event should happen or not. For the games in this chapter, though, we won't need this function.

10.3   *Example 1: Bulls and Cows*

Our first game will be based on an old code-breaking game called Bulls and Cows. It might remind you of the game Wordle (but don't worry if you haven't played Wordle before). We'll be able to play this game against the computer. Randomness plays a critical role in this game, as we'll see.

10.3.1   *How the game works*

In this game, Player 1 thinks up a secret code, which is a sequence of four digits. Player 2 has to figure out what that secret code is. In our version of the game, the computer will be Player 1, and the human player will be Player 2.

Here's how it works. The computer will randomly choose four distinct digits (duplicate digits aren't allowed) as the secret code. For example, it might choose the digits 1862. Then, you'll guess what you think the computer's four digits are. For example, you might guess 3821.

For each guess, you're told two things. First, you're told how many digits in your guess match the corresponding position in the secret code exactly. We'll refer to digits that are in the correct place in the secret code as "correct." Say that the secret code is 1862, and you guess 3821. The second digit in both your guess and the secret code is 8, so that's a match. There are no other matches, so you would be told for this guess that the number of correct digits is 1.

Second, you're told how many digits in your guess exist at some other position in the secret code. We'll refer to digits that are in the secret code but in a different location as "misplaced." Let's again use 1862 for the secret code and 3821 for your guess. The third digit in your guess is 2. It doesn't match the third digit of the secret code (that's a 6), but there is a 2 somewhere else in the secret code. Similarly, the fourth digit in your guess is a 1. It doesn't match the fourth digit of the secret code, but there is a 1 somewhere else in the secret code. All told, two of your digits (1 and 2) exist in the secret code, although they don't match their expected position. You would be told from this guess that the number of misplaced digits is 2. You can use these clues to narrow down what the secret code could be.

Wordle

If you've played Wordle before, you might notice some similarities between Wordle and our game here. Wordle uses letters, and ours uses digits, but the type of feedback you receive for your guesses is similar. In both cases, you're told about letters or digits that are in the right or wrong place. In Wordle, you're given a clue about each of your letters on its own. For example, if the first letter of your guess is *h*, you might be told that the *h* is in the word but in the wrong place. By contrast, in our game, you're not given hints about each digit individually but instead are given hints about your guess in aggregate. Still, we hope you're struck by these similarities and by the fact that you're building something that resembles a recent, worldwide phenomenon of a game!

We found a free version of Bulls and Cows that you can play at www.mathsisfun.com/games/bulls-and-cows.html. We recommend that you play a few rounds of the game before continuing, just so the way the game works is crystal clear in your head. (Note that they use the terminology *bulls* instead of *correct* and *cows* instead of *misplaced*.)

In table 10.1, we've provided an example interaction with the game. We've included a Comments column to convey our thinking and what we learned from each guess.

Table 10.1   Example of playing the game

Guess	Misplaced	Correct	Comments
0123	1	0	One of 0, 1, 2, 3 is in the answer; none are in the correct location.
4567	3	0	Three of 4, 5, 6, 7 are in the answer; none are in the correct location.
9045	0	1	Because one number from 0123 and three numbers from 4567 are in the answer, we know 8 and 9 aren't in the answer. We know at least one of the numbers 4 or 5 must be in the answer from prior guesses and that 0 could be in the answer. One correct means that either 4 or 5 is in the correct location, either 4 or 5 isn't present in the solution, and 0 isn't in the solution.
9048	0	0	We know 8, 9, and 0 aren't in the answer from prior guesses. Zero correct and zero misplaced tells us 4 is also not in the answer, and from the previous guess, we now know that 5 is the last digit.
1290	1	0	Going back to the original guess, we want to know which digit of 1, 2, and 3 is in the answer. We know 9 and 0 aren't in the answer, so one misplaced means either 1 or 2 is in the answer and 3 isn't in the answer. In addition, whichever of the numbers 1 and 2 are in the answer, it's currently in the wrong spot.

Table 10.1 Example of playing the game *(continued)*

Guess	Misplaced	Correct	Comments
6715	2	1	Because 4 isn't in the solution, we know from the second guess that 5, 6, and 7 are. Our guess here tells us that 1 isn't in the answer and that 6 and 7 are in the wrong place. Since 1 isn't in the answer, 2 must be (from the previous guess). Because 5 is at the end and we've tried 2 in the second and third position previously with zero correct, 2 must be in the first position. Because we've tried 6 in the first and third position and neither were correct, 6 must be in the second position. That leaves 7 for the third position. We've got it.
2675	0	4	Yes, this is correct.

The challenge of the game is that you have a limited number of guesses in which you must successfully guess the computer's secret code. In our example from table 10.1, we took seven guesses to guess the code 2675. For each guess, we were given the number of digits misplaced and the number of digits correct to guide our thinking.

In the free version of the game that we just mentioned, you're not allowed to include the same digit multiple times in your guess. For example, the guess 1231 wouldn't be allowed because of the two 1s. We'll maintain this restriction in our version of the game as well.

10.3.2 *Top-down design*

Our overall task is to write a program to play the Bulls and Cows game against the computer. Let's do top-down design on this large task, just as we did in chapters 7 and 9. What has to happen during this game? Answering that question will help us break down the game into smaller tasks. To help us with this, we took the rules of the game and our example and thought through what happens at each step of the game. Each of those high-level steps appears in figure 10.2, so let's break them down one by one.

We'll start with the setup. For us to be able to play the game, the computer has to randomly generate a secret code. We need to ensure that the secret code doesn't have any duplicate digits. To us, this sounds like something that's sufficiently complicated and self-contained, so it should be its own subtask function.

After the computer generates its secret code, we can move to the gameplay itself. Here's where the player starts making their guesses. We might think that we could just use input to ask the player for their guesses and thereby avoid having a separate function for this. But we do need to ensure that the player enters the correct number of digits and that they don't include duplicate digits in their guess. This is more than we can do with a single call of input, so we'll make this its own function as well.

Once the player makes their valid guess, we need to figure out two things: How many digits are correct, and how many digits are misplaced? Should we have one function to carry out both of these tasks? Or, maybe we should have two functions, one for the correct information and one for the misplaced information? We see good arguments on

Game Setup:

Randomly generate secret code

Gameplay:

```
while the player has not won and the player has
       guesses left:
   tell player to input their guess
   read in valid player guess
   compare guess against secret code
   if guess == secret code:
       player wins, notify player
   else
          give feedback to player about guess
   update number of guesses
```

The player is out of guesses, so tell the player the answer and end the game.

Figure 10.2   Steps in the Bulls and Cows game

each side. If we put the tasks together into the same function, we keep the player feedback centralized in one place, and that may make it easier for us to confirm it's written correctly. On the other hand, having two separate functions would make it easier to test each type of feedback (correct or misplaced) at the expense of spreading out the logic for the feedback across two functions. We somewhat arbitrarily chose to use a single function here, but if you were hoping to have two separate functions, we encourage you to try that on your own after you finish working through this section.

Let's take stock. We have a function to generate the computer's secret code. We have a function to get the player's next guess. We have a function to get the correct/misplaced clues for the player's guess. Those are three major subtasks that we're happy to split out of our top-level function.

Is there any other subtask to split out? There's certainly a little more work to do in our top-level function. For example, we need to detect if the player's guess matches the secret code and end the game in that case. We feel that we don't need a separate function for that, though. To determine whether the user's guess equals the secret code, we can use Python's `==` operator, which tells us directly whether two values are equal. And to end the game, we can use a `return` statement to end the top-level game function and thereby stop the program. Similarly, if the player uses all of their guesses without getting the secret code, then we need to tell them that they lost the game, but again, we should be able to do this with a small amount of Python code. As such, we'll stop here with our main top-level function calling three subtask functions.

When we worked through our spelling suggestions problem in chapter 7, we needed to break one of our subtasks into sub-subtasks. But here, each of our three subtasks will be manageable as a single function.

For example, let's think again about our first subtask: generating the computer's secret code, with no duplicate digits allowed. Could we split any sub-subtasks out of here? Maybe we could have a function to check whether there are any duplicate digits in a proposed secret code. Then, we could keep generating secret codes, calling our sub-subtask function until it tells us that there are no duplicates. That would work, but we could also just generate the secret code digit by digit and not allow a duplicate to be added to the code in the first place. This latter plan seems to not need any sub-subtask to be split.

Now let's think about our second subtask: getting the player's next guess. We could split out a sub-subtask to tell us whether a guess is valid (i.e., it has the correct length and has no duplicates). While we could surely do that, it's not much of a stretch to do this with a couple of checks in the subtask function itself. (Did your mind just go back to our example in chapter 7 about valid passwords and detecting valid passwords, where we split the check for validity into its own function? If so, the difference is that checking whether a password is valid is likely a more substantial task than the validity checks we need here.) It would certainly be okay to break this into another sub-subtask, but we'll move forward without doing so. We've already argued that our third subtask is fine as is, so we'll stop our top-down design here.

We'll name our top-level function `play`. In it, we'll call three functions corresponding to the three subtasks that we just identified. We'll call the function for our first subtask (generating the computer's secret code) `random_string`, the function for our second subtask (getting the player's next guess) `get_guess`, and the function for our third subtask (providing feedback to the player) `guess_result`. See figure 10.3 for this top-down design depicted as a tree.

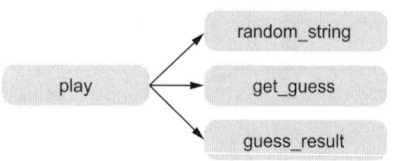

Figure 10.3   Top-down design for the Bulls and Cows game. The top-most (left-most) function is `play`, **which calls** `random_string`, `get_guess`, **and** `guess_result`.

10.3.3 *Parameters and return types*

Normally, we define the types of parameters and return value for each function during the top-down design itself, but we wanted to discuss that separately here because there are some subtle aspects this time. For example, you may already be imagining that we'll use integers to represent the secret code and guesses; but, as we'll see shortly, this isn't the best choice. We'll make some decisions about how we'll represent the data for all the functions before we write each one.

The `play` function is our top-level function and the starting point for our game. It would be possible to have this function take no parameters. Somewhere in the code of the function, we'd have to hard-code the fact that the secret code has four digits and that the player gets, say, 10 guesses. But that wouldn't be very flexible. What if we wanted to play a version of the game where the secret code is seven digits and the player gets 100 guesses? We'd have to go into the code and make all the necessary changes. So, to make the game easily configurable, we can provide some parameters to this function. For example, rather than always having the secret code be four digits, we could use a parameter to allow the length of the secret code to be set to whatever we want. Similarly, rather than putting the maximum number of player guesses directly into the function, we could make that a parameter as well so that we can easily change it. Then, all we need to do to alter the gameplay is to call this function with different values for these parameters, without having to mess around with the code of the function itself.

Using parameters and variables to avoid magic numbers

The number of allowed guesses and the number of digits in the secret code are good examples that we can use to explain an important principle in code design. This principle is that when we write code, if a number can be a parameter or variable, it should be. This principle ensures the code is as versatile as possible. When programmers see a number being used, rather than a friendly name, they call this a "magic number" and that's what we want to avoid. In our discussion about the number of guesses the player gets or the number of digits for the secret code, those should be parameters if we abide by this principle. At some point, these parameters need to be given concrete numbers for the code to work, but we should assign them values at the highest level of the code as possible (e.g., the player might set these parameters when the game starts).

To help adhere to this general principle, whenever you see a raw number (e.g., 4) in the code, ask yourself if that could be a parameter or variable. More often than not, it should be.

Adding these parameters is another example, as per our discussion in chapter 3, of making functions general purpose rather than unnecessarily restrictive. Our `random_string` function is the function that generates the computer's secret code. Why did we put `string` in this function name? Shouldn't we be returning a random integer, like 1862? What does a string have to do with this?

Well, the problem with returning an integer is that the secret code might start with 0. A secret code like 0825 is a perfectly valid four-digit secret code. But 0825 as an integer is 825, which doesn't have enough digits. The string '0825' is just four characters that happen to each be digits, so there's no problem with starting a string like this with a '0'.

Beyond that, let's think ahead about what we'll eventually need to be doing with the computer's secret code. We'll need to compare it digit by digit with the player's guess to determine which digits match. Using indexing on strings will give us easy access to each character of the string, which is exactly what we need. It's more challenging to access each individual digit of an integer: integers don't support indexing!

So, our `random_string` function will take the required number of digits of the secret code as a parameter and will return a random string of that length, where each character in the string is a digit character. When we talk about digits in a string, all we're referring to are the characters of the string. They happen to be digit characters, but they're still characters, just like 'a' or '*'. Don't be confused by the fact that the string might look like a number! Here's an example showing that these strings work the same way every other string works:

```
>>> s = '1862'
>>> s[0]            ◁───┤  We access characters of
'1'                       the string as we always do.
>>> s[1]
'8'
>>> s[2]
'6'
>>> s[3]                      We can't add a
'2'                           string and an
                              integer.
>>> s + 1           ◁───┘
Traceback (most recent call last):
  File "<stdin>", line 1, in <module>
TypeError: can only concatenate str (not "int") to str
>>> s + '1'         ◁───┐
'18621'                 │  This is string concatenation,
                        │  not numeric addition.
```

What about get_guess, the function to get the next guess from the player? As with random_string, this function will need to know the number of digits of a valid guess, so we'll make that a parameter. It will return a string giving the player's guess.

Finally, let's talk about guess_result, the function that tells us how many digits are correct and how many are misplaced. This function will need both the player's guess string and the computer's secret code string in order to make comparisons between them, so we'll need this function to take those two parameters. We need to return two pieces of information—the number of digits that are correct and the number of digits that are misplaced—so we'll return a list of two integers.

10.3.4 *Implementing our functions*

Having completed our top-down design, we can now work with Copilot to write the code for each of our functions. As always, we're going to write the functions in order from bottom to top. This means that we'll first implement our three subtask functions and then ultimately implement our top-level play function.

RANDOM_STRING

As always when working with Copilot to generate code, we provide the def line and docstring and then Copilot writes the code. In each code listing, we'll also provide some guidance about how the code works.

We want our random_string function to take the number of digits in a secret code as a parameter and return a random secret code without duplicates. In the code for this function, we might expect Copilot to use random.randint in a loop that contin-ues running as long as we don't have enough digits. To avoid adding duplicate digits, the code would add a random digit to the secret code only if that digit isn't already in there. We found such a solution in our Copilot results, and that's the one we've chosen to present in the following listing.

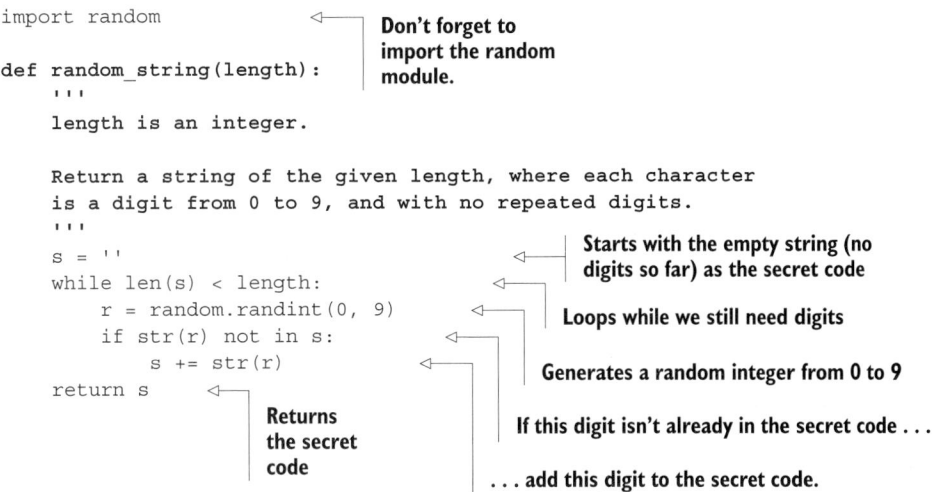

Listing 10.1   Function `random_string` for generating a secret code

```
import random                         ◁──┐   Don't forget to
                                          import the random
def random_string(length):                module.
    '''
    length is an integer.

    Return a string of the given length, where each character
    is a digit from 0 to 9, and with no repeated digits.
    '''
    s = ''                            ◁──────  Starts with the empty string (no
    while len(s) < length:            ◁────    digits so far) as the secret code
        r = random.randint(0, 9)      ◁──      Loops while we still need digits
        if str(r) not in s:           ◁──
            s += str(r)               ◁──      Generates a random integer from 0 to 9
    return s    ◁──
                    Returns           If this digit isn't already in the secret code . . .
                    the secret
                    code              . . . add this digit to the secret code.
```

We're not focusing on testing in this chapter, but even if we were, we wouldn't include exact tests in our docstring for this function. That's because this function has a random result. Randomness can make testing functions difficult because it's hard to control the random values you get. What we could do is add a test to our docstring that at least checks that the generated secret code contains the correct number of characters, that there are no duplicate characters, and that each character is a valid digit. You can also test such functions by running them and observing that their result is always within the bounds of your random range and that the results appear random.

If you did carry through with testing, you'd find that we have a perfectly fine implementation of this function and that there's no need to do more. If you just want the game to work, you can skip to where we start writing the `get_guess` function. If you'd like to learn more about Python and function design, we'd like to take this opportunity to spend a bit more time looking at different solutions to this function.

We encourage you to check out the Copilot suggestions in the window that appears when you press Ctrl-Enter to see some of the other possibilities. For example, we can start with a list of all the integers from 0 to 9 and then use a function called `random.shuffle` to shuffle that list into random order. Then, all we do is take the first `length` integers from that shuffled list (where `length` is the length of the secret code), and that's the secret code! We're guaranteed not to get any duplicate digits because the original list that we shuffle doesn't have any duplicate digits. That version of the function might look like the following listing.

```
import random
def random_string(length):
    '''
    length is an integer.

    Return a string of the given length, where each character
    is a digit from 0 to 9, and with no repeated digits.
    '''
    digits = list(range(10))
    random.shuffle(digits)
    return ''.join(str(d) for d in digits[:length])
```

Creates the list [0, 1, 2, 3, 4, 5, 6, 7, 8, 9]

Shuffles the list in a random order

Returns the first "length" digits from the shuffled list

If you want to learn more about what this code is doing, you have the tools to do that! Don't assume that the code is out of your grasp. You can ask Copilot to explain the code. You might get an explanation like the following.

Human   What does my `random_string` function do?

GitHub Copilot   The code is a Python function called `random_string` that takes an integer `length` as input and returns a string of the given length, where each character is a digit from 0 to 9, and with no repeated digits.

The function first creates a list of digits from 0 to 9 using the `range` function and the `list` constructor. It then shuffles the list using the `shuffle` function from the random module. This ensures that the digits are in a random order.

Finally, the function uses a list comprehension to convert the first `length` digits of the shuffled list to strings and join them together into a single string using the `join` method.

Overall, the `random_string` function generates a random string of digits with no repeated digits, which can be useful for generating unique identifiers or passwords.

What's a *list comprehension*? You don't need to figure this out on your own, you can ask Copilot to explain it.

Human   How does that list comprehension work?

GitHub Copilot   The list comprehension in the `random_string` function is used to convert the first `length` digits of the shuffled list to strings and join them together into a single string using the `join` method.

Here's a breakdown of how the list comprehension works:

1 `str(d) for d in digits[:length]` is the expression that generates the list of strings. It takes each digit in the first `length` elements of the `digits` list, converts it to a string using the `str` function, and returns the resulting string.

2 `digits[:length]` is the iterable that the list comprehension operates on. It takes the first `length` elements of the `digits` list, which have been shuffled randomly.

3 The entire list comprehension is enclosed in square brackets, which creates a new list from the elements generated by the expression.

Finally, the `join` method is called on the resulting list of strings to join them together into a single string with no separator between them.

Some of this text from Copilot may not be completely understandable, but you could keep asking it to explain what you're unsure about until you're satisfied you understand how this is working.

We didn't need to show this second working solution for this function, but we want to take this opportunity to remind you of how far you've come. As you've progressed through the book, you've been developing tools and techniques to understand and create software as well as the confidence to learn and keep learning more! Getting back to the problem at hand, let's code our next function.

GET_GUESS

Our `get_guess` function takes the number of required digits as a parameter and returns a valid guess from the player. Remember that for a guess to be valid, it must contain the right number of digits, and it must not have any duplicate digits. Here's what we got from Copilot in the following listing.

Listing 10.3 Function `get_guess` for user input

```python
def get_guess(length):
    '''
    length is an integer.                           First tries to get
                                                    a valid guess from
    Keep asking the player to enter a string where each character
    is a digit from 0 to 9, until they enter a valid guess.
    A valid guess has the given length and has no repeated digits.
    '''
    guess = input('Enter a guess: ')
    while len(guess) != length or not guess.isdigit()\
            or len(set(guess)) != length:            While length is
        guess = input('Enter a guess: ')             wrong, or the guess
    return guess                                     isn't all digits or has
                                                     duplicates . . .
```

First tries to get a valid guess from the player

Returns the valid guess

. . . subsequently tries to get a valid guess from the player

While length is wrong, or the guess isn't all digits or has duplicates . . .

That `while-loop` condition is a complex one! The final part, `len(set(guess)) != length`, is responsible for checking whether the user entered any duplicate digits. It's using a Python set to do that. We did see this trick back in chapter 7, section 7.7.7, but that was a while ago! So, if you need a refresher, don't hesitate to ask Copilot for an explanation of that line.

GUESS_RESULT

Our `guess_result` function takes two strings as parameters: the player's most recent guess and the secret code. It returns a list of two integers: the number of correct digits and the number of misplaced digits.

This is a tricky function to get right, so even though we haven't been showing the tests we'd want to run in prior functions, we're going to provide some explicit tests in the docstring for this function. We're adding these docstring tests because the logic for this function is going to be complex enough that it will be hard to determine whether the code is correct by solely reading the code. For our docstring tests, we'll need some good example cases of different secret codes and user guesses to ensure the number of correct and misplaced digits returned by the function are as expected. Of course, per chapter 6, you'd likely want to add even more test cases if you were interested in doing serious testing. Our first test case is

```
>>> guess_result('3821', '1862')
```

The correct return value here is [1, 2] because there's one digit that's correct (the 8), and two misplaced digits (the 2 and the 1). Our second test case is

```
>>> guess_result('1234', '4321')
```

The correct return value this time is [0, 4] because there are zero correct digits, but all four digits of the guess are misplaced. Here's our complete docstring, including test cases, and the code from Copilot.

Listing 10.4 Function `guess_result` to get the result of a guess

```
def guess_result(guess, secret_code):
    '''
    guess and secret_code are strings of the same length.

    Return a list of two values:
    the first value is the number of indices in guess where
    the character at that index matches the character at the
    same index in secret_code; the second value is the
    number of indices in guess where the character at that
    index exists at a different index in secret_code.

    >>> guess_result('3821', '1862')
    [1, 2]
    >>> guess_result('1234', '4321')
    [0, 4]
    '''
    correct = 0
    misplaced = 0
    for i in range(len(guess)):
        if guess[i] == secret_code[i]:
            correct += 1
```

This variable is for the correct digits.

This variable is for the misplaced digits.

Goes through each index of the digit strings

This digit is correct.

Increases correct count by 1

```
    elif guess[i] in secret_code:        ◁───┐  This isn't a match but is misplaced.
        misplaced += 1          ◁───────────┘
return [correct, misplaced]  ◁──────┐
                                    │        Increases misplaced count by 1
                                    │
                                    └──────  Returns both results in a list
```

The use of `elif` is subtle here. If it were written as `if` rather than `elif`, then the code would be wrong! Do you see why? If not, try conversing with Copilot before continuing to read our explanation here.

Suppose that the `if` condition `guess[i] == secret_code[i]` is `True`. In that case, we increase `correct` by 1, and we skip the `elif` statements. (Remember, the `elif` statements run only if the preceding `if` and any preceding `elif` conditions are `False`.)

Now, imagine we changed the `elif` to an `if`. If the `if` condition `guess[i] == secret_code[i]` is `True`, we'd still increase `correct` by 1. But then, we'd check the `guess[i] in secret_code` condition, and this one would be `True` as well. After all, we just said that `guess[i] == secret_code[i]`, which proves that `guess[i]` is indeed somewhere in `secret_code`. So, we'd erroneously do the `misplaced += 1`, which we certainly don't want to do (it's a matched digit, not a misplaced one too)!

PLAY

We're done with our subtask functions! Now all we need to do is write the `play` top-level function.

Our `play` function takes two integers as parameters: the number of digits in the secret code and guesses, and the number of guesses that the player has to guess the secret code. It doesn't return anything—it just plays the game! Our final prompt and code for this function is given in the following listing.

Listing 10.5 Function `play` for playing the game

```
def play(num_digits, num_guesses):
    '''
    Generate a random string with num_digits digits.
    The player has num_guesses guesses to guess the random
    string. After each guess, the player is told how many
    digits in the guess are in the correct place, and how
    many digits exist but are in the wrong place.
    '''
    answer = random_string(num_digits)
    print('I generated a random {}-digit number.'.format(num_digits))
    print('You have {} guesses to guess the number.'.format(num_guesses))
    for i in range(num_guesses):
        guess = get_guess(num_digits)
        result = guess_result(guess, answer)
        print('Correct: {}, Misplaced: {}'.format( \
                    result[0], result[1]))
```

Annotations:
- Generates the computer's secret code → (`answer = random_string(num_digits)`)
- Loops once for each possible player guess → (`for i in range(num_guesses):`)
- Gets the next valid guess from the player → (`guess = get_guess(num_digits)`)
- Gets the "correct" and "misplaced" feedback for this guess → (`result = guess_result(guess, answer)`)
- Tells the player the hints → (`print('Correct: {}, Misplaced: {}'...`)

```
    if guess == answer:
        print('You win!')
        return
print('You lose! The correct answer was \
            {}.'.format(answer))
```

Player correctly guesses the secret code!

Exits the function; this ends the game.

If we get here, then the player ran out of guesses.

If we ran our program now, nothing would happen. That's because we haven't called the `play` function yet! We always need to remember to call our top-level function. To call it, we can add this line below the `play` function:

```
play(4, 10)
```

The `4` means that we're playing with four-digit codes and guesses, and the `10` means that we have 10 guesses to correctly guess the secret code. You can change these arguments to tune the game how you like.

Let's give our game a whirl before we continue. We'll show our first few guesses and then our final guess:

```
I generated a random 4-digit number.
You have 10 guesses to guess the number.
Enter a guess: 0123
Correct: 1, Misplaced: 0
Enter a guess: 4567
Correct: 1, Misplaced: 0
Enter a guess: 8901
Correct: 2, Misplaced: 0
Enter a guess: 8902
Correct: 2, Misplaced: 1
...
Enter a guess: 2897
Correct: 1, Misplaced: 3
You lose! The correct answer was 8927.
```

We've succeeded in designing a computer game, which is a very different kind of program than the other programs we've written in this book. Our computer game interacts with the user, has randomness, involves two players (the human player guessing and the computer player providing the correct/misplaced clues), and has winning and losing conditions. That's a lot of new stuff! However, we also hope that you see how much we've learned and brought forward from prior chapters. We're still doing top-down design, still designing functions, still testing code, still reading code, and still conversing with Copilot. You hadn't written a game prior to this chapter, but essentially, you already had the skills to do that. Don't let a seemingly new type of program or app stop you from trying to do it.

10.3.5 *Adding a graphical interface for Bulls and Cows*

You might be disappointed that our game doesn't look much like a game you've recently played because there are no graphics, just text. For example, there's no nice area to type in, no buttons to click, and no graphical interface at all. We've already argued why we focus on text games in this chapter, but it doesn't mean that turning this game into a graphical interface version is entirely out of your grasp because you could interact with Copilot to see if it can help you get started.

The challenge is that programmers create graphical user interfaces using a style of programming called *event-driven programming*, which we haven't taught you yet and is too large to teach in this chapter. You can likely read through event-driven programming code and make some sense of it, and that's what you'd need to do if you ask Copilot to write code to produce a graphical interface. That said, if Copilot doesn't give you what you want, it may be difficult to fix without first becoming familiar with event-driven programming. There's a nice book on game programming that includes graphical user interfaces and event-driven programming in Python called *Invent Your Own Computer Games with Python* [3] if you'd like to learn more.

> **Event-driven programming**
>
> Event-driven programming is commonly used for programs that interact with users. At a high level, the program sets up a way for the user to interact with the program (e.g., by pressing buttons or entering text) and then just sits and waits for the user to do something, sometimes updating the state of the game while waiting for the user input. Once the human interacts with the game, the code recognizes this interaction as an *event*, and each event has code associated with it that should execute when the event occurs. For example, when a user clicks the Quit Game button, it triggers the code that needs to be executed when the user wants to quit (e.g., saving the state of the game and exiting the program).

We were quite impressed by what Copilot gave us when we asked it to create the graphical interface for Bulls and Cows, so we'd like to show you how well it did. The code is somewhat readable even without knowing event-driven programming. For example, you can probably find the title of the game and change it. To do this, we asked Copilot Chat the following question:

> **Human** Can you convert this program to use a graphical interface instead of a text interface?

Copilot responded to us by laying out, step by step, the changes that we'd need to make to do so. It then rewrote the code so that the game now used a graphical interface with buttons and edit boxes, rather than a text interface. See figure 10.4 for the new interface. The code to generate this interface is on the website for the book in case you're interested in running it yourself or learning about the code.

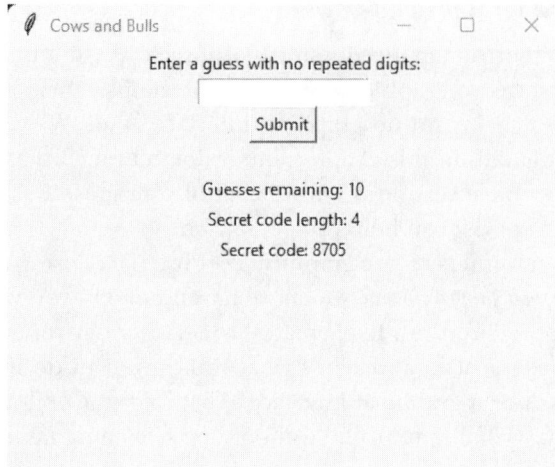

Figure 10.4 The graphical interface for the game as provided by Copilot. Note that it shows the secret code, presumably to help with testing (you'd want to remove that before playing the game).

10.4 Example 2: Bogart

Our second game will be a two-player dice game. In Bulls and Cows, one of our players was human and the other was the computer. This time, we'll write a game for two human players. Randomness again will play a key role. Once we're done, you can play against a friend or family member!

10.4.1 How the game works

The game that we'll be writing here is called Bogart and was designed by Crab Fragment Labs. This is a dice game for two players. The game also uses a pot of chips or coins. We obviously won't need actual dice or chips, though, as we're implementing this as a computer game.

> **Bogart**
>
> The Bogart game was designed by James Ernest (© 1999 James Ernest and Cheapass Games, used by permission; https://crabfragmentlabs.com/). You can download the instructions for the original game for free as part of a .pdf file of games: https://crabfragmentlabs.com/shop/p/chief-herman-1. If you enjoy the game and can't stop playing our re-creation, we encourage you to support the work that Crab Fragment Labs is doing. We thank them for letting us use their game here!

When the game starts, the pot of chips is empty (has no chips in it). One of the two players is randomly chosen to start the game. From there, each player takes turns until the game is over. We'll first explain what it means for a player to take a turn and then give the rules for when the game ends. Figure 10.5 provides an overview of the flow of the game as well.

At the beginning of a player's turn, one chip gets added to the pot, and that player rolls one die. If that die is a 1, then the player's turn is over, and they don't collect any chips. If that die isn't a 1, then the player gets to decide whether to continue their turn or not. If they decide not to continue their turn, they collect all the chips from the pot (making the pot empty).

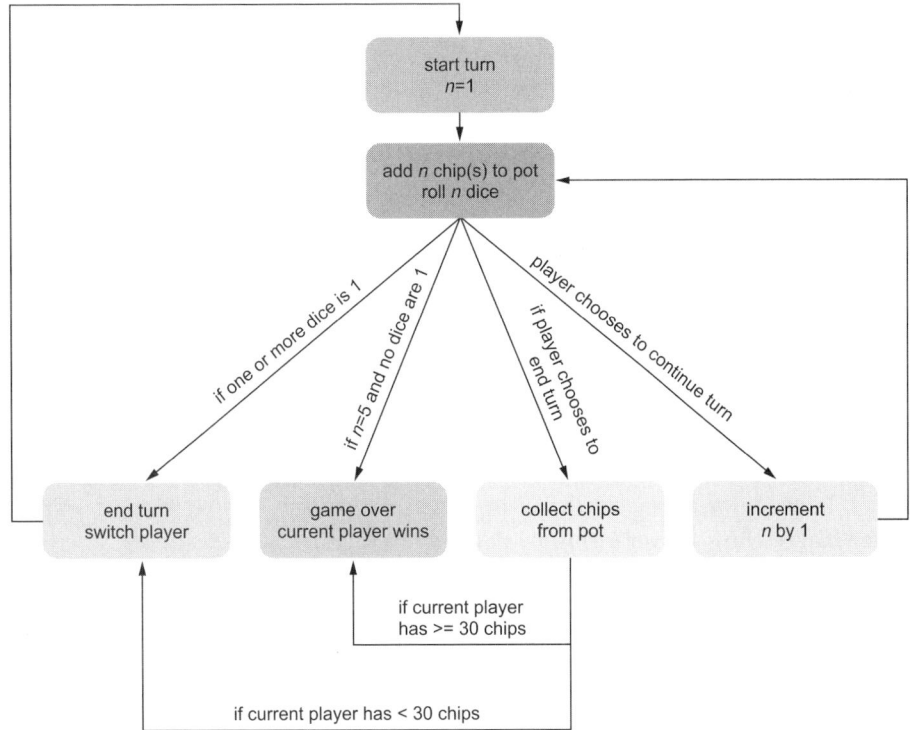

Figure 10.5   Player turn in Bogart

If they do decide to continue their turn, then two chips get added to the pot, and they roll two dice. If one or both of those dice is a 1, then the player's turn is over. Otherwise, the player again gets to decide whether to continue their turn or not.

If they continue their turn, then they roll three dice, then four dice, and then five dice. (Players can't choose to skip a number of dice; they must work through the number of dice sequentially starting from one die.) If they ever roll a 1, then their turn ends, and they don't collect any chips. If they decide not to continue their turn, then they collect all the chips from the pot.

Rolling a 1 in this game is bad news for the current player. When rolling one die, the probability of rolling a 1 is low, only 1 in 6 (about 17%). When rolling two dice, the probability of rolling at least one 1 is higher, this time about 31%. It's higher still when rolling three dice (42%), four dice (52%), or five dice (60%). So, the longer you extend your turn, the higher the probability that you'll eventually roll a 1 and get nothing for your turn. Worse, you'll likely leave the pot quite full for the other player to collect if they play more conservatively than you. At the same time, the longer you extend your turn, the faster the chips in the pot accumulate and the more chips you can collect assuming that you do successfully end your turn eventually. The whole trick is to decide when to press your luck for more chips and when to take what you've got.

This is how a player's turn works. Players alternate turns, rolling dice and collecting chips, until the game ends. There are two ways that the game can end:

1 If a player collects a total of 30 or more chips, then that player wins.
2 Say a player on their turn rolls one die, then two dice, then three, then four, and then five, never once rolling a 1. Then, that player instantly wins. It doesn't matter how many chips they've collected: if they get to five dice of which none are a 1, they win.

EXAMPLE GAME OF BOGART

Let's play out a few turns of the game to make sure we're clear on how it all works. The pot starts out empty. Let's say that Player 1 is the player randomly chosen to go first. We add one chip to the pot, and Player 1 rolls one die. Let's say that they roll a 5. Now Player 1 has to decide whether to end their turn and take the one chip from the pot or continue their turn.

Let's say that they continue their turn. We add two chips to the pot; now the pot has three chips. Player 1 rolls two dice. Let's say they roll a 4 and a 2.

Should they end their turn and take the three chips? Nah, nah. They want more. They continue their turn. We add three chips to the pot; now the pot has six chips. Player 1 rolls three dice. This time, they roll a 6, a 5, and—oh no!—a 1. Player 1's turn is over. They got no chips, and they left a juicy six chips in the pot for Player 2.

Now it's Player 2's turn. We add one chip to the pot—that's seven chips now!—and Player 2 rolls one die. Let's say that they roll a 2. If Player 2 ends their turn now, they'll collect the seven chips from the pot. That feels like a lot, so let's say that Player 2 does decide to end their turn.

Now the pot is empty, and it's back to being Player 1's turn. Player 1 has some catching up to do: they have 0 chips and Player 2 has 7 chips. We'll stop here, but the game will continue until one of the players racks up 30 or more chips or they get to roll five dice and manage not to roll a single 1.

10.4.2 Top-down design

As was the case when we implemented our Bulls and Cows game, implementing Bogart is a large problem for which we need top-down design. We'll offer that design now, but here we encourage you to try it on your own before continuing. We recommend this because we found an effective top-down design to be subtle for this game due to the number of interacting elements. For example, a player's turn can end in one of three ways: collect the chips, don't collect the chips, and instantly win. We need to be able to determine which of these situations happened. As another example, after each player's turn, we need to switch to the other player—except, unfortunately, not always: if a player wins the game, we want to stop the game right there and declare them the winner, not switch to the other player! We'll primarily focus on our successful top-down design here, but we'll occasionally justify why we made our decisions and what went wrong with other decisions.

We'll name our top-level function `play`. Here are the main subtasks that we'll need to solve for our game:

1 Initialize the pot, and start Player 1 and Player 2 with zero chips. This is part of the game setup phase.

2 Randomly choose Player 1 or Player 2 to start the game. This too is part of the game setup.

3 Now we enter the gameplay phase. While the game isn't over, do the following:

   3a Print the number of chips in the pot, number of chips Player 1 has, and number of chips Player 2 has.

   3b Take a full turn for the current player.

   3c If the current player won chips, give the chips to the current player, and reset the pot to have zero chips.

   3d Switch to the other player's turn.

4 Print the name of the player (Player 1 or Player 2) who won the game.

At this point in the book, we suspect you've become familiar enough with the code from Copilot to have some nice intuition about which of these tasks will require separate functions. Task 1 is just a few variable assignments, so we don't need a separate function for that. Other tasks for which we don't need a separate function are task 2 (just a call to `random.randint`), 3a (just a few `print` calls), and 4 (a `print` call). We'll capture each of the remaining subtasks in a function. The following subsections describe each of the remaining subtasks.

TASK 3. WHILE THE GAME ISN'T OVER

We'll have a `while` loop that continues while the game isn't over, so we'll need a function to tell us whether the game is over! How can the function know whether the game is over? It'll need to know the current number of chips that Player 1 has and the current number of chips that Player 2 has. That way, it can check whether one of these is at least 30. But remember that there's another way for the game to end, and that's when a player rolls five dice, none of which is a 1. Therefore, this function will also need to know the most recent dice rolls for the current player.

We'll name this function `game_over`. It will take three parameters: Player 1 chips, Player 2 chips, and list of rolls. It will return `True` if the game is over and `False` otherwise. The code for this function will need to check a few conditions, but we should be able to do that without splitting it out into further subtasks.

TASK 3B. TAKE A FULL TURN FOR THE CURRENT PLAYER

We'll name this function `take_full_turn`. The function *needs* to know how many chips are in the pot right now, so that it can update that as needed. It'll also need to return the updated number of chips in the pot. Beyond that, there's a lot that we need to manage to carry out a full turn, so we're going to need to keep the complexity of this function under control. Here's what comes to mind for what this function may need to do:

1 Allow the player to roll one die, then two dice, then three dice, and so on until the player's turn is over.

2 Update the current player's number of chips based on what happened on this turn. We could add an additional return value to communicate this updated information to whoever called this function.

3 Determine whether the game is over. We could add an additional return value where `True` means that the game is over and `False` means that it isn't.

We initially tried to have the function do all three of these things but were unable to receive satisfactory code from Copilot. This isn't too surprising because we're asking the function to do too much. This led us to focus on the core of this function, which is point 1.

But OK, if we focus only on point 1, then how are we going to update the current player's number of chips (point 2), and how will we know whether the game is over (point 3)? For point 2, the solution we thought of is to not update the current player's chip count at all in this function, instead returning the total number of chips in the pot after this turn.

For example, if there were 10 chips in the pot and this player's turn generated 6 chips, then we'd return 16. The player may or may not get to collect these 16 chips—it depends on how their turn ended—but we won't deal with that here (this is for the calling function to manage now).

For point 3 (knowing whether the game is over), our solution is to have the function return the most recent list of rolls as part of its return value. (This list of rolls will also be needed by the calling function for point 2.) The function that calls this one can then use those rolls to determine whether the game is over.

In summary, our function will take the number of chips in the pot as a parameter and will return a list of two values: the new number of chips in the pot after the player's turn and the most recent list of rolls.

To take a full turn, we'll need to be able to roll dice: first one die, then two dice, then three dice, and so on. We'll split this out into a function named `roll_dice`. It will take the number of dice to roll as a parameter and will return a list of rolls. For example, if we ask the function to roll three dice, we might get back `[6, 1, 4]`.

We'll also need to be able to determine whether the turn is over based on the most recent list of rolls. If the player rolled any 1s or rolled five dice none of which is a 1, then the turn is over. We'll split that out too into a function named `turn_over`.

It will take the list of rolls as a parameter and will return `True` if the turn is over and `False` if not.

If the turn isn't over, then we'll need to ask the player whether they want to continue their turn. We'll ask for a yes (y) or no (n) response. We can do that using a call to the `input` function. If the player wants to keep going, we can again call `roll_dice`. We don't need a separate function for asking for user input, so we won't break this part down any further. If we wanted to validate the user's input (rejecting any response that's not y or n), that would increase the complexity enough so that we'd probably split it out.

In summary, we've split out two subtasks for our `take_full_turn` function: `roll_dice` and `turn_over`. These functions don't need to be broken down any further. For `roll_dice`, we can use `random.randint` in a loop to generate the rolls that we need. And, `turn_over` will amount to a couple of checks on the dice rolls to determine whether they ended the turn for which we won't need any further breaking down.

TASK 3C. IF THE CURRENT PLAYER WON CHIPS

When a player's turn ends, we're furnished with the new number of chips in the pot and the final list of rolls that ended the turn. We need to determine whether the player gets those chips or not. (If the final list of rolls doesn't contain a 1, then the player collects the chips; otherwise, they don't, and the chips stay in the pot.)

We'll split out a function to tell us whether the player collects the chips or not. We'll name it `wins_chips`. This function will take the most recent list of rolls as a parameter and will return `True` if the player wins the chips and `False` otherwise.

TASK 3D. SWITCH TO THE OTHER PLAYER'S TURN

We'll name this function `switch_player`. Suppose that the current player has just finished their turn. We need to switch to the other player's turn, but only if the game isn't over yet. Our function will encapsulate this logic. It will need to call `game_over` to determine whether the game is over, so we need at least three parameters for `switch_player`: player 1's chips, player 2's chips, and the most recent list of dice rolls. We'll also need a parameter to indicate the current player (1 or 2), so that we can return the number of the new current player. So, the function will take those four parameters, and it will return a 1 or a 2 indicating the player that we're switching to next.

If the game is over, this function won't do anything. And if the game isn't over, then we'll need to change a 1 to a 2 or a 2 to a 1. We already have the `game_over` function, and that's sufficient for breaking down this function.

We've finished our top-down design! Check out figure 10.6 for our tree of functions.

10.4.3 *Implementing our functions*

Now it's time to work with Copilot to write the code for each of our functions. As always, we'll start with leaf functions and move our way up (left in the diagram), implementing our top-level `play` function only when all other functions have been implemented. We can start with any leaf function. We'll start with the `game_over`

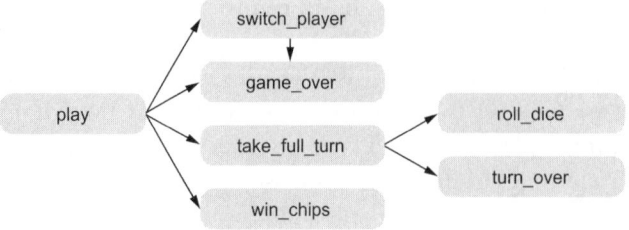

Figure 10.6   Top-down design for the Bogart game

function because it's needed both by `play` and by `switch_player`. Then, we'll move on to other functions.

GAME_OVER

This function takes three parameters: the number of chips that Player 1 has, the number of chips that Player 2 has, and the most recent list of rolls. It returns `True` if the game is over, and `False` if not, as shown in the following listing.

Listing 10.6   `game_over` function in Bogart

```
def game_over(player1, player2, rolls):
    '''
    player1 is the number of chips that player 1 has.
    player2 is the number of chips that player 2 has.
    rolls is the last list of dice rolls.

    Return True if the game is over, False otherwise.

    The game is over if player1 has at least 30 chips,
    or player 2 has at least 30 chips,
    or there are 5 rolls none of which is a 1.
    '''
    return player1 >= 30 or player2 >= 30 or \          The three ways that
           (len(rolls) == 5 and not 1 in rolls)         the game is over
```

Remember that there are three ways for the game to be over: Player 1 has at least 30 chips, Player 2 has at least 30 chips, or a player managed to roll five dice on their last turn without rolling a 1.

Returning a Boolean directly

You may have expected to see the code this way, with the use of `if-else` and actual `return True` and `return False` lines:

```
if player1 >= 30 or player2 >= 30 or (len(rolls) == 5
        and not 1 in rolls):
    return True
else:
    return False
```

This would work, but it's more common to see programmers use a `return` statement directly with the `True`/`False` expression. It works because the result of the expression is what is being returned. If the expression is true, `True` gets returned, and if the expression is false, `False` gets returned. That's exactly the same thing that the `if-else` version does!

ROLL_DICE

This is the function that rolls our dice and adds randomness to our game. It takes the number of dice to roll as a parameter, and it returns the list of dice rolls. We'll expect Copilot to make use of `random.randint` here, as shown in listing 10.7.

In addition to returning the list of rolls, it's also helpful if this function prints each dice roll. That way, the player can see exactly what they rolled. In the docstring, we ask Copilot to print the rolls (in addition to returning the list of rolls).

Listing 10.7 `roll_dice` **function in Bogart**

```python
import random
def roll_dice(n):
    '''
    Create a list of n random integers between 1 and 6.
    Print each of these integers, and return the list.
    '''
    rolls = []                        # List of dice rolls (integers between 1 and 6), starts empty
    for i in range(n):                # Loops n times, once per roll
        roll = random.randint(1, 6)   # Uses "randint" to generate a random integer between 1 and 6
        print(roll)                   # Prints roll for players to see
        rolls.append(roll)            # Adds roll to list of rolls
    return rolls                      # Returns list of rolls
```

TURN_OVER

This function takes the most recent list of rolls and uses that to determine whether the current player's turn is over or not. It returns `True` if the turn is over, and `False` if not, as shown in the following listing.

Listing 10.8 `turn_over` **function in Bogart**

```python
def turn_over(rolls):
    '''
    Return True if the turn is over, False otherwise.

    The turn is over if any of the rolls is a 1,
    or if there are exactly five rolls.
    '''
    return 1 in rolls or len(rolls) == 5    # The two ways for the turn to be over
```

There are two ways for the player's turn to be over. The first is when there's a 1 in the list of rolls. The second is when the player has rolled five dice.

Is len(rolls) == 5 really enough for the turn to be over? Don't we have to check whether there were any 1s rolled? No, if the player rolls five dice, then their turn is over no matter what, regardless of what the dice rolls were. If they rolled any 1s, then the turn is over because they rolled a 1 (and they won't collect any chips). If they didn't roll any 1s, then the turn is still over (and they'll win the game automatically in this case).

TAKE_FULL_TURN

We're ready for take_full_turn now, as shown in listing 10.9. This function takes the number of chips currently in the pot as a parameter. It will process all the rolls from a full turn for the current player and then returns a list of two values: the new number of chips in the pot and the final list of rolls.

Listing 10.9 take_full_turn **function in Bogart**

```
def take_full_turn(pot_chips):
    '''
    The pot has pot_chips chips.

    Take a full turn for the current player and, once done,
    return a list of two values:
    the number of chips in the pot, and the final list of dice rolls.

    Begin by rolling 1 die, and put 1 chip into the pot.
    Then, if the turn isn't over, ask the player whether
    they'd like to continue their turn.
    If they respond 'n', then the turn is over.
        If they respond 'y', then roll one more die than last time,
        and add 1 chip to the pot for each die that is rolled.
        (for example, if 3 dice were rolled last time, then
        roll 4 dice and add 4 chips to the pot.)
    If the turn is not over, repeat by asking the player again
    whether they'd like to continue their turn.
    '''
    rolls = roll_dice(1)                                   ← Rolls one dice
    pot_chips += 1                                          ← Adds one chip to the pot
    while not turn_over(rolls):                            ← While the current player's turn isn't over . . .
        keep_going = input('Continue? (y/n) ')            ← . . . asks the player if they want to continue their turn.
        if keep_going == 'y':                             ← If they do want to continue their turn . . .
            rolls = roll_dice(len(rolls) + 1)             ← . . . rolls one more dice than last time.
            pot_chips += len(rolls)                       ← Adds new chips to the pot
        else:
            break                                          ← Gets out of the while loop
    return pot_chips, rolls                               ← Returns both number of chips in the pot and the final list of rolls
```

WINS_CHIPS

This function takes a list of rolls as a parameter. If the rolls are good (i.e., contain no 1s), then the player will collect the chips. If the rolls contain any 1s, then the player won't collect the chips. This function returns `True` if the player gets to collect the chips, and `False` otherwise, as shown in the following listing.

Listing 10.10 `wins_chips` **function in Bogart**

```
def wins_chips(rolls):
    '''
    Return True if the player wins chips, False otherwise.

    The player wins the chips if none of the rolls is a 1.
    '''
    return not 1 in rolls            ⟵⎯│ Returns True when there are no
                                        1s, and returns False otherwise
```

SWITCH_PLAYER

This function takes four parameters: the number of chips that Player 1 has, the number of chips that Player 2 has, the most recent list of rolls (rolled by the current player), and the number of the current player. If the game isn't over, this function returns the number of the other player. If the game is over, then the function returns the current player (because there's no turn for the other player!). See the following listing.

Listing 10.11 `switch_player` **function in Bogart**

```
def switch_player(player1, player2, rolls, current_player):
    '''
    player1 is the number of chips that player 1 has.
    player2 is the number of chips that player 2 has.
    rolls is the last list of dice rolls.
    current_player is the current player (1 or 2).

    If the game is not over, switch current_player to the other player.
    Return the new current_player.
    '''
    if not game_over(player1, player2, rolls):    ⟵⎯│ If game isn't over . . .
        if current_player == 1:                 ⟵⎯┐ . . . switches from 1 to
            current_player = 2                       │ 2 or from 2 to 1.
        else:
            current_player = 1
    return current_player            ⟵⎯│ Returns new
                                        current player
```

PLAY

We've made it all the way up to our `play` function! We've decided to write this function without any parameters. You might wonder if we could make the code more flexible by adding, say, a parameter for the number of chips required to win (currently 30). You could certainly do that; we haven't done that here to keep the number of parameters smaller throughout the code. This function doesn't return anything. Instead, it plays the game, as shown in the following listing.

Listing 10.12 `play` function in Bogart

```
def play():
    '''
    Play the game until the game is over.

    The pot starts with 0 chips, and each player starts with 0 chips.

    Randomly decide whether player 1 or player 2 goes first.

    Before each turn, print three lines of information:
    1. The number of chips in the pot
    2. The number of chips that each player has
    3. Whether it is player 1's turn or player 2's turn

    Take a full turn for the current player.
    If they won the chips, add the chips in the pot to the
    total for that player and reset the pot to have 0 chips.

    Then, switch to the other player's turn.

    Once the game is over, print the current player
    (that's the player who won).
    '''
    pot_chips = 0
    player1 = 0
    player2 = 0
    current_player = random.randint(1, 2)
    rolls = []
    while not game_over(player1, player2, rolls):
        print('Pot chips:', pot_chips)
        print('Player 1 chips:', player1)
        print('Player 2 chips:', player2)
        print('Player', current_player, 'turn')
        pot_chips, rolls = take_full_turn(pot_chips)
        if wins_chips(rolls):
            if current_player == 1:
                player1 += pot_chips
            else:
                player2 += pot_chips
            pot_chips = 0
        current_player = switch_player(player1, player2,
                                       rolls, current_player)
    print('Player', current_player, 'wins!')
```

Starts pot and players with 0 chips

Randomly makes Player 1 or Player 2 start the game

While the game isn't over . . .

. . . prints the current state of the game.

Lets the current player have their turn

If current player wins chips . . .

. . . and it's Player 1 . . .

. . . gives Player 1 the chips from the pot; . . .

Prints out who wins

Resets pot to now have 0 chips

Switches to the other player's turn

. . . otherwise, gives Player 2 the chips from the pot.

We now have all the code that we need for the game. Just add

```
play()
```

below all of your existing code to call our `play` function, and then you'll be able to play!

CUSTOMIZING THE GAME

We're happy with what Copilot has given us, and the game is certainly playable. But, admittedly, the interaction with the players could be a little more user-friendly. For example, here's how the game might start when we run it and press y a few times:

```
Pot chips: 0
Player 1 chips: 0
Player 2 chips: 0
Player 2 turn
4
Continue? (y/n) y
5
2
Continue? (y/n) y
3
1
4
Pot chips: 6
Player 1 chips: 0
Player 2 chips: 0
Player 1 turn
2
Continue? (y/n)
```

There's no welcome message. Numbers like 4, 5, 2, and so on are just there, with no context of what they mean. The game asks us whether we want to "Continue? (y/n)." Continue what, though? It isn't clear.

We can make the interaction with the players more pleasant by spicing up the `print` calls in our functions. We can just put what we want in each `print` statement ourselves. Why not just use Copilot? It's likely easier to just do it rather than trying to cajole Copilot to print exactly what we want. For example, the following listing shows a new version of `play` where we've added more `print` calls to explain what's going on and to better format the game output.

Listing 10.13   `play` function in Bogart with better formatting

```python
def play():
    '''
    Play the game until the game is over.

    The pot starts with 0 chips, and each player starts with 0 chips.

    Randomly decide whether player 1 or player 2 goes first.

    Before each turn, print three lines of information:
    1. The number of chips in the pot
```

2. The number of chips that each player has
3. Whether it is player 1's turn or player 2's turn

Take a full turn for the current player.
If they won the chips, add the chips in the pot to the
total for that player
and reset the pot to have 0 chips.

Then, switch to the other player's turn.

Once the game is over, print the current player
(that's the player who won).
'''
```python
pot_chips = 0
player1 = 0
player2 = 0
current_player = random.randint(1, 2)
rolls = []
```

```python
print('Welcome to Bogart!')   ⟵──┐ Prints welcome message
print()                        ⟵──── Prints a blank line
```

```python
while not game_over(player1, player2, rolls):
    print('Pot chips:', pot_chips)
    print('Player 1 chips:', player1)
    print('Player 2 chips:', player2)
    print('Player', current_player, 'turn')
    pot_chips, rolls = take_full_turn(pot_chips)
    if wins_chips(rolls):
        print('Player', current_player, 'gets',     ⟵┤ Prints message saying that
              pot_chips, 'chips!')                       the current player got chips
        if current_player == 1:
            player1 += pot_chips
        else:
            player2 += pot_chips
        pot_chips = 0
    current_player = switch_player(player1, player2,
                                   rolls, current_player)

    print()
    print()
    print('-=' * 20)   ⟵┤ Separates each turn
    print()                from the next
```

```python
print('Player', current_player, 'wins!')
```

We encourage you to add `print` calls elsewhere as well to make the game interaction even better! For example, in `roll_dice`, you could add a `print` call to tell the players that dice are about to be rolled (**ROLLS** in the following output). In `take_full_turn`, you could add a `print` call to print the number of chips in the pot prior to asking the player whether they'd like to continue their turn. Here's what an interaction with our game looks like after we made those changes:

Welcome to Bogart!
Pot chips: 0
Player 1 chips: 0
Player 2 chips: 0
Player 2 turn
ROLLS
2
The pot currently has 1 chips.
Continue turn? (y/n) y
ROLLS
6
3
The pot currently has 3 chips.
Continue turn? (y/n) y
ROLLS
1
1
6
-=-=-=-=-=-=-=-=-=-=-=-=-=-=
Pot chips: 6
Player 1 chips: 0
Player 2 chips: 0
Player 1 turn
ROLLS
5
The pot currently has 7 chips.
Continue turn? (y/n)

Try making such changes to your code as well. Make the game yours!

In this chapter, we used Copilot to help us write two computer games: a logic game (similar to Wordle, but with numbers), and a two-player dice game. We were able to do this using the skills we've honed throughout the book, including problem decomposition, writing clear docstrings, and interacting with Copilot Chat.

10.5 Exercises

1 There is an error in the following `guess_result` function that leads to incorrect counts of correct and misplaced digits. Identify and fix the error:

```
def guess_result(guess, secret_code):
    correct = 0
    misplaced = 0
    for i in range(len(guess)):
        if guess[i] == secret_code[i]:
    correct += 1
```

```
    if guess[i] in secret_code:
        misplaced += 1
return [correct, misplaced]
```

2   Modify the `get_guess` function from this chapter to include error messages that guide the player to enter a valid guess. Ensure that these messages are clear and helpful. Be creative! Here are some examples:

     a   "Error: Guess must contain only digits."

     b   "Error: Guess must not contain repeated digits."

3   Why did we choose to pass the number of digits and the number of guesses as parameters to the `play` function for the Bulls and Cows game? How does this decision enhance the flexibility of the game?

4   Implement a simple dice game where the player rolls two dice. If the total is 7 or 11, the player wins. If the total is 2, 3, or 12, the player loses. For any other total, the player continues to roll until they either match their initial roll (win) or roll a 7 (lose). Think carefully about how you want to divide the main problem here into smaller subproblems!

5   Implement a version of the Bogart game where one player is human and the other is the computer. To do this, you'll need to come up with some rules that the computer can use to end their turn. For example, the computer will certainly want to stop rolling dice when the number of chips that they've already accumulated on their turn is enough for them to win the game! The computer will also likely want to stop rolling once it can earn a large number of chips on its current turn.

6   *The Price Is Right* game show is a great source of little games that may be fun to implement. For example, you can try implementing the game called Any Number:

https://priceisright.fandom.com/wiki/Any_Number

In your game, the player should continue to choose numbers until all the digits of one of the prizes are revealed; that's the prize that the player wins.

7   Create a simple game using the Pygame library. In this game, the player controls a character that moves left and right to collect falling objects. The objective is to collect as many objects as possible without missing them. You can be flexible here with how the objects in your game look, so have fun with it! As a potential extension: Can you think of how you would keep track of the player's high score?

Summary

- Games have a common program flow that includes game setup and gameplay.
- Randomness is an important ingredient of many games.
- We can add randomness to our Python games by using functions in the random module.
- We can implement games with Copilot using the same workflow that we've used throughout the book, with problem decomposition playing a key role.

11

Creating an authorship identification program

This chapter covers

- Writing an authorship identification program using top-down design
- Learning about refactoring code and why you would do it

In chapter 7, we learned about problem decomposition and top-down design when we wrote our Spelling Suggestions program. Here, we're going to take top-down design to the next level and solve a much larger problem. We're still doing the same thing as in chapter 7: dividing a problem into subproblems, and further dividing those subproblems into sub-subproblems as needed. And, just like before, we're looking to design functions with a small number of parameters that return a meaningful and useful result to their caller. It's also a good sign if we're able to design functions that are called by multiple other functions—that helps reduce code repetition!

We're including this chapter because we wanted to provide a more authentic example than the Spelling Suggestions problem we solved in chapter 7. We hope our example here is motivating and feels like a real problem that you could imagine yourself wanting to solve.

In this chapter, we're going to write a program that tries to identify the unknown author of a mystery book. It'll be an example of a program that uses artificial intelligence (AI) to make a prediction. We couldn't resist the opportunity to include an AI example in a book about programming with AI!

11.1   Authorship identification

This problem is based on an assignment created by our colleague Michelle Craig [1]. Let's start by taking a look at these two book excerpts:

- *Excerpt 1*—I have not yet described to you the most singular part. About six years ago—to be exact, upon the 4th of May 1882—an advertisement appeared in the Times asking for the address of Miss Mary Morstan and stating that it would be to her advantage to come forward. There was no name or address appended. I had at that time just entered the family of Mrs. Cecil Forrester in the capacity of governess. By her advice I published my address in the advertisement column. The same day there arrived through the post a small card-board box addressed to me, which I found to contain a very large and lustrous pearl. No word of writing was enclosed. Since then, every year upon the same date there has always appeared a similar box, containing a similar pearl, without any clue as to the sender. They have been pronounced by an expert to be of a rare variety and of considerable value. You can see for yourselves that they are very handsome.
- *Excerpt 2*—It was the Dover Road that lay on a Friday night late in November, before the first of the persons with whom this history has business. The Dover Road lay, as to him, beyond the Dover mail, as it lumbered up Shooter's Hill. He walked up hill in the mire by the side of the mail, as the rest of the passengers did; not because they had the least relish for walking exercise, under the circumstances, but because the hill, and the harness, and the mud, and the mail, were all so heavy, that the horses had three times already come to a stop, besides once drawing the coach across the road, with the mutinous intent of taking it back to Blackheath. Reins and whip and coachman and guard, however, in combination, had read that article of war which forbade a purpose otherwise strongly in favour of the argument, that some brute animals are endued with Reason; and the team had capitulated and returned to their duty.

Suppose we asked you whether these two excerpts were likely written by the same author. One reasonable assumption you might make is that different authors write differently, and that these differences would show up in metrics that we could calculate about their texts.

For example, whoever wrote the first excerpt seems to use quite a few short sentences in terms of number of words compared to the second excerpt. We find short sentences like "There was no name or address appended" and "No word of writing was enclosed" in the first excerpt; those kinds of sentences are absent from the second. Similarly, the sentences from the first excerpt seem to be less complex than those in the second; look at all of those commas and semicolons in the second excerpt.

This analysis may lead you to believe that these texts are written by different authors, and, indeed, they are. The first is written by Sir Arthur Conan Doyle, and the second by Charles Dickens.

To be fair, we've absolutely cherry-picked these two excerpts. Doyle does use some long, complex sentences. Dickens does use some short ones. But, on average, at least for the two books that we took these excerpts from, Doyle does write shorter sentences than Dickens. More generally, if we look at two books written by different authors, we might expect to find some quantifiable differences on average.

Suppose that we have a bunch of books whose authors we know. We have one written by Doyle, one written by Dickens, and so on. Then, along comes a mystery book. Oh no! We don't know who wrote it! Is it a lost Sherlock Holmes story from Doyle? A lost *Oliver Twist* sequel from Dickens? We want to find out who that unknown author is, and to do that, we'll turn to a basic AI technique.

Our strategy will be to come up with a *signature* for each author, using one of the books we know they wrote. We'll refer to these signatures as *known signatures*. Each of these signatures will capture metrics about the book text, such as the average number of words per sentence and the average sentence complexity. Then, we'll come up with a signature for the mystery book with an unknown author. We'll call this the *unknown signature*. We'll look through all the known signatures, comparing each one to our unknown signature. We'll use whichever is the closest as our guess for the unknown author.

Of course, we have no idea if the unknown author is really one of the authors whose signatures we have. It could be a completely new author, for example. Even if the unknown author *is* one of the authors whose signature we have, we still might end up guessing wrong. After all, maybe the same author writes books in different styles (giving their books very different signatures), or we simply fail to capture what is most salient about how each of our authors writes. Indeed, we're not after an industry-strength author identification program in this chapter. Still, considering the difficulty of this task, we think it's impressive how well the approach that we'll show you here works.

Machine learning

Authorship identification, as we're doing here, is a *machine learning* (ML) task. ML is a branch of AI designed to help computers "learn" from data in order to make predictions. There are various forms of ML; the one we're using here is called supervised learning. In supervised learning, we have access to training data, which consists of objects and their known categories (or labels). In our case, our objects are book texts, and the category for each book is the author who wrote it. We can train (i.e., learn) on the training set by calculating features—average number of words per sentence, average sentence complexity, and so on—for each book. Later, when we're provided a book whose author we don't know, we can use what we learned in the training to make our prediction (or guess).

11.2   *Authorship identification using top-down design*

Alright, we want to "write a program to determine the author of a book." This seems like a daunting task, and it would be if we were trying to do this in one shot, using a single function. But just like in our Spelling Suggestions example in chapter 7, we're not going to do that. We're going to systematically break this problem down into subproblems that we can solve.

In chapter 7, we solved the Spelling Suggestions problem by using the model of reading input, processing that input, and producing an output result. We can think about our authorship identification program as following that model as well:

- *Input step*—For the input step, we need to ask the user for the filename of the mystery book.
- *Process step*—For the process step, we need to figure out the signature for the mystery book (that's the unknown signature), as well as the signature for each of the books whose author we know (those are the known signatures). Creating the signature for each book is commonly called the training phase in ML. We also need to compare the unknown signature to each known signature to figure out which known signature is closest. These comparisons are the prediction phase in ML.
- *Output step*—For the output step, we need to report to the user the unknown signature that's closest to the known signature.

That is, to solve our overall authorship identification problem, we need to solve these three subproblems. We're starting our top-down design!

We'll name our top-level function `make_guess`. In it, we'll solve each of the three subproblems we identified.

For the input step, we're simply asking the user for a filename. That's something we can do in a small number of lines of code, so we probably don't need a separate function for that. The output step seems similar: assuming that we already know which known signature is closest, we can just report that to the user. By contrast, the process step looks like a lot of work, and we'll certainly want to break that subproblem down further. That's what we'll do next.

11.3   *Breaking down the process subproblem*

We'll name our overall process function `process_data`. It will take the mystery book filename and the name of a directory of known-author books as parameters and return the name of the closest known signature.

Looking at our description for the process step, it seems that we have three subproblems to solve here:

- *Figure out the signature for the mystery book.* That's our unknown signature. We'll name this function `make_signature`.
- *Figure out the signature for each of the books whose author we know.* These are our known signatures. We'll name this function `get_all_signatures`.

- *Compare the unknown signature to each known signature to figure out which known signature is closest.* Because close signatures will have small differences, we'll name this function `lowest_score`.

We'll work on our top-down design for each of these subproblems in turn. Figure 11.1 shows a diagram of what we have so far.

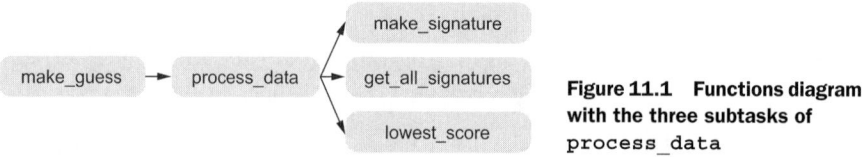

Figure 11.1   Functions diagram with the three subtasks of `process_data`

11.3.1 *Figuring out the signature for the mystery book*

The function for this task, `make_signature`, will take the text for our book as a parameter and return the book's signature. At this point, we need to decide on the features that we'll use to determine the signature for each book. Let's break this down by thinking back to the previous example passages. We noticed there are differences in the authors' passages based on the complexity and length of sentences. You may have also suspected that the authors may differ in the length of words used and ways they use words (e.g., some authors may be more repetitive than others). As such, we'll want some features to be based on the structure of the author's sentences, and we'll want others based on the words that the author uses. We'll look at each of these in detail.

FEATURES RELATED TO THE STRUCTURE OF THE AUTHOR'S SENTENCES

In our earlier Doyle versus Dickens example, we talked about using the average number of words per sentence as one feature. We can calculate this by dividing the total number of words by the total number of sentences. For example, consider the following text:

> *The same day there arrived through the post a small card-board box addressed to me, which I found to contain a very large and lustrous pearl. No word of writing was enclosed.*

If you count the words and sentences, you should find that there are 32 words (card-board counts as one word) and two sentences, so we'll calculate the average words per sentence as $32/2 = 16$. This will be the *average number of words per sentence* feature.

We also noticed that the complexity of sentences may vary between authors (i.e., some authors have sentences with many more commas and semicolons compared to other authors), so it makes sense to use that as another feature. More complex sentences have more phrases, which are coherent pieces of sentences. Breaking a sentence into its component phrases is a tough challenge in its own right, and although we could try to do it more accurately, we'll settle here for a simpler rule of thumb.

Namely, we'll say that a phrase is separated from other phrases in the sentence by a comma, semicolon, or colon. Looking at the previous text again, we find that there are three phrases. The first sentence has two phrases: "The same day there arrived through the post a small card-board box addressed to me" and "which I found to contain a very large and lustrous pearl." The second sentence has no commas, semicolons, or colons, so it has only one phrase. As there are three phrases and two sentences, we'd say that the sentence complexity for this text is $3/2 = 1.5$. This will be the *average sentence complexity* feature.

We hope that these sentence-level features intuitively make sense as things we could use to differentiate how authors write. Next, let's start looking at the ways that authors may differ in their use of words.

FEATURES RELATED TO THE AUTHOR'S WORD SELECTION

You can probably think of your own metrics for word-level features, but we'll use three here that in our experience work well. First, it's likely that some authors use shorter words on average than other authors. To that end, we'll use the average word length, which is just the average number of letters per word. Let's consider this sample text that we created:

A pearl! Pearl! Lustrous pearl! Rare. What a nice find.

If you count the letters and words, you should find that there are 41 letters and 10 words. (Don't count punctuation as letters here.) So, we'll calculate the average word length as $41/10 = 4.1$. This will be the *average word length* feature.

Second, it may be that some authors use words more repetitively than others. To capture this, we'll take the number of different words that the author uses and divide it by the total number of words. For our previous sample text, there are only seven different words used: *a, pearl, lustrous, rare, what, nice,* and *find.* There are 10 words in all, so our calculation for this metric would be $7/10 = 0.7$. This will be the *different words divided by total words* feature.

Third, it may be that some authors tend to use many words a single time, whereas other authors tend to use words multiple times. To calculate this one, we'll take the number of words used exactly once and divide it by the total number of words. For our sample text, there are five words that are used exactly once: *lustrous, rare, what, nice,* and *find.* There are 10 words in all, so our calculation for this metric would be $5/10 = 0.5$. This will be the *number of words used exactly once divided by total words* feature.

In all, we have five features that will make up each signature. We'll need to store those numbers together in a single value, so we'll end up using a list of five numbers for each signature.

Let's dig into how we'll implement each of these features, starting with the word-level ones and proceeding to the sentence-level ones. We'll go in this order:

- Average word length
- Different words divided by total words

- Words used exactly once divided by total words
- Average number of words per sentence
- Average sentence complexity

For each one, we'll ultimately end up writing a function. We have an updated diagram with function names for each of these five new functions that will help us implement `make_signature` in figure 11.2. Do we need to further break down these problems, or are they OK as is? Let's see!

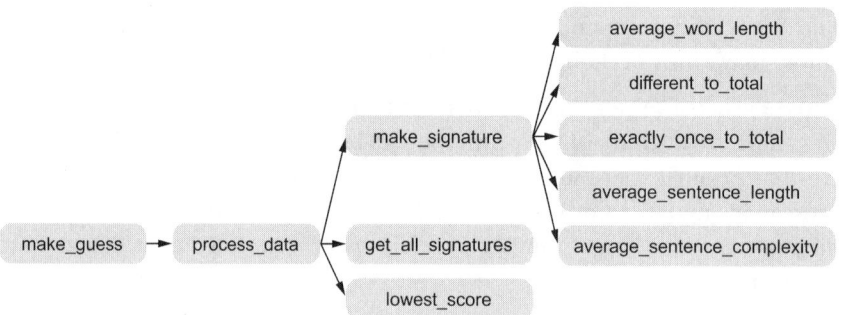

Figure 11.2 Functions diagram with the additional five subtasks of `make_signature`

AVERAGE WORD LENGTH
The function for this task, `average_word_length`, will take the text of the book as a parameter and return the average word length. We might start solving this task by using the split method on the text. As a reminder, the `split` method is used to split a string into a list of its pieces. By default, `split` will split around spaces. The book text is a string, and if we split around spaces, we'll get its words! That's exactly what we need here. We can then loop through that list of words, counting up the number of letters and number of words.

That's a good start, but we need to be a little more careful here because we don't want to end up counting nonletters as letters. For example, "pearl" has five letters. But so does "pearl." or "pearl!!" or "(pearl)". Aha—this sounds like a subtask to us! Namely, we can divide out the subtask of cleaning up a word into its own function to be used by `average_word_length`. We'll call that cleanup function `clean_word`.

There's another benefit to having our `clean_word` function, and that's to help us identify when a "word" is actually not a word. For example, suppose one of our "words" in the text is . . . . When we pass this to `clean_word`, we'll get an empty string back. That signifies that this in fact isn't a word at all, so we won't count it as such.

DIFFERENT WORDS DIVIDED BY TOTAL WORDS
The function for this task, `different_to_total`, will take the text of the book as a parameter and will return the number of different words used divided by the total number of words.

As with `average_word_length`, we need to be careful to count only letters, not punctuation. But wait—we just talked about a `clean_word` function that we needed for `average_word_length`. We can use that function here as well! In fact, we'll use `clean_word` in most of our five feature tasks. This is the sign of a useful general-purpose function! Our top-down design is going well. We can see how the `clean_word` function will be called by both functions in our updated function diagram in figure 11.3.

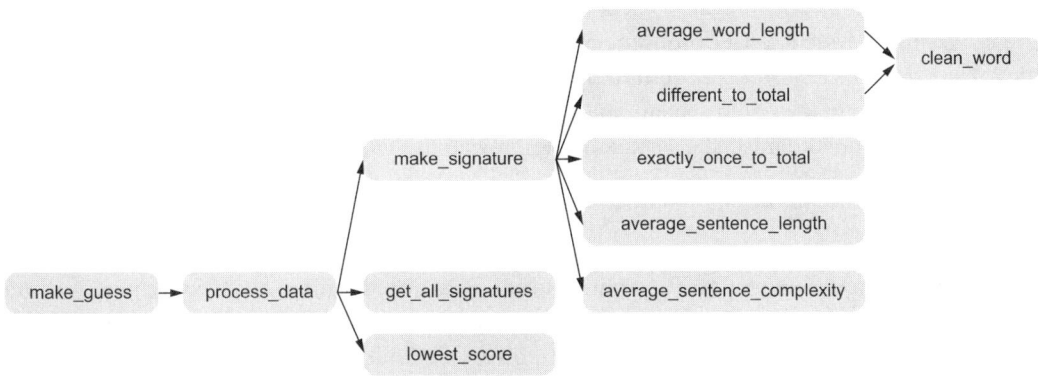

Figure 11.3   Functions diagram with two functions, both using our `clean_word` function to help

There's one extra complication here, though, and it involves words like *pearl, Pearl,* and *PEARL.* We want to consider those to be the same words, but if we simply use string comparisons, they will be treated as different words. One solution here is to split this off into another subproblem to convert a string to all lowercase. We could also think of this as another part of cleaning up a word, right along with removing the punctuation. We'll go with this second option. What we'll do, then, is make our `clean_word` function not only remove punctuation but also convert the word to lowercase.

You might wonder whether we need to split off another subtask here, one that determines the number of different words. You could do that, and it wouldn't be a mistake to do so. However, if we persevere without doing that, we'll see that the function remains quite manageable without this additional subtask. Practice and experience over time will help you anticipate when a task needs to be further broken down.

WORDS USED EXACTLY ONCE DIVIDED BY TOTAL WORDS

The function for this task, `exactly_once_to_total`, will take the text of the book as a parameter and will return the number of words used exactly once divided by the total number of words. We're going to need our `clean_word` function here as well for reasons similar to why we needed it in the prior two tasks: to make sure we're working only with letters, not punctuation. Again, while we could split out a subtask to determine the number of words that are used exactly once, we'll find that it doesn't take much Python code to do this, so we'll just leave this task alone without splitting it further.

AVERAGE NUMBER OF WORDS PER SENTENCE

The function for this task, `average_sentence_length`, will take the text of the book as a parameter and will return the average number of words per sentence. To split our text into words for the previous three tasks, we can use the string split method. How do we split our text into sentences? Is there a string method for that?

Unfortunately, there isn't. For that reason, it will be helpful to split out a task to break our text string into sentences. We'll call the function for that subtask `get_sentences`. The `get_sentences` function will take the text of the book as a parameter and will return a list of sentences from the text.

What's a sentence? We'll define a sentence as text that is separated by a period (.), question mark (?), or exclamation point (!). This rule, while convenient and simple, is going to make mistakes. For example, how many sentences are in this text?

I had at that time just entered the family of Mrs. Cecil Forrester in the capacity of governess.

The answer is one. Our program, though, is going to pull out two sentences, not one. It'll get tricked by the word *Mrs.*, which has a period at the end. If you continue with authorship identification past this chapter, you could work on making your rules more robust or, use sophisticated natural language processing (NLP) software to do even better. For our purposes, however, we'll be content with this rule that sometimes gets sentences wrong because most of the time we'll get them right. If we're only wrong once in a while, the errors won't have an appreciable effect on our metric.

AVERAGE SENTENCE COMPLEXITY

We'll name the function for this task `average_sentence_complexity`. It will take the text of a sentence as a parameter and return a measure of the sentence complexity.

As we discussed previously, we're interested in quantifying sentence complexity using the number of phrases in a sentence. Much as we used punctuation to separate sentences from each other, we'll use different punctuation to separate phrases from each other. Namely, we'll say that a phrase is separated by a comma (,), semicolon (;), or colon (:).

It would be nice to have a subtask to break a sentence into its phrases, just like we had a subtask to break text into its sentences. Let's make that happen! We'll call the function for that subtask `get_phrases`. The `get_phrases` function will take a sentence of the book as a parameter and return a list of phrases from the sentence.

Let's pause for a moment and think about what we're doing with our `get_sentences` and `get_phrases` functions. They're both quite similar, come to think of it. All that distinguishes them is the characters that they use to make the splits. `get_sentences` cares about periods, question marks, and exclamation points, whereas `get_phrases` cares about commas, semicolons, and colons. We see an opportunity for a parent task that would simplify both of these tasks!

Namely, imagine that we had a `split_string` function that took two parameters, the text and a string of separator characters, and it returned a list of pieces of text separated by any of the separators. We could then call it with `'.?!'` to split into sentences and `',;:'` to split into phrases. That would make both `get_sentences` and `get_phrases` easier to implement and reduce code duplication. This is a win!

At this point, we've fully fleshed out the functions necessary to support the higher-level function `make_signature`, as reflected in figure 11.4. We'll next turn to the `get_all_signatures` function.

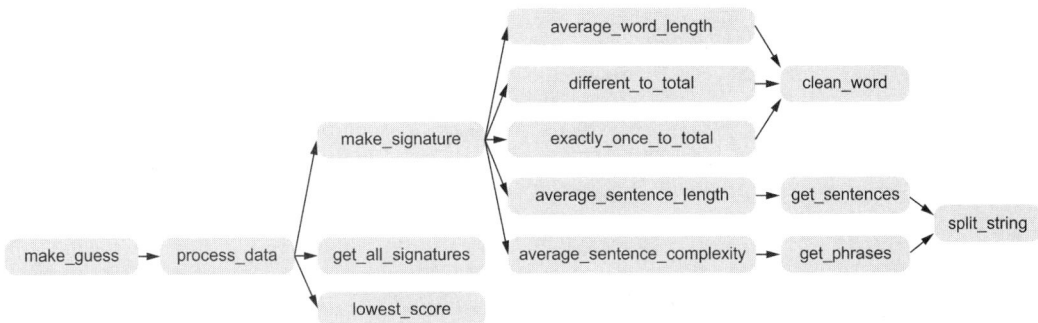

Figure 11.4 Functions diagram with all the supporting functions for the `make_signature` function complete

FIGURING OUT EACH KNOWN SIGNATURE

We just worked hard to break down our `make_signature` function into five main tasks, one for each feature of our signatures. We designed that function to determine the unknown signature—the signature for the mystery text whose author we're trying to identify.

Our next task is to figure out the signature for each of the books for which we know the author. In the resources for this book, under the ch11 folder, you'll find a directory called `known_authors`. In there, you'll find several files, each named as an author. Each file contains a book written by that author. For example, if you open Arthur_Conan_Doyle.txt, you'll find the text of the book *A Study in Scarlet* by Arthur Conan Doyle. We need to determine the signature for each of these files.

Amazingly, we have far less work to do to solve this problem than it may seem. That's because we can use that same `make_signature` function, the one we designed to determine the signature of the mystery book, to also determine the signature for any known book!

We'll name the function for this task `get_all_signatures`. It wouldn't make sense for this function to take the text of one book as a parameter because it's supposed to be able to get the signature for all of our known books. Rather, it will take a directory of known books as a parameter. Its behavior will be to loop through the files in that directory, calculating the signature for each one.

We need the function to tell us which signature goes with which book. In other words, we need it to associate each book with its corresponding signature. This kind of association is precisely why Python has dictionaries! We'll therefore have this function return a dictionary, where the keys are names of files, and the values are the corresponding signature. Our function diagram didn't need any *new* functions to support the `get_all_signatures` function, so our updated diagram in figure 11.5 just shows how `get_all_signatures` calls `make_signature`.

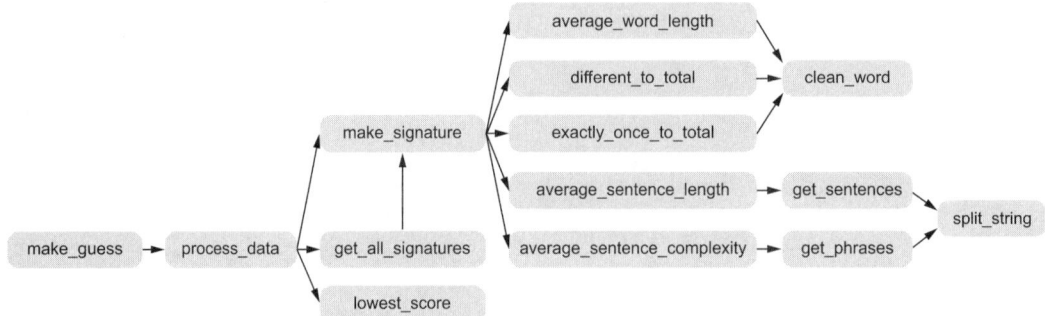

Figure 11.5   **Functions diagram updated for `get_all_signatures` to call `make_signature`**

FINDING CLOSEST KNOWN SIGNATURE

Let's recap what we've designed so far:

- We've designed our `make_signature` function to get us the unknown signature for the mystery book.
- We've designed our `get_all_signatures` function to get us all of our known signatures.

Now, we need to design a function that tells us which of those known signatures is best; that is, which known signature is closest to our unknown signature. Each of our signatures will be a list of five numbers giving the quantity for each of our five features. The order of these numbers will be the same order we used before: average word length, different words divided by total words, words used exactly once divided by total words, average number of words per sentence, and average sentence complexity.

Suppose that we have two signatures. The first one is [4.6, 0.1, 0.05, 10, 2] which means that the average word length for that book is 4.6, the different words divided by total words is 0.1, and so on. The second signature is [4.3, 0.1, 0.04, 16, 4].

There are many ways to get an overall score giving the difference between signatures. The one we'll use will give us a difference score for each feature, and then we'll add up those scores to get our overall score.

Let's look at the values of each signature for the first feature: 4.6 and 4.3. If we subtract those, we get a difference of 4.6 − 4.3 = 0.3. We could use 0.3 as our answer for this feature, but it turns out to work better if we *weight* each difference using a different weight. Each weight gives the importance of that feature. We'll use some weights ([11, 33, 50, 0.4, 4]) that in our experience have proven to work well. You might wonder where the heck these weights come from. But note that there's no magic about them: in working with our students over the years, we've just found that these weights seem to work out. This would be only a starting point for a stronger authorship identification program. When doing this type of research, people routinely *tune* their training, which means to adjust weights to obtain stronger results.

When we say that we're using weights of [11, 33, 50, 0.4, 4], it means that we'll multiply the difference on the first feature by 11, the difference on the second feature by 33, and so on. So, rather than getting a difference of 0.3 for the first feature, we'll get $0.3 \times 11 = 3.3$.

We need to be careful with features like the fourth one, where the difference is negative. We don't want to start with $10 - 16 = -6$ because that's a negative number, and that would *undo* some of the positive difference from other features. Instead, we need to first make this number positive and then multiply it by its weight. Removing the negative sign from a number is known as taking the absolute value, and the absolute value is denoted as abs. The full calculation for this fourth feature, then, is $abs(10 - 16) \times 0.4 = 2.4$.

Table 11.1 gives the calculation for each feature. If we add up all five scores, we get an overall score of 14.2.

Table **11.1** Calculating the difference between two signatures

Feature Number	Value of Feature in Signature 1	Value of Feature in Signature 2	Weight of Feature	Contribution of Feature
1	4.6	4.3	11	$abs(4.6 - 4.3) \times 11 = 3.3$
2	0.1	0.1	33	$abs(0.1 - 0.1) \times 33 = 0$
3	0.05	0.04	50	$abs(0.05 - 0.04) \times 50 = .5$
4	10	16	0.4	$abs(10 - 16) \times 0.4 = 2.4$
5	2	4	4	$abs(2 - 4) \times 4 = 8$
Sum				14.2

Remember where we are in the top-down design: we need a function that tells us which known signature is best. Well, now we know how to compare two signatures and get the score for that comparison. We'll want to make that comparison between the unknown signature and each known signature to determine which known signature is best. The lower the score, the closer the signatures; the higher the score, the more different the signatures are. As such, we'll want to ultimately choose the signature with the lowest comparison score.

We'll name the function for this task lowest_score. It will take three parameters: a dictionary mapping author names to their known signatures, an unknown signature, and a list of weights. The function will return the signature that has the lowest comparison score with our unknown signature.

Think about the work that this function will need to do. It needs to loop through the known signatures. We can do that with a `for` loop—no need for a subtask there. It will need to compare the unknown signature to the current known signature. Oh! That's a subtask right there, embodying the scoring mechanism that we outlined in table 11.1. We'll name the function for that subtask `get_score`. Our `get_score` function will take two signatures to compare and the list of weights and return the score for the comparison between these two signatures.

11.4   Summary of our top-down design

We did it! We've broken down our original big problem into several smaller problems that are amenable to being implemented as a function.

Figure 11.6 depicts all the work that we've done during the process of decomposing the problem. Remember, we started with a `make_guess` function, which will solve the overall problem. To help us with `make_guess`, we created a `process_data` function that will do some of the work for `make_guess`. To help `process_data`, we created three more functions, `make_signature`, `get_all_signatures`, and `lowest_score`, that each have their own helper functions, and so forth. Having sketched out the functions we'll need to solve our problem, our next step will be to implement them.

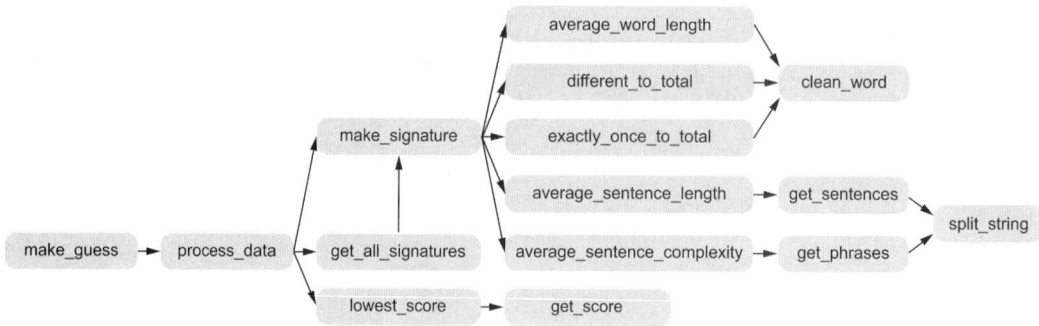

Figure 11.6   Full functions diagram for `make_guess`

11.5   Implementing our functions

Now we're ready to ask Copilot to implement each function that we need. We designed our functions by starting from the top—the biggest problem—and working down to smaller problems. But remember from chapter 7 that this isn't the order that we implement the functions; instead, we implement the functions in the opposite order, from bottom to top (or right to left in figure 11.6).

Just as in our example in chapter 7, we're not going to focus much on testing, prompt engineering, debugging, or code reading. We do encourage you to run doctest on the docstring tests that we've provided, and further encourage you to add additional tests for each function.

11.5.1 *clean_word*

We'll start with our `clean_word` function. As usual, we provide the function header (the `def` line) and docstring, and we let Copilot fill in the code. We also provide some annotations to briefly illustrate how the code works.

Remember that we want our `clean_word` function to remove punctuation that might show up around the word and to convert the word to lowercase. But we don't want to mess with punctuation in the middle of the word, such as the "-" in *card-board*. We've written the docstring to make clear what we want.

Listing 11.1   Clean words for analysis

```
def clean_word(word):
    '''
    word is a string.

    Return a version of word in which all letters have been
    converted to lowercase, and punctuation characters have been
    stripped from both ends. Inner punctuation is left untouched.

    >>> clean_word('Pearl!')
    'pearl'
    >>> clean_word('card-board')
    'card-board'
    '''
    word = word.lower()                        ◁────  Converts the word
    word = word.strip(string.punctuation)  ◁──        to lowercase
    return word                                        Uses the string module to
                                                       strip punctuation from ends
```

When working on our password functions in chapter 3, we saw Copilot using the string module, and we see Copilot doing that again here. We know from our work in chapter 3 that this won't work unless we import string first, so add

```
import string
```

above this function as we've done in the following listing.

Listing 11.2   Clean words for analysis, complete

```
import string
def clean_word(word):
    '''
    word is a string.

    Return a version of word in which all letters have been
    converted to lowercase, and punctuation characters have
    been stripped from both ends. Inner punctuation is left
    untouched.

    >>> clean_word('Pearl!')
    'pearl'
    >>> clean_word('card-board')
```

```
'card-board'
'''
word = word.lower()
word = word.strip(string.punctuation)
return word
```

This completes the `clean_word` function, so we can mark this as complete in our functions diagram in figure 11.7.

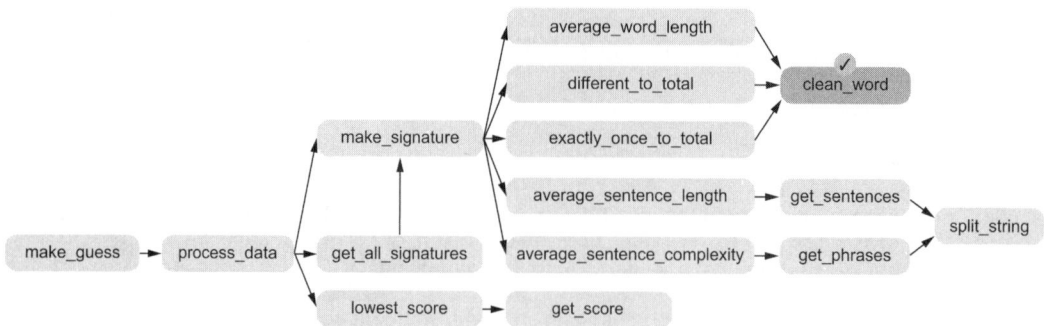

Figure 11.7   Full functions diagram with `clean_word` now finished

11.5.2 *average_word_length*

Now let's tackle the first of our five signature feature functions: `average_word_length`. It needs to determine the average number of letters per word, but we don't want to count surrounding punctuation as letters nor include words that don't have any letters. We want to use our `clean_word` function here, as shown in the following listing. As always, we've written the docstring in a way that we hope directs Copilot to make these decisions.

Listing 11.3   Average word length

```
def average_word_length(text):
    '''
    text is a string of text.

    Return the average word length of the words in text.
    Do not count empty words as words.
    Do not include surrounding punctuation.

    >>> average_word_length('A pearl! Pearl! Lustrous pearl! \
Rare. What a nice find.')
    4.1
    '''
    words = text.split()        ◁
    total = 0                   ◁
    count = 0                   ◁──────
    for word in words:          ◁─┐
```

Splits string into its words

total will count the total number of letters across all words.

count will count the number of words.

Loops through each word

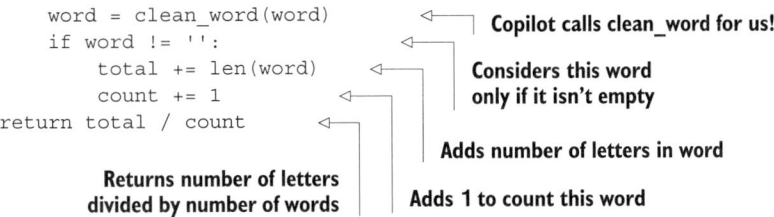

You'll notice in the doctest here that we've split our string over two lines, ending the first line with a \ character. The reason we did this is that the string wouldn't otherwise fit on one line in the book. We also needed to keep the second line without any indentation; otherwise, doctest would use that indentation as spaces in the string. On your computer, you can type the string on a single line and not worry about the \ or lack of indentation.

We can now mark `average_word_length` as done in our updated figure (figure 11.8). Although satisfying, marking these off in the figure one by one might be a bit too much noise, so we'll revisit the figure only periodically going forward.

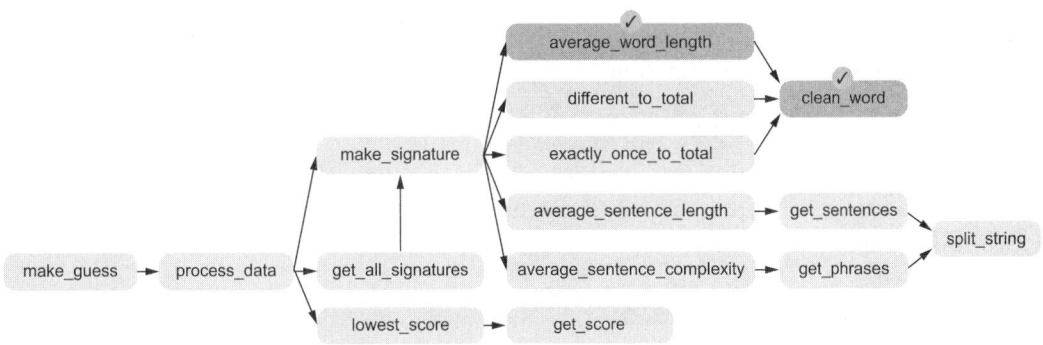

Figure 11.8 Full functions diagram with `average_word_length` now finished

11.5.3 different_to_total

This is the second of our signature features. We need this one to calculate the number of different words used divided by the total number of words. Again, we don't want surrounding punctuation or empty words.

Listing 11.4 Different words divided by total number of words

```
def different_to_total(text):
    '''
    text is a string of text.

    Return the number of unique words in text
    divided by the total number of words in text.
    Do not count empty words as words.
    Do not include surrounding punctuation.
```

```
>>> different_to_total('A pearl! Pearl! Lustrous pearl! \
Rare. What a nice find.')
0.7
'''
words = text.split()
total = 0
unique = set()
for word in words:
    word = clean_word(word)
    if word != '':
        total += 1
        unique.add(word)
return len(unique) / total
```

Splits string into its words

total will count the total number of nonempty words.

A set of the unique words found

Copilot again calls clean_word for us!

A set is like a list but doesn't accept duplicates.

Returns the number of different words divided by total number of words

This code uses a Python set, rather than a Python list, to store the unique words that it finds. A set is similar to a list except that it doesn't accept duplicates, so if you try to add the same word multiple times, it retains only one copy of the word. That's why we can use `len(unique)` in the return statement to get the total number of unique words.

We don't need to know any more about Python sets to continue here. But if you're interested in learning more, you can ask Copilot for a code explanation and/or do a Google search for information on Python sets.

11.5.4 *exactly_once_to_total*

We're ready to implement our third signature feature. This one calculates the number of words used exactly once divided by the total number of words, as shown in the following listing. We provided the prompt to Copilot and received the following function.

Listing 11.5 Fraction of words used just once: Try 1

```
def exactly_once_to_total(text):
    '''
    text is a string of text.

    Return the number of words that show up exactly once in text
    divided by the total number of words in text.
    Do not count empty words as words.
    Do not include surrounding punctuation.

    >>> exactly_once_to_total('A pearl! Pearl! Lustrous pearl! \
Rare. What a nice find.')
    0.5
    '''
    words = text.split()
    unique = set()
    total = 0
    for word in words:
        word = clean_word(word)
        if word != '':
            if word not in unique:
```

```
                unique.add(word)
          else:
                unique.remove(word)      ◁——  Removing a word
          total += 1                           from the unique set?
    return len(unique) / total
```

When we skim that code, it looks like `unique` is a set that keeps track of the unique words. At the end, we divide that number of unique words by the total number of words.

However, run our test case using doctest, and you'll see that our code fails the test. We need the result to be 0.5, but our code is unfortunately giving us 0.6. Our code is wrong. We need to stay vigilant!

Let's review the code to see why it was wrong. Imagine that a word is used three times in a text. The first time our code finds it, the code will add it to `unique`. The second time, it will *remove* it from `unique`. That's fine so far because the word isn't being used exactly once anymore, so it shouldn't be in there. But then the third time, it will add that word back to `unique`! So, our code is going to count some words as being used exactly once when in fact they were used more than once. We looked through the list that appears when you press Ctrl-Enter and found this alternate version, which is correct, as shown in the following listing.

> **Listing 11.6 Fraction of words used just once: Try 2**

```
def exactly_once_to_total(text):
    '''
    text is a string of text.

    Return the number of words that show up exactly once in text
    divided by the total number of words in text.
    Do not count empty words as words.
    Do not include surrounding punctuation.

    >>> exactly_once_to_total('A pearl! Pearl! Lustrous pearl! \
    Rare. What a nice find.')
    0.5
    '''                                      Keeps track of all
                                             words we've seen
    words = text.split()
    total = 0                                Keeps track of words used
    unique = set()          ◁————            exactly once—what we
    once = set()            ◁————┘           ultimately care about
    for word in words:
        word = clean_word(word)              We're seeing
        if word != '':                       the word again.
            total += 1
            if word in unique:       ◁——     So the word has to be
                once.discard(word)   ◁——     removed from once.
            else:
                unique.add(word)     ◁——  We've now seen this word.
                once.add(word)       ◁——  So far, the word is used exactly once.
    return len(once) / total     ◁——
                                     Returns the number of words used exactly
                                     once divided by the total number of words
```

This code is tricky! To understand it, start by focusing on the `else` code. That's the code that runs the first time we see each word. That word gets added to both the `unique` and `once` sets. It's the `once` set that's going to keep track for us of the words used exactly once.

Now imagine that we see a word for a second time. The `if` code is going to run when this happens because the word is already in `unique` (we added it there the first time we saw this word). Now, because we've seen the word more than once, we need it gone from the `once` set. That's exactly what the `if` code does: it uses `once.discard(word)` to remove the word from `once`.

To summarize, the first time we see a word, it gets added to `once`. When we see it again, it gets removed from `once` with no way to ever have that word added back to `once`. The `once` set is correctly tracking the words used exactly once.

11.5.5 split_string

We've finished our three word-level signature feature functions. Before we can move on to our two sentence-level signature feature functions, we need to write `get_sentences`. But to write `get_sentences`, we first need `split_string`, which is what we'll work on now.

Our `split_string` function is supposed to be able to split a string around any number of separators. It inherently has nothing to do with sentences or phrases. We've included one docstring test to highlight this fact: even though we're going to use it to split sentences and phrases, it's more general than that. Look at the following listing.

Listing 11.7   Split a string around separators

```
def split_string(text, separators):
    '''
    text is a string of text.
    separators is a string of separator characters.

    Split the text into a list using any of the one-character
    separators and return the result.
    Remove spaces from beginning and end
    of a string before adding it to the list.
    Do not include empty strings in the list.

    >>> split_string('one*two[three', '*[')
    ['one', 'two', 'three']
    >>> split_string('A pearl! Pearl! Lustrous pearl! Rare. \
    What a nice find.', '.?!')
    ['A pearl', 'Pearl', 'Lustrous pearl', 'Rare', \
    'What a nice find']
    '''
    words = []
    word = ''
    for char in text:
        if char in separators:
```

A better variable name would be all_strings.

A better variable name would be current_string.

Current string ends here.

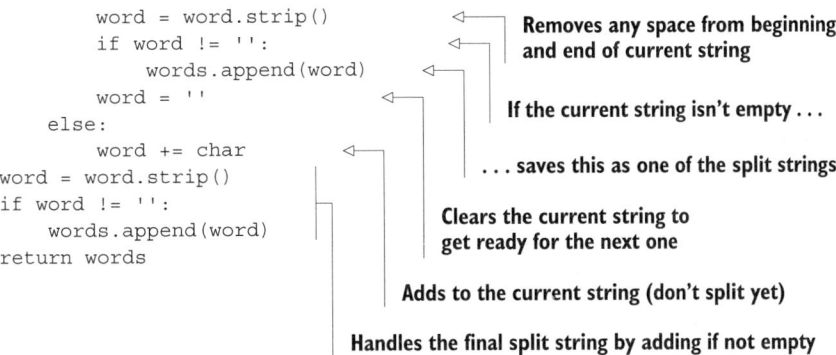

You might be curious about the code after the `for` loop and before the `return` statement. It seems to be duplicating some of the code from within the `for` loop, so what's it doing there? This code is there because the loop only adds a split string to our list of strings when it finds one of the separator characters. If the text doesn't end with a separator character, the loop won't add the final split string. The code below the loop ensures that this final split string isn't lost.

It's been a little while since we updated our diagram with functions we've completed. Time for an update! This also serves as a reminder that we're finishing functions from the bottom up (right-to-left in the diagram). As such, figure 11.9 has our functions completed so far.

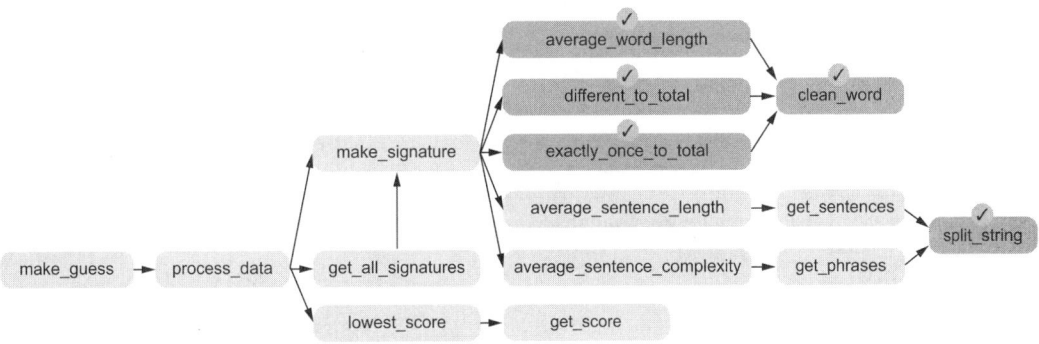

Figure 11.9 **Full functions diagram updated with** `different_to_total`, `exactly_once_to_total`, **and** `split_string` **now finished**

11.5.6 *get_sentences*

In our top-down design, we kicked most of the work for `get_sentences` off to the `split_string` function. Therefore, what we're hoping for is that Copilot implements `get_sentences` by making a suitable call to `split_string`.

We don't want our sentences to have any space at the beginning or end, and we don't want any empty sentences. We initially had these requirements in the docstring, but even without them Copilot correctly calls `split_string`, and that function handles these edge cases anyway.

Listing 11.8   Return list of sentences in text

```
def get_sentences(text):
    '''
    text is a string of text.

    Return a list of the sentences from text.
    Sentences are separated by a '.', '?' or '!'.

    >>> get_sentences('A pearl! Pearl! Lustrous pearl! Rare. \
What a nice find.')
    ['A pearl', 'Pearl', 'Lustrous pearl', 'Rare', \
'What a nice find']
    '''
    return split_string(text, '.?!')          ◁──┤ Calls split_string with the
                                                   sentence separator characters
```

11.5.7   *average_sentence_length*

Now that we have `get_sentences`, we can proceed with `average_sentence_length`, our fourth signature feature. This one calculates the average number of words per sentence. We provided the prompt to Copilot and received the function shown in the following listing.

Listing 11.9   Average number of words per sentence

```
def average_sentence_length(text):
    '''
    text is a string of text.

    Return the average number of words per sentence in text.
    Do not count empty words as words.

    >>> average_sentence_length('A pearl! Pearl! Lustrous pearl! \
Rare. What a nice find.')
    2.0
    '''
    sentences = get_sentences(text)          ◁──┤ Gets a list of sentences
    total = 0
    for sentence in sentences:               ◁──┤ Loops through the sentences
        words = sentence.split()             ◁──┤ Breaks current sentence
                                                  into its words
        for word in words:                   ◁──┤ Loops through sentence's words
            if word != '':
                total += 1
    return total / len(sentences)            ◁──┤ Returns number of words
                                                  divided by number of sentences
```

11.5.8   *get_phrases*

Much liked we needed `get_sentences` before we could implement `average_sentence_length`, we need `get_phrases` before we can implement `average_sentence_complexity`.

As with `get_sentences`, we expect Copilot to call `split_string` to get the phrases. That is what it has done for us here, as shown in the following listing.

Listing 11.10   Return list of phrases from a sentence

```
def get_phrases(sentence):
    '''
    sentence is a sentence string.

    Return a list of the phrases from sentence.
    Phrases are separated by a ',', ';' or ':'.

    >>> get_phrases('Lustrous pearl, Rare, What a nice find')
    ['Lustrous pearl', 'Rare', 'What a nice find']
    '''
    return split_string(sentence, ',;:')
```
⟵ Calls split_string with the phrase separator characters

11.5.9   *average_sentence_complexity*

With `get_phrases` completed, we can now prompt for an implementation of `average_sentence_complexity`. The code is shown in the following listing.

Listing 11.11   Average number of phrases per sentence

```
def average_sentence_complexity(text):
    '''
    text is a string of text.

    Return the average number of phrases per sentence in text.

    >>> average_sentence_complexity('A pearl! Pearl! Lustrous \
pearl! Rare. What a nice find.')
    1.0
    >>> average_sentence_complexity('A pearl! Pearl! Lustrous \
pearl! Rare, what a nice find.')
    1.25
    '''
    sentences = get_sentences(text)
    total = 0
    for sentence in sentences:
        phrases = get_phrases(sentence)
        total += len(phrases)
    return total / len(sentences)
```

⟵ We changed a period to a comma to make this 5/4 = 1.25.

⟵ Gets a list of sentences

⟵ Loops through the sentences

⟵ Gets a list of phrases in the current sentence

⟵ Adds the number of phrases in the current sentence

Returns the number of phrases divided by the number of sentences

We're really coming along now! We've finished all the functions needed to create `make_signature`, as shown in figure 11.10.

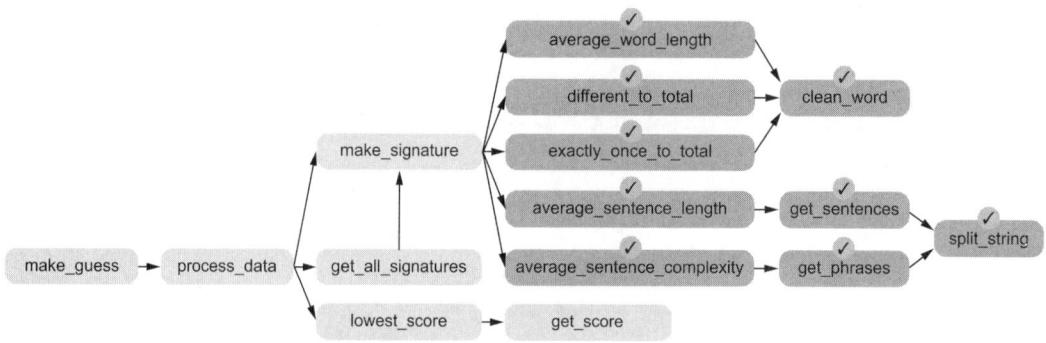

Figure 11.10   Full functions diagram updated to show that we're now ready to write `make_signature`

11.5.10 make_signature

We've written nine functions to this point, and while they're all important, we may feel a little unsatisfied right now because we're not even dealing with text signatures yet. We've got some functions that clean words, split strings in various ways, and calculate individual features of signatures, but no function to make a full signature.

That changes now because we're finally ready to implement `make_signature` to give us the signature for a text. This function will take the text of a book and return a list of five numbers, each of which is the result of calling one of our five feature functions.

Listing 11.12   Numeric signature for the text

```
def make_signature(text):
    '''
    The signature for text is a list of five elements:
    average word length, different words divided by total words,
    words used exactly once divided by total words,
    average sentence length, and average sentence complexity.

    Return the signature for text.

    >>> make_signature('A pearl! Pearl! Lustrous pearl! \
Rare, what a nice find.')
    [4.1, 0.7, 0.5, 2.5, 1.25]
    '''
    return [average_word_length(text),
            different_to_total(text),
            exactly_once_to_total(text),
            average_sentence_length(text),
            average_sentence_complexity(text)]
```

Each of our five feature functions is called.

Notice that this function can be implemented as nothing more than a call to each of our five feature functions. It's important to pause now to think about just how messy this function would have been without having done a solid top-down design first. The code for all five of the functions that we're calling here would have had to be in a single function, with all of their own variables and calculations mingled together into a real mess. Lucky for us, we're using top-down design! Our function is therefore easier for us to read and easier to convince ourselves that it's doing the right thing.

11.5.11 get_all_signatures

Our `process_data` function has three subtasks for us to implement. We just finished with the first one (`make_signature`), so now we'll move on to its second subtask, which is our `get_all_signatures` function.

From now on, we'll assume that your working directory has your code and that it also has the subdirectory of books that we've provided. We need this function to return the signature for each file in our directory of known authors. We're hoping for Copilot to call `make_signature` here to make this function far simpler than it otherwise would be.

Copilot did do that for us, but the code we got still had two problems. Our initial code is shown in the following listing.

Listing 11.13   Obtain all signatures from known authors: Try 1

```
def get_all_signatures(known_dir):
    '''
    known_dir is the name of a directory of books.
    For each file in directory known_dir, determine its signature.

    Return a dictionary where each key is          Our dictionary, initially
    the name of a file, and the value is its signature.   empty, maps filenames
    '''                                            to signatures.
    signatures = {}
    for filename in os.listdir(known_dir):         Loops through each file in
        with open(os.path.join(known_dir,          the known authors directory
                                filename)) as f:   Opens the current file
            text = f.read()                        Reads all text
            signatures[filename] = make_signature(text)   from the file
    return signatures
                                                   Makes the signature
                                                   for text and stores it
                                                   in the dictionary
```

Try running this function from the Python prompt as

```
>>> get_all_signatures('known_authors')
```

and you'll get the following error:

```
Traceback (most recent call last):
  File "<stdin>", line 1, in <module>
  File "C:\repos\book_code\ch11\authorship.py", line 207,
  in get_all_signatures
    for filename in os.listdir(known_dir):
                    ^^
NameError: name 'os' is not defined
```

The error is telling us that the function is trying to use a module named os, but we don't have this module available. This module is built-in to Python, and we know what to do in this case: import it! That is, we need to add

```
import os
```

above this function. After that, we still get an error:

```
>>> get_all_signatures('known_authors')
Traceback (most recent call last):
  File "<stdin>", line 1, in <module>
  File "C:\repos\book_code\ch11\authorship.py", line 209,
  in get_all_signatures
    text = f.read()
           ^^^^^^^^
  File "…\Lib\encodings\cp1252.py", line 23, in decode
    return codecs.charmap_decode(input,self.errors,decoding_table)[0]
           ^^^^^^^^^^^^^^^^^^^^^^^^^^^^^^^^^^^^^^^^^^^^^^^^^^^^^^^^
UnicodeDecodeError: 'charmap' codec can't decode byte 0x9d in
position 2913: character maps to <undefined>
```

You might be wondering what a UnicodeDecodeError is. You could google it or ask ChatGPT if you're interested in a technical explanation. What we need to know is that each file that we open is encoded in a specific way, and Python has chosen the wrong encoding to try to read this file.

We can, however, direct Copilot to fix it by adding a comment near the top of our function. (When you encounter errors like these, you can try placing a comment directly above the erroneous code that was generated. Then, once you delete the incorrect code, Copilot can often generate new code that is correct.) Once we do that, all is well, as shown in the following listing.

Listing 11.14   Obtain all signatures from known authors: Try 2

```
import os

def get_all_signatures(known_dir):
    '''
    known_dir is the name of a directory of books.
    For each file in directory known_dir, determine its signature.

    Return a dictionary where each key is
    the name of a file, and the value is its signature.
    '''
    signatures = {}
    # Fix UnicodeDecodeError                          ◁————  This prompt tells
    for filename in os.listdir(known_dir):                   Copilot to fix the error
        with open(os.path.join(known_dir, filename),        we saw previously.
                encoding='utf-8') as f:
            text = f.read()
            signatures[filename] = make_signature(text)
    return signatures
```

Now, if you run this function, you should see a dictionary of authors and their signatures, like this:

```
>>> get_all_signatures('known_authors')
{'Arthur_Conan_Doyle.txt': [4.3745884086670195,
0.1547122890234636, 0.09005503235165442,
15.48943661971831, 2.082394366197183],
 'Charles_Dickens.txt': [4.229579999566339,
0.0796743207788547, 0.041821158307855766,
17.286386709736963, 2.698477157360406],
 'Frances_Hodgson_Burnett.txt': [4.230464334694739,
0.08356818832607418, 0.04201769324672584,
13.881251286272896, 1.9267338958633464],
 'Jane_Austen.txt': [4.492473405509028,
0.06848572461149259, 0.03249477538065084,
17.507478923035084, 2.607560511286375],
 'Mark_Twain.txt': [4.372851190055795,
0.1350377851543188, 0.07780210466840878,
14.395167731629392, 2.16194089456869]}
```

For simplicity, we haven't added a test in the docstring for this function. If we did, however, we would create a fake, small book, along the lines of what we did in our second example in chapter 6. We'd like to proceed here with our overall purpose of function decomposition, though, so we'll leave that exercise to you if you'd like to pursue that. As shown in figure 11.11, we've gotten two `process_data` subtasks out of the way. Let's keep going!

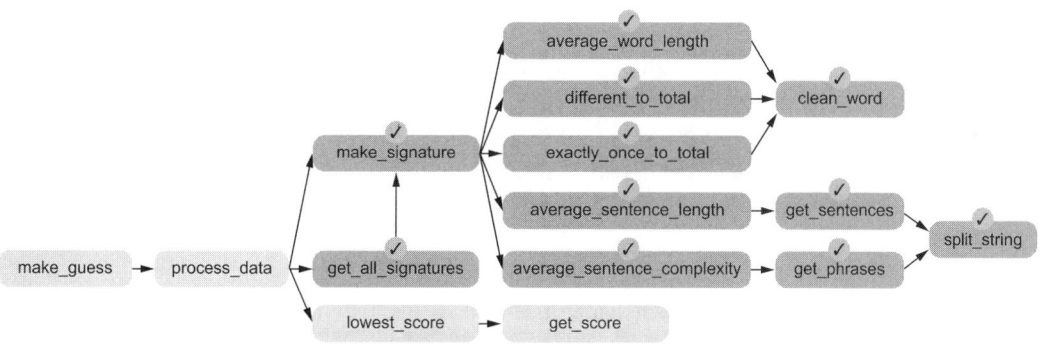

Figure 11.11   Full functions diagram updated to show that `make_signature` **and** `get_all_signatures` **are finished**

11.5.12 get_score

Let's implement `get_score`, where we need to encode the way that we compare signatures. Remember the whole thing where we find the difference on each feature, multiply it by a weight, and then add everything together into an overall score? That's what we want `get_score` to do.

It would be a challenge to explain this formula in the docstring. And we're not even sure that it should go there: a docstring is supposed to explain how someone can use your function, not how it works internally. And, arguably, users of our function won't care about this specific formula anyway. What we can do is use a general docstring, without our specific formula, and see what Copilot does with it. Here we go in the following listing.

Listing 11.15   Compare two signatures

```
def get_score(signature1, signature2, weights):
    '''
    signature1 and signature2 are signatures.
    weights is a list of five weights.

    Return the score for signature1 and signature2.

    >>> get_score([4.6, 0.1, 0.05, 10, 2],\
                  [4.3, 0.1, 0.04, 16, 4],\
                  [11, 33, 50, 0.4, 4])
    14.2
    '''
    score = 0
    for i in range(len(signature1)):
        score += abs(signature1[i] - signature2[i]) \
                * weights[i]
    return score
```

These weights, [11, 33, 50, 0.4, 4], worked well for us.

Loops through each signature index

Adds the weighted difference to score

Copilot has implemented exactly the formula that we wanted. Now, before we start thinking that Copilot mind-melded us or anything like that, remember that the formula we've used here is a very common metric for comparing signatures. Many students and other programmers over the years have implemented authorship identification using this very formula. Copilot is just giving that back to us because it occurs so often in its training data. If Copilot happened to give us a different formula, we could have tried to describe what we want in a comment or, failing that, changed the code ourselves to get what we want.

11.5.13 lowest_score

Our `lowest_score` function will finally wrap up everything we need to implement `process_data`. The `get_score` function that we just implemented gives us the score between any two signatures. Our `lowest_score` function is going to call `get_score` once for each known signature to compare the unknown signature to each known signature. It will then return the known signature that has the lowest score with the unknown signature, as shown in the following listing.

Listing 11.16   Closest known signature

```
def lowest_score(signatures_dict, unknown_signature, weights):
    '''
    signatures_dict is a dictionary mapping keys to signatures.
```

```
unknown_signature is a signature.
weights is a list of five weights.
Return the key whose signature value has the lowest
score with unknown_signature.

>>> d = {'Dan': [1, 1, 1, 1, 1],\
         'Leo': [3, 3, 3, 3, 3]}
>>> unknown = [1, 0.8, 0.9, 1.3, 1.4]
>>> weights = [11, 33, 50, 0.4, 4]
>>> lowest_score(d, unknown, weights)
'Dan'
'''
lowest = None
for key in signatures_dict:
    score = get_score(signatures_dict[key],
                      unknown_signature, weights)
    if lowest is None or score < lowest[1]:
        lowest = (key, score)
return lowest[0]
```

Using variables in the doctest to make the test itself easier to read

This line is easier to read because we're using our variables.

Loops through each author name

Gets a score for comparing this known signature to the unknown signature

If this is the first comparison or we've found a lower score . . .

. . . this stores both the best key and score for that key.

lowest[0] is the best key.

The first parameter, `signatures_dict`, is a dictionary that maps names of authors to their known signatures. That will ultimately come from the `get_all_signatures` function. The second parameter, `unknown_signature`, will ultimately come from calling `make_signature` on the mystery book. The third parameter, `weights`, will be hard-coded by us when we call this function.

11.5.14 process_data

Only two functions to go! One of them is `process_data`—it feels like it took us forever, but we're finally ready for it.

Our `process_data` function is going to take two parameters in the following listing: the filename of a mystery book and the directory of known-author books. It will return the author that we think wrote the mystery book.

Listing 11.17   Signature closest to the mystery author

```
def process_data(mystery_filename, known_dir):
    '''
    mystery_filename is the filename of a mystery book whose
                     author we want to know.
    known_dir is the name of a directory of books.

    Return the name of the signature closest to
    the signature of the text of mystery_filename.
    '''
    signatures = get_all_signatures(known_dir)
    with open(mystery_filename, encoding='utf-8') as f:
```

Gets all the known signatures

Copilot uses our prior work to get the encoding right this time.

```
    text = f.read()
    unknown_signature = make_signature(text)
return lowest_score(signatures, unknown_signature,
                    [11, 33, 50, 0.4, 4])
```

Reads text of the mystery book

Gets the unknown signature

Returns the signature with the lowest comparison score

Again, notice how much we're relying on our earlier functions. This massively useful `process_data` function is now really nothing more than a carefully sequenced list of function calls.

In the book resources for this chapter, we've included a few unknown author files, for example, unknown1.txt and unknown2.txt. Those should be in your current working directory along with your code (and the subdirectory of known author files).

Let's call `process_data` to guess who wrote `'unknown1.txt'`:

```
>>> process_data('unknown1.txt', 'known_authors')
'Arthur_Conan_Doyle.txt'
```

Our program guesses that Arthur Conan Doyle wrote unknown1.txt. And if you peek at the text of unknown1.txt by opening the file, you'll see that our guess is right. The book is called *The Sign of the Four*, which is a well-known Arthur Conan Doyle book.

11.5.15 make_guess

To guess the author of a book, we currently need to type the Python code to run `process_data`. That's not very friendly to users; it would be nice if we could run the program and have it ask us which mystery book file we want to work with.

We'll put that finishing touch on our program by implementing `make_guess`, our top-most function! This function will ask the user for a filename of a mystery book, get the best guess using `process_data`, and tell the user about that guess, as shown in the following listing.

> **Listing 11.18   Interacts with user and guesses text's author**

```
def make_guess(known_dir):
    '''
    Ask user for a filename.
    Get all known signatures from known_dir,
    and print the name of the one that has the lowest score
    with the user's filename.
    '''
    filename = input('Enter filename: ')
    print(process_data(filename, known_dir))
```

Asks the user for the filename of the mystery book

Calls process_data to do all the work and report our guess

This completes all the functions from our diagram! Figure 11.12 shows that we've checked off every function from the bottom to the very top of our diagram.

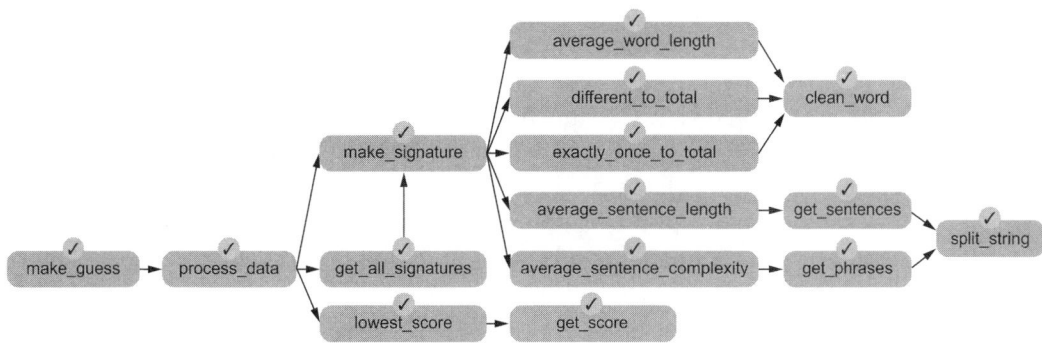

Figure 11.12   All the required functions for `make_guess` are now complete!

If you have all of our code in your Python file, you'll be able to run it to guess the author of a mystery book after you add the following line of code at the bottom of that file:

```
make_guess('known_authors')
```

For example, here's what happens when we run our program and type `unknown1.txt` as the unknown book:

```
Enter filename: unknown1.txt
Arthur_Conan_Doyle.txt
```

It correctly tells us that unknown1.txt is written by Arthur Conan Doyle! Try running it for each of the other unknown book files that we've provided. How many of those does it guess correctly? Which ones does it get wrong?

Congratulations! You've completed your first real-world top-down design. And look at what we've managed to accomplish—an authorship identification program that any beginning programmer should be proud of. Your program uses AI to learn how individual authors write (do they use shorter or longer words on average, shorter or longer sentences on average, etc.?) by using the text of books in its training data. It then applies that learning to make a prediction on a mystery book by determining which author the mystery book most closely emulates—very cool! We managed to solve a very difficult problem, and we did it by breaking down the problem and letting Copilot write the code for each of the subproblems.

11.6   *Going further*

After people do a top-down design, they often see opportunities to refactor their code, which means making the code cleaner or better organized without changing its behavior. It's possible to refactor our program in several ways. For example, you might notice that many of our signature feature functions split the string into words and then ignore empty words. This task (returning a list of nonempty words from a string) could be split off into its own subtask function, which would further simplify any function that calls it.

We might also decide that weights should be passed to `process_data`, rather than hard-coding the weights in that function. The weights would then be hard-coded in `make_guess`, moving the decision higher in the function hierarchy and therefore making it easier to find and change if needed.

It's also possible to improve the program in terms of its features or efficiency. For features, right now, our program simply prints its best guess for the mystery book author. But we don't know anything about that guess. Was there a second author that was very close to the one that was guessed? If so, we might want to know that. More generally, we might want to know the top few guesses rather than just the top guess. That way, we have useful information about who the author might be even if the top guess happens to be wrong. These are additional features that we could add to our program.

For efficiency, let's think about that `get_all_signatures` function again. That function does a lot of work! If we have five books in our known directory, then it will read each of the five files and calculate each signature. Big deal, right? It's only five files, and computers are really fast. But imagine if we had 100 files or 10,000 files. It may be acceptable to do all that work as a one-time-only thing, but that's not what our program does. In fact, every time we run the program to get a guess for the author of a mystery book, it runs that `get_all_signatures` function, which means re-creating those signatures every single time. That's a huge amount of wasted effort; it would be nice if we could just store those signatures somewhere, never having to calculate them again. Indeed, if we were to redesign the code for efficiency, a first step would be to ensure that the signature for a known text is only computed once and reused thereafter.

That's exactly what tools like Copilot do! OpenAI trained GitHub Copilot just once on a huge corpus of code. That took thousands or millions of computer hours. But now that the training is done, it can keep writing code for us without having to train from scratch every time. The idea of doing the training once and then using that training for many subsequent predictions is a common paradigm throughout all of ML.

11.7   Exercises

1 Which of the following isn't a step in the AI-based authorship identification process described in this chapter?
   a Calculating the average word length of the mystery book
   b Comparing the mystery book's signature to known signatures
   c Asking the user for the filename of the mystery book
   d Finding the total number of pages in the mystery book

2 Build a classifier that can distinguish between spam and non-spam (ham) emails based on email content. Use features like word frequency, presence of certain keywords, and email length. Here are the steps you'll need to take:
   a Collect a dataset of spam and non-spam emails. You can find publicly available datasets online, such as the Enron spam dataset.

b Preprocess the emails (remove stop words, punctuation, etc.).

c Extract features (e.g., word counts, presence of certain words).

d Train a classifier using our labeled data (supervised learning). A simple and effective choice for the classifier is the Naïve Bayes classifier (feel free to use a Python library to help you).

e Test the classifier with a separate set of emails to check its accuracy.

3 In this exercise, you'll create a simple text generation program using n-grams. N-grams are contiguous sequences of *n* items from a given sample of text or speech. You'll use these n-grams to generate new text that mimics the style of the input text. The key idea is to build a model that is trained to know which words commonly follow other words (i.e., "cat eats" makes sense, "tissue eats" does not) and then, among the possible choices, randomly select the next one. Feel free to look up n-grams for more information. Here are the steps you'll need to take:

a Choose input text that you can load into Python. You can use something like: "Pride and Prejudice" by Jane Austen.

b Preprocess the text by converting it to lowercase and removing punctuation.

c Create n-grams from the input text. An n-gram is a contiguous sequence of *n* items from a given text. For simplicity, we'll use bigrams ($n = 2$) in this example.

d Use the generated n-grams to produce new text. Start with a random n-gram, and keep adding new words based on the n-gram model until the desired length is reached.

Summary

- Top-down design becomes more and more critical as the complexity of our programs increase.

- Author identification is the process of guessing the author of a mystery book.

- We can use features about words (e.g., average word length) and sentences (e.g., average number of words per sentence) to characterize how each known author writes.

- Machine learning is an important area of computer science that investigates how machines can learn from data and make predictions.

- In supervised learning, we have some training data in the form of objects (e.g., books) and their categories (who wrote each book). We can learn from that data to make predictions about new objects.

- A signature consists of a list of features, one signature per object.

- Refactoring code means to improve the design of the code (e.g., by reducing code repetition).

Future directions

This chapter covers

- Using prompt patterns to write and explain code
- Current limitations and future directions of generative AI tools

In this final chapter, we want to give you a glimpse of the creative ways people are currently using generative AI tools such as GitHub Copilot and ChatGPT. For example, it's possible to make Copilot Chat ask you the questions, rather than the other way around. And it's possible to make Copilot take on a different persona to be even more helpful to your current programming task. We're going to keep this brief, and it's not clear how much of this will become standard practice, but we want to take this opportunity to demonstrate the power of being creative with these new tools. We'll also talk about some of the current limitations of generative AI tools (you've seen some of them already in this book!) and offer our thoughts on what may be next.

12.1 Prompt patterns

Throughout the book, we've conveyed why programming directly in Python is a very different experience compared to programming using Copilot. Rather than writing code, our focus shifts to writing prompts and interacting with the generated code to determine whether or not it's correct, and then fixing it if needed. But along with those differences, there are surprising similarities between coding without Copilot and coding with Copilot.

When programmers write code, they don't start from scratch each time they write a new program. Researchers and programmers have created catalogs of design *patterns*, that is, general-purpose ways of organizing programs to make them easier to write, debug, and extend. The most famous such catalog is a book called *Design Patterns: Elements of Reusable Object-Oriented Software* [1], also known as the "Gang of Four book" because it was written by four authors. It requires familiarity with object-oriented programming, which we haven't taught in this book, so we don't recommend picking up that book quite yet. Just know that thousands of programmers have saved thousands of hours using the patterns in this book and not reinventing the wheel.

As just one example of a design pattern, suppose that you're writing a computer game where a human player plays against the computer. You want to implement several AI opponents of varying difficulties (e.g., beginner, intermediate, advanced, and expert) to provide different skill levels of opponents for the human. Each AI opponent will have its own code for determining its behavior. It would be possible to use `if` conditions to determine what the AI opponent should do:

```
if ai_opponent == 'beginner':
    # make decision consistent with beginner AI opponent
elif ai_opponent == 'intermediate':
    # make decision consistent with intermediate AI opponent
...
```

The downside to doing it that way, though, is organizational. We'd have all the AI code for the various AI opponents in the same place. We know from what we've learned in this book that huge functions like that aren't easy to design and test.

The clean way to organize this kind of program is using a pattern called the *strategy pattern*. We're not going to go into details of that pattern here, but the important thing is that people have documented this pattern [1] for others to use. The pattern documentation tells you its intent (purpose), motivation for why we would use it, the structure of the code needed to implement it, and example code.

Researchers are beginning to catalog patterns that can be used with generative AI tools like GitHub Copilot and ChatGPT [2]. They're called *prompt patterns*, and similar to design patterns, they tell you how to construct a prompt to achieve a desired goal. The documentation for each of these patterns is similar to the documentation for design patterns, but rather than example code, we get example prompts that we can use.

In this book, we've spent most of our time on two types of AI responses: generating code (by pressing Tab in VS Code) and explaining code (by using Copilot Chat). The new prompt patterns that are emerging can help generative AI tools go beyond these to help with other code-related tasks.

To give you a flavor of the state of the art in prompt patterns, we'll sample a couple of them here. For many more, we encourage you to check the catalog of prompt patterns that we've used [2]. Be warned, though: we're referring you to an academic paper, rather than a beginner's guide because we're not aware of any beginner's guides at this time (this is still new stuff).

> ### Copilot Chat may not engage in these prompt patterns
>
> At the time of writing, Copilot Chat refuses to engage in some of the cataloged prompt patterns, claiming that they are unrelated to programming assistance. While some may be less specifically related to programming, they are all designed to help programmers. Unlike ChatGPT, Copilot has been designed to try to always stay squarely on the topic of programming. If you decide to explore the variety of patterns further, you may wish to do so using ChatGPT when your interaction with Copilot isn't productive.

12.1.1 *Flipped interaction pattern*

To this point, we've been the one requesting code and asking questions, and Copilot has been the one answering. But it's possible to flip the script so that Copilot does the asking and we do the answering. This is called the *flipped interaction pattern.*

The intent of this pattern is to help us interact with the AI when we don't know what information it needs to perform a task. The motivation is that the AI may know what to ask us to get to its goal faster than if we provided incomplete or unhelpful information. The structure of our prompt will look like this:

> I would like you to ask me questions to achieve X. You should ask questions until we achieve this goal, where X is the goal we'd like to achieve.

This structure isn't meant to precisely dictate the prompt that we should use. Rather, it cues us to the key ideas that we need to convey in the prompt. Here, for example, the key ideas are that we want Copilot to ask the questions and that we don't want it to stop until our goal has been achieved.

In chapter 3, we wrote a function to keep asking the user for a password until they typed a strong password. Suppose we weren't sure how to design this function. We could ask Copilot to design it for us by providing a code prompt, but then it might make decisions that we don't agree with. Instead, we can have Copilot ask us the questions. Let's use Copilot Chat to do this.

> **Human** I would like a Python function that keeps asking the user for a password until they provide a strong password. Ask me questions one at a time until you can write that Python function.
>
> **GitHub Copilot** Sure, I'd be happy to help you write a Python function that keeps asking the user for a strong password! Here are some questions to get started:

1 What do you consider to be a strong password?

2 Should the function have any input parameters?

3 What should the function return?

4 Should the function have any side effects, such as printing messages to the console?

5 Should the function have any error handling, such as handling invalid input from the user?

Copilot failed to follow our instruction to "Ask me questions one at a time." Let's remind it.

Human Ask me the questions one at a time.

GitHub Copilot Sure, let's start with the first question:

1 What do you consider to be a strong password?

Now we can start answering the questions. Copilot will use the answers to these questions to write the code for us.

Human The password must have at least one uppercase character, at least one number, and at least one punctuation mark.

GitHub Copilot Great, thanks for letting me know! Here's the next question:

2 Should the function have any input parameters?

Human I don't know. What would they be used for?

GitHub Copilot Input parameters are used to pass data into a function so that the function can perform some operation on that data. For example, if we want to write a function that adds two numbers together, we would need to pass those two numbers into the function as input parameters.

In the case of our password function, we might want to pass in some parameters that define the requirements for a strong password. For example, we might want to pass in the minimum length of the password, the required number of uppercase characters, the required number of numbers, and the required number of punctuation characters.

Alternatively, we could hard-code these requirements into the function itself, but using input parameters would make the function more flexible and reusable.

Human Please hard-code them.

GitHub Copilot Sure, we can hard-code the password requirements into the function itself. Here's the next question:

3 What should the function return?

Human It should return the user's strong password.

GitHub Copilot Great, thanks for letting me know! Here's the next question:

4 Should the function have any side effects, such as printing messages to the console?

We'll stop here as we don't think it's interesting to read our full interaction. We continued our conversation with Copilot and answered questions 4 and 5, and Copilot had the information it needed to write the code we wanted. The code we ultimately received, after answering all five questions, is shown in the following listing.

Listing 12.1 Function designed via the flipped interaction pattern

```python
import string

def get_strong_password():
    '''
    Keep asking the user to enter a password until they provide
    a strong password.
    A strong password has at least one uppercase character, one
    number, and one punctuation character.
    '''
    # Print the password requirements
    print("Your password must contain at least:")
    print("- One uppercase letter")
    print("- One number")
    print("- One punctuation character")

    # Keep asking for a password until a strong one is provided
    while True:
        password = input("Enter a password: ")

        # Check if the password meets the requirements
        if not any(c.isupper() for c in password):
            print("Password does not contain an uppercase letter.")
        elif not any(c.isdigit() for c in password):
            print("Password does not contain a number.")
        elif not any(c in string.punctuation
                     for c in password):
            print("Password does not contain a punctuation character.")
        else:
            print("Password is strong!")
            return password
```

There's no way to make this True condition False!

If there's no uppercase character in the password

If there's no digit character in the password

If there's no punctuation character in the password

This is how we get out of the "while True" loop.

In our `while` loops to this point, we've always used a loop condition that we hope eventually becomes `False` (otherwise, we'd have an infinite loop). For example, we could imagine having a loop that says, in effect, "while the password is not valid." But here, the code is using `while True`, and `True` is a condition that can never become

`False`. There must be some other way out of the loop—and there is! We get out of the loop through a `return` statement when the password is valid. That is, instead of "while the password is not valid," the logic here is "loop forever; if the password is valid, stop looping." The `while True` form of `while` loops is a common alternative structure to the style that we've seen throughout the book.

This code does a good job of implementing our task. It starts with some `print` calls to tell the user the rules for strong passwords. It also tells the user what's wrong with their password if, in fact, it isn't strong. It keeps looping until the user enters a strong password. And, when we eventually have a strong password from the user, we return it.

Now, we already knew how to write this function because of our work in chapter 3. And your Python knowledge by this point is sufficiently strong that you can cut to the chase and write the function signature for Copilot to write the code as we've been doing throughout the book. But for tasks with which you're less familiar and may not know where to start, this flipped interaction pattern may help.

12.1.2 *Persona pattern*

The intent of this pattern is to have the AI take on a particular persona or point of view. Why would we ever be motivated to do this? Well, here's an example: say you're a student in an introductory Python programming course. Your instructor is using Copilot as part of the course, but they are disallowing some Python features that they feel detract from learning introductory Python. You could ask Copilot to take on the persona of that instructor and then help you check your code to find and, if necessary, remove any disallowed Python features. The structure of our prompt will look like this:

> From now on, act as persona X. Provide outputs that persona X would create.

We'll fill in X with a particular persona. Let's try this with our introductory programming instructor persona. We'll ask Copilot to play the part, disallowing a list of more advanced Python concepts. (Don't worry if you've never heard of these!)

> **Human** From now on, act as an introductory Python programming instructor. In the course that you're teaching, the following Python features aren't allowed: list comprehensions, generators, "lambda", and the "any" function. I will provide code, and you'll review the code for any Python features that aren't allowed and suggest how to rewrite the code to not use those features.

> **GitHub Copilot** Sure, I can do that! Please provide the code you would like me to review.

Let's feed it the `get_strong_password` function from the previous section. It uses the `any` function, and by our persona rules, that function isn't allowed. Here's our original code and what Copilot does in response.

Human

```
def get_strong_password():
    '''
    Keep asking the user to enter a password until they provide
    a strong password.
    A strong password has at least one uppercase character, one
    number, and one punctuation character.
    '''
    # Print the password requirements
    print("Your password must contain at least:")
    print("- One uppercase letter")
    print("- One number")
    print("- One punctuation character")

    # Keep asking for a password until a strong one is provided
    while True:
        password = input("Enter a password: ")

        # Check if the password meets the requirements
        if not any(c.isupper() for c in password):
            print("Password does not contain an uppercase letter.")
        elif not any(c.isdigit() for c in password):
            print("Password does not contain a number.")
        elif not any(c in string.punctuation for c in password):
            print("Password does not contain a punctuation character.")
        else:
            print("Password is strong!")
            return password
```

GitHub Copilot   The `get_strong_password` function uses the `any` function, which is not allowed in your course. Here's a modified version of the function that does not use the `any` function:

```
import string

def get_strong_password():
    '''
    Keep asking the user to enter a password until they provide
    a strong password.
    A strong password has at least one uppercase character, one
    number, and one punctuation character.
    '''
    # Print the password requirements
    print("Your password must contain at least:")
    print("- One uppercase letter")
    print("- One number")
    print("- One punctuation character")

    # Keep asking for a password until a strong one is provided
    while True:
        password = input("Enter a password: ")

        # Check if the password meets the requirements
        has_uppercase = False
```

```
has_number = False
has_punctuation = False
for c in password:                    ⟵ ┤ The loop that
    if c.isupper():                       replaces "any"
        has_uppercase = True
    elif c.isdigit():
        has_number = True
    elif c in string.punctuation:
        has_punctuation = True
if not has_uppercase:
    print("Password does not contain an uppercase letter.")
elif not has_number:
    print("Password does not contain a number.")
elif not has_punctuation:
    print("Password does not contain a punctuation character.")
else:
    print("Password is strong!")
    return password
```

> This version of the function uses a `for` loop to iterate over each character in the password and check if it meets the requirements. This approach is more verbose than using the `any` function, but it does not use the disallowed Python features.

As Copilot Chat indicated, this program doesn't use the `any` function. Copilot has rewritten the program to avoid that function, thereby following the rules set by our Python programming persona.

The `any` function returns `True` if one or more values in its argument are true, and `False` if all values in its argument are false. Behind the scenes, `any` must be looking at each value to check whether it's true or false. Sounds like a loop, right? Indeed, a loop is exactly what Copilot has used here to replace the `any` function calls.

12.2 Limitations and future directions

In our experience working with Copilot (and students) and reading the research literature published while we were writing this book, we've observed some limitations and future possibilities of generative AI models that we wanted to share.

12.2.1 Where Copilot (currently) struggles

We found that Copilot struggles in three different types of scenarios: contrived problems, ill-defined problems, and large tasks.

CONTRIVED PROBLEMS

Shortly after ChatGPT and GitHub Copilot took the world by storm, programming instructors feverishly worked to find types of tasks that these tools couldn't do well. One early proposal was to use contrived tasks: tasks made obscure and convoluted in an attempt to misdirect tools like Copilot to have them generate incorrect code. To us, such tasks seem wholly uninteresting and unfair to students, and their use seems to be a last-ditch attempt to retain the previous style of programming courses without acknowledging the disruption wrought by tools like Copilot. Our sense is that these contrived tasks will eventually be solved by Copilot as the models continue to improve, but even if they aren't, these types of problems aren't generally important to solve anyway.

ILL-DEFINED PROBLEMS

An ill-defined problem is a problem that hasn't been precisely specified, meaning we don't exactly know or haven't decided what we should do in all cases. For example, asking Copilot for a function to determine whether a password is strong is ill-defined until we define what we mean by "strong password." Your first thought may be that Copilot can't possibly get better at solving these kinds of problems. After all, if we struggle to precisely specify the behavior we want, how are we going to communicate the required behavior to Copilot? Ill-defined problems are certainly challenging for Copilot, but they aren't impossible. Remember the flipped interaction prompt pattern that we discussed earlier in the chapter? Perhaps, one day soon, Copilot will automatically switch into that mode when it doesn't have enough precision from you to solve the problem.

LARGE TASKS

We've spent a lot of time throughout the book teaching you how to design small functions and how to organize those functions using top-down design to solve large problems. We did this because Copilot struggles when given a monolithic task to solve. Is this an inherent limitation of tools like Copilot, or can AI get past it? We don't know. Right now, Copilot struggles with problem decomposition, and even if it could get that right, probabilities aren't in its favor. Specifically, it has a higher probability of getting something wrong the more code it writes. For example, if it needs to write 20 functions to solve a task with each function averaging 10 lines, it's almost certainly going to make a mistake somewhere. But it's also foolish to bet against these systems. With advancements in how Copilot learns, perhaps this isn't that far off after all.

12.2.2 Is Copilot a new programming language?

When we write computer code in a language like Python, there's a compiler behind the scenes converting the Python to an assembly code or machine code that the computer can understand. There was a time when programmers wrote code in an old computer language like Fortran or C, ran the compiler to produce code in assembly language, and then checked the assembly code to make sure it was correct. We weren't around then, and it probably didn't happen that much, but we can understand why programmers didn't trust compilers back then. Compilers were a new technology, and it took time to work out the bugs. In addition, the code output from compilers was probably fairly inefficient compared to handwritten assembly. But after decades of improvements both to correctness and efficiency (compiler optimizations are a really exciting and interesting topic for anyone curious!), very few programmers ever look at the output of compilers. Could there be a point when humans simply use large language models (LLMs) as the primary interface to computers and don't spend much time examining the code they produce? Let's think about both possible answers to this question.

WHY LLMS MAY NOT REPLACE PROGRAMMING LANGUAGES

There are reasons to think LLMs won't become the primary interface for humans to program computers. The principle one is that LLMs aren't a stringent programming language. We trust compilers because there's a programming language specification for each programming language and there's a specified, exact behavior expected from each line of code. LLMs don't have this. It's just someone writing English or another natural language to an LLM. The LLM isn't bound to interpret the natural language in a particular way. It doesn't have to output the answer based on any rigorous specification. And, randomness and nondeterminism make it so the answer it gives us could vary or be wrong! Compilers are deterministic and by now are a mature, trusted technology. They don't face these problems.

WHY LLMS MAY REPLACE PROGRAMMING LANGUAGES

There are also reasons to believe that, like compilers, LLMs will get better and become our primary programming interface. In fact, for data science, this is already starting to happen.

As we've learned throughout the book, a key challenge to working with Copilot is determining whether the generated code is correct. In a sense, it isn't fair to nonprogrammers: we give Copilot natural language (our preference), and it gives us back code that's not in a natural language (the computer's preference). It would be nice if we could "skip the code" and use natural language not only to communicate with Copilot but to receive our answer.

Researchers are beginning to explore this possibility in restricted domains of interest to millions of computer users. As one example, let's think about data science. Data scientists make sense of data by exploring the data, visualizing the data, and using data to make predictions. Much of what they do involves manipulating data in constrained, well-understood ways, such as merging spreadsheets, cleaning particular columns of data, or conducting analyses such as clustering the data into meaningful categories or simplifying data to focus only on its core underlying structure. Data scientists who use Python use many libraries to work with their data, but one extremely popular library is called pandas.

Researchers have successfully "skipped the code" in this context of doing data science with pandas [3]. Here's how it works:

1 The user expresses their intent in a natural language such as English.
2 The AI generates Python code and runs it to get the result (e.g., a table of results for an analysis or a new spreadsheet) for the user. Importantly, the user doesn't see this Python code.
3 The AI converts the code back to natural language and presents that (not the Python code!) back to the user. The natural language that the user gets back is in a consistent format that can be reliably interpreted by the AI. The researchers

describe the purpose of the response from the AI like this: "This is how you should ask the system to do what the system thinks you just asked it to do." The response helps the user understand the capabilities of the AI and the types of queries that are effective.

4 The user can edit the natural language from step 3 if it's not correct. If the user makes an edit, they can submit the new prompt, which repeats the cycle.

An example provided by the researchers clarifies this process [3]. Suppose we have a spreadsheet with one astronaut per row. Each row has three relevant columns: the astronaut's name, their total time in space, and a comma-separated list of missions that they participated in. We want to calculate the average mission length for each astronaut.

In step 1, the user writes a prompt like "calculate average mission length." In step 2, the AI generates code corresponding to that prompt. It runs the code and adds a new column to the user's spreadsheet containing the average mission length. In step 3, the AI converts the code to a list of tasks in natural language, such as the following:

1 Create column "Mission Length."
2 Column "Space Flight(hr)" divided by (count "," from column "Missions" + 1).

In step 4, the user can edit the natural language from step 3 and resubmit the updated tasks to the AI. Might we be able to "skip the code" in the far broader area of "Python programming" rather than the more restricted setting of "data science with pandas"? It's too early to tell. Data manipulation has the benefit of working in a visual medium, with spreadsheets and graphs that can be directly presented to the user, who may be able to discern whether the analysis looks correct or if further prompt engineering is needed. Such visual representations aren't readily apparent for general-purpose programming.

Still, we can imagine a new era where humans continue to perform important tasks like problem decomposition, specifying program behavior, writing tests, designing algorithms, and so on but where the programming of functions is entirely done using LLMs. The human tells the AI tool what the program is required to do and provides the test cases, and the AI generates the code. The human can then check that the program works properly without ever needing to see the code.

For another take on whether LLMs will replace programming languages, we recommend the blog post written by Chris Lattner [4], a programming and compiler expert. Lattner argues that, at least in the short term and possibly longer, programming languages won't go away because the code from LLMs can be subtly wrong. So, if programming languages are sticking around for a while, the question is: Which programming languages should we be using? Lattner says, "The best language for an LLM is one that is highly usable and easy to read for humans, but whose implementation can scale to many different use cases and applications" [4]. Do existing languages meet this goal? Can we do better by designing a programming language that's easier to read than, say, Python? Stay tuned!

OK, so maybe programming languages go away, or maybe they don't; maybe they change. Regardless, do we need to worry about programmer jobs? We think not. Anyone who has worked at a software company will tell you that writing code isn't the only or even main thing that programmers do with their time. Programmers also meet with clients to determine what they need. They specify what programs do and how they fit together. They check systems for performance and security concerns. They work with other teams to coordinate the design of huge pieces of software. If the writing code step gets easier, maybe we just get more useful software. That's what happened when we got high-level languages. No one is going to code the next killer app in assembly! Compilers improve how we make software. Used thoughtfully, we think LLMs can do this too.

AN EXCITING FUTURE

Although we're partially unsure of what's to come, it's clear LLMs are going to dramatically change the future of programming. Perhaps, for now, they are just aids to help software engineers write better code. Perhaps five years from now, however, the majority of software will be written by LLMs and only a small subset of software engineers will be writing code from scratch. Whichever outcome proves true, changes are coming fast, and they'll likely lead to more people being able to write software to meet their needs.

As of writing, we already have some insights into how these tools are being used. In one survey, 92% of software developers reported using these tools on a regular basis [5]. Recent studies have found evidence that developers who use these tools are more productive than without the tools [6]. In one particularly interesting research study conducted at UC San Diego, researchers found that professional developers use these tools in two ways: acceleration and exploration [7]. In the acceleration phase, developers use these tools to help generate code faster than if they wrote it themselves. In the exploration phase, developers use these tools to help them find libraries that may be helpful or to understand the existing codebase. These findings align with what we've been learning in this book, and we look forward to the research to come.

More than anything else, we hope that you're now able to make your own, informed decision on how you'll use LLMs to program and what LLMs may mean for the future of programming. At times like these, with some fervently proclaiming, "Programming is over!" and others equally fervently proclaiming, "Programming won't change much at all!" [8], it's important for us to be able to weigh the arguments ourselves and the ways that this change may affect us and everyone else. Can these tools help us? We think so. We should therefore use them, but use them responsibly. Are there concerns? Again, we think so, as we've discussed throughout the book. We should take steps, such as testing and debugging, to mitigate those concerns.

The approach to teaching programming that we've taken in this book is new. Teachers and professors like us have just begun incorporating tools like Copilot into programming courses [9], though we're still working on the balance between when we want learners to use Copilot and when we don't. No matter the balance that programmers choose to learn programming, we want to stress to you that you've learned absolutely essential skills that everyone needs to create good software, whether you're writing code occasionally at work to automate tedious tasks or you're planning to become a professional software engineer. You have a strong foundation going forward, wherever your path may take you.

12.3 *Exercises*

1 Explain how the persona pattern can be used to enforce coding standards in a company. For example, a company may ask its employees to always use camel case (e.g., xVal, ZValOut). Provide an example of a prompt you could use to have GitHub Copilot act as a manager enforcing specific coding standards.

2 You want to create a Python function that generates a username based on a user's preferred username and full name. The function should follow these rules:

   a If the preferred username is available (i.e., not already taken), use it.

   b If the preferred username is taken, generate a new username by appending a single digit (e.g., 1, 2, 3, 4 . . .) to the preferred username.

   c If the generated usernames are also taken, use the user's full name to generate a username by combining parts of their first and last name.

   d The function should keep asking for a new preferred username if the generated usernames are also taken.

   Which interaction pattern (flipped interaction pattern or persona pattern) would you use to design this function with the help of GitHub Copilot? Justify your choice, and outline how you would start the interaction.

Summary

- A prompt pattern is a template to help us construct a prompt to meet a given goal.
- The flipped interaction pattern flips the script: rather than posing questions to the LLM, the LLM poses questions to us.
- The flipped interaction pattern is useful when we don't know how to effectively prompt the LLM.
- The persona pattern is used to have the AI take on a particular persona, such as "introductory programming instructor," or a specific point of view.
- The persona pattern is useful when we want the LLM to respond from a given perspective.
- Copilot currently struggles with tasks that are contrived, not well defined, or large.
- Some believe that LLMs will replace programming languages; others believe that programming languages are here to stay.

- LLMs are helping people perform data science tasks without those people ever seeing the underlying programming language code.
- It may be that programming languages themselves aren't replaced, but that the leading languages will be developed to be more readable than today's languages.

references

Foreword

[1] M. Kazemitabaar, J. Chow, C. Ka To Ma, B. Ericson, D. Weintrop, and T. Grossman. "Studying the Effect of AI Code Generators on Supporting Novice Learners in Introductory Programming." ACM CHI Conference on Human Factors in Computing Systems, Apr. 2023.

Introduction

[1] D. M. Yellin. "The Premature Obituary of Programming." *Commun. ACM*, 66, 2 (Feb. 2023), 41–44.

[2] XKCD. "Real Programmers." https://xkcd.com/378/. Accessed Feb. 1, 2023.

Chapter 1

[1] G. Heyman, R. Huysegems, P. Justen, and T. Van Cutsem. "Natural Language-Guided Programming." In *2021 Proc. ACM SIGPLAN Int. Symp. on New Ideas, New Paradigms, and Reflections on Programming and Software* (Oct. 2021), 39–55.

[2] N. A. Ernst and G. Bavota. "AI-Driven Development Is Here: Should You Worry?" IEEExplore. https://ieeexplore.ieee.org/document/9713901/figures#figures. Accessed Feb. 7, 2023.

[3] M. Chen, J. Tworek, H. Jun, Q. Yuan, H. P. D. O. Pinto, J. Kaplan, et al. "Evaluating Large Language Models Trained on Code," 2021. arXiv preprint. https://arxiv.org/abs/2107.03374. Accessed Feb. 7, 2023.

[4] R. D. Caballar. "Ownership of AI-Generated Code Hotly Disputed > A Copyright Storm May Be Brewing for GitHub Copilot." *IEEE Spectrum*. https://spectrum.ieee.org/ai-code-generation-ownership. Accessed Feb. 7, 2023.

[5] P. Denny, V. Kumar, and N. Giacaman. "Conversing with Copilot: Exploring Prompt Engineering for Solving CS1 Problems Using Natural Language," 2022. arXiv preprint. https://arxiv.org/abs/2210.15157. Accessed Feb. 7, 2023.

[6] A. Zilber. "AI Bot ChatGPT Outperforms Students on Wharton MBA Exam: Professor." *New York Post*, Jan. 1, 2023. https://nypost.com/2023/01/23/chatgpt-outperforms-humans-on-wharton-mba-exam-professor/. Accessed Feb. 7, 2023.

[7] A. Mitchell. "ChatGPT Could Make These Jobs Obsolete: 'The Wolf Is at the Door.'" *New York Post*, Jan. 25, 2023. https://nypost.com/2023/01/25/chat-gpt-could-make-these-jobs-obsolete/. Accessed Feb. 7, 2023.

Chapter 2

[1] C. Alvarado, M. Minnes, and L. Porter. "Object Oriented Java Programming: Data Structures and Beyond Specialization." www.coursera.org/specializations/java-object-oriented. Accessed Apr. 9, 2023.

[2] S. Valstar, W. G. Griswold, and L. Porter. "Using DevContainers to Standardize Student Development Environments: An Experience Report." In *Proceedings of 2020 ACM Conference on Innovation and Technology in Computer Science Education* (July 2020), 377–383.

[3] Visual Studio Code. "User Interface." https://code.visualstudio.com/docs/getstarted/userinterface. Accessed Apr. 9, 2023.

[4] Kaggle. Kaggle Inc. www.kaggle.com/. Accessed Apr. 9, 2023.

Chapter 3

[1] J. Sweller. "Cognitive Load Theory." *Psychology of Learning and Motivation* (Vol. 55, pp. 37–76). Academic Press, 2011.

Chapter 4

[1] R. Lister, C. Fidge, and D. Teague. "Further Evidence of a Relationship between Explaining, Tracing and Writing Skills in Introductory Programming." In *ACM SIGCSE Bulletin*, 41, 3 (Sept. 2009), 161–165.

Chapter 6

[1] R. D. Pea, "Language-Independent Conceptual 'Bugs' in Novice Programming." *Journal of Educational Computing Research*, 2, no. 1, pp. 25–36. 1986.

Chapter 7

[1] J. Ousterhout, "A Philosophy of Software Design." www.youtube.com/watch?v=bmSAYlu0NcY&ab_channel=TalksatGoogle. Accessed June 6, 2024.

Chapter 8

[1] "Debugging." https://code.visualstudio.com/docs/editor/debugging. Accessed June 7, 2023.

[2] "Python Tutor." https://pythontutor.com/. Accessed June 7, 2023.

[3] J. Gorson, K. Cunningham, M. Worsley, and E. O'Rourke. "Using Electrodermal Activity Measurements to Understand Student Emotions While Programming." In *Proceedings of the 2022 ACM Conf. on Intl. Comp. Education Research*, 1 (Aug. 2022), 105–119.

Chapter 9

[1] M. Odendahl. "LLMs Will Fundamentally Change Software Engineering." https://dev.to/wesen/llms-will-fundamentally-change-software-engineering-3oj8. Accessed June 2, 2023.

Chapter 10

[1] Pygame. www.pygame.org/. Accessed July 20, 2023.

[2] Unity Real-Time Development Platform. https://unity.com/. Accessed July 20, 2023.

[3] A. Sweigart. *Invent Your Own Computer Games with Python, 4th Edition*. No Starch Press, 2016.

Chapter 11

[1] M. Craig, "Nifty Assignment: Authorship Detection." http://nifty.stanford.edu/2013/craig-authorship-detection/. Accessed Apr. 9, 2023.

Chapter 12

[1] E. Gamma, R. Helm, R. Johnson, and J. Vlissides. *Design Patterns: Elements of Reusable Object-Oriented Software.* Addison-Wesley Professional, 1994.

[2] J. White, Q. Fu, S. Hays, M. Sandborn, C. Olea, H. Gilbert, et al. "A Prompt Pattern Catalog to Enhance Prompt Engineering with ChatGPT." https://arxiv.org/abs/2302.11382. Feb. 2023.

[3] M. X. Liu, A. Sarkar, C. Negreanu, B. Zorn, J. Williams, N. Toronto, et al. "'What It Wants Me to Say': Bridging the Abstraction Gap Between End-User Programmers and Code-Generating Large Language Models." In *Proc. of the 2023 CHI Conf. on Hum. Fact. in Comp. Syst.,* 598 (Apr. 2023), 1–31.

[4] C. Lattner. "Do LLMs Eliminate the Need for Programming Languages?" www.modular.com/blog/do-llms-eliminate-the-need-for-programming-languages. Accessed July 4, 2023.

[5] I. Shani and GitHub Staff. Survey Reveals AI's Impact on the Developer Experience. https://github.blog/2023-06-13-survey-reveals-ais-impact-on-the-developer-experience/. Accessed June 22, 2024.

[6] K. Z. Cui, M. Demirer, S. Jaffe, L. Musolff, S. Peng, and T. Salz. "The Productivity Effects of Generative AI: Evidence from a Field Experiment with GitHub Copilot." An MIT Exploration of Generative AI, March 2024. https://doi.org/10.21428/e4baedd9.3ad85f1c.

[7] S. Barke, M. B. James, and N. Polikarpova. Grounded Copilot: How Programmers Interact with Code-Generating Models. Proc. ACM Program. Lang. 7, OOPSLA1, Article 78. Apr. 2023.

[8] A. J. Ko. "Large Language Models Will Change Programming . . . A Little." https://medium.com/bits-and-behavior/large-language-models-will-change-programming-a-little-81445778d957. Accessed July 4, 2023.

[9] A. Vadaparty, D. Zingaro, D. Smith, M. Padala, C. Alvarado, J. Gorson Benario, and L. Porter. (2024). "CS1-LLM: Integrating LLMs into CS1 instruction." In *Proc. of the 29th ACM Conf. on Innovation and Technology in Computer Science Education (ITiCSE).* (July 2024), 297–303.

index